T0003662

FROM THE
STREETS OF SHAOLIN

ALSO BY S. H. FERNANDO JR.

The New Beats:
Exploring the Music, Culture, and Attitudes of Hip-Hop

"So much has been written about the Wu-Tang Clan, but finally we have the entire story in one place. S. H. Fernando Jr., one of the first-ever journalists to cover the group, walks us through not only the backstories of the founding members, but also the specific conditions that led to Wu-Tang's formation. Economic/racial inequality, the drug trade, the teachings of the Nation of Gods and Earths, kung fu cinema, and the early days of New York hip-hop are explained in full detail, as well as production techniques and the machinations of the music industry, with analyses of the albums (both as a group and solo projects) that took the world by storm and helped define a generation. This is an essential text for any fan of hip-hop culture or American history in general."

—Ben Merlis, author of *Goin' Off: The Story of the Juice Crew & Cold Chillin' Records*

Praise for *From the Streets of Shaolin:*
The Wu-Tang Saga

One of SLATE's "Must-Reads for Summer" (2021)

"This sweeping history of the Wu-Tang Clan, the nine-man rap crew from Staten Island whose eclectic sound transformed the genre, traces the journey of its members from their childhoods in New York City housing projects to their current role as elder statesmen of American hip-hop. If the Clan's initial success was surprising, in an early-nineties rap scene dominated by a slick, West Coast style, its longevity has been astonishing; its various artists have produced nearly a hundred albums. Fernando dutifully narrates the group's origin story, but his real contribution lies in a careful analysis of how its mastermind, RZA, that 'mystic, majestic magus from the slums,' created a dynasty."

—*The New Yorker*

"An undisputed labor of love, this is the account diehard fans have been waiting for."

—*Publishers Weekly*

"An authoritative history of seminal hip-hop collective the Wu-Tang Clan.... Fernando vividly evokes the hardscrabble landscape of the group's home turf of Staten Island, where RZA first brought them together with an ambitious vision.... The go-to source for anyone interested in one of the most significant hip-hop groups of all time."

—*Kirkus Reviews*

"Wu-Tang Clan led a revolution, and S.H. Fernando Jr. was on the front lines—at the shows, in the studio, and on set for the video shoots where these nine hip-hop warriors changed the world. With vivid reporting and sharp critical analysis, *From the Streets of Shaolin* offers a chronicle of the Wu in real time, and truly allows the reader to enter the 36 Chambers."

—Alan Light, former Editor-in-Chief of *Vibe* and
Spin magazines, author of *What Happened,*
Miss Simone?: A Biography and *Let's Go Crazy:*
Prince and the Making of Purple Rain

"Playing chess, not checkers, author S. H. Fernando Jr. has written a blunted history of the Wu-Tang Clan that reads like a textual tapestry weaving together New York history, old school hip-hop, gritty futurism, crack corners, Five-Percent Nation knowledge, kung-fu flicks, Times Square tricks, Blaxploitation aesthetics, vintage soul, Asian philosophy, Black power, and streetwise poetics. Like the Wu crew, Fernando was driven by passion, knowledge, and the desire to drop science. Master-mixing journalistic discipline and research with gonzo enthusiasm, *From the Streets of Shaolin: The Wu-Tang Saga* is a masterful contribution to the culture and beyond."

—Michael A. Gonzales, Senior Writer, *Wax Poetics*

"S. H. Fernando Jr. is the original Wu-Tang chronicler. His early work is foundational, and his latest tome delivers the titillating travels of these original men with more flavor than Flav."

—Sacha Jenkins, Director, *Wu-Tang Clan: Of Mics & Men*

"To truly tell the story of a group like Wu-Tang, a writer needs to see so much more than just the music, and look deeper into the culture, sociohistorical context, and sheer rawness of the streets that these young gods emerged from.
It's rare that a writer so poignantly unravels the riddle wrapped in a mystery inside an enigma that is the Wu.
S. H. Fernando Jr.'s unprecedented early access and immersion into the golden era of hip-hop lends to a deeper story of Wu-Tang's brotherhood, visual inspirations, and the gritty ecosystem that informs Wu-Tang's come-up story. From the Nation of Gods and Earths to The Zulu Nation to Raekwon's immortal Snow Beach Polo parka, Fernando lyrically illustrates why the life and times of the Wu stand as a great American story.
Beautifully nuanced and lushly written, Fernando's telling of the Wu-Tang story shows (and proves) that it can, indeed, all be so simple."

—Vikki Tobak, author and curator of *Contact High: A Visual History of Hip-Hop*

FROM THE
STREETS OF SHAOLIN

THE WU-TANG SAGA

S. H. FERNANDO JR.

hachette
BOOKS
NEW YORK

Copyright © 2021 by S. H. Fernando Jr.

Jacket design by Terri Sirma
Jacket Illustration © David Choe
Cover copyright © 2021 by Hachette Book Group, Inc.

Hachette Book Group supports the right to free expression and the value of copyright. The purpose of copyright is to encourage writers and artists to produce the creative works that enrich our culture.

The scanning, uploading, and distribution of this book without permission is a theft of the author's intellectual property. If you would like permission to use material from the book (other than for review purposes), please contact permissions@hbgusa.com. Thank you for your support of the author's rights.

Hachette Books
Hachette Book Group
1290 Avenue of the Americas
New York, NY 10104
HachetteBooks.com
Twitter.com/HachetteBooks
Instagram.com/HachetteBooks

First Trade Paperback Edition: November 2022

Published by Hachette Books, an imprint of Perseus Books, LLC, a subsidiary of Hachette Book Group, Inc. The Hachette Books name and logo is a trademark of the Hachette Book Group.

The Hachette Speakers Bureau provides a wide range of authors for speaking events. To find out more, go to www.hachettespeakersbureau.com or call (866) 376-6591.

The publisher is not responsible for websites (or their content) that are not owned by the publisher.

Library of Congress Control Number: 2021938237

ISBNs: 978-0-306-87446-8 (hardcover); 978-0-306-87445-1 (ebook); 978-0-306-87443-7 (trade paperback)
Printed in the United States of America
LSC-C
Printing 1, 2022

For Johnny

CONTENTS

PREFACE

"I smoke on the mic like 'Smokin' Joe' Frasier / The Hellraiser, raising hell with the flavor." When Inspectah Deck launched into his iconic opening lines from "Protect Ya Neck" during a 2018 Wu-Tang Clan performance on *Jimmy Kimmel Live!*, I couldn't help but crack a smile and feel the goosebumps rising. The nine MCs gliding smoothly and nonchalantly across the stage, now grown men in their late forties and early fifties, were still doing it—maybe not with as much gusto as twenty-five years earlier, but the ecstatic crowd was loving it, and so was I. Flashbacks of the Clan's record release party at New York's Webster Hall in November 1993—the world premiere of these grimy, young upstarts from the mysterious shores of Staten Island—replayed in my mind. Like a title bout, the place was packed to the rafters with industry types and media, along with a colorful assortment of playas, hustlers, floozies, and a who's who of New York's hip-hop massive, who turned out to fete the crew behind "Protect," a breakout street hit that had dominated rap's collective consciousness for most of the year. As Wu-Tang swarmed the stage with what seemed like half their housing projects, no one even knew who was in the group until they started rhyming. No question, they brought one hell of a ruckus that night, putting Staten Island, or Shaolin, as they called it, on the map. Their unveiling also marked the beginning of a new chapter in hip-hop—the Wu era.

Emerging from New York's forgotten borough, the original nine-man collective hit like a Scud missile with *Enter the Wu-Tang: 36 Chambers* (Loud/RCA, 1993), an explosive debut that permanently altered the rap landscape. Hijacking the charts with a raw, underground sound and storming the gates of the music industry like Attila's hordes, the Clan kept on coming with an unrelenting assault of solo releases that furthered their choke hold on rap between 1993 and 1997. Today, with over forty million records sold worldwide, music attests to only part of their epic saga. At this point, it's fair to say they have even transcended the rap game, claiming their place in the cultural zeitgeist.

Man for man, the nine unique personalities of Wu-Tang, each oozing with witty, unpredictable talent and natural game, composed an all-star lineup never before seen in hip-hop. But the chemistry they exhibited as a team was what made them truly special. Commercial success almost overshadowed the fact that one of the main reasons they received so much love was that they represented the underdog everywhere, defying insurmountable odds to make it to the top. Even their whole DIY approach, which was grass roots and underground, made their impact on the mainstream all the more impressive. For generations of youth who grew up under the full sway of hip-hop in the seventies, eighties, and nineties, they are our equivalent of the Beatles or the Rolling Stones.

The Clan first appeared on my radar in October 1992, before "Protect Ya Neck" started tearing up the underground. After a year of barrio living in Manhattan's Spanish Harlem while working on my master's degree at the Columbia School of Journalism, I had just made the move to Williamsburg,

Brooklyn—at the time, a Shangri-la of artists, eccentrics, and delinquents, all drawn by the immense but affordable industrial spaces. One night, a college buddy, Jon Shecter, came over to check out the new digs. Along with fellow classmate Dave Mays, he had started hip-hop's premier publication, *The Source*, which gave me my first byline. Coming straight from the new *Source* offices on lower Broadway, Shecter brought a cassette that had him pretty hyped. After rolling up the requisite blunt, we popped in the tape, and I heard those iconic karate chops that open "Protect Ya Neck" for the first of what was to be many times.

Over a galloping kick and snare beat, RZA cut up the siren-like saxophone wail that opened "The Grunt" by the J.B.'s—the same iconic sample that powered Public Enemy's classic "Rebel Without a Pause"—to sinister effect. Random stabs of a guitar riff from LL Cool J's classic "Rock the Bells" added some unexpected rock 'n' roll swagger. Above the glorious mayhem, eight MCs with distinctly different styles and flows battled for our attention in a nonstop lyrical assault, uninterrupted by hooks. We had to rewind the tape a few more times to even catch some of their witty, intricate wordplay, which was heavy on the slang.

A couple of months later, in January 1993, Kid Capri played "Protect Ya Neck" for the first time on his mix show on WBLS. No doubt underground faves Stretch and Bobbito on WKCR and Funkmaster Flex on Hot 97 also helped break the single to a wider audience, but New York's urban commercial powerhouse playing an independent release from a then-unknown, unsigned group proved to be a game changer for this ragtag outfit from Staten Island. Upon hearing "Protect Ya Neck" on the radio for the first time, Raekwon the Chef, who stands about five foot five, reportedly jumped so high, he almost hit his head on the ceiling. He probably had no idea that his life and those of his fellow clansmen and their families would never be the same again. Of course, neither would the world of music.

The opening salvo in the Wu revolution lit up the airwaves across the Rotten Apple. The antithesis of the slick, smooth-sounding G-funk of Dr. Dre and his disciples on the West Coast who dominated commercial radio and the charts, Wu-Tang's gritty basement sound recalled hip-hop's halcyon days. With roots reaching back into the Bronx bedrock, they were reclaiming rap for the city that started it all. You always knew what was hot on the streets from the sounds booming out of passing SUVs, and "Protect Ya Neck" ricocheted across the concrete canyons of Gotham like an emergency broadcast from hell. Taking a page from the DIY punk rock manual, as well as their own checkered past, the group pressed the single themselves, pushing it on the streets like a controlled substance. Well acquainted with the drug game, they applied that same kind of hustle to flipping product and moving units. By the time they got rid of that initial run of two thousand records, the major labels came calling.

Of course, Wu mastermind RZA had a plan. He had already been burned once by the music industry after being briefly signed and dropped as a solo artist by Tommy Boy. To do battle again in that cutthroat biz, he needed the support of his whole team. At the same time, he was aware that one record deal wouldn't be enough to feed everyone. RZA's genius, then, was signing the group as a single entity while retaining the rights to sign each individual member to solo deals with other labels—a practice unheard of at the time. It took a fairly new, unproven imprint called Loud Records to agree to such terms, but they paid the group only $60,000, a relative pittance by the standards of the day. The autonomy and creative control that RZA secured in return, however, to fully realize his vision proved to be priceless. Few records of that time can compare with *36 Chambers'* raw, dusted aesthetic, which in drug parlance represented that pure, uncut dope.

A few months after first hearing "Protect Ya Neck," Loud contacted me to write a bio for the group. As a hip-hop journalist about to publish my first book, *The New Beats: Exploring the Music, Culture, and Attitudes of Hip-Hop*, I had pretty much interviewed all the major players in hip-hop by then. Yet my conversation with the RZA left an impression like a fatcap. Speaking to me by phone from his studio in Staten Island, he launched into an animated discussion about martial arts as a metaphor for the group's lyrical prowess—that Wu-Tang was a sword style, and the sword represented a sharp tongue. "We flip flows like kung-fu and take niggas' heads with our lyrics," he told me in no uncertain terms. RZA was also heavily into numerology and kicked a lot of Five-Percenter jargon—though I was ignorant to it at the time—breaking down words and numbers into alternative meanings. In an art form filled with unique and memorable characters, he came off like some mystic, majestic magus from the slums. Behind thick ghetto slang compounded by a rhotacism, I clearly recognized someone of innate intelligence—the kind you don't acquire at school— who was incredibly passionate and laser-focused on where he was going. A lot of rappers talk the talk, but I knew this guy was the real deal.

I finally met the RZA a few months later at Firehouse Studio in Manhattan. The group Gravediggaz, of which he was a member, was working on their first album, and their producer, Prince Paul, a friend of mine, had invited me down to voice a skit for the album, playing a crooked lawyer on the intro of a song called "Diary of a Madman." I remember walking into the studio, proudly holding the January 1994 issue of *The Source*, hot off the press, featuring my first cover story on Das EFX—an issue that also happened to contain the magazine's initial coverage of the Clan, whose album had just dropped. Raekwon, who was hanging out with a few guys, spotted the magazine in my hands and approached me holding a pair of garden shears with ten-inch blades. "Yo, kid, that the new joint?" he asked. "Let me peep that right quick." Though I didn't really know who Rae was at the time, I wasn't about to argue with a guy holding those nasty-looking shears. Needless to say, I never got my copy of *The Source* back. But I did meet RZA, who struck me as incredibly humble and hungry. With an album on the verge of blowing up, he looked like he had just rolled off a park bench before coming to the studio. I mentioned our prior conversation for the press release for "Protect Ya Neck," and he actually thanked me for writing it. Since graciousness was not a quality I usually associated with rappers, it confirmed what I already thought about him.

So began my long association with RZA and the group. My initial dealings with the "Abbot" of the Clan grew into a great rapport with him over the years as I wrote about Wu-Tang for such publications as *The Source, Rolling Stone, Vibe,* and many others. In addition to conducting multiple interviews with all the members between 1994 and 2002, I was lucky enough to be a fly on the wall as they worked on the first round of solo releases and their follow-up to *36 Chambers.* During the making of Genius's album, I was pulled out of my usual role as observer when RZA drafted me into playing the drug dealer, Mr. Grieco, on the skit that opens "Killah Hills 10304."

Without much forethought, he simply told me, "Follow my lead," and in a moment of adrenaline-pumping exhilaration, we acted out a deal gone bad. By the end of it, he was shouting at me, spittle flying, and even grabbing me by the throat for emphasis as GZA, Killah Priest, Dreddy Kruger, and Masta Killa crowded around. Masta Killa, incidentally, had just been in the news for punching friend and fellow journalist Cheo Coker in the face because he didn't like the artwork that ran with Coker's article on the Clan in *Rap Pages*, so I was already a little wary. Even though it felt like I was on the verge of a beatdown, I was somehow able to improvise my lines in a faux foreign accent. Thank God we nailed it in one take. As well as providing one hell of a story, the incident gave me an up close and personal look at the spontaneous and often unconventional methods the Clan used to create. Nothing was out of bounds, and there were no rules to any of it.

Though never compensated for my performance, I have enjoyed amazing access to the group over the years. I've been out to Staten Island numerous times and to the Wu Mansion in the woods of rural New Jersey, poking my video camera into the vocal booth while they were recording and taking a beating on the chessboard at the hands of GZA and Masta Killa. I joined the group in Los Angeles when they were working on *Wu-Tang Forever*, arriving the day after Notorious B.I.G. was gunned down. But, mostly, as a journalist I've just been around—to video shoots, live performances, studio sessions, award shows, and other events. I should note that interviewing anyone from the Clan is never a simple affair. Extreme tardiness is, of course, a given. I've spent entire days following RZA around town from record label offices to a chess game in the park to Indian restaurants to Sam Ash

Music or B&H Photo in Midtown, and finally to the studio, where we might not get to talking until well past the witching hour. While most rappers spend their money on cars or jewelry, he once dropped $50,000 on an Avid video-editing system, paying for it with an American Express black card. I've seen him chop it up with a homeless bum one minute and then Richard Branson the next. Basically, it's never a dull moment when you're hanging with the Wu. During this time, I built up a formidable Wu archive, including pages of unpublished interviews, videos of the group in action in the studio, and several notepads of on-the-spot observations and accumulated memories.

Drawing on this wealth of exclusive material, as well as the bounty of open-source public information, I recount the Clan's rise from humble beginnings to cultural icons in *From the Streets of Shaolin: The Wu-Tang Saga*. Wu-Tang, like hip-hop itself, represents a movement from the bottom that slowly and organically percolated to the top, constantly upping the ante on creativity, innovation, and originality and redefining music in the process. Beyond documenting their incredible rise, the book offers the most detailed and comprehensive look to date inside a true musical phenomenon, providing the social and cultural context to understand why Wu-Tang are as revered today as during their heyday in the nineties and how such a lasting and profound impact made them the greatest hip-hop group the world has ever known.

On a personal note, as a huge Wu fan myself, I have a far deeper relationship with their catalog than your average music journalist, and I approached this project not only with a commitment to truth and accuracy but also with the utmost love and respect. The Clan has seen me through many dark and difficult times. I remember one instance, in particular, when I was working for a media outfit in Iraq at the beginning of the war and living in a private residence outside the Green Zone. Our accommodations were rocked by a massive truck bomb that targeted the Australian Embassy next door. The first free elections since the ouster of Saddam were taking place at the end of the month, and insurgent violence was ratcheting up all over Baghdad. They were even threatening to close the airport, from which we hoped to make our escape. We didn't know what was happening from one moment to the next, and the only thing that got me through those final hairy days was having Wu-Tang on repeat on my iPod. It was the perfect soundtrack to war because theirs is a music of strength, survival, and transcendence, and you can never defeat the gods.

S. H. Fernando Jr.
Baltimore
December 2020

RUCKUS IN B MINOR (THE PRELUDE)

You know, the man just upped my rent last night
'Cause Whitey's on the moon
No hot water, no toilets, no lights
But Whitey's on the moon

—*Gil Scott-Heron, "Whitey on the Moon," 1970*

"You start out in 1954 by saying nigger, nigger, nigger. By 1968
you can't say nigger, that hurts, there's a backlash, so you say
stuff like forced busing, states' rights and all that stuff. And
you're getting so abstract now, you're talking about cutting
taxes, and all of these things you're talking about are totally
economic things and a byproduct of them is, blacks get hurt
worse than whites."

—*Lee Atwater, Republican strategist, 1981*

Despite the hard-won gains of the civil rights era, Black America, like the rest of the nation, was in a state of disarray by the end of the sixties. While white youths were protesting the Vietnam War and trashing the constricting social mores of the fifties with psychedelic drugs and free love, the revolution went a little deeper for Black folks. Discrimination in housing, jobs, and education; scarcity of resources and opportunities; and high rates of heroin addiction and incarceration were issues crying out for attention. Yet the incremental pace of change within the System couldn't keep up with the groundswell for substantive reforms, which were, inevitably, deferred. The struggle had also decimated Black leadership—the assassinations of Medgar Evers in '63 and Malcolm X in '65—and when they finally gunned down Nobel Peace Prize recipient the Reverend Dr. Martin Luther King Jr. on April 4, 1968, pushing people past the breaking point, Blacks burned down their own neighborhoods in one hundred cities across America, from Brooklyn and the Bronx to Cabrini Green and Watts. The nonviolent King had called riots "the language of the unheard," and since he was the last person who could have kept the peace, his dream of an equal, just, and equitable society was also deferred. Groups like the Black Panthers, who favored an opposite approach, picked up the struggle but, like those before them, were infiltrated and promptly neutralized by J. Edgar Hoover's FBI. Beneath the full powers of the state, Black liberation and resistance were effectively snuffed out.

Meanwhile, the real America, of military-industrial complex and empire, was too busy focusing on external threats to take stock of its own domestic failings. The so-called red scare had inspired the multibillion-dollar space race, and the US was sinking tremendous resources into a superficial show of force—ostensibly to also test technologies that could be used in Vietnam. On the evening of July 15, 1969, as the Apollo 11 spacecraft sat on its launchpad, poised to deliver the first Americans to the moon, the Reverend Ralph Abernathy led a Poor People's Campaign of twenty-five African American families in two mule-driven wagons to the west gate of Kennedy Space Center in Florida. He wasn't protesting the launch as much as the country's messed-up priorities, saying, "We may go on from this day to Mars and to Jupiter and even to the heavens beyond, but as long as racism, poverty and hunger and war prevail on the Earth, we as a civilized nation have failed."[1]

Space travel may have represented a symbolic future to some, Abernathy implied, but what good was technology if it could not be put to the practical purpose of feeding people at home? The real future was the children—like Bobby Diggs (a.k.a. the RZA), a brand-new arrival to planet Brooklyn, along with his cousins, Gary Grice (a.k.a. the GZA) and Russell Jones (a.k.a. ODB), both still in diapers. Products of the post–civil rights era, they suffered the consequences of their country's misplaced priorities and outright neglect. Growing up in the seventies, they were pretty much left to fend for themselves in an increasingly hostile society that offered them little assistance and fewer opportunities. They also came of age during the scourge of crack cocaine in the eighties, which disproportionately affected the Black community.

Compare the way that the fentanyl epidemic gripping suburban white America has been treated as a public health crisis to the way that crack became an issue of law and order, spawning the destructive war on drugs that led to epidemic rates of incarceration and further disintegration of the Black family. When it was discovered that the CIA was actually responsible for pumping crack into communities of color in order to fund their anti-communist activities in Nicaragua, the costly toll on those communities was regarded as simply collateral damage. But Republican strategist Lee Atwater inadvertently gave up the goods, laying out his party's racist agenda, which saw the slashing of vital social programs and the establishment of the prison-industrial complex during the Reagan-Bush years. So the war against Blacks is nothing new, and it continues to this day.

This new generation, including the future members of Wu-Tang, emerged with few positive role models and little guidance or mentorship to help structure their lives. With absent fathers and working single mothers, more often than not, TV and pop culture were their teachers. Cassettes and vinyl records were their entertainment—especially old records—and running wild in the streets was their recreation. For this generation there were no marches or slogans, yet their protests were very real. The simple and proud expression of who they were was an act of rebellion against a society stacked against them. Creativity and imagination were their weapons, and like so many who came before, freedom was their ultimate goal. Starting from scratch, the hip-hop generation changed everything.

PART 1

KNOWLEDGE BORN

1. Knowledge—to look, listen, and observe
9. Born—to bring into existence

From "Supreme Mathematics"
The Nation of Gods and Earths

CHAPTER 1

SOMETHIN' IN THE SLUM WENT RA-PA-PUM-PUM

"Say it loud. I'm black and I'm proud."
James Brown

Hip-hop was always for the children—especially the Black and brown children of the Bronx, who had scarcely anything else. Living on the fringes of a bankrupt city, enduring poor schools and worse neighborhoods, ridden with crime, drugs, and gangs—everything you'd expect in the depths of poverty—they were the victims of a savage society that barely acknowledged their existence. But instead of being eaten alive by their environment and circumstances, they transcended them. See, scarcity and limitation also fostered ingenuity and resourcefulness, and using what little they had at their disposal—their parents' old records, a turntable, a mic, and their own fertile imaginations—they created a musical phenomenon that swept the world.

Defying all odds and expectations, hip-hop stands as one of the ultimate underdog success stories of all time as it rose from nothing to become a pop-culture Galactus, gobbling up millions in profits and leaving a wide swathe of influence in its wake. As far as underdogs go, the same could be said for the

Wu-Tang Clan. Nine young Black men from the projects—most high school dropouts and ex-felons from broken homes who were never supposed to amount to anything—joined together for a common cause, not only beating the odds but profoundly changing hip-hop in the process. At a time when the corporate music industry controlled rap, pushing pop sellouts or smooth G-funk for mass consumption, Wu-Tang bum-rushed the boardroom, bringing the art form back to its essence—the streets. In the process, they became veritable superheroes to a generation, eventually attaining the kind of cultural cachet that few artists ever achieve.

"The reason why people took hold of our shit was because they fiendin' for hip-hop," explains RZA, architect of the Clan. "See, it's like when hip-hop was first in the streets, know what I'm sayin', everybody was into it. But then when it got to the radio and it started getting watered down, started getting into pop music, everyone started getting away from it for a minute. But we came back with a nice revival, you know what I'm sayin'? And I think our revival has been the strongest revival as of date." After years of corporate dominance, Wu-Tang ushered in a renaissance of real hip-hop, a core reason behind their huge impact and appeal. "Wu is hip-hop—classical, vintage hip-hop," RZA declares. "We the bridge between old and new. We like the bridge between the old school and the new generation of hip-hop." In restoring the integrity of the art form and culture, Wu-Tang spearheaded a movement of their own, assuring their place as rap royalty.

Hip-hop's humble origins can be traced back to the South Bronx of the seventies, a study in urban decay and neglect that provided unlikely fertile ground for this explosion of creativity from the bottom. Poor Black and Hispanic youth, lacking even a basic social safety net or opportunities for improvement, took it upon themselves to create something for their own edification and entertainment. From a dee-jay cutting and scratching records while an MC dropped rhymes on the mic to B-boys "goin' off" during the extended percussive sections known as "the breaks," contorting their bodies like pretzels or spinning on their heads, only a flimsy piece of cardboard separating skull from concrete, this new movement was born in the parties or "jams" held in housing-project recreation rooms or outside in the public parks. It came to encompass street fashion and other facets of urban culture, including the unseen rebels who threw up elaborate, stylized "tags" on the sides of abandoned buildings using cans of aerosol paint, soon to switch to subway cars as their canvases.

For youth mired in poverty and all of its negative effects, the various elements of hip-hop provided a means of express-ing themselves and making a mark on their environment. It soon became a source of pride, a path to respect and rec-ognition in the neighborhood, and something they could call their own. For us, by us. At a time when the Bronx was synonymous with bad news—in the form of street gangs, slums, smack, and serial arson, which turned the area into a postapocalyptic wasteland—hip-hop offered nothing short of salvation.

Few genres of music can claim an exact date of ori-gin, but, among the cognoscenti, it is generally agreed that August 11, 1973, provided the jump-off. That night, a young Jamaican immigrant named Clive Campbell, a.k.a. DJ Kool Herc, threw his first party in the rec room of 1520 Sedgewick Avenue in the West Bronx, where he lived. What started off as a simple neighborhood bash, attended by mostly teens, to raise money for his younger sister Cindy's back-to-school wardrobe, triggered a movement that influenced the world.

A twelve-year-old Campbell had arrived in the Bronx from Kingston in November 1967, joining his mother, Nettie, a nurse, who had emigrated the previous year. His father, Keith, and five younger siblings soon followed. Awkward and unsure in his new surroundings, Campbell must have felt like he had just fallen off the turnip truck. Eager to assimilate, as are most immigrants, he found an accelerated path to acceptance through sports, winning medals for cross-country and track-and-field in junior high.

By the time he reached Alfred E. Smith High, they were calling him "Hercules" (or "Herc" for short) due to his muscular build and athletic prowess. He had also tamed his thick patois by listening to American music—the sounds of the Temptations, Nat King Cole, and James Brown—as well as copping the style of popular New York radio disc jockeys such as Cousin Brucie and Wolfman Jack. The gang members and Five Percenters, who comprised his classmates, also hipped him the lingo of the streets. By 1970, Campbell was among the hordes of Bronx youth caught up in graffiti's first wave. He wrote, "CLYDE AS KOOL," a tag that combined the name people mistakenly called him and a TV ad for the popular menthol cigarette brand.[1]

However, one part of his Jamaican identity that he maintained and, in fact, nurtured was a passion for music. One of his cherished childhood memories was of Kingston's mobile sound systems, known for setting up massive speaker boxes outside and playing music for the people of the ghetto. Herc, who wanted to somehow re-create that experience in his new home, received crucial support from his father, an avid record collector. Soon after moving to the Bronx, Keith Campbell started sponsoring a local R&B band, investing in a professional PA system with towering Shure speakers. He asked Herc to play records in between sets at their gigs. In exchange, the budding deejay was allowed to borrow the sound system for his own parties. Though it took some tinkering to get everything sounding nice at maximum level, Herc was able to hook up two Bogart amps and two Girard turntables into a preamp, using its channel knobs as his mixer.[2] When he started deejaying, he added the "KOOL" from his graffiti tag to become Kool DJ Herc, the man with the Bronx's first boomin' system. Though the sheer volume of Herc's set could easily drown out any competition, wattage wasn't the only thing he had going for him.

Unlike other deejays, who just played the hits of the day, Herc further distinguished himself by his eclectic selection. His genius was identifying certain records that had an extended percussive section that he called the "get down," because that's the part when dancers really let loose. He used records like Rare Earth's cover of the Temptations' "Get Ready," which had a two-minute percussive breakdown, or "Apache," a funky instrumental jam by the Incredible Bongo Band that became his calling card. While other deejays played a whole song from start to finish, Herc reveled in these breaks, whose appeal boiled down to pure polyrhythms—the kind that made your body move in all different directions at once. Because most breaks were usually brief, however, he experimented, buying double copies of a record and mixing back and forth between them in what he called the "merry-go-round." The extended groove he created came to be known as the "break beat," the primary building block of hip-hop. The breaks inspired young dancers known as "break boys," or

B-boys for short, to bust out the acrobatic moves that came to be dubbed "break dancing." Great for wilding out on the dance floor, the breaks served another purpose as well.

Herc unleashed his ferocious medley of funky break beats at Cindy's back-to-school bash. For crowd control, he used a microphone attached to a Space Echo box, like the dee-jays used to do back home in Jamaica, sending his bellowing baritone soaring above the music. But as Herc focused more on playing records, his buddy Coke La Rock, seized by the inspiration of the moment, grabbed the mic and started dropping simple rhyming phrases like "Yes indeed, you rock with the rockers and jam with the jammers and boogie with the boogiers" in the jive-talkin' tradition of *Hustler's Convention* (Celluloid, 1973), an album of prison toasts and pimp talk that was a ghetto favorite at the time.[3] He also shouted out his friends' names, saying, "My mellow in the house." In the process, he inadvertently became rap's first master of ceremony, or MC. "That first party was epic," says Curtis Fisher, one of Herc's early fans, who started attending all his jams. "Afterwards, everybody attempted to recreate the energy of that night, because that sparked everything."[4] Indeed, even Fisher was eventually inspired to pick up the mic, rapping under the alias Casanova Fly, a.k.a. Grandmaster Caz.

Word of Herc's phenomenal splashdown spread quickly through the neighborhood, leading to packed monthly parties in the Sedgewick Avenue rec room as well as guest appearances at a couple of area high schools. By the summer of 1974, with his crowds growing too large, he brought his set outside, playing records in nearby Cedar Park and inspiring legions of youth by his example. At this point, there was no looking back. From the parks, he moved on to the local clubs—long-forgotten spaces like the Twilight Zone,

Hevalo, and Executive Playhouse—and by 1976, his name rang bells far beyond the borough. The excitement sparked by Herc ignited the Bronx like the flames of arson that had once plagued the neighborhood. His innovations were copied by others, who took what he was doing and added their own spin.

Only fifteen at the time, Joseph Saddler was intrigued by what he had seen in Cedar Park. An immigrant from Barbados, he lived with his parents and four sisters at Fox and 163rd Streets in the Bronx, smack-dab in the middle of the notorious gang territory known as Fort Apache. A self-professed nerdy kid, he preferred spending his time fixing broken radios or appliances rescued from the piles of trash to hanging out in the mean streets outside his windows. Any chance he got, he delved into his father's extensive record collection, even recognizing some of the songs he heard that night in the park.

But Saddler, who approached everything in a very scientific manner, felt that Herc's practice of randomly dropping the needle where he thought the groove began led to sloppy, offbeat transitions. As an electronics wiz at Samuel Gompers Vocational High, he had a fix for that. The enterprising teen actually built his own mixer with a cue switch—like the ones that disco deejays like Pete DJ Jones used—allowing him to audition one record in the headphones while the other was playing. Using this simple innovation, he could seamlessly interlock the beats as he segued between turntables.

Calling himself "Grandmaster Flash" in homage to the karate films that were popular at the time and the blazing speed at which his hands worked the vinyl, Saddler single-handedly pioneered the art form of turntablism, or using the turntable itself as an instrument. He demonstrated his mastery with the

innovation of scratching, or manually manipulating the record with his hands as it spun to create sharp rhythmic noises.
Though his younger protégé "Grand Wizard" Theodore Liv-
ingston, who was only thirteen at the time, accidentally discovered the technique, Flash was the first to debut this new
trick, stopping the party in its tracks. As everyone gathered
around to stare at him in awe, he realized that this was not
exactly the desired effect. Therefore, in order to divert attention from what he was doing, Flash was the first to employ
multiple MCs, starting with the Glover brothers—Melvin,
a.k.a. "Melle Mel," and Nathaniel, a.k.a. "Kid Creole"—and a
former Black Spade gang member, Keith "Cowboy" Wiggins,
whose lyrical stylings gave us the term "hip-hop."

On the other side of the borough, another Black Spade
from the Bronx River projects, Afrika Bambaataa, was also
paying close attention to Herc and taking notes. Though only
a student at Stevenson High, he had a lot of the same records himself—including James Brown, the Incredible Bongo
Band, Baby Huey, and the Jimmy Castor Bunch. As warlord
for one of the most powerful street gangs in New York, Bambaataa commanded so much respect of the streets that he
could freely move through all the treacherous gang turfs in
the Bronx. He assumed his distinctive title, meaning "affec-
tionate leader," after winning an essay contest in high school
that afforded him a life-changing trip to Africa. Seeing Black
people in the motherland running their own thriving society
without whites proved to be nothing short of inspirational.
As a child of the civil rights era and a natural leader and orga-
nizer, Bambaataa wanted to establish a similar model in the
Bronx. During the waning influence of the gangs, he had the
foresight to start a street-based organization called the Universal Zulu Nation, uniting the various elements of hip-hop

under a single banner and helping to spread their influence far beyond the borough.

When he first started deejaying, he positioned his speakers out the windows of his project apartment, which he shared with his mother, a nurse. After getting more comfortable with his skills, he started throwing parties in the Bronx River Community Center, located in the middle of the projects. With crates upon crates of vinyl, Bam, who was dubbed "Master of Records," expanded hip-hop's palette of funk, soul, and R&B to include jazz, rock, world music, and obscure rarities, as well as interludes, like the theme from *The Munsters*, which he taped off TV and played in his mixes.

At a time when R&B and later disco was bumping in the clubs and on commercial radio, hip-hop issued forth from the streets, the parlance of poor Blacks and Hispanics partying for their right to exist and be recognized—the original Black Lives Matter. Before it even had a name, the art form was both dynamic and democratic, constantly honed and improved upon in the communal parties called "jams," where anyone with talent could make a name for themselves. Those early formative years, respectfully regarded as the "Old School," set the tempo for everything to follow. A more fitting description would be "True School" because the pioneers who grew and established the art form represented the truest form of hip-hop. Before money and fame entered the equation, they were doing it largely out of love and respect. In today's commercial era, we often lose sight of their invaluable contributions, but what they started impacted generations of youth to come— especially those who were following right on their heels.

"If my homeboy came to me and I was hangin' out somewhere playin' handball, and he'd come over and say, 'Yo, they jammin' down in such and such,' I might do something I've never done before right on the spot, like do a backflip off a car because that's how much we loved hip-hop and still do," says Gary Grice, fifty-five, otherwise known as the GZA or Genius, a founding member of Wu-Tang Clan.[5] He was born in Brooklyn on August 22, 1966, and his parents separated when he was young, so he split time between his mother in Brooklyn and Staten Island and his father in the South Bronx's Soundview projects.

A quiet, contemplative child, Grice gravitated toward the nursery rhymes of Mother Goose, which he memorized word for word. He discovered a different kind of poetry at his aunt's house, however, when he was first introduced to the fiery rhetoric of the Last Poets, a revolutionary group of poets and musicians, formed on Malcolm X's birthday on May 19, 1968, for the uplifting of Black consciousness. (Coincidentally, Jalal Nuriddin, a member of that group, is also responsible for the influential *Hustler's Convention* album under the alias Lightnin' Rod.) "At that time, albums didn't have explicit stickers on them," Grice says. "So, some of the songs had profanity on them, and I was moved by that. I would listen to the songs, to the flow, and I would balance it back and forth with the nursery stuff I had."[6] Making the leap to MCing was nothing, as Grice adds, "When hip-hop came in, I already had that kind of flow, you know, that knack for rhyming and delivering lyrics in a certain way."[7]

His initial exposure to rapping and deejaying came while spending summers with his father in the Soundview projects. "It's like every motherfucker that would get on the mic in the South Bronx was incredibly ill, you know, how I saw it then," he says, inspiring him to start writing his own rhymes. "So, I used to go back and forth from the Bronx to Staten Island, pickin' up on my skills, coming back, kickin' some uptown shit from the Bronx," he continues. "You know how it is when you start—we all go through it, you know what I'm sayin'? It's just payin' respect to niggas that's dope—say they lyrics, you know. And as time went on, I started to advance in my skills." He also introduced his cousin from his mother's side, Bobby Diggs, who would become Wu-Tang mastermind RZA, to this new movement that was bubbling up from the streets and spreading to low-budget neighborhoods around the five boroughs.

As the nation celebrated its two hundredth birthday in July 1976, Bobby, then seven, was visiting Gary, a.k.a. Buck, who was three years older and living in Staten Island's Park Hill projects at the time. That afternoon, a guy known as DJ Jones had set up his turntables, mixer, and speakers between two of the project buildings, jacking power from a streetlight. He started cutting and scratching records as his MCs, Punch and Quincy, traded simple rhymes on the mic: "Dip, dip, dive, and you socialize / Clean out your ears and you open your eyes."[8] Having never seen guys talking over beats before and feeling the energy of the crowd and the whole vibe of something fresh and new happening, Bobby's mind was officially blown. He stayed out until well past eleven, soaking up the atmosphere and dancing the night away. Though his mother gave him an ass whipping, it was a small price to pay for falling in love for the first time. "These words and this music, they were a call—a call to something deep inside me," he recalled in his memoir.[9] But, he says, "it wasn't until fourth grade at the age of nine that I wrote my first rhyme. But once I wrote my own, I never stopped."[10]

The following summer, Gary accompanied Bobby to his baptism at the source—the South Bronx. The journey, which took about two hours, required hopping a bus to the ferry, then taking the train all the way uptown to another bus before finally arriving at Morrison/Soundview. The payoff was getting to hear Disco King Mario play records, flanked by a wall of fourteen Cerwin Vega speakers set up outside in the project courtyard. On that sticky summer day, they danced with the girls until a break beat like "Apache" or "Dance to the Drummer's Beat" came on, instantly transforming them into B-boys. "I would just dive in the air crazy high, land on my hands, goin' crazy, all a that," Grice recalls.[11] Though the man behind the wheels of steel was still the main attraction, the budding MC cast an envious eye at the roped-off area behind the turntables, where the deejay's crew took turns rocking the mic. Then, all the way home on the train, the cousins imitated those MCs, kicking rhymes back and forth to each other. "For us, it was just a passion and a hobby—it was something that is so much a part of my makeup," says Grice. "It was something I loved so much. We didn't know it was going to change or revolutionize the world as a music genre."[12]

Born in Brooklyn, King's County Hospital, on July 5, 1969, Robert Fitzgerald Diggs—named after the martyred Kennedy brothers, whom his mother admired—didn't stay in New York for long. Only three years old when his parents split up, Bobby was sent to live with a great-uncle in Murfreesboro, North Carolina. His mom's father's brother, Uncle Hollis, a practicing physician who owned six hundred acres of land on which he grew tobacco and peanuts and raised animals, provided him with probably his first and only positive male role model. Bobby grew very fond of Hollis, whom he described as "Solomon-wise" and who also instilled in him a love of learning. He encouraged Bobby to read and study, and one of the first books he gave the four-year-old was *Mother Goose Nursery Rhymes*, which he enjoyed as much as his cousin Gary. Bobby also credited his great-uncle with teaching him manners and how to carry himself. He enjoyed a very proper and comfortable upbringing on Hollis's sprawling estate, even attending Southern Baptist church services every Sunday, where people regularly broke out in hysterics, apparently overcome by the Holy Spirit. But even as a kid, Bobby exhibited a wisdom beyond his years and wasn't buying it. Despite the separation from his immediate family, those early years were happy ones for him.[13]

Everything changed, however, in 1976, when his mother, Linda, brought him back to Brooklyn. While playing the numbers, she hit a winner for almost $4,000 and was able to get a lease on a three-bedroom unit in the Marcus Garvey Village Apartments in Brownsville for herself and eight of her eleven kids. The newly built public housing project stood in stark contrast to the Betsy Head Pool, the city's first public outdoor pool and bath house built in 1914, which sat right across the street. Here, youth from all the nearby projects— including the Brownsville, Tilden, and Van Dyke Houses— went to beat the heat. They also learned, firsthand, the law of the concrete jungle, as daily fights and muggings made it the kind of place that if you went in wearing nice sneakers, you were walking home barefoot.

But Brooklyn builds character, or so the saying goes. A guy known around the block as "Bighead" Mike would hang at the basketball court next door to the pool.[14] Bullied incessantly for his high-pitched voice and lisp, Mike, the son of sex workers, earned his lumps here, learning to fight just to survive. Involved in muggings and petty crime, he was arrested thirty-eight times by the age of thirteen. Finally, he ended up at the Tryon School for Boys, a reformatory in Johnstown, New York, where he was able to turn things around and hone his raw power into a formidable prowess in the boxing ring. The champ Mike Tyson eventually escaped the hell that was Brownsville. But Bobby was new to these mean streets.

More than a hundred years earlier, in 1866, a developer named Charles S. Brown put the neighborhood on the map. After acquiring some subdivisions in the east of Brooklyn through a foreclosure auction, he started touting "Brownsville" as an alternative for working-class Jews crammed into Manhattan's Lower East Side. By the turn of the century, the neighborhood's population had swelled, earning it the nickname of Little Jerusalem. In the meantime, it had also become a hub of manufacturing. Along with factories came low-income tenements to house the workers, which was how Brownsville became designated as a slum. The neighborhood's reputation for crime originated as early as the thirties and forties, when the notorious mob enforcers known as Murder Inc., including legendary Jewish gangsters Meyer Lansky and Bugsy Siegel, established their base there.

Brownsville remained predominantly Jewish up until the fifties. Then the building of several new high-rise public housing projects within a one-mile radius—to accommodate a burgeoning lower-income Black population, who were part of the postwar migration from the South—triggered white flight. According to US Census figures from 1970, Brownsville's population of 138,000 was 77 percent Black and 19 percent Puerto Rican. The unemployment rate stood at a whopping 17 percent, twice that of the rest of the city, while the neighborhood also claimed the highest poverty rate. Surveying a landscape scarred by arson and the 1968 riots, Mayor John Lindsay called it "Bombsville."[15] Its empty lots and burned-out buildings rivalled even the apocalyptic squalor of the South Bronx. Racism and redlining had created neglected communities of color just like this across the nation, where the living was not easy, to say the least.

But the Garvey Houses stood in stark contrast to the Ville's typical high-rise projects. Finished in February 1975, this development of modular three-story buildings in brown brick with gray trim and large white numbers demarcating the individual units looked more like modernist college dorms. It even won kudos for its design, featured at an exhibition at the Museum of Modern Art three years earlier. In the Garvey Houses, front doors opened directly onto the street instead of hallways, and some units even boasted private backyards. But they were still smack-dab in the middle of an impoverished neighborhood with the second-highest crime rate in the city.

Just before moving in, Bobby's family became official Brooklynites when all their belongings, including furniture, toys, and bikes, were stolen right out of their new apartment. The culprit, who revealed himself years later, turned out to be their next-door neighbor, a drug dealer named Chili-Wop, whom Bobby eventually befriended.[16] If being a victim of grand larceny wasn't enough, on his second night in Brownsville, three teenagers mugged Bobby at the corner store. His mom was so incensed that she actually brought him back to look for them in her nightgown, butcher knife in hand. But crime was as normal a part of life here as the mail delivery. Bobby's older brother Mitchell was routinely robbed for his stack of quarters when he went to do the family laundry at the Laundromat, and the boys witnessed their first shooting in the park directly across the street from where they lived.[17]

It's no mystery how "Crooklyn" earned its reputation back then.

Bobby attended PS 384 Francis E. Carter Elementary in neighboring Bushwick, where, in second grade, he met future collaborator Corey Woods (a.k.a. Raekwon the Chef). As per Hollis's influence, he remained a conscientious student who attended church every Sunday with his family. The four Diggs brothers shared a room with two twin beds like they shared their clothes and everything else. Once, after heavy rains, their basement apartment on Dumont Avenue flooded, backing up the toilet and spewing raw sewage everywhere. With the slimmest of means, Bobby's mother still tried her best to make the place into a suitable home. She assigned all the kids chores so that they could contribute to the household and learn some responsibility, and she encouraged them to look out for one another. Though life was hard, being poor was not something Bobby could really grasp at that age—especially surrounded by poverty. After about a year in Brooklyn, he got word that Uncle Hollis had died of a heart attack in North Carolina at the age of forty-five. Absolutely crushed by the news, Bobby cried more than any other time in his young life. In tough situations like these, however, it helped to have a large extended family for support.[18]

Since returning to Brooklyn, Bobby had become close with another cousin, Rusty, who was a year older. Rusty's father, William Jones, and Bobby's grandmother, Mae, were siblings from a large family from Franklin, Virginia, who had both ended up in New York. Born Russell Tyrone Jones on November 15, 1968, Rusty became a man of many aliases, the most popular being Ol' Dirty Bastard, the third founding member of Wu-Tang Clan. But his original nickname came from his mother, Cherry, who combined the first letters of his first and middle names.

When Rusty's family—including his parents and five siblings (two brothers and three sisters)—were living in the Linden Plaza apartments in East New York, Bobby visited practically every weekend. Sometimes they spent Sundays at Rusty's grandmother's house at 112 Putnam Avenue in Bed-Stuy, where Gary often met them as well, playing records and coming up with rap routines in the basement. Bonded by their love of hip-hop, the trio soon became inseparable, whether hanging out in Brooklyn or Staten Island or stomping around Manhattan's Times Square.

Meanwhile, as hip-hop continued to flourish across the five boroughs, it started experiencing the inevitable growing pains. In 1977, Herc was stabbed during an altercation at the door of one of his parties at the Sparkle in the Bronx. Afterward, he receded from the scene, never really reclaiming his former glory. With him, the whole art of deejaying itself seemed to fade from the spotlight—especially when the MCs came to captivate the crowd. By 1978, Grandmaster Flash and the Three MCs had grown into the Furious Five, and they started packing them in at a Bronx club called Disco Fever on Jerome Avenue and 167th Street. Other popular acts who performed there included Grand Wizard Theodore and the Fantastic Five, Funky Four Plus One More, and the Cold Crush Brothers, boasting two deejays, Charlie Chase and Tony Tone, along with MCs Easy AD, JDL, Almighty Kay Gee, and Grandmaster Caz. From rap's inception, then, big groups were the norm, living out their hyperbolic names with flamboyant outfits and creative routines. In this formative era driven by competition, battling on the mic became a way to gain notoriety, and early MCs engaged in a literal war of words to crush their opponents and move the crowd with their verbal dexterity. Before records, bootleg tapes captured the energy of these live jams, circulating throughout the tri-state area and beyond.

"We based ourselves on what came before us," says Grandmaster Caz, who ultimately credits Harlem's DJ Hollywood, a disco deejay, for laying the blueprint of rhyming on the microphone to complement the music. He says, "Kool Herc or Coke La Rock would have a little saying, you know what I mean? And we would just copy it and embellish it or change it, you know what I'm sayin', to fit our particular format. Other people started doing it, and the more it happened, the more it grew."[19] One of those people was a young Bobby, who says, "I'm nine years old, listening to them, and I start writing based on what I'm hearing them do, and so I'm like a student."[20]

But as hip-hop migrated to the clubs, it also underwent its first major reckoning. Would it remain true to its roots or become watered down for mass consumption? Since then, two diverging camps—commercial and underground—have been battling for the soul of the art form. Initially, rap provided an alternative to disco, but as it expanded, it merged with its former nemesis in a bid for wider appeal. The culmination of rap's crossover came with the release of a record that epitomizes the never-ending conflict between art and commerce, clearly separating the hustlers of culture from those who were doing it from the heart.

It all started when Sylvia Robinson, a former singer herself and co-owner of the Sugar Hill record label with her husband, Joe, was looking to get into something new. She had seen a guy named Lovebug Starski (Kevin Smith) talking over disco tracks and driving the crowd crazy at Harlem World at 116th and Lenox and wanted to re-create that same energy on a record. When she approached the MC, however, he rebuffed her, saying that what he did was only meant to be done live at a club. Later on, at an Englewood, New Jersey, pizzeria, Robinson heard Henry Lee "Hank" Jackson rapping to a tape of the Cold Crush Brothers. She told him she was putting together a group to record a rap.

Hank was no MC, but a club bouncer who had aspirations of becoming an artist manager. In fact, he already had a relationship with Cold Crush, but instead of tipping them off to this opportunity, he asked one of the members, Grandmaster Caz, a.k.a. Casanova Fly, if he could borrow his book of rhymes. Caz consented, and the rest, as they say, is history. "Big Bank" Hank, along with Michael "Wonder Mike" Wright and Guy "Master G" O'Brien, three random dudes put together by Robinson, ended up making a record called "Rapper's Delight," a six-minute song with no hook that soared up the charts, becoming an international hit. As amazing and groundbreaking as it sounded, it really had nothing to do with what was going on in the Bronx. It wasn't even the first rap on wax—preceded months earlier by a record called "King Tim III (Personality Jock)," by the Fatback Band, released on the independent Spring Records, run by Julius Rifkind. Nevertheless, "Rapper's Delight," a catchy, funky novelty hit based on Chic's disco sensation "Good Times," became most people's introduction to this new sound from the streets of New York. As rap got its first taste of stardom, becoming the flavor of the moment, hip-hop remained hidden from view, oozing up from the asphalt like black gold.

Change was in the air all over. Back in Brownsville, the Diggs family, four months behind in rent, got evicted from their apartment in Marcus Garvey Village. Bobby and his two elder brothers were sent to live with their grandparents at Sixty-Four Targee Street in Staten Island. It was, by no means, the first, or last time, he would change addresses. But music remained a constant in his life and something that kept him grounded. The breakout success of "Rapper's Delight" planted a seed inside the impressionable ten-year-old's mind. He realized not only the possibility of making a rap record—a completely novel concept at the time—but also that it could be hugely popular and make money. Full of dreams and possibilities, he made a conscious decision to dedicate himself to that goal.

CHAPTER 2

LIFE AS A SHORTY

"Children are the constructors of men whom they build, taking
from the environment language, religion, customs and the
peculiarities not only of the race, not only of the nation, but
even of a special district in which they develop. Childhood
constructs with what it finds. If the material is poor, the
construction is also poor. In order to build himself, he has to
take by chance, whatever he finds in the environment."

Dr. Maria Montessori, in a letter to world governements, 1947

In the wake of Columbus's accidental "discovery," another
Italian explorer, Giovanni de Verrazzano, became the first
European to lay eyes on what is now New York Bay in 1520.
After navigating the bay's narrow entrance, he anchored his
ship, *La Dauphine*, only for the night—but long enough to
secure his place in history. On November 21, 1964, when
they cut the ribbon on what was then the longest suspen-
sion bridge in the world—an astounding feat of engineering
at a span of 4,260 feet—his name was immortalized in steel
and concrete. Connecting the boroughs of Brooklyn and
Staten Island, the Verrazzano Narrows Bridge, championed
by city planner Robert Moses, the man behind the Cross
Bronx Expressway and other major urban renewal projects
that changed the face of New York in the forties, fifties, and

sixties, promised to bring the city closer together while also promoting expansion to the isolated fifth borough of Staten Island, which had only been accessible by ferry. Now families from Brooklyn had a physical escape route from the poverty, crime, and neglect that was consuming their neighborhoods. The Verrazzano threw them a lifeline, as it were, and many seized it. Due to the high volume of traffic on the bridge, a lower deck was added in June 1969.[1]

All those cars stacked up in multiple lanes, horns blaring and engines idling as they waited to pay the toll, might have looked like one hot mess, but Bobby, now eleven, and his older brother Mitchell, twelve, saw an opportunity. Displaying a precocious entrepreneurial spirit and work ethic, they started selling newspapers to the morning commuters for fifty cents a pop, palming a ten-cent commission per paper for themselves. A couple of hours of work could net them ten to twelve dollars each, which, at the end of the week, added up to sixty or seventy dollars. "That's enough to buy me a pair of Pumas, a pair of Lees, or help out my mother," says RZA.[2] Sometimes Gary joined them, as well as Mitchell's buddy from PS 57, Oliver "Pook" Grant, and his cousin Kevin. The impetus behind their collective hustle was simple. "We saw the struggle," says Grant. "We all had families, and it was not so much just to buy your own shit, it was just like to take some burden off the family, 'cause, you know we had little brothers and shit."

Though the struggle was as real here as in any other borough, Bobby's new home distinguished itself from the rest of the city with a suburban vibe of its own. "One thing about Staten Island that was different from Brooklyn was the ability to walk from one neighborhood to another, to actually have a break from project life," he says. "For instance, in

Brownsville, in Brooklyn, if I walked from the Marcus Garvey projects to go see my cousin Vince, who lived in the Van
Dyke projects, I had to walk through four projects to get
there—and each project could be considered 'turf.' In fact,
each building could be considered turf."[3] On Staten Island,
however, he says, "You can walk from the Park Hill projects
to the Stapleton projects, and in between those two projects
is something else—'normal' hardworking homeowners, you
know, not projects. I saw what we'd consider mansions then,
big homes. And I think seeing another side of life that wasn't
ghetto life—I think there was something healthy about that."[4]
In addition to selling newspapers, he says, "When I was living in Staten Island in sixth grade, when a snowstorm happens, guess what I'm able to do—I'm able to get out, pull out
a shovel, and make $15 hustling, shoveling snow. That wasn't
available in Brownsville. You had breathing space. You were
able to walk a few blocks, not worried about fighting, defending, stealing, robbing—things that happen every day in the
projects."[5]

Though saddled with the unenviable nickname of the Forgotten Borough, Staten Island's unique history contributed
to its misfit status, lending an aura of mystique as well. Even
the native Munsee tribes that originally lived there called it
Aquehonga Manacknong, or Place of the Enchanted Woods.[6]
Unlike Manhattan, which Dutch colonists supposedly purchased from the local Lenape Indians in 1626 for the bargain price of trinkets worth roughly sixty guilders (about US
$1,000 back then), this neighboring island proved far more
difficult to acquire. Though the Dutch gained a foothold there
in 1661, naming it *Staaten* Island in homage to their parlia-
ment back home, territorial disputes with the natives raged

on. Finally, in 1670, the British kicked everyone out, and the former Dutch holding, anglicized to Staten Island, joined the colony of New York. Designated as Richmond County (after Charles Lennox, the first duke of Richmond), and later the Borough of Richmond, it did not become a part of New York City until much later, in 1898.[7]

"It is greener, quieter and more open on Staten Island," wrote the *New York Times* in 1972, capturing the place's ultimate paradox of being a suburb within a city. "Still, Staten Island does have 333,000 people in its 60 square miles, which means that an area three times the size of Manhattan has about one-fifth of its population."[8] Ironically, both rank-and-file cops and Mafia dons had already discovered this quiet corner of New York as an ideal place to raise families or keep a low profile. Throughout the seventies, however, the city started encouraging others to take advantage of the plentiful space and cheaper rents, and the exodus from other boroughs began.

Radio ads touting the Park Hill Apartments, located in the Clifton section of Staten Island, attracted people like Lamont Hawkins (a.k.a. U-God) and his mom. Like many parts of New York, the area had a storied history. Originally owned by the wealthy Vanderbilt family in the 1830s, the land became property of the Fox Hills Golf Club by the turn of the century and was later requisitioned as a military barracks during World War II. Built in the sixties after the opening of the Verrazzano, Park Hill originally attracted middle- and working-class whites. The six-story brick buildings, situated on a six-block radius around Vanderbilt and Park Hill Avenues, boasted carpeted hallways, doormen, and even vending machines in the lobbies. Looks could be deceiving, however, because the buildings were found to be structurally unsound and began falling apart, forcing the owners to apply for federal funding. But by opening the doors for government subsidies, they were also obliged to accept low-income, predominantly Black, section-eight applicants, who soon supplanted the mostly white residents. As whites packed up and left, they took many of the local businesses with them—including the cleaners, the fish market, and the shoe repair—gradually hollowing out the community.[9] It was the same story in practically every city in America where Blacks sought suitable housing.

Born in Brooklyn on November 10, 1970, Lamont spent his early years in the Brownsville projects before moving out to Staten Island. A child of generational poverty, he never knew his father, and his mother was also a product of public housing, raised in Brownsville's Howard Houses. In fact, she grew up in the same building—1543 East New York Avenue—as Andrea Woods, who had also just relocated to Park Hill with her young son, Cory, born January 12, 1970, who was Lamont's age. Coincidentally, Lamont's mom also knew Bobby's mom, Linda, who had lived in the neighboring Van Dyke Houses.[10] Indeed, despite all the downsides of project life, they did, at least, help foster lasting friendships and a sense of community.

"Growing up how we did, you'd think it was all hard times," Lamont recalled in his memoir. "We were too young to know we were 'disadvantaged.' You sort of have a feeling something's not right, but you're a kid, so you adapt and learn how to have your fun anyway."[11] That meant playing with the neighborhood kids in a patch of undeveloped land behind the projects that even included a small wooded area with two ponds. As a child of the asphalt, he felt a sense of liberation being around so much nature and living out a

Huck Finn fantasy, catching frogs and crawfish or skipping stones across the water. Reality only intruded if they happened to venture to the other side of the big pond, where the white kids would chase them back, openly taunting them with the N-word. Blacks, in fact, were expected to observe the unspoken, racially segregated boundaries that separated their immediate area of Clifton and neighboring Stapleton from the predominantly Italian neighborhoods of the North Shore, such as Rosebank, which they labelled "Mini Mississippi." If they didn't, they could expect to be chased out by an angry white mob.

White bullies were not the only threat. The Avenue Crew, a gang of Black teens who hung out on the corner, relentlessly terrorized the younger kids. It didn't take long for Lamont and his friends to figure out that there was strength in solidarity. While in elementary school at PS 57, he, Cory, and a few others formed the Baby Crash Crew (BCC) to protect themselves from their teen tormentors. "It was really some neighborhood shit, you know. It was like hangin' out with friends that you grew up with," says Raekwon. "We was running around, getting into shit, getting into trouble, but it more started from going to school together."[12]

Yet the same people they feared were the ones they emulated. "For me, say around '82, '83, I was a kid and just growing up in the neighborhood and watching the older dudes," Raekwon recalls. "Everything they did, from what they wore, to where they was goin', to what they ate. My generation of cats that was living in the neighborhood, we was just wanting to follow the procedure and do the same shit."[13] Estranged from his father, a drug addict, Raekwon looked to these older dudes on the corner as his only male role models. With a strict mother, any bad habits he picked up came from these streets, where it was easy to be robbed of the innocence of childhood. By junior high, BCC had morphed into DMD, or Dick 'Em Down crew, which in turn became the Wreck Posse in high school.[14]

The area youth attended junior high at IS 49 Bertha A. Dreyfus School on Warren Street, directly across from the Stapleton Houses. Here, Lamont and Cory first came into contact with Jason Hunter (a.k.a. Inspectah Deck), Dennis Coles (a.k.a. Ghostface Killah), and Oliver Grant (a.k.a. Power, CEO of Wu-Wear). Jason and Cory were assigned to the same special education classroom for problem students, where many young Black males were railroaded for any excuse at all.[15] Neglected and ignored by teachers, administrators, and the system itself, they were often set on a path that led directly to reform school and, later, prison.

As with most teens, school and learning were hardly priorities in their lives. "I was a straight class fuckin' clown, yo," says Jason. "I'm one of them niggas that was makin' everybody else laugh, had no respect for the teacher, but when test time came, I was the mu'fucka that got the 100."[16] The highlight of their day was lunch, when guys took turns banging out beats on the cafeteria tables with their fists and palms. Jason showed off his poppin' and lockin' skills while Dennis, who sported a puffy afro and perpetual grin, spun on the ground like a member of the Rock Steady Crew. "We used to battle every day like it was *Beat Street* the movie," Deck recalls, referencing one of Hollywood's initial attempts to depict hip-hop culture in 1984.[17]

Born in the Bronx on July 6, 1970, Jason, the youngest child of Frank and Cynthia Hunter, spent his early years shuffling between Brooklyn, the Lower East Side, and Queens before finally settling in Staten Island. If losing his father at the tender age of six wasn't traumatic enough, Jason faced the humiliation of eviction as well, seeing all of his family's belongings tossed into the street. "I watched my moms come back from that with us," he recalls. "She threw us on her back, and she went like fuckin' She-Hulk. I respect her for that, and she made me strong by seeing her be like that."[18] More of an introvert, Jason didn't come outside too much, but he liked to draw, which eventually led to him writing graffiti as "Deck." Living on the top floor of 160 Park Hill, a building known for drug dealing, he also spent a lot of time staring out the window, observing the happenings on the streets below.[19]

Dennis was the only native Staten Islander among the bunch. Since his birth, on May 9, 1970, he had known no other home than the Stapleton Houses, the imposing eight-story buildings erected in 1962, which looked more like a prison— with exposed hallways, like cell-block tiers, covered in chain-link fence to prevent jumpers. When his parents threw parties, he'd have to stay in the room, and one of his fondest early memories was falling asleep to the sounds of the Delfonics, Temptations, or other popular soul and R&B of the era. But when Dennis was only six, his father walked out, leaving him as the man of the household.[20] Under the weight of raising a family alone and on public assistance, Diane, his mom, leaned on the bottle for support, leaving her oldest son to take care of his two younger brothers, both of whom suffered from muscular dystrophy and were confined to wheelchairs.

Like the others, Dennis was also well-acquainted with working at an early age. His first jobs were selling newspapers and bagging groceries at the A&P. Until the federally funded Summer Youth Jobs Program was suspended by the Reagan administration in the early eighties, he also helped clean up the parks. Despite the hardships of growing up in poverty, he managed to retain some of the trappings of a regular childhood, like watching *Tom & Jerry* cartoons after school or playing his favorite video games, *Asteroids* and *Defender*, at the corner store.[21]

IS 49 offered an after-school program where Lamont struck up a friendship with a charismatic youth named Clifford Smith (a.k.a. Method Man), who could pass as the seventh member of New Edition when he busted moves to their 1983 hit, "Candy Girl." Born March 2, 1971, in Hempstead, Long Island, Cliff, who went by "Shotgun," was yet another product of a broken home, splitting time between his dad in Long Island and his mom in Staten Island. In better times, when the family was still together, he was a conscientious student who also excelled on the athletic field, playing football and lacrosse. Like any child, he always looked forward to Christmas when there were a lot of presents under the tree. In third grade, however, everything changed when he, his mother, and two sisters, Terri and Missy, temporarily ended up in a shelter for battered women in Manhattan. Because Umi, the lady who managed the facility, lived in Park Hill, they were able to get a place there and stayed for several years. Then, when Cliff was fourteen, his mom picked up and moved the family to Indianapolis. He only returned to Staten Island a year and a half later for high school.

While the worldwide success of "Rapper's Delight" had opened the floodgates for rap, leading to an avalanche of new artists and releases, many outside the culture still perceived it as a passing fad or novelty. But in the projects, they had been living hip-hop for years. Before records, bootleg cassette tapes of the latest jams or rap battles circulated across the tristate area. They reached Lamont's ears through his uncle

Matt, who came out to Staten Island to lay low whenever he got into trouble. "He'd bring tapes of live performances from Harlem World, a popular club that hosted everyone who was anyone in hip-hop, like Grandmaster Flash and the Furious Five, Lady Smiley, Busy Bee Starski, Doug E. Fresh and Kool Moe Dee," U-God recalls.[22] By July 1982, hip-hop had also arrived on commercial radio in the form of *Mr. Magic's Rap Attack* on 107.5 WBLS, New York's top urban station. Through a variety of formats—vinyl, cassette, and now radio—rap was on a roll, growing and expanding while continuing to inspire minions of youth in the hood.

Saving up from his job selling newspapers at the bridge, Bobby was eventually able to buy a pair of Technics turntables and a DJ mixer. The following year, he added an echo box, a microphone, and a beat machine, which spit out simple preprogrammed rhythms including such styles as waltz, bossa nova, and rock. "If you pushed two buttons together, it might make a different kind of beat," he explains, adding, "Me and Dirty used to make hundreds of beats with that beat machine."[23] He recorded everything on his dual-cassette deck, which also allowed him to dub copies to pass around. By the age of twelve, the young prodigy linked up with local talent—deejay Dr. Rock, from Staten Island's first rap group, the Force MCs (later the Force MDs)—and started making a name for himself around the way.

One summer day, while deejaying outside in the courtyard of the Stapleton Houses, Bobby ran into Lamont, who had come to support his neighbor and buddy Tom, who was also spinning. By this time, with his grandparents' place getting too crowded, Bobby had moved into the projects at 350 Park Hill. Meanwhile Lamont and his mom, after getting kicked out of building 260, settled in across the street at

339 Vanderbilt. Recognizing each other from the neighborhood, the boys kicked it for the first time, planting the seeds of friendship.[24] But that would have to wait, as Bobby soon relocated back to Brooklyn for a couple of years, only returning to Staten Island for high school.

When Gertrude Cuffie bought the former funeral parlor at 112 Putnam Avenue in Bed-Stuy, Brooklyn, in 1954, she needed the four-story brownstone to hold her huge brood—she gave birth to twenty children, only half of whom survived. The three sons and seven daughters who did grow up in that house remained close by, even after having families of their own. Some, like the youngest, Cherry, even lived there for the first couple of years of her marriage, until she and her husband, William Jones, could get on their feet and find a place of their own. But even when they did, 112 Putnam remained a family compound where they were always welcome.

The Cuffie family, who sang church songs together every Sunday in the basement, were all musically inclined. But Cherry, who played violin, clarinet, saxophone, piano, and vibes, stood out for her amazing voice. As early as fifth grade, she won a spot on the citywide school chorus. Then, as teens, she and her sister Paulette started singing in local hotspots like the 521 Club, around the corner at 1134 Fulton Street, where sixties stars like Millie Jackson, Little Johnny Taylor, and the Persuasions often played. When soul singer Billy Preston saw her perform there at age sixteen, he wanted to sign her immediately to Columbia Records, but, obviously, her strict mother wouldn't allow it. Later, after she was married, Cherry and her husband often hosted parties at their apartment in Linden Plaza, singing duets of popular songs and passing on their love of music to their six children.[25]

The firstborn, William Jr., nicknamed Ramsey after jazz great Ramsey Lewis, exhibited an early predilection for banging on pots, pans, and furniture, so they bought him a drum set by age five, encouraging him on the path to becoming a professional musician. If Cherry wasn't able to realize her ambitions, there was no reason one of her children couldn't. But Rusty, who was three years younger than Ramsey, was the last person she'd expect to fulfill that role. With more heart than talent, he crooned into the end of a broom handle, emulating the fancy footwork of his crazy uncle Fred, who was known for his James Brown imitation. Forever clowning, Rusty kept his family entertained, prompting his sisters to give him his first stage name, "The Wizard of Do It Land."[26] The kid was up for anything. At parties, he and his sister Dione stole the show with their rendition of the popular Rick James and Teena Marie duet "Fire and Desire" as cousins, aunts, and uncles eagerly egged them on. Partial to Billie Holiday, Marvin Gaye, and his mother's favorite singers—Gladys Knight, Aretha Franklin, and Chaka Khan—Rusty was also influenced by his older brother's eclectic taste in music, which was informed and encouraged by their father.

William Sr. prized his extensive record collection and listened to all kinds of music. Scattered among the soul, jazz, and R&B platters, for example, you could find the Beatles' *White Album* and *Are You Experienced* by Hendrix. He introduced his elder son to Greenwich Village, exposing him to all the new and used record stores there. Ramsey's aunt Cat, who lived in Clinton Hill, rescued some of her neighbor's collection from the trash—including records by Black Sabbath, the Beach Boys, and Led Zeppelin—passing them on to her nephew as well. Whatever their big brother played, the others listened to as well, so Rusty absorbed it all.

Although recipients of public assistance, both parents worked full-time—William for the transit authority and Cherry as a 911 dispatcher—providing a stable home for their family. Such a powerful example was not lost on Bobby when he came to visit. As a child, he was impressed that the Joneses always had milk in the fridge and two boxes of cereal in the cupboard. On Saturdays, Cherry made pancakes for the kids, and William, on his time off, took his sons fishing out by Jamaica Bay. Rising early, they took the A Train out to Far Rockaway, returning home later in the day with porgies, bluefish, and black fish to fry. "I never could catch a black-fish," Jones recalled. "Dirty [Rusty] would sit there and catch them back-to-back. His brother Mark couldn't catch them either. You hear a lot of guys who say they've been fishing all their lives; they say a black fish is hard to catch."[27] Apparently, Rusty already had a certain attraction about him.

Bobby began spending more time with his cousin after moving back to Brooklyn. "When I was thirteen, I had a job as food peddler," he recalls. "Me and ODB would get up early in the morning, and we would go unload apples and oranges and peaches and put 'em into a fruit stand in down-town Brooklyn where we were selling all day."[28] Other times, they passed out flyers, earning up to eighty-five dollars a week, which gave them pocket money to spend on what they pleased. Aside from buying a pair of pants or sneakers or helping out their families, they channeled these funds toward their passion, hip-hop.

In the same basement where the Cuffies gathered every Sunday to sing and pray and the Cuffie boys, Fred Jr. and Pete, got their hair processed, Bobby and Rusty set up their turntables and mixer and started practicing rap routines with Gary. "They used to be down in my grandmother's basement," recalls David Turner (a.k.a. Popa Wu), also known as Free-dum Allah, their older cousin, "and my grandmother used to say, 'Turn the music down!' And they'd be all night long with the turntables. And I used to sit there, 'I'm your manager.' They didn't have nobody to listen to 'em so they come to me. 'Listen to this, listen to this.' All they had to do was buy me a pint of wine. So, I'd be sitting there drinking my little wine, listenin' to 'em."

Around this time, the trio formed their first short-lived group, FOI, or Force of the Imperial Master, which eventually turned into the All in Together Now Crew. Originally called the "Genius," Rusty became the "Specialist" for his skill at beatboxing. Gary, who was far and away the best rapper among the bunch and taught the other two how to write rhymes, then naturally assumed the title of "Genius." Into the technical wizardry of the turntables, as well as cerebral rhymes, Bobby called himself the "Scientist." From jump, they set themselves apart by not taking the typical flashy MC names, while their group initials, FOI, also stood for Fruit of Islam, the Nation of Islam's security wing.

Though Bobby was the youngest, he was tall and lanky and used height to his advantage. According to ODB, "RZA, he used to make me rhyme. He used to fight me to rhyme. If I ain't rhyme, he'll fight me. That's one thing. The GZA organized my style because I listened to the GZA, and he organized my style. And then I took the Beatles and Marvin Gaye and Teddy Pendergrass and the Temptations and all that put together, and I just made it one thing, man, and it worked, man. It was called singin' rappin', and nobody was doin' it."[29]

While Rusty's style of singin' rappin' was still years ahead of its time, another trio emerged on the scene and totally changed the rap game once again, taking the art form in a new and exciting direction. Joseph "Run" Simmons, Darryl "DMC" McDaniels, and Jason "Jam Master Jay" Mizell, three friends from middle-class Hollis, Queens, recorded a single called "It's Like That / Sucker MCs" with the help of Simmons's brother Russell, a rap promoter and manager. Released on August 10, 1983, on the independent Profile Records, the record did surprisingly well, peaking at number fifteen on the Billboard R&B charts. When their eponymous debut dropped the following year, it became the first rap album to go gold, selling five hundred thousand units. Rebelling against the disco-fied sound that had become the norm since "Rapper's Delight," Run-DMC recorded a hard, abrasive album, full of stripped-down drum-machine beats punctuated by electric guitar riffs, which were not usually associated with rap. They presented a rugged style to match, wearing black leathers, fedoras, Adidas sneakers, and chunky gold ropes, mimicking the drug dealers around their way rather than their more flamboyant predecessors. In this back-to-basics approach, they reclaimed rap for the streets, showing the youth that you didn't need all that theatrical shit to rock the mic right. The three cousins who would go on to form the core of Wu-Tang took note.

When Bobby moved back to Staten Island for high school, Gary and Rusty, who both lived in Brooklyn, naturally spent more time with each other. Inspired by Run-DMC, they recorded their first rhyme around 1984, "True Fresh MC," with Rusty doing the beatbox. That was followed by other songs, like "All in Together Now," which they dubbed on cassettes that circulated around the city. Though only teenagers with big dreams of rap stardom, they already had one foot up in the game, pursuing their passion with the urgency of youth.

CHAPTER 3

SUPREME CLIENTELE

When David Turner was just a twelve-year-old, living in Coney Island with his mother, Hilda, a single parent, in 1968, he says, "I noticed these guys in long cashmere coats walking around with briefcases, but they didn't go to work. They used to be on the corners saying, 'The Black man is God.'"[1] Those five words alone were enough to stop the impressionable youth in his tracks, but the slick linguistics with which they delivered their street ministry—equal parts preacher and pimp—drew him in.

"I was like, damn, I wanna talk like this brother. I like the way this brother talk," David recalls. "The things he was saying brought tears to my eyes. I ain't ever heard no Black man talk like that"—pausing a beat before adding—"That's deep." In addition to adopting Muslim-sounding names, the brothers on the corner greeted each other with the phrase "Peace, God." Such proclamations of their own divinity were accompanied by the assertion that the one responsible for all their troubles—the white man—was the devil incarnate. An additional takeaway impressed upon their mostly young audience was to stop eating pork, which they considered to be poison and a "slave food."

Profoundly affected by what he heard that day, David left the impromptu gathering clutching three sheets of paper,

which he was told to go home and memorize. The first, entitled "Supreme Mathematics," assigned a symbolic meaning to
all of the prime numbers between zero and nine. The second,
the "Supreme Alphabet," offered the same treatment to each
of the twenty-six letters of the alphabet. The third, simply called
the "Twelve Jewels," provided a checklist of sorts to which each
person should strive in order to lead a fulfilling life. One first
needed to gain knowledge, wisdom, and understanding, for
example, in order to attain freedom, justice, and equality. That
would, in turn, allow one to secure food, clothing, and shelter
and eventually achieve love, peace, and happiness.

Of course, to a junior high school student, memorizing
stuff sounded suspiciously like homework, for which David
had no inclination. But the next time he came outside, he
ran into those same righteous brothers, who tried to test him
on the material they had provided. After pleading ignorance,
he was given a warning: memorize what was on those pages
or catch a beatdown next time. Since leaving the house was
becoming a hazard, David felt compelled to complete this
extracurricular assignment, and when next confronted by
the older gods, he was able to hold his own. He soon graduated to studying the "Supreme Wisdom Lessons," or "the
120," as they were called, which represented the bulk of
Five-Percenter philosophy. Each time he learned to recite
a lesson or "degree," he was given another one to master,
thereby advancing on his path. After a certain point, this rote
learning started to sink in.

"I went into a deep study, and I started seeing that it
was education," he says. "It wouldn't put money in your
pocket, it wouldn't do nothin', but it was education, givin'
you knowledge that the teachers in school don't teach you.
It was all about self-awareness." In keeping with the practices

of the group, after he had mastered the entirety of the 120 "Supreme Wisdom Lessons," he assumed the righteous name of Freedum [*sic*] Allah when he was only fourteen. Already a gifted speaker at such a young age, his name signified that he was "freeing the dumb" with knowledge. "Allah" or God was a title all members shared. Thus began his journey with the Nation of Gods and Earths, otherwise known as the Five Percenters, who had a huge impact on generations of Black youth growing up in New York in the seventies and eighties. So, too, would Freedum, affectionately dubbed "Popa Wu" by his younger cousin ODB, become a spiritual mentor to the future members of Wu-Tang Clan, all of whom adopted the teachings of the Five Percent as teens.

"Freedum was actually the wisest one out of my family," RZA declares. "If anyone enhanced my knowledge and increased it and sent it further than anybody, it was Freedum. He was a very logical, practical man."[2] He regarded his cousin's cousin, thirteen years his senior, as more of a hip, funky uncle. "When Wu-Tang became famous and I was dealing with the business side of things, I needed somebody who was a strong scientist that could be around the brothers while I did what I had to do, and I went to Freedum, nah mean?" says RZA. "He had a job working for transit. He wasn't into this hip-hop shit—he was a silk-suit brother, know what I mean? And I was like, 'Yo, God, I want you to come and be with us, nah mean? I want you to teach these brothers 'cause I got a lot of things that I gotta do in the business world, and I ain't gonna be there every day.' And he agreed. So, I put him on tour with Wu-Tang, and he was the one who put a lot of wisdom in their heads, every day."[3]

If gaining "knowledge of self," shorthand for being initiated into the Five Percenters, proved to be the great awakening, being mentored by others who reinforced the Lessons daily was essential to sustaining the grassroots movement. "Everybody in our whole camp is righteous," says Freedom, noting the difference between other crews and the Clan, who shared a philosophy of self-sufficiency and empowerment. "Most of Wu-Tang were black sheeps in their family that nobody gave a fuck about. We had to make ways for ourselves, but the most important thing is that we all got knowledge of self. We all talk the same language. We say we got the same father and different mothers. Our father's Allah."

Defying the critics and naysayers who have described them as a "gang," "cult," or "false religion," the Nation of Gods and Earths, an offshoot of the Nation of Islam, actually lay claim to a compelling history that cannot be so easily dismissed, in the very least, for the indelible impression they have left on hip-hop culture. So much slang from the rap lexicon— words and phrases like "bomb," "cipher," "droppin' science," "break it down," "show and prove," "right and exact," "word is bond," and even using "peace" as a greeting—derived from Five-Percenter vernacular. In addition, influential rappers from Rakim to Big Daddy Kane, Brand Nubian to Poor Righteous Teachers proudly touted their affiliation with the group.

But the origins of the Nation of Gods and Earths extend back to an era before most rappers were born. Heir to the almost mythical "Blood Brothers," an unofficial alliance of street kids banded together against the rampant police brutality that was going on in Harlem at the time, the Gods first gained traction in 1964 during a major rift in the Nation of Islam, which was founded in 1930. Building on all the ideologies of Black liberation that emerged during the beginning of the twentieth century—including Marcus Garvey's United

Negro Improvement Association (UNIA) and Noble Drew Ali's Moorish Science Temple—the Black Muslims created a mass movement dedicated to the spiritual, mental, social, and economic upliftment of Blacks in North America. But ongoing tensions between Elijah Muhammad, the self-proclaimed prophet or messenger of the Nation, and his most important minister, the charismatic Malcolm X, led to Malcolm's ousting from the group to which he had devoted his life and that he'd helped greatly expand during the course of the fifties.

After making a pilgrimage to Mecca and seeing the diversity of Muslims from around the world, Malcolm renounced his prior views about a white "devil," forming a new organization called Muslim Mosque, Inc. Grounded in classical Sunni Islam, it aimed to be more political than the Nation. The Gods actually benefitted from this schism and found an eager audience among "mainly adolescent boys who may have respected Elijah's anti-white rhetoric but held no interest in wearing bowties or quitting music and girls. While Malcolm would have scolded youths for gambling, Allah [Five Percent founder, Clarence 13X] assured them that shooting dice revealed the mathematical properties of the universe. Rather than impose rules and regulations, he gave the powerless a means by which they would command the unknown."[4]

According to Freedum, "Allah went to the youth. Nobody gave a fuck about the youth in the '60s. All Five Percenters was nothing but kids 12–16 years old. Clarence 13X said, 'I know how to beat the city, I'm going to snatch all these little brothers out here, 15, 16 years old that's shooting dope in their arm and give them knowledge.' So, he went and told them the truth. He gave them a culture, a way of life, something they could adapt to." Far from being a religion, it provided a blueprint for negotiating an inhospitable world.

By the time Freedum joined their ranks in 1968, the Gods were a movement on the rise. In order to quell some of their more militant leanings, the City of New York and Urban League had given the group a cheap lease on a building at 2122 Seventh Avenue in Harlem—called the Allah School in Mecca—to serve as a community center or "street academy" where various self-improvement courses were taught. The numbers of the address proved auspicious, as they added up to seven, the number of God in Supreme Mathematics. From this base, they held their "universal parliaments," where members could "build" or exchange ideas, and they eventually expanded their reach into other boroughs as well. Though the Gods explicitly rejected any association with classical Islam, they were still attracted to Arabic names, remaking New York into a map of the Middle East. If Manhattan represented Mecca, then Brooklyn was Medina, Islam's second holy city. The Bronx became Pelan (another name for the Greek isle of Patmos, where St. John received the Book of Revelation), Staten Island was Savior's Island, and Queens was known as the Desert.

Following Martin Luther King Jr.'s assassination on April 4, Mayor John Lindsay brought the Gods to prominence when he enlisted them to walk the streets of Harlem with him to prevent rioting. Five-Percenter founder Clarence 13X Smith, simply known as "Allah," or "the Father," who inspired tremendous respect on these streets, stood shoulder to shoulder with him, front and center. For helping to keep the peace that night, he and the mayor made the cover of *New York Magazine* on April 22, 1968, under the headline "The City on the Eve of Destruction."[5]

An unlikely leader, Smith's background revealed a man of many contradictions and flaws. Born in Danville, Virginia, on February 22, 1928, he moved to Harlem with his mother in 1946. A high school dropout, he quickly adapted to the ways of the street, hanging out with hustlers and numbers runners and developing an affinity for shooting dice. He had a reputation for getting around with the ladies as well. In 1950, after marrying Dora Smith and starting a family, he also fathered two children with mistress Willieen Jowers. Like many young Blacks with few prospects, he joined the army, despite the racism he encountered as a youth growing up in Virginia. He fought for his country during the Korean War from 1952 to 1954 and subsequently served in the army reserves until 1960. After returning to Harlem, he found that Dora had become a member of the very strict and discipline-oriented Nation of Islam. Despite a partiality for gin, reefer, cocaine, gambling, and women, he decided to sign up as well.[6]

The couple joined the congregation of up-and-coming Minister Malcolm X at Mosque No. 7, on the corner of 116th and Lennox. In keeping with NOI tradition, Clarence dropped his surname or "slave name" to become Clarence 13X, which meant he was the thirteenth member of the organization so named. An avid student of the Supreme Wisdom Lessons, which laid out the Nation's doctrine, he committed them to memory in no time. Thanks to his military background and martial arts training, he also rose quickly in the ranks of the FOI or Fruit of Islam, the Nation's security detail. But his progress as a Black Muslim didn't alter the fact that this charismatic character, a master with the dice, still had one foot in the streets. When Malcolm got wind of his extracurricular activities, Clarence was suspended from the NOI more than once. By the end of 1963, he left for good, though the exact reasons remain unclear.[7]

It could have been a crisis of faith, as Clarence reflected deeply on the Lessons—with the help of a little reefer—stumbling upon some glaring inconsistencies. The root problem for him went all the way back to the Nation's origins, in which Allah had appeared in the form of Wallace D. Fard, a light-skinned man of mixed ancestry. Arriving in Detroit in 1930, Fard was a silk merchant who claimed to have come from the East, and he disappeared just as mysteriously three years later. In the interim, however, the Lost-Found Nation of Islam that he built with Elijah Poole (a.k.a. Muhammad), his assistant and first disciple, began attracting followers with its message to uplift the Black man of North America. Its central tenets lay embedded in the Supreme Wisdom Lessons, a question-and-answer session between Fard and Elijah Muhammad, who eventually took over the helm of the Nation, proclaiming himself as the Messenger of Allah.

Clarence considered the first question in the Lessons: "Who is the Original Man?" The answer was: "The Original Man is the Asiatic Blackman, the Maker, the Owner, Cream of the Planet Earth, Father of Civilization, God of the Universe." But if he believed this to be true, then how could Fard, who was half white, have been Allah? The Black Muslims, after all, believed in a "true and living god" and considered a "mystery god" to be a grand deception or trick to keep the masses pacified. But where was Fard now, and how and why had he disappeared? Not content to simply cast doubts on the legitimacy of the Nation's founder, Clarence took it a step further, declaring that he, as the Original Man, was God, as the lesson stated. To underscore this point, he called himself "the Father" or "Allah." A lover of wordplay, he broke down the Arabic word for "god" into an English backronym that stood for "Arm, Leg, Leg, Arm, Head," which, like da Vinci's famous Vitruvian Man illustration, represented the human form.[8] According to Clarence's interpretation, every Black man represented Allah as well.

Digging deeper into the Supreme Wisdom Lessons, which classified humanity into three distinct groups, he found further inspiration. The first group, known as the "uncivilized," who were easily led in the wrong direction and hard to lead in the right, made up 85 percent of the population. Another 10 percent comprised the rich slave owners, who kept the masses in servitude while denying them the truth. Only the remaining 5 percent of the population, known as the poor, righteous teachers, had knowledge of the truth and wanted to expose it. Clarence viewed himself and his followers as the latter. He and fellow NOI defector John 37X (who later became Abu Shahid) continued studying the Lessons even after they left the Nation and, in the years that followed, revised and refined them, adding Supreme Mathematics and the Supreme Alphabet, which comprised the body of Five-Percenter ideology.

Of course, such revisionist views of Elijah Muhammad's teachings would have been seen as sacrilegious by the Messenger and his followers had they not had a much more serious problem with Malcolm X in 1965. After a messy split with the Nation of Islam—one in which they even reclaimed the house they had given him to use as minister of Mosque No. 7—Malcolm ended up exposing Elijah Muhammad's numerous illicit affairs with several teenage secretaries, which all but guaranteed his fate. A recent Netflix documentary, *Who Killed Malcolm?*, revealed that on February 21, the outspoken former minister was gunned down by no less than five assassins from the Nation's Mosque No. 25 in Newark, just before he was scheduled to speak at Harlem's Audubon Ballroom.[9]

Meanwhile, Allah had begun teaching his "Suns of the Almighty God Allah" the Supreme Wisdom Lessons, which had previously been reserved for only registered members of the NOI, who were also obliged to observe strict rules of conduct for that privilege. No such rules—whether a dress code or behavioral guidelines—applied to Allah's young followers. His nine initial disciples, who came to be known as the "First Born," were youths ranging in age from thirteen to twenty, who otherwise hung out on the street. Some perhaps sold weed to get by or formed crews of "boosters" to steal from downtown department stores. But, hungry for guidance and a path forward in life, they also faithfully memorized the Lessons, assuming Arabic- or African-sounding names to distinguish themselves from the 85 percent and show their commitment to the cause. Allah had a firm allegiance to these youth as well, whom he rightfully saw as the future. He bade them to go out and recruit others. In this manner, the Gods expanded organically, their ranks swelling with a very youthful membership.[10]

Their growth continued even after Allah's arrest in May 1965 following a violent confrontation between his followers and the NYPD. Because he had identified himself as "God" when taken into custody, he was sent to Bellevue Hospital for psychiatric evaluation and eventually upstate to Matteawan State Hospital for the Criminally Insane. But as a person of interest to the FBI, who had been monitoring his activities since 1961, these charges seemed more like a convenient ploy to remove him from the streets. Regardless, incarceration did not deter Allah, who continued to proselytize in prison and gain new followers, including the first white Five Percenter, John Michael Kennedy, whom he dubbed "Azreal," the name for the Angel of Death in the Hebrew and Islamic traditions.

While some Gods on the outside visited him, his two years behind bars actually forced the group to develop some degree of independence and autonomy, one of the main reasons the Five Percenters were able to survive after his death.

Whether Allah eventually ran afoul of the Nation of Islam or got caught up in some beef on the streets, he, too, met a violent end like Malcolm. In the twilight hours of June 13, 1969, after a night of shooting craps, he went to his wife Dora's apartment at 21 West 112 Street in Harlem's Martin Luther King Towers. As he was about to get on the elevator, he was ambushed from behind, taking bullets to the head, legs, and torso. The assassins, three Black men who allegedly fled in a white Chevy, were never caught.[11] Though it was clearly a hit, Minister Louis Farrakhan, who had ascended in the ranks of the NOI following Malcolm's death, denied any culpability, saying that they had a good relationship with the Five Percenters. Others speculate that the murder might have been over a gambling debt. Regardless, it was a heavy blow to the Five Percenters, who initially seemed to dissolve and disperse.

But the lack of an anointed heir or even a hierarchical structure worked in the group's favor as individuals took it upon themselves to continue studying and teaching the Lessons to others. By the early seventies, the Nation of Gods and Earths experienced a resurgence in their ranks, proving that you cannot kill an idea whose time had arrived. The message of self-awareness, independence, responsibility, and Black pride promoted by Allah and his followers started to filter down to a whole new generation of sufferers in the ghetto.

Gary first heard about the Nation of Gods and Earths through his brother-in-law, who kept a pack of flash cards of the Supreme Mathematics under his bed. Each card displayed a picture of a stylized number between zero and nine with a Black man standing next to it. As a child, he was initially attracted by the artwork. He didn't learn the meaning of the numbers until much later on, at fourteen, when his older cousin Life Allah and a friend named Infinite gave him knowledge of self. Mathematics provided Gary with another way of viewing the world. "In the simplest form, it's the study of measurements, you know, weighing and judging and adding things up," he says. In addition to mastering the Supreme Wisdom Lessons, or the 120, he stopped eating pork and eventually chose the righteous name "Allah Justice."

Bobby first noticed a change in his cousin when he went to hang out one day in the spring of 1980. Gary, who was then living at 55 Bowen Street in Park Hill, had a new attitude to go with his new name. He told Bobby, "He's not a spirit. God is you—he's inside you."[12] It was a daunting concept to digest, especially for an eleven-year-old. But Bobby, a precocious youth, hungry for knowledge and guidance, took the leap of faith and quickly advanced. After mastering Supreme Mathematics, the Supreme Alphabet, and Twelve Jewels, he started studying the 120—initially with his older brother Randy. Then, after they got into a fight, he strayed from his studies for a time. Finally, he resolved to lock himself in the bathroom every night, allowing his brain to soak up the degrees like a sponge. Exercising this kind of discipline and commitment, he mastered the Lessons in only a year. By his twelfth birthday, he had become one of the youngest to claim a righteous name, settling on Prince Rakeem Allah.[13]

"Getting knowledge of yourself is the key to life," says RZA. "If a man don't know hisself, he can't know nobody else. When it came to Supreme Mathematics, the first thing they taught us was knowledge, which was 1, and that means to look, listen, observe, and respect where you at. Then you act upon it, which is wisdom. Wisdom is just a manifestation of knowledge. So those principles actually saved my life dozens and dozens of times because I'm able to take a look first or listen first before I just jump out there, know what I mean? Most people, especially young urban people in our community, do something first and find out later. But if a kid knew the results of his actions ahead of time."[14] Such were the practical insights he gained from being a member of the Five Percenters.

In his memoir, he summed it up, saying, "If you were poor and black, Mathematics attacked the idea that you were meant to be ignorant, uneducated, and blind to the world around you. It exposed the lies that helped treat your forefathers as animals. And it wasn't until someone like the Father came to actively disseminate this information to poor black men—saying, 'Hold on, your people are the fathers of civilization'—that people like me were set free. That's what the lessons did for me. They gave me guidance, understanding, and freedom."[15]

With several cousins already involved in the Nation of Gods and Earths, it was only a matter of time before Rusty was brought into the fold by Freedom. After gaining knowledge of self and mastering the Lessons, he changed his name to Ason Unique at the age of fourteen. When he went home and told his mother, a devout Jehovah's Witness, that he was God, like any sensible parent, she almost choked him. "There's only one God in my house and that's Jesus," she declared, furious at her nephew Freedom as well for filling Rusty's head with such thoughts. Her reaction was hardly surprising, though, considering that the Five Percenters had a reputation for being troublemakers, rabble-rousers, and even a gang. Because they proselytized in prisons and on street corners in the hood in order to reach their prime audience— the ghetto youth—they were automatically associated with negativity, even though their ultimate goal was the awakening and redemption of those who needed it the most.

"It's like in any organization, in anything, you have real, and you have fake. You have right and you have wrong," GZA observes. "You know, you might have brothers that wear our flag and go out and do crime. That don't make 'em part of us, so you have to really know the individual, and then see how he live through his ways and actions because many men can speak great, but it's what you live."

Since hip-hop and the Nation of Gods and Earths were both quintessential products of New York in the seventies, it was inevitable that they would eventually cross paths and cross-pollinate. Five Percenters were among the crowds at Kool Herc's parties in the Bronx and, in fact, provided security at some of these early jams. As a prominent presence of project life, their colorful lingo also heavily influenced rappers, many of whom eventually got down with the cause themselves. But the MC most closely associated with the Nation of Gods and Earths, who also made the most powerful and enduring impression on hip-hop, was none other than Rakim Allah.

Born William Michael Griffin Jr. on January 28, 1968, in Wyandanch, Long Island, Rakim was actually a contemporary of Gary, Bobby, and Rusty. His unique background, skills, and connections, however, placed his career on a vastly different trajectory from the founding members of the Clan. For starters, he hailed from a staunchly middle-class enclave of single-family homes and well-tended yards—not the hood. The youngest of five kids, Rakim had the guidance of two nurturing parents and came from a very musically inclined family. Everyone sang or played an instrument, and his aunt Ruth Brown was dubbed the "Queen of R&B." Introduced to hip-hop at an early age, he wrote his first rhyme by the time he was seven and continued to excel at his craft through high school, where he made mixtapes as Kid Wizard. But for him, rapping remained only a hobby that gave him respect around the way. As a high school senior and star quarterback for the Wyandanch Warriors, he hoped to play college ball at Stoney Brook in the fall. The universe, however, had other plans.

One day, his homeboy Alvin Toney introduced him to a promotions guy at New York's WBLS named Eric Barrier, or Eric B. for short. Eric worked for Marley Marl, who was Mr. Magic's assistant on the first-ever rap show on the radio, *Mr. Magic's Rap Attack* (1982–1988). Marley also happened to be the hottest producer in the game, with hits like Roxanne Shante's "Roxanne's Revenge" (1984) and MC Shan's "The Bridge" (1986) under his belt. After hearing five minutes of Kid Wizard rap, Eric said, "Yo, we can go to Marley Marl's crib and make a record right now."[16] Talk about a huge break for the unknown seventeen-year-old, who gained knowledge of self that year as well. So much for football and "Kid Wizard." Rakim Allah became the first MC to proudly flaunt his righteous name as his stage name.

In his memoir, he recounted that first session with Marley Marl, whose studio was the living room of his sister's apartment in the notorious Queensbridge Houses, which have spawned so much rap talent. It's a humorous story because the legendary MC said he delivered the rhymes to "My Melody," one of his many hits, in that cool and calm manner that fans have come to know and love. But Marley, the hit maker, didn't initially approve of his delivery and tried to make him redo it with more energy. "I wanted to be more thought-provoking, and if people were going to really hear my ideas and the intricacies of my rhymes, it was better to have a calmer delivery," Rakim explained. "I liked being more conversational because then I could have more control over the tones in my voice, and you'd be better able to really hear me. If you could hear me, then you'd have to think about what I was sayin.'"[17] Style and flow were, of course, essential to rapping, but Rakim contributed another important component: lyrical complexity.

Sticking to his guns, he obviously won that battle with his producer, and when his album with Eric B., *Paid in Full* (4th & Broadway / Island, 1987), finally dropped, it was like an extinction-level event for what had been rap up to then, ushering in a new age of lyricism. He spat lyrics like John Coltrane, one of his idols, played the sax (the MC studied sax as well). Utilizing such devices as internal and multisyllabic rhymes, he banished Mother Goose MCs to the playground, elevating minds with a mastery of vocabulary and concepts. On "My Melody," he even rhymes about rhyming itself: "The rhyme is rugged, at the same time sharp / I can swing off anything even a string of a harp / Just turn it on and start rocking, mind no introduction / 'Til I finish dropping science, no interruption." Rakim basically sent other MCs scurrying back to the drawing board.

While not overtly rapping about the Five Percenters, he laced his lyrics with their lingo and represented the Gods to the fullest, thereby earning the nickname the God MC. Not attempting to conceal his affiliation, he appeared on the cover of his follow-up, *Follow the Leader* (4th & Broadway

/ Island, 1988) wearing a Dapper Dan exclusive with his name stitched above the universal flag of the Five Percent. This symbol depicted the numeral 7 in the center of an eight-pointed sun, surrounded by a crescent moon and star to represent man, woman, and child—the Black family.

Rakim may have been the first Five Percenter to make an impression on the mic, but he certainly wasn't the last, surrounded by such talent as Big Daddy Kane, Just-Ice, King Sun, and later Busta Rhymes and groups such as Brand Nubian, Poor Righteous Teachers, and obviously Wu-Tang, who were huge fans and greatly influenced by his music when they were coming up. Through such artists, the Five-Percent message of self-awareness and empowerment has pervaded rap, not only giving depth and dimension to the art form but also imbuing it with a certain transformative power. An analogous example would be the relationship of Rastafarianism to reggae music. Rastafarianism is to reggae as the philosophy of the Five Percent is to hip-hop, a spiritual and cultural foundation that flavors the language and attitude of the music, elevating it to much more than simply entertainment.

"It made me what I am today," says GZA. "Comin' into the Nation of Gods and Earths is something that enabled me to see, enabled me to hear and observe—to question a lot of things. It was all about learning certain things when we were younger or learning certain lessons and knowin' it word for word, bein' able to add onto other things and apply it."[18] This powerful oral tradition passed on by the Five Percenters not only evoked the griots of west Africa but also proved to be essential training for an MC.

As RZA noted, "The power of the Lessons didn't just come from the information they provided; it also came from their actual vocabulary and cadence. It's like how they say that the Koran can be truly understood only in Arabic because of the cadence of the language. The act of internalizing these lessons transforms you; it strengthens your mind."[19] Thus, the same memorization and oratorical skills involved in learning to recite the Lessons could be applied to the art of MCing.

"The brothers was showin' and provin' a better way of livin', you know what I'm saying?" says Corey Woods, who assumed the righteous name of Shallah Raekwon at seventeen. "I was so infatuated as a young brother. I would always be around the older gods and they would be on my ass only due to the fact that they wanted me to recognize who I am. So, they would take me through the degrees."[20] A high school dropout, his education was actually furthered by the Gods. "When I started getting into the Five Percent Nation, it was always about reading," he says. "So reading was definitely something fundamental to me. You had to read though, know what I mean. If you didn't read, you didn't know how to write."[21] Echoing his brothers, Raekwon reaffirmed how studying the Lessons actually aided his abilities as an MC.

Lamont gained knowledge of self at the age of fourteen through his enlighteners, Dakim and Love God, assuming the name Universal God Allah, or U-God for short. "The word *universal* means multi-dimensional, infinite, comprehensive," he explains. "Basically, anything I put my mind to, I will figure out how to get it done. I was given the Universal name because I carry the ambassador torch every day. I can go anywhere, I can talk to anyone, it's just who I am."[22]

Explaining what drew him to the philosophy of the Five Percent, he says, "It's a mental thing. It's a self-esteem thing for Black kids 'cause it deals with our history, how we got here: slavery, four hundred years ago, how we were tricked in certain situations and stripped of our last name. And know-ing this at a young age, you know, kind of gives you an under-standing of what you're up against in this world."[23] While low self-esteem may be common among teenagers regardless of race, U-God's involvement in the Nation of Gods and Earths provided what was missing for him and his homeboys. "It's a great source of pride and takes a lot of reflection because as a kid you get bombarded by so much white America that you don't know that blacks have contributed massive amounts of things to this world," he says.[24]

One cannot underestimate the influence of the Nation of Gods and Earths in the ghettoes of New York in the seventies and eighties. They appeared at a time when they were needed most and, like hip-hop, captured the youth who badly needed guidance and a path out of hell. As an affirmation of their success, RZA sums it up when he says, "I can now say that if it wasn't for Mathematics, I wouldn't have achieved anything. I would never have imagined that a poor black motherfucker like me would grow up to respect the world, his fellow man, or himself."[25]

CHAPTER 4

SHAOLIN VS. WU-TANG

If New York City in the seventies was one hot mess, Times Square at Forty-Second Street between Seventh and Eighth Avenues—a strip known as the Deuce—represented its seething cesspit of sleaze, a place where folks of all color, class, persuasion, and kink came to satisfy their every vice and craving. Dominated by grind house theaters whose flashing marquees, awash in neon, created a canopy of light over the sidewalk like some devilish carnival of delights, the block comprised a world of its own with triple-X bookstores, twenty-five-cent peep shows, and shops selling everything from bowie knives big enough to disembowel a deer to bootlegged brand-name knockoffs and plastic Statues of Liberty—made, of course, in China. In the open-air market of the street, however, the sky was the limit, as hustlers peddled the high of your choice while hookers offered raw, carnal satisfaction back behind a dumpster. Once lauded as "the crossroads of the world" for the millions who passed through its busy transit hub, the Deuce had devolved into the most notorious red-light district in the country. "With both sides of the street cluttered with a mixture of upright citizens, low-down schemers, bullhorn screaming preachers, high-heeled hookers, and sidewalk scavengers of every variety who'd come to the strip to lay down their hustle, even the most native of New Yorkers had to be cautious," says writer Michael Gonzales, recalling his first impressions of the place as a child, adding, "Although most of the city looked as though someone had dumped a giant garbage can over it, Times Square was especially grimy."[1]

This seedy reputation stretched as far back as the nineteenth century, when the formerly named Long Acre Square was known as the Tenderloin or "Satan's Circus" for its blocks of brothels and bars nestled in the shadow of Broadway. The entertainment first arrived in 1895 when theater impresario Oscar Hammerstein, grandfather of the famous lyricist, developed a complex of three theaters called the Olympia, ushering in the age of gilded halls. With cavernous interiors, grand balconies, and red velvet curtains, these elegant spaces hosted lavish spectacles like the Ziegfeld Follies before eventually becoming burlesque striptease halls and, finally, being converted to movie theaters in the sixties. Mayor George B. McClellan gave Times Square its name in 1904 after the newspaper relocated there, razing the Hotel Pabst and erecting the Times Tower at 1475 Broadway—incidentally, the same location where the ball is dropped from the roof every New Year's Eve, a tradition inaugurated by *Times* publisher Adolph S. Ochs in 1908.[2]

Times Square, however, never managed to live up to the faded glory of its past. By the sixties, according to the book *Sleazoid Express*, "The Deuce grindhouses were showcases for the wildest and most extreme films in cinematic history, and ticket buyers were of all sorts: depressives hiding from jobs, sexual obsessives, inner-city people seeking cheap diversions, teenagers skipping school, adventurous couples on dates, couples-chasers peeking on them, people getting

high, homeless people sleeping, pickpockets. This disenfran-
chised audience had nowhere else to go, and the grindhouses
were where they all wound up."[3]

Neither were these theaters completely safe, as robber-
ies were not uncommon. "During the screenings, two mug-
gers would take seats on either side of their intended victim,
then grab his arms holding him in place. One of the robbers
would flash a pocket-knife or razor. Audience members who
noticed knew it was some sort of shakedown in which they
would not want to get involved. The mark would quickly turn
over his money and the assailants would beat it to cop their
drug fixes or hide out."[4]

The Times Square movie houses also provided convenient
shooting galleries for heroin addicts and other drug users.
"Inevitably, somebody would be getting high smoking angel
dust, which has a distinct chemical stink that seems buried
in incense. Patrons were wary of the sickly-sweet aroma that
would occasionally waft through the auditorium—no one
wanted to be near a potentially crazy outburst or breathe it
in and have an involuntary bad trip. And no one wanted to
be kicked when the dust head got too into the movie and let
loose with some deranged chop-socky missteps of his own."[5]

Add to that the lurking perverts, stained seats, sticky
floors, and people talking out loud or even throwing stuff at
the characters on the screen, and "the Deuce remained the
most intense venue one could ever hope to see a movie in."[6]
With the advent of porn in 1972, the Mob, which had already
monopolized the sex trade, entered the movie business as
well, controlling all facets of production and distribution.
But these new landlords were hardly invested in revital-
izing theaters that were mostly dirty, dingy, and in serious
disrepair. To get the most bang for their buck, they started

screening porn twenty-four hours a day, supplemented by blaxploitation and eventually imported kung fu films, two other low-budget genres that sold tickets. In this virtual terror dome, Bobby Diggs acquired his love of cinema.

The first film he ever saw on the big screen, *Star Wars* (1977), became an instant favorite, until the competition came along. The following year, when he was nine, his cousin Vince took him up to the Deuce one Saturday to see a triple feature for $1.50. The first movie, *Fury of the Dragon* (1972), was really several episodes of the 1966 TV series *Green Hornet*, starring martial arts legend Bruce Lee, edited together to make a full-length feature. The next one, *Black Samurai* (1977), a blaxploitation / martial arts mash-up, featured Jim Kelly, a Black actor and martial artist who also played opposite Lee in the kung fu classic *Enter the Dragon* (1973).[7] Having never experienced anything like these films, with their unique form of hand-to-hand combat, augmented by over-the-top sound effects, Bobby was glued to the screen. By the time the credits rolled on the last feature on the bill, *Five Deadly Venoms* (1978), a clash between five kung fu fighters whose different styles were based on venomous animals, he was hooked. "Seeing *Five Deadly Venoms* sparked my imagination," says Bobby.[8] He had just read Kurt Wiese's classic children's book *The Five Chinese Brothers*, about five brothers with different superpowers, and the film, he says, "just resonated with me at a high level,"[9] adding, "This is actually the movie that made me become a kung-fu fanatic."[10]

Though *The Five Venoms*, as it was originally titled, was neither the first nor best martial arts film to penetrate the US market, it quickly became a cult favorite. According to *The Ultimate Guide to Martial Arts Movies of the 1970s*, "It is curious because the film had few fights compared to other kung fu films, and the actors were performing well below their skill levels. However, it had a simple story and the costumes and wire work were completely different from anything American audiences had seen up until that point."[11] Those wires allowed the characters to walk up walls and execute fighting techniques that defied the laws of physics. With each of the Venoms boasting a special power and wearing a signature Lucha libre–style mask, they also appealed to the American appetite for superheroes.

"I think from 1979 to 1983, the majority of movies played on the Deuce was kung fu, and I must have seen a hundred, two hundred films," Bobby recalls. "I went to the movies every weekend, and then when I was twelve, thirteen, me and ODB cut school so many days, scraped up $1.50 and sat in those theaters from nine, ten a.m. until closing. And mind you, these movies are rated R; no one under seventeen permitted. I remember giving the local glue sniffer an extra dollar to buy my ticket."[12]

Once inside, he continues, "We'd be sittin' beside—in those days—guys sniffing glue, some guy over here is smoking weed, some guy is trying to fondle his girlfriend and get his rocks off. Here go two kids just watchin' movies, escaping our reality and finding an alternate reality. To think, I could go and watch a movie that takes me back, yunno, fifteen hundred years to China or to a galaxy far, far beyond, it has some magic to it, and it actually helped me as an individual, you know? That was my therapy."[13] Indeed, for an underprivileged child living in crowded conditions at home, to be able to steal away for a few hours to one of these decaying movie palaces like the Lyric, one of his favorite theaters, and allow his imagination to take flight was nothing short of magical. But Bobby was not alone in his appreciation of martial arts movies. "These films definitely resonated a lot in the Black community," he says. "It's the underdog thing, it's the brotherly thing, and also I think its escapism 'cause you can go and watch these movies, and it's not even America. It's like a whole 'nother world."[14]

Hong Kong cinema was, indeed, a world unto itself, and the story of how an African American audience came to embrace it leads directly through Bruce Lee, the most influential martial artist of all time. He was born in San Francisco on November 27, 1940—in both the year and hour of the Dragon, a powerful omen according to the Chinese zodiac—and his family moved to Hong Kong when he was only three months old. As the son of Chinese opera stars, he was introduced to the theater early and found his way into acting, starring in over twenty films by the time he was eighteen.

But Lee also got into a lot of fights in school, so, at sixteen, his parents enrolled him in martial arts training—specifically a style called *Wing Chun*, which his father practiced, characterized as being more free-form and favoring speed over strength. He also took up Western-style boxing. In 1959, at the age of nineteen, Lee returned to the US to work and study, attending the University of Washington, though he never finished his degree. Instead, he married a white American, Linda Emery, and opened a kung fu school, where he was one of the first *sifus*, or masters, to start training non-Asians, a move that did not endear him to the Chinese kung fu community.[15]

Lee's first break stateside came in 1964, when TV producer William Dozier noticed him at a martial arts exhibition in Long Beach, California. The event marked one of the few times that he demonstrated the "one-inch punch," knocking a man down from a punch launched from an inch away with no windup or recoil. Such skills helped him land the role of Kato, the superhero's sidekick in the series *The Green Hornet*, which had a brief run on TV from September 1966 to March 1967.

Left without work after the show's cancellation, Lee founded another school, where he started developing his own signature style of kung fu known as Jeet Kune Do, "a synthesis of *Wing Chun*, Japanese jiujitsu, and African American boxing" that also reflected his philosophy of life.[16] According to Lee, "Jeet Kune Do favors formlessness so that it can assume all forms and since Jeet Kune Do has no style, it can fit in with all styles. As a result, it utilizes all ways and is bound by none and, likewise, uses any techniques or means which serve its end."[17]

Not giving up on acting, however, he also worked on developing a series called *The Warrior*, in which he played a kung fu warrior who battles injustice, pitching it to several major studios, including Paramount and Warner Bros. Supposedly, Warner had been developing a similar idea about a Shaolin monk roaming the Wild West and considered Lee for the role, but, ironically, his accent took him out of the running. Like the dumbed-down Chinese food they ate, Americans, apparently, weren't deemed ready for the real thing. Instead, the starring role of Caine in *Kung Fu*, which first aired in 1972, was given to American actor David Carradine, who didn't even study martial arts at the time.

Finally, frustrated with negotiating Hollywood's racial politics and landing only supporting roles, Lee decided to return to Hong Kong, where the dominoes started falling fast for him. Unaware that his role as Kato had made him famous back home, he had the cachet to sign a two-movie deal with

Raymond Chow's Golden Harvest Productions, which, along with Shaw Brothers, was one of the top two studios in China. Shaw Brothers actually had the chance to work with Lee first but passed, allowing former employee and current competitor Chow to make the deal. Lee's first film, *The Big Boss* (1971), made him a huge box-office draw in Asia, followed by *Fist of Fury* (1972)—released in the US as *The Chinese Connection*—which cemented his stardom. Renegotiating his deal with Golden Harvest for his third picture, *Way of the Dragon* (1972), he was given complete creative control over all aspects of the film as writer, director, fight choreographer, and star. With Lee in the driver's seat, his career was finally on a roll.

While in production for his fourth film, *Game of Death* (1973), which featured former student and basketball star Kareem Abdul-Jabbar, who, at twenty-four, had led his Milwaukee Bucks to their first NBA championship in 1971, payback was at hand. Warner Bros., the same studio that had dissed Lee by not casting him in the *Kung Fu* TV series, offered him the starring role in *Enter the Dragon* (1973), which would be the first joint production between Hong Kong and Hollywood (represented by Golden Harvest; Warner; and Concord, Lee's own production company). The collaboration came at a time when Warner was not doing well and needed the biggest bang for their buck.

Made for only $850,000, the film, which was considered a low-budget James Bond knock-off, received rave reviews when it opened. Costarring John Saxon and blaxploitation favorite Jim Kelly, the multiracial cast was designed to appeal to the broadest possible audience. Shooting commenced in Hong Kong on January 1973, and after principal photography, they overdubbed all the sound and effects, as was standard practice with kung fu films. But only six days before the film's release, on July 20, 1973, Lee died of cerebral edema, or swelling of the brain, as a result of an allergic reaction to a painkiller he had taken. He was only thirty-two. When *Enter the Dragon* premiered in the US a month later, it went on to become one of the highest-grossing films of the year, earning $90 million worldwide (about $518 million today) and cementing Lee's status as a martial arts legend.

The film played especially well among Black audiences. According to author Sundiata Keita Cha-Jua, "What differentiated Lee from other cinematic martial artists were his exceptional athletic abilities and fighting skills. Second, the nationalist politics embedded in his films paralleled dominant trends in African American political culture and were a central theme in blaxploitation movies. Lee's third attribute that endeared him to African American audiences was his open, multiracial, and polycultural cultural politics. Fourth, his class politics also broadly mirrored a major theme in blaxploitation films."[18] In addition, Lee's immense talent and skills helped push the genre toward greater realism. He also presented a rare nonwhite lead who wasn't afraid to share the spotlight with brothers like Kelly and Abdul-Jabbar. While blaxploitation and martial arts movies enjoyed equal popularity in the early seventies, the staying power of the latter—especially among Blacks—was telling. Author Darius James went so far as to crown Bruce Lee "the greatest blaxploitation hero of all time."[19]

When it came to martial arts movies, Lee also changed the game. Whereas earlier films in the genre, known as *wuxia*, relied primarily on fantasy tales set in an ancient past, he updated the stories, making them morality plays for the present. He also made the fighting scenes more authentic and less like a choreographed dance routine. But there was also more to his films than gratuitous violence. As Cha-Jua says, "Lee and the formula he established for kung-fu films were political in much the same way as blaxploitation films; that is, they were nationalist visions of self-defense or retaliatory violence against racial oppression, albeit fueled by individual grievances," adding, "His nationalism was anti-imperialist and imbricated with racial and class consciousness."[20]

The timing could not have been better, as the evolving Black Power movement, influenced by Chinese communism, was gaining an awareness of its place within a greater Pan-African struggle that united oppressed peoples around the world. When Muhammad Ali, for example, famously refused to serve in Vietnam, he demonstrated that solidarity with other people of color, saying, "Man, I ain't got no quarrel with them Viet Cong. Why should they ask me to put on a uniform and go ten thousand miles from home and drop bombs and bullets on brown people in Vietnam while so-called Negro people in Louisville are treated like dogs and denied simple human rights?"[21] Ali, a high-profile member of the very controversial Nation of Islam, was not only the greatest in the ring but also a champion of his people outside of it.

The sixties had taken its toll on the civil rights struggle, and in the absence of iconic figures like Malcolm and Martin, the only nonwhite heroes could be found on celluloid. In blaxploitation, the pimps, pushers, and hustlers filled that role. But the kung fu archetype of the underdog or lone rebel fighting against a ruling class that represented the establishment or the Man was definitely something brothers could relate to as well. As David Desser writes, "Through pairing kung-fu films with blaxploitation movies in inner city movie houses, black and brown audiences were disproportionately exposed to the latest offerings from Shaw Brothers and Golden Harvest."[22] After *Five Fingers of Death* (originally titled *King Boxer*) first played on the Deuce in March 1973, thirty more martial arts films followed that year, including *Enter the Dragon*, ushering in America's first kung fu craze.

By this time, David Carradine's *Kung Fu* series had become a popular hit on prime-time TV. The following year, Jamaican singer Carl Douglas's catchy "Kung Fu Fighting" soared to the top of the Soul Singles chart on its way to selling eleven million copies worldwide. Meanwhile, youths like Richie "Crazy Legs" Colon and Ken "Ken Swift" Gabbert were sitting in those same Times Square theaters as Bobby, awed by the acrobatic fighting they were seeing onscreen. B-boy pioneers of the Rock Steady Crew, they started incorporating these moves into their own form of physical competition, known as break dancing, part of the burgeoning movement of hip-hop in the Bronx.

On May 2, 1981, WNEW Channel Five in New York inaugurated its *Drive-In Movie* series, which aired on Saturday afternoons at three o'clock, with *Bruce Lee: His Last Days, His Last Nights* (1976). For a program promising the best in B-movies, that particular selection was a strange choice, since Bruce Lee was not even in it. Instead, Betty Ting Pei, the last person to see him alive, talked about what kind of person he was while actors dramatized fight scenes from his movies. But the film definitely qualified as exploitation because anything with Bruce Lee's name in the title was guaranteed viewers.

Thankfully, Channel Five redeemed themselves a few weeks later on June 6, when they showed *Master Killer*, originally titled *The 36th Chamber of Shaolin* (1977), which, Fanon Che Wilkins says, "ranks as one of the all-time classics of Asian martial arts films and was at the forefront of a new form of martial arts moviemaking that showcased the skill and practice of Shaolin kung fu."[23] Somehow this movie had managed to evade Bobby at the Deuce, but when he saw it for the first time on TV that day, he was blown away. "*The 36 Chambers* movie was the one that—after seeing the Bruce Lee genre and all the spinoffs, and *The Mystery of Chess Boxing*, all the amazing fantastical ones—this movie for some reason resonated as a reality story to me," he recalls. "I felt like I was watching a piece of history in a period of time that kind of was shielded from us in America."[24] In his memoir he wrote, "I had knowledge of self, had mastered the 120 faster than anyone my age, and was teaching Mathematics to others. When I saw *The 36th Chamber*, I felt like I was living it."[25]

Period pieces were nothing new to Hong Kong cinema, but *The 36th Chamber of Shaolin* proved to be a groundbreaking production on many levels. For one, its director, Lau Kar-leung, a martial arts practitioner, actor, and choreographer, "became part of a new wave of martial artists who brought true fighting skills to film and successfully explored the spiritual and philosophical dimensions of Chan [Zen] Buddhism that endowed many of their protagonists with a sense of moral cause and ethical justice, a device used to good effect in *The 36th Chamber of Shaolin*."[26] So, in addition to the reality of the fighting and its historical accuracy, eternal truths lay embedded in the story's core, which sent Bobby searching for books on Eastern philosophy.

The film is divided into three acts that, together, represent the epic journey of protagonist San Te, as played by Gordon Liu, a character based on a real eighteenth-century disciple of the Shaolin Temple. When we are introduced to San Te, he is just a naïve student, Liu Yude, who stumbles into the resistance movement against the Manchu invaders from the north. In the course of suppressing the rebellion, this powerful enemy wipes out his family and school, leaving San Te with no recourse but revenge. After seeing one of his friends use kung fu to break open a box, San Te asks him where he learned it and decides to journey to the prestigious martial arts academy, the Shaolin Temple, to acquire these skills for himself. At first, he is rejected because he is not a monk, but the abbott of the temple sees something in him and allows him to train there, which is where act two picks up.

Located in the mountains of Henan province in central China, Shaolin is a place steeped in a rich history that often blurs the lines with mythology. Founded in 495 CE by Indian monk Bodhidharma, or "Damo" in Chinese, the monastery is one of the oldest and most respected kung fu schools in the country, combining martial arts training with the spiritual practices of Chan (Zen) Buddhism. Akin to modern-day Five Percenters, Damo placed the goal of reaching enlightenment on the individual and "advocated that seekers of the dharma (the way) be self-motivated and practice self-awareness and self-recognition in their daily lives."[27] Shaolin kung fu supposedly developed out of the yoga-based movements that Damo taught the monks to deal with the rigors of meditation. In feudal times, it was also a means of protecting themselves from invaders. But the monks' approach was never about violence for violence's sake. According to their philosophy, "If a person studied Shaolin and learned little more than kung-fu, he was not Shaolin. All the arts of the temple were aimed at leading one close to enlightenment by providing tools to make a person whole."[28]

Unfortunately, San Te embarks on his training with the wrong intention—revenge. But he has plenty of time to think about it, as he spends his first year confined to cleaning and sweeping the temple grounds. Only when demonstrating humility and showing respect for the other monks is he given the opportunity to go through the temple's thirty-five chambers, each of which showcases a different style or technique of martial arts. So act two finds him, like Rocky Balboa, struggling through various physical tasks designed to bolster his discipline, stamina, and strength, both mental and physical. After getting off to a rough start, he starts practicing after-hours, eventually finding his groove and becoming the temple's star pupil. "So, that journey of that character really resonated with me," says Bobby.[29] "That really inspired me—started me doing push-ups, punching walls, going to Chinatown to buy kung-fu books. But it also confirmed the path I was already on. It was like an echo of the Lessons [of the Five Percent] from another world, a reflection that made my situation clear."[30]

Finally, after San Te masters all thirty-five chambers, which takes seven years, the abbott bestows upon him the honor of teaching the chamber of his choice. But the newly minted Shaolin monk counters with a proposal of his own—to start a thirty-sixth chamber to teach laypeople kung fu. Of course, the elders view such plans as sacrilegious, but with a nod and a wink, they kick him out of the temple, allowing him the freedom to carry out his intended plans. The third act finds him returning to his village, where he starts recruiting followers to help him defeat the Manchus. After he attains victory, the final shot of the film takes place back at the Shaolin Temple, where San Te's dream of teaching laypeople kung fu is finally realized, as he establishes a thirty-sixth chamber.

Of course, as soon as the credits rolled at five o'clock, everyone in the neighborhood was outside sparring with each other, trying to re-create the amazing moves they had just witnessed on TV. But for Bobby, already a seasoned connoisseur of martial arts cinema, the physicality of the fighting was only one part of the attraction. "I noticed, having the brain that I had, the chivalry of the martial arts; the discipline of training to become the best; the honor, you know, if you say my brother. And those energies started to resonate," he says.[31]

He adds, "If *36 Chambers* never had a fight in it, it's still a great drama; it's still a great story of discipline, of struggle through oppression, shall we say. It inspires you."[32] The film motivated him enough to go to Chinatown in Manhattan to buy his first karate manual, *Tiger-Crane Style*, which, coincidentally, happened to be one of the main styles used in the movie. Channel Five's *Drive-In Movie* continued to provide New York City youths with the best of grind house kung fu until the summer of 1988, when the show was canceled. But Bobby's obsession only grew stronger.

Even though he could now watch the flicks from the comfort and safety of his own home, Bobby's fascination with the Deuce persisted through high school—one could even say in lieu of school, since he cut class so many times to see films there. But in the eighties, when Forty-Second Street was really going downhill and twenty-four-hour porn theaters started taking over, he says, "To see kung fu you had to go to the bummiest theaters, where a homeless guy lived, and those theaters were a funky, motherfuckin' place."[33]

Early one morning in 1981, after a night of carousing and rabble-rousing in Times Square, he and Rusty were looking for a warm place to crash. They found shelter in a scummy theater on the corner of Forty-Second Street and Seventh

Avenue. On the verge of passing out, Bobby caught the tail end of a movie that woke him right up. He was so determined to see it in its entirety that he waited through the whole next feature until it was screened again. Of that film, *Shaolin vs. Wu Tang* (1983), he says, "At that point, I'd have to say this was the best kung-fu movie I'd ever seen. The sword fighting alone was from another planet. Then there was the attitude of the Wu Tang themselves. The Wu Tang were defectors from the Shaolin Temple, warriors that had trained at Shaolin then developed a sword style that was invincible. In a lot of kung-fu films—like *Fist of the White Lotus* or even *Kill Bill*—the Wu Tang are actually the bad guys."[34]

Shaolin vs. Wu Tang, directed by Gordon Liu, star of *The 36th Chamber of Shaolin*, who also plays one of the lead characters in this film, presents another epic period piece with all its convoluted side stories and dramatic plot twists but also some of the best fight scenes, including those involving the *jian*, or Chinese straight sword. The story revolves around an evil feudal lord who pits two rival kung fu academies in competition in order to learn their secrets and make them destroy each other. His plan is foiled at the end, however, when the Shaolin Temple's Chao Fung-Wu and Hung Jun-Kit of the Wu Tang Academy, who happen to be best friends, join forces against their common enemy. In the process, they create a new fusion of their traditional styles.

From a philosophical perspective, the real Shaolin and Wu Tang actually did represent the yin and the yang, inhabiting opposite ends of the martial arts spectrum. Developed in the Taoist monasteries of the Wudang Mountains in Hubei Province, *Wudangquan* referred to a branch known as *nèijia*, which represented the internal or "soft" arts such as t'ai chi. Here, emphasis was placed on awareness of the mind, the spirit, the breath, and the use of relaxed leverage over brute strength, as opposed to the quick, explosive movements of the external style. But *Wudangquan* also involved weapons training—including the sword, which had a special resonance for Bobby.

"I kind of took the analogy from the Bible, where it says in the book of Revelations, 'When the Son of Man comes, out of his mouth will be a double-edged sword and he will change the nations with it,'" he says. "And I don't think a sword could come out a man's mouth, but I kinda reasoned that his sword was his tongue, which is symbolic to a sword, which could save you or kill you."[35] Echoing his cousin, Genius says, "Wu Tang is a sword style of kung fu. Our tongue is a sword, and we use it verbally and keep it sharp, and that's the whole point about it. We liked them flicks, so we applied that to the hip-hop shit.

"If you go back to the flicks, usually there was always someone who was skilled trying to challenge someone else who was skilled. That's kinda what hip-hop is—that's what it was for us back then," Genius continues, connecting it all back to the art form of MCing. After seeing kung fu films at the Deuce or on TV, he and his cousins, or sometimes his friend Walter Reed (a.k.a. Killah Priest) combed the city looking for a rhyme battle. "We used to travel from borough to borough, neighborhood to neighborhood, town to town, and we would just look for whoever was said to be the best in that town, and we would just challenge them, yunno, pull out our sword, and challenge 'em and that's usually what a lot of kung fu and martial arts flicks is about, yunno, challenging—friendly battles, though, not to the death," he adds.

Since moving back to Brooklyn, he had settled in at 719 Munroe Avenue in Bed-Stuy, which was not far from Ason.

Once the cousins battled a local crew called the Dissmasters, who lived around the corner. Mike Ski and Raven T., who had just released a twelve-inch called *Small Time Hustler*, were feeling themselves and ready to rumble. "They was coming with all kinds of foul profanity, 'Your mother' this, 'Your mother' that," Genius recalls. "And we damn near got into a fight. But we never used to come like that. But after we went home and we started writing rhymes like that just to have, but that wasn't what we was really about. We were about keepin' it lyrical, keepin' that flow and keepin' it sharp."[36]

Speaking of memorable battles, Genius and Ason also ended up going toe-to-toe with a guy named Q-Tip (Kamaal Ibn John Fareed), then a student at Murry Bergtraum High School for Business Careers in Manhattan, who went on to form A Tribe Called Quest with his three friends from Queens, Ali Shaheed Muhammad, Phife Dawg (Malik Taylor, RIP), and Jarobi White. In a similar fashion, they crossed paths with another young MC from Brooklyn's Marcy projects named Jay-Z (Sean Carter). The incident occurred at the Ansaaru Allah Community Center on Bushwick Avenue, where they served wheat pizzas and sponsored youth talent shows. "We wasn't performing against each other, but we just happened to run into him out there and we like, 'Yeah, we're MCs.' And then we went back and forth with a couple of darts, yunno, and that was that," says Genius.[37] "Yunno, he was very arrogant at the time, and he still is. He was very cocky. But he was rhyming much, much faster. He was superfast back then, but, yunno, he's a clever MC. He's always been, and he's still nice. I give it to him," he adds.[38]

"Wu-Tang Clan truly did take a martial arts approach to hip-hop—to the sound of the music, the style of the lyrics, the

competitive wordplay of the rhyming, the mental prepara-
tions involved. I think we really did bring a new school to
the world," says RZA, who remains a walking encyclopedia
of the martial arts movie genre.[39] These films were not a passing fad for him but an obsession, forever intertwined with
his formative years. He learned to appreciate them not only
for the fighting but also for the cultural and spiritual aspects
they illuminated. In retrospect, his own path followed a similar trajectory to the plot of 36 Chambers of Shaolin in that
it took extensive training, discipline, and time to hone and
refine his art and craft, which was hip-hop. When Wu-Tang
appeared on the scene, they practically provided a blueprint
for others to follow, in much the same way that San Te started
a thirty-sixth chamber and democratized the study of Shaolin kung fu. The sound of karate chops or film dialogue in
their music was far from gimmick or cultural appropriation
but part of an earnest desire to synthesize the influences of
their youth into an expression of who they were and what
they represented. After all, salvaging shards of sonic and cultural detritus and placing them in a new context have always
been part of hip-hop's MO, and the influence of Eastern philosophy and discipline represent the Clan's contribution to
the mix.

CHAPTER 5

THE CRIME SIDE

Cocaine business control America
Ganja business control America
KRS-ONE come to start some hysteria
Illegal business controls America

—Boogie Down Productions

Kung fu was not the only genre that played well with urban Black audiences. The movie *Scarface*—the rags-to-riches story of a Cuban émigré who works his way up from lowly dishwasher to powerful cocaine kingpin—opened to a fairly tame reception upon its release in 1983, taking in $46 million at the box office, making it only the sixteenth-highest-grossing film of the year. Despite being directed by Brian De Palma; written by a young Oliver Stone, just off an Oscar win for his screenplay adaptation of *Midnight Express* (1978); and starring the iconic Al Pacino, the film was regarded by critics—still a decade away from Tarantino—as a glorified B-movie, citing the gratuitous, bloody violence and Pacino's hyperbolic performance. Apparently, they couldn't see past the mountain of blow on Scarface's desk or the customized M-16 A1 assault rifle with grenade launcher that he referred to as "my little friend" to appreciate the principled gangster with his own code of ethics. After all, how many bad guys would refuse to take down a mark accompanied by his wife and child, hastening Scarface's own demise in a hail of bullets? The critics missed the nuances and contradictions in an otherwise brutal persona that made Scarface the kind of three-dimensional antihero for whom audiences rooted. They also failed to recognize that, instead of sensationalizing the rising specter of a nationwide drug crisis or glamorizing an excessive lifestyle, the movie actually hit the nail on the head, presenting a very real cautionary tale.

But none of this was lost on legions of youth in the hood, who embraced the film after it went to video in 1984, seeing a reflection of their own circumstances within all the negativity and carnage. To them, *Scarface* represented a warped but attainable version of the American dream in which a self-made player, starting out with nothing, could achieve enormous success, albeit illegally. Furthermore, the character of Tony Montana was machismo personified, an alpha male who pursued his desires—whether it be a woman, a fancy car, or simply status—with verve and gusto. His loyalty was unquestionable, and his work ethic, or grind, relentless. He also lived by the credo "All I have in this world is my balls and my word, and I don't break them for no one," another admirable quality from an otherwise unsavory character. Scarface was determined to make it by any means necessary, displaying a strength of will that allowed him to power past any obstacles. The only caveat—as everyone involved in the drug game knows—was that, at some point, you wind up dead or in prison. To an audience raised on blaxploitation heroes, who usually operated outside the law, *Scarface* provided a familiar face, updated for the modern era.

"I think *Scarface* was such an influential movie because it's the movie we all saw during the period of having dreams of American success," says RZA. "It's a rags-to-riches story even though it's painted in blood. It spoke to a generation at that time who was livin' that life. There was no other way for us to see the American Dream besides selling drugs."[1] Raekwon, who entered the drug game when he was about fifteen, would agree, saying, "That movie pretty much guided us on how to be a hustler."[2] It told a parable of the streets, and even though Scarface goes down at the end, countless young, impressionable teens wanted to emulate his rise to the top.

While cocaine gave America's favorite beverage, Coca-Cola, its name—and, for a time, its main ingredient—the drug's march to infamy began in the early seventies in Latin America— specifically the nations of Colombia, Ecuador, Bolivia, and Peru, where the coca plant was indigenous. In fact, in a country like Peru that straddled the Andes, practically the entire population chewed raw coca leaves for their mild stimulant effect and to relieve the debilitating effects of headaches and shortness of breath that came with living at higher altitudes. Extracting the psychoactive alkaloid cocaine from coca leaves, however, involved a sophisticated laboratory process using several chemical solvents, which delivered a more concentrated product. When snorted, the drug stimulated the release of those feel-good compounds dopamine and serotonin, giving the user a sense of exhilaration and confidence. One was capable of all kinds of feats of folly under the influence, as the drug lowered inhibitions and impaired judgment as well. While processing powder cocaine, jungle chemists also found a cheap and crude method of making a paste called *basuco*, or base, which could be smoked.

The drug's equivalent to moonshine, *basuco* was simply mashed-up coca leaves mixed with a solvent such as ether or gasoline. Though it tasted nasty, was highly flammable, and was chock-full of questionable adulterants, it hit like a hurricane. Base found a strong following among the poor, who could never afford powder, a rich man's high. They even preferred smoking, or freebasing, as it was called, for the shorter but more intense rush, since the lungs provided swifter delivery of the drug to the brain than the nasal passages did. Real cocaine connoisseurs came around to this method as well.[3]

Just ask comedian Richard Pryor, who, in June 1980, became the poster child for the hazards of freebasing when he accidentally set himself on fire during a coke binge. He ended up running naked down the streets of LA, trying to put out his blazing afro and suffering severe burns.[4] In America, freebasing cocaine did not gain popularity until the mid- to late seventies, and even then, the drug was still associated with a whole different class of people—mostly celebrities and the wealthy. All that changed in the early eighties, however, thanks to the Colombian cartels, who supplied the Scarfaces of the world, flooding the market and creating a glut of product. In 1983, the same year the movie premiered, the DEA estimated that sixty-five tons of cocaine were smuggled into the country—mostly through Miami.[5]

Some of this massive amount of contraband made its way through the Bahamas, where local dealers, looking to unload their surpluses, started catering to the substantial low-end market of *basuco* smokers. Their new form of smokable "rock" was made by combining powder cocaine with baking soda and boiling it down into a solid form. According to author David Farber, "Crack's fierce and nearly instant high was a huge hit with coke users of all kinds, especially poorer folk who could not afford the price of a gram of powder cocaine but could buy a cheap hit of the highly potent 'rock.'"[6] By 1980, Caribbean immigrants introduced this new sensation to Miami, and from there it spread to several other major US cities—including LA, San Diego, and Houston.

Farber further states, "LA had a big cocaine trade by the late '70s, but it became America's cocaine capital in the mid-1980s because of an external disruption in the US supply networks. Earlier, federal authorities had targeted the Columbian cartels' supply routes and distribution networks in South Florida. But rather than give up and find a new way to make a living, the Colombian suppliers worked with Mexican narcotics trafficking organizations—experienced in bringing heroin and marijuana into the United States—to transport their cocaine. LA offered opportunity. It was conveniently located near the border; economically bustling; and it had a heavily trafficked and decentralized highway system. Thus, LA became the Mexican smugglers' cocaine hub."[7]

The last link in the chain of this underground economy were the street retailers—usually young Black men like Rick Donnell Ross, better known as "Freeway Ricky," a frustrated high school tennis star and unlikely entrepreneur who was single-handedly responsible for making crack or "ready rock," as he called it, the hottest-selling commodity on the streets of South Central, a predominantly Black and impoverished area of LA. From 1982 to 1989, he became the original crack kingpin, moving tons of blow through the City of Angels using the Bloods and Crips. According to investigative journalist Gary Webb's compelling exposé *Dark Alliance*, which was originally a series of articles for the *San Jose Mercury News*, the CIA was involved in bringing cocaine into the country to fund arms sales to the Contras in Nicaragua. Rick was just the expendable Black guy who eventually took the fall, serving thirteen years behind bars. But with a recipe for success, the Bloods and Crips started franchising the drug game as they spread eastward to other cities and towns.

On the East Coast, the situation played out quite differently. While Colombia's second-biggest crime syndicate, the Cali Cartel, handled importation to New York, Dominicans, who had carved out a niche for themselves in the northernmost tip of Manhattan known as Washington Heights since the sixties, controlled operations on the ground. According to journalist Michael Massing, "The Colombians found dependable customers in the Dominicans of Washington Heights. The two groups got along well, joined not only by a common language but also similar entrepreneurial values. The Dominicans became New York's chief middlemen. As sales boomed to aspiring young dealers outside Washington Heights, the city was eventually carved up along ethnic lines with Dominican-supplied blacks controlling Harlem, Queens and Brooklyn, and Dominicans dominant in upper Manhattan and the South Bronx."[8]

In the early eighties, the Dominicans started experimenting, cutting powder cocaine with lidocaine, a prescription anesthetic they called "comeback," to make freebase before realizing that baking soda was cheaper and more readily available. Washington Heights bodegas may have been short on staples like bread and milk, but stacks of Arm & Hammer, whose shares probably went through the roof, lined the shelves. Cooking equal amounts of cocaine and baking soda in water yielded a single solid mass that could be broken up. The small, pebble-like shards dealers sold made a crackling sound when torched, giving the product its name, "crack," which grabbed the national media spotlight toward the end of 1985. By this time, the drug had already devastated poor neighborhoods around New York as well as in LA and

Miami, the other major distribution points for cocaine. But the epidemic spread even farther into the heartland thanks to the power of the Jamaican posses, who changed the game, upping the ante on violence and brutality.

"Yardies," as they were sometimes known (since Jamaicans often referred to their home as their "yard"), started flocking to the US after the pivotal 1980 elections in their own country. Many were former "gunmen" or enforcers who worked for Jamaica's two opposing political parties—the US-backed Jamaica Labor Party (JLP) and the Castro-backed People's National Party (PNP). After claiming victory for the JLP, Reagan disciple Edward Seaga vowed to crack down on these political enforcers, who were responsible for killing some eight hundred people in the run-up to the elections. Consequently, many fled to East Coast cities such as Washington, DC, Baltimore, Philadelphia, New York, and Boston, all of which offered established Caribbean communities into which they could easily disappear.

Most, like Delroy "Uzi" Edwards, who went on to lead the infamous Rankers Posse, entered on a tourist visa and stayed illegally. Like Edwards, they may have started out in the weed business, hustling dime bags at a neighborhood "gate," or drug spot, but as soon as they saw the potential for crack, there was no turning back. When Jamaicans moved to take over a block, they did it with overwhelming force and firepower, reminiscent of the posses in Hollywood Westerns from which their name was derived. They introduced Uzis and AK-47s to the drug game, as well as the concept of shoot first so that no one asks questions later. In 1987, when rapper KRS-ONE declared in faux patois that "illegal business control America," he was hardly overstating the problem.

"I think crack probably came out like a month or two after *Scarface* came out," says Raekwon, a freshman at New Dorp High School at the time. "So the drug life was equivalent to a lot of money in my neighborhood. It seemed like all the older people turned into addicts, and I was like, 'Oh, shit! This drug is really fuckin' up people's minds.'"[9] Nonetheless, the lure of making fast money in the streets when opportunities were few, if any, proved to be too powerful to resist. "You know how it goes," he says. "Maybe one of my friends will start sellin', then the next thing you know them two start selling, next thing you know they on it, and I'm lookin' at my sneakers like, shit, I'ma bout to be on it too."[10]

"Material stuff is so enticing when you don't have shit," says U-God, echoing these thoughts. "It's not that we were even materialistic like that, but when you've got old-ass clothes and last year's boots on in winter, it's hard to have a righteous attitude. My mom provided the bare minimum, but that was all she could afford. If I wanted to get fresh and have some money to eat, I had to come up with my own plan."[11]

Raekwon adds, "Far as gettin' jobs was concerned, it was tough because of the neighborhood we was livin' in. So, a lot of times we were already judged before we even get to go do that, to go try and get a job. I remember my mom used to wake me up at 8 o' clock in the morning like, 'You gon' get a job.' And I'm like, 'Aight, I'm down to do it.' And I try it, and it's like it never worked. So, I come back and be like 'I tried,' and she be like, 'Yeah, you tried, but you gon' try again.'"[12] For those without prospects or a proper education, U-God calls the drug game "the last stand for survival," and he and Raekwon were the two members of the Clan to get most deeply involved.[13]

Sometime in 1985, a crew of dreadlocked West Indians from Brooklyn stormed Park Hill practically overnight, setting up shop in an apartment on 55 Bowen Street, where they introduced crack to the neighborhood. Their leader, the charismatic Dusty Fats, a Guyanese dread who flashed a smile full of gold teeth, was always freshly "dipped" in crisp FILA tracksuits and Clark's wallabees. He drafted a fourteen-year-old U-God as one of his first workers.

On his first day serving the fiends, it was practically like Black Friday in the spot as an endless stream of rumpled bills came through a small hole in the front door. He serviced vials of crack in return. But after a while, his Spidey senses tingling, U-God decided to close up shop early—only minutes before the police battered down the door. It wasn't the last time his gut instincts saved his ass. Afterward, he ran into Dusty, who was surprised that his new worker had not been busted and peeled off three C-notes from a fat wad as a reward. But U-God was pissed that he had taken such a big risk for peanuts and had to fall back from the drug game for a minute.[14]

Dusty redeemed himself, however, when he took the young hustler under his wing later on. "I got trained by the best drug dealers that was out there. The best," says U-God, who returned to that life at seventeen. Adopting a patois accent, he continues, "He said, 'Redmon, c'mon let me tell you, mon. You see dat ting dere? Dat's a kilo. Dat ting there, dat's eighteen Gs.' Dropped the whole thing in a bucket, he cook it up, splashed it right in front of my face. I'm like, 'Godammit, that's how they do it?,' 'Yeah, mon, gimme a razor.' Chop, chop, chop, boom. Showed me the whole thing. Bagged a few, know what I'm sayin. 'Dis a G-pack—G at a time, hear. But the eighteen, mon, I make it forty.' And he showed me and told me how it was."[15]

Dusty was basically passing on trade secrets—namely, the simple formula for transforming powder cocaine into the smokable form known as "crack," which was fast becoming the scourge of the streets with its short and intense but highly addictive high. The recipe amounted to boiling the powder in water with equal parts baking soda until a single solid mass formed. Small pieces were shaved off that big "rock" with a razor blade and could be packaged in vials that sold for five or ten dollars, depending on the size. Dealers distinguished their product with different-colored caps—red tops, green tops, and so on—as well as catchy brand names like "Beam Me Up, Scotty."

Crack transformed the cocaine trade from a high-end business catering to an upscale clientele to a McDonald's Dollar Menu, where any aspiring entrepreneur could easily start a franchise and tap into a huge market of low-income repeat customers in the ghetto. The fact that you could more than double your money on a kilo while keeping the customers coming back for more explained why crack boomed into such a lucrative business. David Farber writes, "Between 1985 and 1989, according to the Office of National Drug Control Policy, cocaine use had doubled in the United States. And much of that increase was due to the popularity of crack. Federal authorities estimated that 50 percent of the cocaine smuggled into the United States was cooked into crack."[16]

At the same time, jails and prisons were filling up with an endless supply of low-level street dealers per Reagan's war on drugs. Due to such draconian legislation as the Rockefeller Drug Laws, passed in 1973, which created mandatory minimum sentencing of fifteen years to life for possession of four ounces of narcotics, many young Black and brown hustlers trying to get a leg up in life got ensnared in a crooked criminal justice system instead. According to *Time*, "Drug offenders as a percentage of New York's prison population surged from 11% in 1973 to a peak of 35% in 1994, according to the state's Corrections Department. The surge was mostly a result of convictions for 'nonviolent, low-level drug possessions and drug sales.'"[17] The racial disparities in convictions and sentencing were nothing less than staggering, disproportionately affecting the Black community. Ava DuVernay's illuminating documentary *13th*, which argues that slavery never really ended but rather transformed into the prison-industrial complex, projected that one in three Black males will spend time behind bars in their lifetime, as compared to one in seventeen white males.

For the moment, however, U-God, who was lucky to escape arrest once, decided to try legal employment. At age fifteen, he got a job working at the Statue of Liberty concessions counter, where he was soon reunited with his old friend Cliff, a.k.a. Shotgun, recently returned to Park Hill from Indianapolis. Like everybody else in the neighborhood, Shotgun became a Five Percenter and changed his name to Shaquan. Enrolled at New Dorp, he says, "Once I got to high school, it got deep because it wasn't my academics that were low, yunno. It was basically, I didn't like going to school because it turned into a fashion show. Everybody was so conscious of how they looked, and I didn't have shit, so I didn't like going to school."[18]

"When you grow up inside the hood, or, as they call it, the projects," says Bobby, "you hang with your older cousins or older kids on the block, and you wind up just following their lead. And with so many kids, my mother couldn't keep a hold of all of us, and I would go hang out with the local drug dealer or something like that and get involved in all kind of things. And it's funny because you don't see yourself goin' down a narrow path. You think it's fun or something—anything to escape. If you don't have a father in your house, any older male figure becomes the father. And you start following these people thinking they're your guidance."[19]

At fifteen, Bobby was a hip-hop fiend with dreams of someday making a record, but he was also immersed in the streets. "I was a major influence back then," he boasts. "My clothes, my style, my slang, my braids—niggas wasn't even rockin' braids back then, know what I'm saying? I had all the Polo, I was a king booster, a king thief. Me and ODB used to steal at least $1,000 a day worth of shit, right. Like I got a rep because of my ability to steal. We used to bring bitches with us and shit." By this time, his mother had reunited the family back in Staten Island, renting a two-story wood frame at 88 Laurel Avenue, where Bobby spent his high school years. Though enrolled at Curtis High, he didn't attend very often, skipping school to see kung fu movies in Times Square. But as a naturally gifted student who studied on his own time, he would still show up for tests and get As.

Bobby was at that age, however, where trouble seemed to follow him. He remembers how heartbroken his mother was when she found a gun in his room that his older brother had procured. "She tried so much to keep us away from negativity and try to keep us in church and try to keep us on the right path," he says. "But, yunno, we was tempted by the streets, addicted to the streets, and wanting to be in the streets. And it really broke her heart and she kind of disowned us at that time, and that really broke my heart because my mother, aw man, I love her so much."[20] But guns were a rite of passage in the hood, where threats lurked around every corner, and people often carried for their own protection. Even so, accidents happened, as U-God discovered one day when he and Raekwon, both fifteen, were playing with a loaded gun. He pointed the .38 revolver at Rae's head, but when his friend balked, U-God turned toward the window and pulled the trigger, shattering the glass.

Though Bobby tried to change his ways for a short time, the lure of the streets inevitably pulled him back. In addition to shoplifting, he hustled dime bags of weed to the suits on Wall Street. Around the same time, however, he started messing around with his first drum machines—first the Roland TR-606 and then the TR-707, both borrowed from fellow Staten Island deejays Philly Phil and Dr. Rock. Under the sway of these competing influences, he tried to strike a balance and maintain the righteous path through Mathematics and music.

Others succumbed to the full force of the crack tsunami that was hitting the neighborhood. Oliver Grant, who by then had remade himself as a Five Percenter, claiming "Power" as his righteous name, started operating a gate out of 225 Park Hill Avenue. He simply had the balls to approach Dusty and the dreads, who put him on. At the height of his hustling, he ran a crew of about twenty, including his right-hand man, Raekwon. By the age of sixteen or seventeen, both were rocking designer labels and jewelry and driving Mercedes Benzes. "I used to hang with RZA when I didn't want to get in trouble from being in the neighborhood all the time, you know. It was like, you would either sell drugs or get in trouble, or do something different," Raekwon recalls. "RZA was always the type of dude who was moving through the city a lot. I would hang out with him because it was like a day for me, it would give me something to do, like, 'Oh, I'm gonna fuck with him, you know, he's a good dude. He's on some musical shit.'"[21]

Meanwhile, Jason Hunter, a.k.a. Deck, his classmate from IS 49, started rolling with his older brother's crew, all guys in their midtwenties. "You're seeing coke get chopped on the table, guns, and all kinds of shit at a young age," he says. "That young age is when your mind is the ripest, man. All that information is going on and it gets sucked in. You catalog all that, and that's what you become. You become what your surroundings is. So, kids are forced to be grown men fast."[22]

Unfortunately, he had to find out the hard way when he was arrested at fifteen for selling crack to an undercover officer—the first of two felonies—and shipped off to the Brooklyn House of Detention. "There's grown men—murderous niggas—lookin' at my hat and shit," he recalls. "So you got to learn quick. As a youngster, I had to grasp who I was. I'm like, 'Oh shit, I'm in here and I'm a young nigga. Don't talk too much.' That's when Inspectah was born. That was the nigga that shut up and just started analyzing things. . . . You got to make observations and determine when to make moves, and that's how I became Inspectah. I learned that, came home, and that helped me learn how to survive on the streets."[23]

The name was inspired by Peter Sellers's Inspector Clouseau character from the *Pink Panther* movies. "The chief used to always say, 'Inspectaaah!' And that's what U-God used to say to me when I see him on the streets, and it just stuck, you known what I mean," says Deck. "And then 'Deck' was a graffiti name I used to write. I used to tag up crazy, man. I used to bomb the trains, buses, all of that shit—steal art supplies and everything, you know what I mean?"[24]

Perhaps because he had just returned to Park Hill, Shaquan managed to stay out of the street life for the moment, advancing in his job at the Statue of Liberty gift shop, where he made assistant manager. But after suffering a foot injury at work, things started unraveling fast for him. Laid off and desperate for funds, with his mother stressing him out for rent, he made an "ass" bet at a dice game, which was placing a bet without having the money to back it up. But his luck held out, and he managed to walk away with $800 in his pocket, the price of admission to the drug game.[25]

After moving in with a buddy, Rader Ruckus (Clifton Fuller), and using his winnings to set himself up in business, he found himself on the block, pumping rocks, like everyone else. New to the game, he made amateur mistakes that cost him. "Around my way, there was a little area where we used to hustle at," he says. "Cars would come through, everybody used to run up to the cars, and yunno, if you got fifteen people hustling at the same spot, first one there gets the sale. And you literally got to put your head in the window to get the sale. So, I'm out there by myself this night. This fiend pulls up. 'How many you want?' I put my head inside, got my hand like this [outstretched]. 'What's good. How many you want?' Smacks my hand. Takes off with all my stuff."[26] In addition to cops or rival dealers, even customers presented a potential hazard, making street sales a thankless job. But his situation deteriorated even further after that.

"We was living in this apartment of these people, and the apartment got shot up and firebombed. They tried to put a hit out, you know what I'm sayin'?" says Meth. "When the people moved out, we moved in. We was payin' them to stay there and shit. The next thing you know, the lights go out. We was living by candlelight, cuttin' up crack in that motherfucker, and surviving." After finally moving into a hotel for a couple of weeks, he ended up going home. Though this initial foray into the fast life proved unsuccessful, he ended up working for U-God, who was attending McKee Vocational High School while he hustled.

When the practical-minded U-God returned to the drug game at seventeen, he ran drug spots in several buildings and, like Power, had a crew of about twenty deep working for him at the height of his involvement. But he was a reluctant Scarface. "I didn't want to be a drug dealer," he says. "I was happy with two bricks [kilos] or three bricks. These other dudes, they wanted 100 bricks and to be Pablo Escobar and shit. I didn't want to be Escobar. The street will have you chasing something completely different than what you got in the game for."[27] U-God's plan was to go to college to study mortuary science.

Perhaps his odd choice of major had something to do with what he was witnessing around him on a daily basis. As the crack situation worsened, he says, "Our neighborhood became nothing but a meat factory—straight butchery. Maniacs running around, sticking up people, popping rounds off every day. Motherfuckers getting shot down in the street. At its worst, people were getting hurt or killed almost every day. A lot of people dying. Park Hill soon got the nickname 'Killah Hill.'"[28]

Hip-hop's first golden age in the mideighties paralleled the rise of crack, as drug dealers suddenly became the trendsetters in the hood with rappers reveling in their style and attitude. Art was not only imitating life but colliding with it. According to Raekwon, "The bottom line really is we came up in the streets, and yunno, we were so magnetized to hip-hop, yunno, that we paid attention to the stars. We paid attention to what they was writing. We paid attention to the way they was dressin', the way they aura was, yunno? And I grew up under the Rakims and the Kanes and the KRSes, yunno, Kool G. Raps and N.W.As, and it's like sittin' there, just watchin' they style and they technique and how they made their music. We felt like they was talkin' for us. Yunno, so these songs started to be like paragraphs in our lives and shit."[29] Since this was the era of the downtown hip-hop clubs, they joined the mobs of youth taking the ferry to Manhattan to such venues as the Red Zone, Latin Quarters, and Union Square, where they got a chance to see their idols up close. Plenty of artists also performed in Staten Island, thanks, once again, to the drug dealers.

While Dusty's reign of terror might have transformed the once peaceful Park Hill into "Killah Hill," Bobby says there was another side to him. "Even though he was a very ruthless man and powerful on the negative side, he always promoted positivity to the young people," he says. "And it's funny because sometimes on the law enforcement side, those people are looked at like criminals. But they don't realize that these men actually became icons of our community. Because of their money and everything they attracted us."[30] During Bobby's high school years, Dusty promoted rap shows at a local venue called Park Villas, at 70 Beach Street, where he brought such artists as KRS-ONE, Doug E. Fresh, and Rakim. He also sponsored rap contests at the same venue, which attracted the likes of Bobby, Genius, Ason, Dennis, Deck, Raekwon, U-God, and Shaquan, all battling each other for a cash prize.

On a memorable night in 1986, with all the usual suspects in attendance, Ason beatboxed for Bobby, who performed a song, followed by Genius. Then Darryl Hill (a.k.a. Cappadonna), seventeen, who went by the name Original, took the stage. Known as a member of the Get Busy Crew, Original, along with his brother Lounge Lo, already had a rep in Park Hill as a stylish dresser and slang innovator. He was the terror of project stairwells, where dudes hung out, smoking weed and having rhyme ciphers. When the Park Villa deejay threw on the classic break beat "Impeach the President," by the Honey Drippers, Original launched into a song called "Loungin," where he worked Dusty's name into a verse. As the crowd erupted, easily propelling him to victory, he scooped up the $1,000 grand prize. But, their pride hurt, Brooklyn wasn't having it. Genius stepped to Original, saying, "You ain't win that shit! That shit was whack! What's today's Mathematics?"[31] Always the ferocious competitor, for him it was more about respect than money.

According to RZA, "After that, he [Dusty] brought out EPMD, and we met EPMD and realized, just by meeting these artists, that there's a chance that you can become one of these artists. So, he did that for us." In the end, however, Dusty fared no better than Tony Montana when he was eventually busted in the summer of 1990, receiving two life terms plus eighty years for his criminal activities.[32] He was not an exception but rather the rule. Over the course of the decade, hordes of incarcerated Scarfaces helped push the US prison population past two million, making it the largest in the world. It's no wonder, then, that the legacy of crack left a lasting impression. As RZA says, "This crack culture influenced our music—became part of our music."[33]

CHAPTER 6

LABELS

Melquan Smith, fifty-four, belongs to a generation that knew hip-hop before it was hip-hop. During the summer of 1977, he was just another twelve-year-old who flocked to the jams every Sunday at Valley Park, near the northeast Bronx's Edenwald projects. Hand-drawn flyers or simply word of mouth announced whether DJ Kool Herc and the Herculoids, Grandmaster Flash and the Furious Five, or DJ Breakout and his Sasquatch Sounds would be bringing out their sets and raising a ruckus. "It'd be waves of people walking to the park from different directions—north, east, and south," he recalls. "As you got a little closer, you would hear the bass, and then you gettin' hyped, so you walkin' a little faster." People of all ages attended these park jams like they were going to church, to see the deejay spinning break beats while the MCs rocked the mic. Far more than simply the soundtrack to his youth, "hip-hop inspired me," says Smith.

Another equally looming presence in his life at the time was the Nation of Gods and Earths. At age thirteen, Smith acquired knowledge of self through his enlightener, Qasim Wise Allah, a fellow student at Cardinal Hayes High School. "People always say we [the Gods] ran New York, you know what I'm sayin'? It's because the knowledge spread like wildfire, you know, all across the ghettos," he says. "The Five Percent Nation is a very young nation, and it attracted the youth. And that's, you know, mainly the people we teach—the youth." In fact, Smith met other Five Percenters at the park jams and conducted impromptu ciphers, forming a circle and "building" or expounding on the day's Mathematics. "We're supposed to be having fun, and we'll be building at the jams," he says. Growing up, he watched as hip-hop took over the five boroughs.

Neither an MC nor a deejay, Smith played hoops in high school before heading off to Howard University in DC in 1983. But college wasn't the best fit, and he only lasted two and a half years. "I started getting distracted," he says. "I wasn't doing that well in school. I started getting caught up in fun." But far from frivolous diversion, the party scene showed him how rap records were making a huge impact outside of New York. "Imagine seeing a music come from the streets and then blow up to this industry," says Smith. "It was like us against the world." A hustler at heart—from his days selling baggies of weed in the back room of the Bronx's legendary Disco Fever—he wanted a piece of the action. So, with an eye toward breaking into the music industry, he returned to New York and enrolled in Baruch College.

"But when I was at Baruch, my mind wasn't right," he says. "I wasn't in class; I wasn't even paying attention because I wanted to start a label." Instead of trying to gain some practical experience by working for an established imprint like Def Jam or Uptown, Smith decided to just wing it. He figured that what he lacked in contacts and experience, he made up for in enthusiasm and a total dedication to his cause. Confidence and charisma concealed his naïveté, and he wasn't shy about making cold calls to label execs or approaching someone he didn't know at an industry function. He and his partner Shabazz, another Howard dropout, had a side hustle selling furs on commission from a storefront on Twenty-Seventh Street in the Fur District—a gig they exploited for maximum advantage.

"We used to go to parties, and we would wear these fur coats," Smith recalls. "And we young; I had gold teeth, got fur coats on, like, 'Who the fuck is these young motherfuckers with these fly-ass fur coats?' We look like drug dealers or somethin', you know what I'm sayin'?" Borrowed from the showroom, the coats had to be returned undamaged, but they served their purpose, connecting the young entrepreneurs with the likes of Def Jam impresario Russell Simmons, Uptown's Andre Harrell, and Fly Ty Williams of Cold Chillin', who all became customers. "I go to an industry party back in the days, I would have the magnetic," says Smith. "I got swagger, but I ain't no artist. I'm business. I talk smooth, you know. I'm different. I'm not talking like a street dude. So, I had the charisma, so that's why I know all these people and started getting cool with all these people."

Industry contacts aside, Smith, a native son of the Boogie Down, also had cachet with a lot of rappers from the borough, including KRS-ONE and fellow Five Percenters King Sun and Just Ice, who even gave him a shout-out on his song "Going Way Back" (1987). The following year, none other than Big Daddy Kane, the MC du jour, gave "Melquan & Shabazz" a shout-out on his hit "Set It Off" (1988). Influenced by artists like Kane (King Asiatic Nobody's Equal) and Rakim, one of the first Five Percenters to pick up the mic and incorporate the lingo of the Gods into his rhymes, Smith says, "The Gods have a fantastic way of teaching people, from the highest to the lowest, right? So, I figure if we're going to have entertainment, this is a good way to spread the knowledge or at least influence people through the knowledge, you know what I'm sayin'? I wanted to like make history with the Gods and Earths, so my first group was Divine Force."

He was introduced to the Brooklyn trio, which consisted of Ice T, a.k.a. Lady Nefertiti, Supreme, and Sir Ibu, after running into Ibu on the subway, where they admired each other's fashion sense. Smith was soon dressing the group up in furs for the promo shot of their first twelve-inch single, "T.V. Guide / The Jizer," released in early 1987. Produced by Teddy Riley, a young talent from Harlem's St. Nicholas projects, who was tearing up the charts with the latest funky-fusion sound dubbed "new jack swing" by *Village Voice* journalist Barry Michael Cooper (who also, incidentally, penned the screenplay for the 1991 crack drama *New Jack City*), the single failed to ignite. Smith could have predicted as much, as he didn't think the track was right for his artists. Nonetheless, with that record, he realized his dream of starting a label. His father, James, whom he describes as an "old-school, hardworking dude," was indispensable in making it happen. A fireman for most of his life, the elder Smith made some money in real estate when he retired, and in support of his son's hustle, he invested in the launch of Yamakka Records (a play on "You make a record").

Another twelve-inch, "Holy War / Something Different," followed later that year, featuring only Sir Ibu. But this record created enough of a buzz on the streets that it helped Ibu land a deal at 4th & Broadway / Island, the same label that signed Rakim. Then in 1988, the other two members of Divine Force returned with the single "My Uptown Beat," garnering more underground acclaim for the group. But, unfortunately, just as Smith was building up some momentum, he collided with the realities of running an independent label and ran out of money.

It was around this same time that he got a call from the Genius, who had seen his business card in a Five-Percenter publication called *The Word*. Though working for the transit authority cleaning subway cars, Genius, twenty-two, had not given up on his dream of making it as an MC. He told Smith he admired his work with Divine Force, whom Smith had managed to get covered in popular rap fanzines such as *Right On!*, and arranged a meeting at Smith's home office on Parkside Avenue in Flatbush, Brooklyn.

Genius had been committed to MCing since the age of eleven. While introducing his younger cousins to the art form and mentoring them on their paths, he was also improving his own craft by hanging out with better MCs. "I had another cousin who was a little older than me who had shit locked down on the MCing tip out in Jamaica, Queens," says Genius. "This was in the early '80s, '81, yunno. It was like watching him do his thing, my lyrics just started to advance. It took a while to develop, but lyrically I was on some shit, always analyzing something, writing something." Through his cousin, Genius was introduced to Antonio Moore, a member of the Infinity Machine crew, whose sound system had hosted all the old-school greats from Afrika Bambaataa and Grandmaster Flash to Kurtis Blow and Eddie Cheeba. They used to team up with another local crew, Cipher of Sounds, to host legendary block parties in Jamaica, Queens. "Me and Dirty used to go out there and make demos 'cause they was fuckin' with all types of shit like drum machines," says Genius. "We just had lyrical skills. We just coming through, man, I'm tellin' you, we was goin' for ours, walking miles to go to this nigga house and get on the mic."

Around 1984, Genius, Ason, and Rakeem formed their own crew called All in Together Now. "I think I was more into it than the other guys at the time, maybe because I was older," says Genius, who hosted everyone at his house at 719 Monroe Street in Bed-Stuy. "I used to spend most of the time back then writing the group's routines. Ol' Dirty was more into fashion and lookin' fly back then. He was one of the best beatboxers around, though. I used to write ODB's beats, write out the sounds on paper and orchestrate them," he says.[1] "We definitely had a bugged chemistry," he adds. "We'd make up routines, battle other crews, that kind of thing. Most of our songs were based on popular songs just like Cold Crush Brothers and Treacherous Three used to do."[2] Adapting a well-known ditty that girls used to chant when they jumped rope, the trio dropped their theme song, "All in Together Now," which circulated on a mixtape in 1985. That tape actually made the rounds because even Biz Markie, a popular Cold Chillin' artist at the time, recalled hearing it.

"When I hooked up with the Genius, I thought he was fire, you know what I'm saying? Blew my mind," says Smith. "But I noticed something was wrong, you know, as dope as the stuff he played me." The problem was his nonstop rhyming. "You got to have the hook, you've got to have the bridge, you've got to have the intro," he says. "He didn't have the structure, but he had all the talent in the world. Incredible talent. But I would try to bring structure to it." Genius also played Smith demos he had made with his cousins, eventually bringing them to meet him as well.

"RZA had the personality, man," Smith recalls. "He was real likable, and then when I heard his rhymes, I was buggin', you know what I'm sayin? 'Cause the RZA rhymes are incredible." With a sudden infusion of new talent but no money to release them himself, Smith made the organic transition from label owner to manager as he directed his energies into finding opportunities for his artists, putting them together with producers, and generally "developing them for stardom," he says.

One of the first producers he approached was a fresh face on the scene named Easy Mo Bee (Osten Harvey Jr.). Born in Brooklyn's Bed-Stuy and raised in the Lafayette Gardens projects, Mo belonged to that same first generation that grew up with hip-hop. From the age of ten, he remembered watching local disco deejays such as Grandmaster Flowers, Frankie D, and Vaughn K. spin records in the project courtyard. "I was like amazed, man," he says. "I'm like that's what I want to do." Though growing up in a strict Christian household, Mo credits his father's love of music and playing different types of records—from gospel and soul to funk and jazz—for influencing his own wide-open tastes. In high school, he and some friends from the neighborhood formed a group called Rappin' Is Fundamental, and it was through one of the group's rappers, A. B. Money (Anthony Mosley), that Mo got his first big break in the music industry.

Money attended Sarah J. Hale High School in Boerum Hill with a guy named Antonio Hardy, who was then making a name for himself as one of the hottest MCs in the game, Big Daddy Kane. In 1987, Kane's breakout single "Raw" became an underground hit for Cold Chillin' Records, a gritty independent label that was challenging Def Jam's dominance of the rap market. Though his thundering debut album, *Long Live the Kane* (1988), distributed by Warner Bros., sold gold,

Kane resented the fact that heavyweight producer Marley Marl had taken the lion's share of the production credits, when it was actually Kane who had chosen many of the records they sampled. When it came time for the follow-up, *It's a Big Daddy Thing* (1989), Kane planned to minimize Marley's input by handling most of the production himself and bringing in a few outside producers. Money had been telling Kane about Mo's beats for a while. When Kane's deejay, Mr. Cee (Calvin Lebrun)—who coincidentally lived in the same building as Mo, three floors down—cosigned this recommendation, he sealed the deal.

Mo ended up producing two hype tracks for Kane's album—"Another Victory" and "Calling Mr. Welfare"—making him a known quantity in the industry. For his work, he received a grand sum of $3,000. "Today that would be an insult," he says. "But I was looking at it like, I want in. I want in on the game, you know what I'm sayin'?" With his first earnings in hand, he remembers beelining to Sam Ashe Music, the premier spot for gear, on Forty-Eighth Street in Manhattan and plopping down $2,395 for the latest drum machine on the market, the Emulator SP-1200.

"I forget where I was at," says Mo. "But Melquan walked up on me and was like, 'Peace, I like the stuff that you did on Kane's album, and I've got an artist I'd like you to work with—his name's the Genius.'" Smith also mentioned that Genius was part of a crew of eight or nine artists who had a concept of fusing together martial arts and hip-hop. "The conceptual thing in hip-hop, it was there, but rare," he says. "Everybody was doin' straight hip-hop, so when he threw that concept at me, in my mind I was like, 'Yeah, whatever.'"

But, hungry for more work, Mo couldn't say no. "When Melquan brought Genius to me—shoot, the dude could rap, he was nasty on the mic—I was like c'mon, let's go, you know?" he says. "It was all about staying busy, man. That was it. I didn't want to just produce Kane and then people didn't hear from me anymore. I was just trying to stay as busy as I could while that name was still hot."

That chance meeting with Smith in the fall of 1989 sparked a long and fruitful working relationship between Easy Mo Bee and the Genius, who would come over to Mo's place in the projects practically every weekend to work on demos. He started bringing Rakeem as well. "What I liked about them—RZA and GZA—was that I was just able to be my raw self, know what I'm sayin?" he says. Sometimes Ason Unique would tag along. "He used to tell me, 'Word, G., I got a drunken style, know what I'm sayin'? I call myself Ol' Dirty Bastard,'" Mo recalls. Raekwon even showed up for a session once. He and Rakeem had a group together called Recreation, and they made a song called "In the Streets."[3]

"Back then I was highly influenced by the Stax Memphis sound—Johnny Taylor, Booker T. and the MG's, Rufus Thomas, Carla Thomas," says Mo, "something that I'm not reluctant to say that RZA and them actually picked up from me. Yunno, they called it the 'Al Green' sound." He says Rakeem was also enamored by the SP-1200, which he had never seen before, and peppered him with questions about it.

The rapper was becoming increasingly interested in production at this time, mainly so he didn't have to rely on others for beats. "Now I kept telling my manager that I knew how to make beats, too, but I ain't never have that kind of equipment," says RZA. "I had a Casio RZ-1, but I didn't have that SP, which was the best thing you could ever get, and it took me maybe a year and a half before I finally got a hold of one."[4] Through a producer named Dice, he had also become familiar with the Ensoniq EPS, a keyboard sampler that hit the market in 1988 as one of the first affordable consumer models (retailing for about $2,400).

Melquan also introduced Rakeem to Prince Paul (Paul Huston), the former deejay for Tommy Boy artists Stetsasonic, who had just produced *3 Feet High and Rising* (Tommy Boy, 1989), the platinum-selling debut by De La Soul, a group of misfits from his former high school in Amityville, Long Island. "Melquan played me some stuff, and I was like, 'Yeah, OK, he's dope, you know. I'll work with him,'" Paul recalls. "So we went inside—I think it was Calliope—and I brought my man Double B to do some beats; I brought DBC from Stetsasonic, and we all sat down, and we made probably like three or four songs." Pleased with the outcome of that session, Paul filed them away in his vaults for the moment, as he was busy with other projects.

Rakeem left a positive impression on the platinum producer, who says, "He was very young, but he wanted to learn a lot, which I was really impressed with. You know, like he would ask a bunch of questions and he would question stuff like, 'What's that? Well, why is this?' You know, 'cause usually kids—especially during that time—they were, just like, 'I just want to get on,' but he wanted to learn about things, you know what I'm saying? And I think that's what made me and him closer or made us cool because he wasn't just there to like, get on. Like he really wanted to figure stuff out. And he was very respectful, which I appreciated too."

By 1987, Rakeem's family had moved once again—this time to 67 Warren Street in the Stapleton projects, Dennis Coles's stomping grounds. The Stapleton / Park Hill rivalry, which went back before grade school, could not have been any hotter. "My project was a fighting project. We liked to fight a lot, you know what I mean? Back in the '80s, his project was the 'get fly' project. We used to go up there because they had the weed spot. We had the mescaline and dust spots," says Coles, describing decidedly rougher turf. Going by the name D-Lover at the time, he says, "RZA moved down to my projects and there was just somethin' about RZA, know what I mean? He had an aura about him. He had a lot of people around him, know what I mean? Like, he brought all that 'get fly' shit from the Hill, like Polo, Tommy Hill, Pacific Trail shit."[5]

Rakeem also brought his home-studio setup, which was continuing to expand. In addition to his Technics SL-1200 turntables and dented gold microphone, Scotty Rock, a fellow DJ, lent him a Roland TR-909 drum machine, and from his friend DJ Skane, he borrowed a Yamaha four-track recorder. "I was making an album every month, basically," says Rakeem. "In the neighborhood they knew my albums. At this time, me and Ghost [Coles] was MCing together, and me and Rae been MCing together for years."[6] Shaquan became a frequent collaborator, too, along with Inspectah Deck, whom Rakeem met at a block party.

"One day I saw RZA doing a block party in a neighborhood that is one of the roughest on Staten Island, the kind of place you don't fuck around in, and he was out there all by himself holding it down," Deck recalls. "I was out there by myself, too, so we just cliqued up, and that's when I kicked my first block party rhyme."[7] After witnessing Deck's impressive skills, Rakeem invited him over to the apartment. "We'd be out on the balcony rhymin' with a banged-up mic, all of us, even Pop Da Brown Hornet and Shyhiem [Wu-affiliated artists who would eventually get their own record deals],"

says Deck. "We was out there because his mom wasn't tol-
eratin' all that noise. This is before the Clan even started. We
was there at RZA's every day, man, like the Fat Albert kids
out in the junkyard."[8] These impromptu sessions produced
such songs as "Ra's Ill," "Stay Out of Bars," "Baggin' Bitches,"
"Deadly Venoms," and "Not Your Average Flow." Says Deck,
"Niggas had full-blown songs and all that shit that was
anthems around the way before you ever heard of us."[9]

Shaquan, who first started making tapes in 1986 as
Shaquan the Poet, became a neighborhood sensation when
demos like "Panty Raider" and "My House, My House," made
with a simple Casio keyboard, started making the rounds
in 1988. Even though he, Deck, U-God, and Raekwon were
from Park Hill, they were able to come to Rakeem's place in
Stapleton without any static. "I remember one time, Ghostface's birthday, we had one little radio, and Ra had a tape with
beats on it, and we was out there 'til five in the morning—nine
o'clock that evening 'til five in the morning—and everybody,
a crowd of niggas, outside. No fight, no nothing in Stapleton,"
he says.

It was around this same time that D-Lover, a fan of kung
fu flicks himself, started using the "Wu-Tang slang." "After
they saw the movie, *Shaolin vs. Wu Tang*, the Wu-Tang style
was so fly, anything that was fly was 'Wu-Tang,'" Rakeem
explains. Initially, Ghost started calling Olde English 800, his
favorite brand of malt liquor, Wu-Tang, so Rakeem, a Ballantine Ale drinker, called Ballantine Shaolin. But Wu-Tang
had staying power. "Then what I did really, when niggas was
throwing the word out—like 'Wu-Tang'—I kinda explained
to them what it really was 'cause I knew," says Rakeem. "I'd
been into it for years already, and then what happened and
shit, is that the prime people who was into Wu-Tang, using

that word for a slang or whatever, used to come to my house every night and watch flicks and smoke our little dust or whatever, smoke weed."

By 1988, Rakeem's mother had relocated to Ohio with the girls and younger kids, leaving him in charge of the apartment with his younger brother Born (Terrance Hamlin). Needless to say, with so much traffic coming through, the place looked like a hurricane had hit it, with sneakers and clothes strewn helter-skelter along with empty beer bottles, the guts of cigars, and empty bags of weed. Barely getting by, they subsisted on a diet of Oodles of Noodles, grits, or whatever they could shoplift. "I'd watch Ghostface's back while he'd be stealing canned goods out of the store. That's how bad we had it," says Born. "Ghostface would throw on his big oversized coat and just stack four or five cans in his coat pockets, and we'd walk out and shit. Times was definitely bad back then."[10] At this point, the motley crew, united by their love of martial arts movies, marijuana, MCing, and Supreme Mathematics, looked more like a street gang than a rap group.

Rakeem christened his friends with new alter egos based on the flicks. Known in the streets as a tough customer, D-Lover became Ghost Face Killer, after the murderous supervillain in the film *The Mystery of Chess Boxing* (1979), who left a metal plate with a ghost on it next to his victims. U-God was called Golden Arms, after the hero of the Shaw Brothers' classic *The Kid with the Golden Arm* (1979). Shaquan, who smoked a lot of weed, which was known as method on Staten Island, assumed the title of the film *Method Man* (1979), which was alternatively released as *The Fearless Young Boxer* or *Avenging Boxer*. Ason Unique, the drunken master, whose one-of-a-kind flow was lubricated by alcohol, was already known as Ol' Dirty Bastard after Bamboo Stick, the tipsy but entertaining protagonist of *Mad Mad Kung Fu* (1979), alternatively titled *Ol' Dirty Kung Fu* and *Ol' Dirty & the Bastard*.

On a typical night in 1989, when dudes came over to hang out, Rakeem threw on a VHS tape of *The Eight Diagram Pole Fighter* (1984), a Shaw Brothers film he had seen many times before with his own family. In the film, a story of betrayal and brotherhood, a general and his seven sons are ambushed by the enemy. Only the fifth and sixth sons escape, but the sixth son returns home severely traumatized. The fifth son seeks refuge in a Buddhist monastery, where he is initially rejected but manages to stay on and train, developing the eight-diagram pole-fighting technique.

"Before we were an hour into it, something strange happened in that crib. People got real quiet, some niggas even started crying," Rakeem recalls, "because the movie is real— it's a reflection of the reality we were all living."[11] He explains, "Listen, we're oppressed. It does feel like we as a people were betrayed a long time ago. I can't really describe it any other way. It's real because the issues are alive with us. You're living in the hood and you've got knowledge and dreams and you got wars between neighborhood and neighborhood. Everybody's backstabbing everybody. And when you know someone who's got your back, that's a life or death thing. That's a real bond, a real brotherhood."[12] Such were the ties that connected the members of the Clan. They were brothers who grew up together in the same neighborhood and attended the same schools, brothers whose mothers knew each other, and brothers in the struggle, ensuring virtually indestructible bonds.

The end of the eighties and beginning of the nineties proved to be another pivotal turning point for rap, as the battle raged between the art form's underground roots and its pop aspirations. Long considered a novelty or fad by the music industry, rap was finally coming into its own and gaining attention for its full-frontal assault on the Billboard charts. But aside from Public Enemy and N.W.A, two hugely successful hardcore acts who seemed to inhabit a space of their own, most rap had taken a sharp turn toward pop radio. You could see the writing on the wall as early as the late eighties when new jack swing blurred the lines between R&B and hip-hop, which had previously been regarded as oil and water. Similarly, house music from Chicago, which was also having its breakout moment, started making incursions into hip-hop. It got to a point where even established New York acts like EPMD ("It's Time 2 Party") and Jungle Brothers ("I'll House You") jumped on the hip-house phenomenon to widen their appeal.

Then former gangbanger Tone Lōc (Anthony Terrell Smith) soared to the top of the charts in 1989 with party anthems like "Wild Thing" and "Funky Cold Medina" from his double platinum debut *Lōced After Dark* (Delicious Vinyl), blowing the gates wide open for pop rap. One of the writers of those hits, University of Southern California student Marvin Young, a.k.a. Young MC, went on to enjoy his own success with "Bust a Move," which won a Grammy for best rap performance in 1990, propelling his album *Stone Cold Rhymin'* (Delicious Vinyl) to platinum status.

By the time MC Hammer's *Please Hammer, Don't Hurt 'Em* touched down on February 12, 1990, the pop-rap takeover was complete. That record set the tone for releases to come with its wholesale rip-off of Rick James's "Superfreak," which became the chart-topping megahit "U Can't Touch This." The end of the year saw the rise of the phenomenon known as Vanilla Ice. While this slew of catchy, radio-friendly, and undeniably memorable multiplatinum records helped ease rap into the mainstream consciousness, they didn't really do much to feed the core audience of the streets. But with a proven formula for success, record companies had no incentive to stray from this commercial path.

"It was rough on a hip-hop artist from New York," says Smith. The only ones to really survive and thrive in this new climate were the Native Tongues, a loose collective featuring the Jungle Brothers, Queen Latifah, De La Soul, A Tribe Called Quest, Black Sheep, and child rapper Chi-Ali, who together represented a kinder, gentler, quirkier, and often more abstract form of hip-hop. Yet in spite of the inherent challenges, Smith was still able to get both of his artists signed to labels. Rakeem scored a single deal with Tommy Boy, hot off De La Soul's success and doing big numbers with the "Humpty Dance" from Oakland, California, outfit Digital Underground. Meanwhile, attracted by his lyricism, the more street-oriented Cold Chillin' signed Genius to an album deal, hoping to produce another smooth operator like Big Daddy Kane.

"So, they [Cold Chillin'] had us do a record," Smith continues, "and we had to conform to the style of what's goin' on." Despite the label's reputation as a rap powerhouse featuring the likes of Kane, Biz Markie, and Kool G Rap, their recently inked distribution deal with Warner Bros. made them more beholden to the corporate powers that be, who, of course, pushed for the flavor of the moment. The result was "Come Do Me," a new jack swing–style workout featuring a hook sung by R&B heavy Johnny Kemp. For the album's only single, they shot a predictable video set in a club, where Ason even made an appearance doing his patented moves, the "funky

Ason slide." If you blinked for a second, however, you could miss cameos by Rakeem and Raekwon, who played painters in the background of one street scene. Of the whole experience, Smith says, "We was just trying to go with the times even though that ain't the GZA."

Prince Rakeem had a similar experience at Tommy Boy, a label started in 1981 by Tom Silverman, publisher of the biweekly *Dance Music Report*. After initially releasing early rap and electro twelve-inch singles—including 1982's breakthrough hit "Planet Rock" by Afrika Bambaataa and the Soul Sonic Force—Tommy Boy had carved out a niche for themselves behind Monica Lynch, the label's first employee and eventual president, responsible for signing Queen Latifah, De La Soul, Naughty by Nature, Stetsasonic, Paris, Digital Underground, and many more. Says Rakeem, "I remember giving Tommy Boy a whole album of hardcore lyrics, yunno, Staten Island and Brooklyn style, and they was like, 'Oh, we like the song "Ooh, We Love You Rakeem." We think girls will like you.'"[13]

While not exactly what he expected, he certainly wasn't going to squander the opportunity. If his intro to rap audiences was as a gigolo, he could have fared worse. When it came time to record the track, Rakeem chose Calliope on West Twenty-Eighth Street in Manhattan, where he had previously worked with Prince Paul. In fact, Smith called Paul to come down and kind of oversee the session. "He [Rakeem] was trying to figure out how to put together, 'Ooh, We Love You Rakeem.' Like he had the loop, but he didn't know how to program the beat, like put a drum beat behind it," says Paul. "That's when they had the SP-12 there, and I was showing them how to program the drums on the SP-12." The rhythmic snippet that Rakeem looped came from the song

"Free" by Deniece Williams. As it played, Paul went over to the drum machine and said, "OK, here's an example of a beat" while tapping out a simple pattern. "You know, it was just basic, you know, boom, boom, smack, boom, boom smack," he says. "And he [Rakeem] told me years later that that example for the beat is the drum beat on 'Ooh, We Love You Rakeem.' I programmed it. So, a little fun fact I don't think people know." Even more significantly, that double kick and snare pattern was one RZA returned to often, referring to it as the hip-hop template because practically any one-, two-, or four-bar sample could be made to fit.

Rakeem enlisted Easy Mo Bee to produce the B side, "Sexcapades," which appeared on the final release as two different versions—the "Wu-Tang Mix" and the "DMD Mix," both a nod to his Staten Island crew. He was also able to sneak another one of his own productions, "Deadly Venoms," onto the B side, making the release more of an EP than a single. They recorded the tracks at INS Studios on Park Row in lower Manhattan and mixed them at Greene Street in Soho. Unfortunately, by the time of the release, the label was unable to clear the Deniece Williams sample, forcing Rakeem to replace it. To assuage his feelings, they paid for a slick video for the track but decked him out in a top hat and tails, which was totally antithetical to his street image.

Mo also produced the bulk of Genius's album—ten cuts— while his brother LG Experience (Patrick Harvey) contributed four songs, and Jesse West, another rising talent from the Bronx, produced the single. According to Mo, "Genius didn't really want that as the single. They [the label] pushed that on him. I remember him being really unhappy about that, too, 'cause we had so many other street-sounding songs on the album—like really raw stuff that he wanted to put out."

When their records dropped in 1991—the *Words from the Genius* LP on February 19 and "Ooh, We Love You Rakeem" later on July 1—both artists had the opportunity to go out on the road, doing radio interviews and in-store appearances and seeing different parts of the country for the first time. Rakeem performed in Houston at an artist showcase. Cold Chillin' actually sponsored a ten-city promotional tour featuring their recent signings—Kid Capri, Grand Daddy I.U., and Genius—as well as veteran artists Kool G Rap, Masta Ace, and Biz Markie for select dates.

At the opening gig in south Jersey, an inebriated Ason, Genius's hype man, took the stage first and started insulting and cursing at the crowd, almost starting a riot. The label promptly sent him home as a result. According to Masta Ace, everything went smoothly until the last night of the tour, when the artists discovered that the label was making $60,000 a night, while they were only receiving a $25 per diem. They ended up doing the show but returned to New York livid at the label. Genius, already upset about the weak promotional push behind his album, felt like he had to get out of his contract.[14]

This initial exposure to the music industry proved both eye-opening and humbling, as it took them beyond the creative process of making beats and writing rhymes, which was only a small part of making it as an artist. Being able to perform live, create a charismatic persona, and promote your product were just as important. Where matters of business were concerned, they discovered that so many people at the label had a say in their careers that when it came to making important decisions, their own voices were often drowned out. Young and inexperienced, they were simply expected to fall in line and follow orders, ultimately compromising their own artistic visions to become something they were not. It was an exercise bound for failure, and when both projects were greeted with lackluster sales, Rakeem and Genius were summarily dropped from their respective labels. Chalk it up to youth, inexperience, and just plain bad timing. "Anybody that was true hip-hop got caught in that—it was really just for like two years, hip-hop was fucked up," says Smith.

But not long after the deal had gone south, he actually set up a meeting between Rakeem and Monica Lynch so that they could pitch the Wu-Tang idea that had been percolating for a minute. Representing the best MCs in Rakeem's neighborhood of Staten Island, they combined hip-hop with a kung fu concept. "Monica Lynch was like, 'This is too close to Fu-Schnickens. They do karate stuff too,'" says Smith, referring to the Brooklyn trio whose debut single "Ring the Alarm," a fusion of rap and reggae, had just landed in the top ten of the Billboard Rap Singles chart. The group, composed of Chip Fu (Roderick Roachford), Moc Fu (Joe Jones), and Poc Fu (Lennox Maturine), playfully flirted with kung fu imagery in their lyrics and videos, and their full-length debut, *F.U. Don't Take It Personal* (Jive, 1992), sold gold on the strength of hits like "La Schmoove" and "True Fuschnick." But a Wu-Tang Clan they were not. Despite playing Lynch a six-song demo of hard-core tracks produced by Rakeem, Smith says, "She fronted. She said no."

CHAPTER 7

FORM LIKE VOLTRON

Steubenville, a small Rust Belt town in the easternmost part of Ohio—population about twenty thousand—seemed like an unlikely second act for a rapper out of a record deal, but months behind in rent and running out of prospects in New York, Rakeem was forced to retreat to this quiet enclave on the banks of the Ohio River. His mother had moved here in 1988 after getting remarried to a man who ran a convenience store in Pittsburgh's historic Hill District, a short twenty-five-minute drive. But Steubenville, a mostly white, blue-collar town that established itself on the strength of its once great steel mills and coal mines, was a place most people were dying to escape. Its most famous son, Dino Paul Crocetti, successfully made the leap, transforming into legendary entertainer and Rat Pack member Dean Martin, as did Nora Louise Kuzma, who reinvented herself as teenage porn queen Traci Lords.

Rakeem had been visiting ever since his mom and younger siblings relocated there. He even developed somewhat of a following, as he used to teach the Nation of Gods and Earths Lessons to a group of young people who would regularly meet at the local public library and build. One of these youths, Selwyn Bougard (a.k.a. 4th Disciple), a schoolmate of Rakeem's cousin Freedom, recalls, "We used to have meetings at the public library in Steubenville. Everybody would bring information to the table—whether it was Islam or whatever was spiritual—everybody would bring it to the table and share information. Freedom had brought RZA to one of the meetings early in its inception, and that's when we all first met RZA."[1] Later on, after discovering they shared a common interest in music, Rakeem brought Ghostface and Ol' Dirty to Bougard's grandmother's basement, where they recorded demos on a dusty four-track.

However, things changed after he became a resident of Steubenville. Instead of maintaining the righteous path, which he encouraged others to follow, Rakeem reversed course in his own life. With his music career stymied, he had to come up with a quick solution to put food on the table, and the drug game presented the obvious choice. But Killah Hill was far too competitive and deadly, and he had already lost friends and had people gunning for him. That's when he realized, *I know a place where they aren't as advanced in this game, a place where we could go out and get a hustle on.*[2] In order to finance the product, Rakeem borrowed money from Genius, who was working as a bike messenger. Ghost went so far as to contemplate knocking off a Brink's truck but settled instead on robbing someone they knew had cash. Pooling their funds, they were able to set themselves up in the corner crack game.[3]

In the fall of 1991, Rakeem hopped on an Amtrak train with little more than the clothes on his back; a copy of the 120 Lessons; a .25-caliber pistol; a chunky, gold rope chain to pawn for cash; and, of course, the product. Ghost and ODB soon followed, and it didn't take long for them to set up shop and start getting paid. But that didn't mean they felt good about it. "We made money and were able to feed ourselves, but it was the most negative point in my life," Rakeem recalls. "I never wanted to be a drug dealer—I thought I was killing my own people—but for my own survival I entered that world. I betrayed myself."[4]

In the forties, Steubenville was known as "Little Chicago" for providing a hub for the Mob's illegal gambling activities, which flourished in the back rooms of bars all over town—with a wink and a nod from local cops, of course. The opening of Las Vegas in the fifties shifted operations westward. But the scourge of crack in the eighties brought a different type of criminal organization to town—street gangs, namely the Crips and Bloods. When the New York contingent, backed by their local affiliates, suddenly appeared on the scene out of nowhere, calling themselves the Godz (Rakeem's code name was Jesus, and Ghost went as Moses),[5] they naturally sparked a lot of resentment and competition on the streets. The echo of gunshots after dark became a familiar sound, giving sleepy Steubenville a new nickname, Little New York.

After a couple of months hustling, their situation quickly soured. "The streets [were] not working," says Rakeem. "Every time we get a package, you can make $10,000, but guess what? Somebody got arrested, somebody got shot. I kept seeing a cycle of non-success."[6] Dirty got locked up. Ghost took a bullet to the left side of his neck and was lucky to survive. Local associate Wise God Allah got stabbed (and later on fatally shot), and others landed in jail as well. It all came to a head on Christmas Eve, when Rakeem got involved in an altercation that would change the course of his life.

That night, he borrowed his sister's car to give two girls he knew a ride home. One of the girls had been seeing Ghost, who wasn't even in town at the time. While they were stopped at a traffic light, another car full of dudes pulled up beside them. One of the girls' boyfriends happened to be in that car, and on spotting her with Rakeem, he went ballistic. Jumping out of his vehicle, he started kicking Rakeem's sister's car and banging on the windows as he cursed out his girlfriend. Terrified, the girls screamed for Rakeem to take off, since they knew the other guys were carrying guns. So he floored it, managing to get away and evade them. After laying low for a couple of hours, he went to drop the girls home at around three in the morning.[7]

One of the girls lived on Edgar Avenue, a dead-end street. After making sure she was safely in her house, Rakeem started to leave but was confronted by the same guys from the traffic light, who had been waiting in ambush. It was four against one, and these guys obviously meant business. "They was really kind of aggressive, and real egotistic and they wanted to do the do," he says.[8] Without hesitation, Rakeem pulled out his pistol, squeezing off some shots. One hit the instigator, a guy named Willie Walters, in the right thigh. A second shot grazed Walters's stepbrother Anthony McCleod. Charged with felonious assault, Rakeem spent Christmas in the Jefferson County jail, where he remained for thirty days.[9]

While locked down, he had a lot to ponder. His girlfriend had just told him that she was pregnant, but this otherwise happy news was overshadowed by the gravity of his situation. His mother's utter disappointment weighed heavily on him too, but the family rallied around, and his sister Sophia put up her savings to help cover his $10,000 bail.[10] Assistant prosecutor Chris Becker initially offered a plea deal, which would have given Rakeem sixty days, but after finding out that he was from New York and possibly part of a larger drug organization, he pushed for an attempted murder charge, which carried with it a minimum of eight years. The stakes could not have been higher for Rakeem. No sooner had he made bail than he became a fixture at the Jefferson County Law Library, researching similar cases of self-defense. Like a prizefighter, he gave up smoking and drinking and picked up the Lessons again as he prepared for the bout of his life.

Opening arguments for the three-day trial began on April 21, 1992. Of the ambitious young prosecutor Becker, Rakeem says, "It was his dedication to destroy me that saved me because he went to any means necessary to make me look like the kind of person I really wasn't inside. And the truth showed that I was just a young guy in a bad situation, made a couple of bad decisions, but overall had a good heart, had a brain in my head."[11]

On April 23, in a risky but strategic move, Rakeem's lawyer had him take the stand and tell the mostly white jury the plain and simple truth of the matter—that he was defending himself from a jealous boyfriend and his three buddies, who were armed and threatening him. It was a question of being caught at the wrong place at the right time. Speaking from the heart, he told them of his humble background and how he was trying to pursue a career in music. When the jury left to deliberate, his insides were churning. Two hours later, they returned to deliver a verdict of not guilty.

Those two words were life-affirming for the twenty-two-year-old, who felt a huge weight lift off his shoulders. When he turned around, stunned but ecstatic, the first person he laid eyes on was his mother. "She said, 'Boy, this is your second chance. Don't blow it.' I'll never forget this joy that overcame me," he recalls. "At the same time I had a baby on the way. So, I'm like, 'Yo, Rakeem is greater than this. I gotta be greater than that. I'm going to put Rakeem to the side. I'm going to birth something new. I'm going to birth The RZA.'

When The RZA was born, I decided to walk the path of righteousness and not turn back."[12]

Explaining the etymology behind the name, he says, "I had become dumb. My life had done a zigzag. I was in the right place from ages 11 to 16. Then I got involved with women, drugs, and hip-hop in a street way, with battling, guns, cars, gold cables, drug using and drug dealing."[13] The trial's favorable outcome, however, persuaded him to return to the righteous path. "In the Divine Alphabet, Z stands for Zig-Zag-Zig, which means knowledge, wisdom, and understanding. It's the last letter of the alphabet and represents the final step of consciousness," he says. "So, I zigged back. I became The RZA. Rakeem Zig Zag Zig Allah. It stands for Ruler-Knowledge / Wisdom / Understanding-Allah."[14] RZA was the phoenix rising from the flames in which Rakeem had been purified.

Feeling truly liberated, as if he had just reclaimed eight years of his life, RZA headed back to Staten Island with a fire in his belly. He was able to move back into the Stapleton projects, his last New York address. Though he tried contacting Tommy Boy, he discovered that they weren't interested and had moved on without him, having just signed the white rap group House of Pain. *Fuck 'em*, he figured. *Fuck 'em all.* "The industry was kinda guiding the artist to the way they wanted their music to be instead of letting the music come out freely," he says. "So I was like, yo, I gotta start my own record company, do it myself, and say what we want to say and be free in what you express," taking a page from former manager Melquan and his father's playbook.[15] RZA even contacted their lawyer Bill Warren, picking his brain about strategies for success. He dove headfirst into a study of the music industry—reading Donald S. Passman's industry bible, *All You Need to Know about the Music Business*, as well as books about legendary labels like Stax and Motown that had started from humble beginnings.

During May, June, and July, RZA walked around Staten Island like the prophet Mohammed roaming the desert for forty days, meditating and formulating his master plan. He went from Stapleton to New Brighton to Park Hill to the Staten Island Ferry docks, sometimes talking out loud to himself. "People thought I was crazy because I used to walk and think and talk," he says. "You get so much inspiration from walking and thinking, so I walked around Staten Island until I got an epiphany. It took me a while to get it, but once I had it, I knew what I wanted to do. I went to Ghost first and said Wu-Tang Clan."[16]

Wu-Tang were the renegades and often the bad guys in the kung fu flicks, and a clan represented a family. Ghost, his roommate, was the first to popularize "Wu-Tang" as a signifier for anything "fly" or cool. But RZA laid down the mythology on which to launch a rap super group. "Wu-Tang is an internal martial art," he explains. "Wu-Tang was also the best sword style, and as an MC our tongue is our sword. And I said to myself, 'There's no other ill MCs that I've met than the crew that I know right here on Staten Island, you know what I'm sayin'?' So, we the Wu-Tang. Our style is Wu-Tang. We go out there and chop anybody heads off when it comes to battling on the mic, yunno."[17] Shaolin also no longer signified a beverage but the mystical island of Staten, the foundation, where the brother monks learned and perfected their thirty-six chambers of lyrical styles.

With his vision in place, the next step was lining up the team. RZA already knew he could count on Ghost as well as his cousins Dirty and Genius, who had been down since day one when they were just kids pursuing hip-hop for fun. He went out to Brooklyn to fire them up, saying, "Yo, man, we the illest! We the dopest! I'm tellin' you. I know we could do it."[18] While Genius was still working as a bike messenger, Dirty's situation was a little more precarious.

After his parents separated in the late eighties, he had moved back to his grandmother's house at 112 Putnam Avenue with his mother and younger siblings. While living there, he married his high school sweetheart, Tracey (Icelene), and they promptly had two children. But a couple of weeks after the arrival of their third child in 1991, they moved to a homeless shelter in Brooklyn—ashamed to tell even family about it. During that time, Dirty found work in an auto garage and later at the Marriot Marquis Hotel in Manhattan.[19]

The rest of the crew on Staten Island had not fared much better in the interim. Crack had ravaged the neighborhood, and no one was spared. Divine, RZA's older brother, was locked up on drug charges for more than a year but was able to beat serious time by enrolling in a rehab program. Deck racked up his second felony for selling crack to an undercover cop and spent almost two years in jail, where, he says, "I was able to get my craft sharp."[20] U-God, who was nabbed in Harlem with three and a half ounces of cocaine and an illegal gun, was doing one to three years upstate.[21] Original, who had changed his name to Cappadonna, was in Rikers, serving a three-year bid for a drug charge he wasn't even guilty of. In fact, the only ones who had managed to evade jail time were Shaquan (Method Man) and Shallah Raekwon, who, despite their recent reawakening as Five Percenters, were still doing dirt on the block to survive.

"At that time, we was still street-life niggas, and you know, things that happen in the streets sometimes you could never count on it being over," says Raekwon. "Any beef could catch up to you, you know what I mean?"[22] But, he continues, "at the end of the day, we wanted to go straight, you know what I mean? You had to let something go in order to build something new and fresh again. And the music thing was the legitimate world for us. It was not havin' to worry about never bein' hungry or dealin' with some other shit or some shootin' uptown or whatever, trying to get some drugs."[23]

On the afternoon of July 22, RZA happened to be holding court across the street from 160 Park Hill Avenue, talking to Raekwon and Deck about forming a group, when he spotted Shaquan, who was on his way to cop some weed at the well-known spot known as the "Oo" building. He called over to his friend, who stopped to see who it was before abandoning his mission and running over. Seconds later, a flurry of shots sprayed the front of 160, sending everyone scattering like roaches. When the smoke cleared, Kieim "Poppie" Crabbe, sixteen, a well-liked and respected guy around the neighborhood who did well in school and was not involved in the streets, lay bloodied and dying on the pavement. He was just returning from the store after buying his mom a pack of Newports when he got caught up in the melee, which left four others wounded.[24]

According to RZA, "The guys who shot him were Brooklyn niggas beefing with Staten Island niggas—they were gunning for Meth. Meth later told me, 'Yo, you saved my life that day because I was headed right into that doorway that got shot up.'"[25] As sad and senseless a death as Poppie's was, that was just the daily reality around Killah Hill, underscoring the urgency of RZA's plans.

In August, RZA received a call from Prince Paul. The once hot platinum producer of De La Soul, Big Daddy Kane,

KRS-ONE, and many more had fallen on hard times. His Dew Doo Man label deal with Def Jam had been prematurely nixed by Russell Simmons and Lyor Cohen, and he was no longer working with De La. In the mercurial world of rap, where one minute you're hot and the next you're not, Paul felt like he was at a low ebb in his career. He could only express his frustration through his music, which had taken a dark and somber turn, and he was looking for some kindred spirits to form a group.

Paul approached people like himself, who had been given a similar raw deal by the industry. Frukwan (Arnold Hamilton), his former bandmate in Stetsasonic, was the first person who came to mind because "I already had a relationship with him, and I always thought Frukwan was just dope and underrated," says Paul. He also reached out to Too Poetic (Anthony Berkeley), who had released a moderately successful single on Tommy Boy in 1989 called "God Made Me Funky" / "Poetical Terror." Though the label gave Poetic the budget and approval to make a full album, they ended up dropping him just before its release. In fact, Paul was going to sign him to Dew Doo Man before he himself got dropped. "I had a demo of Poetic, and I was like, 'Yo, he's so dope,'" Paul says. The same went for those first demos that he had done with RZA. "I held on to those demos, man, like for years, and I would listen to him, and like, yo, he's so dope," he says.

RZA was pleased to hear from his old friend and mentor—one of the few people he respected in the industry. He told Paul that he was calling at a good time, since he had just beaten a charge in Ohio. "I'm ready to record, you know, whatever you want to do," RZA said. "It's like I'm trying to put something together myself, but I'm down." Paul invited him to come out to his condo in East Meadow, Long Island, for the first group meeting.

On the appointed day, RZA arrived in his beat-up MPV along with Dirty and Genius. Frukwan and Poetic had arrived separately, and everyone was hanging in Paul's basement studio getting to know each other when a spontaneous rhyme cipher broke out. According to Paul, "One thing I liked about RZA, like I said, he's cocky. So, he says to the other guys, 'Let me hear what you got? Yeah that's cool, that's cool. What you got?' And then everybody's like rhymin'. That's cool. Then he's like, 'Yo, Paul, let me hear those beats. Yeah, I think we could do this.'"

After roughly sketching out the "horror" concept that the group was going for, they turned their attention to figuring out a name. "And I can't say for sure," says Paul. "But I say RZA made the name up, you know, that he came with 'Gravediggaz.' Poetic will always argue he came up with the name, but he, you know, God bless his soul, he passed away so he can't defend himself." They also decided to choose alter egos for the project. RZA said he was going to call himself the Resurrecter, according to Paul: "And I was like, that's cool. He's like, 'But I'ma spell it RZA, the RZArecter.' And I was like, 'Yo, that's ill.'" Poetic became the Grym Reaper, since he was formerly in a group with his two brothers called the Brothers Grym. Frukwan chose to be the Gatekeeper, which had a double meaning in relation to the music industry. When it was Paul's turn to pick an alias, he said, "I'm like, man, who am I going to be? If I be Pallbearer that's gonna be corny." Since he was the guy behind the whole effort, he settled on the Undertaker. After a round of high fives, the Gravediggaz were officially born.

Paul says, "We recorded the first demo that day 'cause I wanted to see how everybody sounded together." The track, titled "The House That Hatred Built," never made the final album, but, years later, Paul posted it on SoundCloud. Though he ended up producing about two-thirds of that initial Gravediggaz album, *6 Feet Deep* (Gee Street / Island / Polygram, 1994), all the group members had a hand in production. Frukwan produced the track "Blood Brothers," while Poetic produced "Here Come the Gravediggaz." RZA limited his contributions to two tracks—"Graveyard Chamber" and "Six Feet Deep"—as he had his hands full with other matters.

With his path carved out, RZA was on a mission, but his life post-trial was anything but stable. After a couple of months in Stapleton, he got kicked out of the projects and wound up moving in with an aunt at nearby 7 Purroy Place. The upstairs apartment where he lived had no electricity, so he had to run a long extension cord down to his aunt's place in order to have power to make beats. At the time, RZA's production setup was still in flux.

After finally acquiring an SP-1200 drum machine through some shady moves, he traded it with fellow producer RNS (Arby Quinn) for an Ensoniq EPS. RNS, a fellow Stapleton resident, produced the debut album by RZA's former young neighbor Shyheim Franklin, *AKA the Rugged Child* (Virgin / EMI, 1994). "He had let me hold the EPS before, and I liked it because it was a keyboard sampler, and whereas the SP-1200 had only two and a half seconds' sampling time per pad, with the EPS you get about twelve, thirteen seconds, but you could use it all at one time on one key," he says. "So, I could sample more than one bar of music."[26] At the time, most hip-hop was limited to sampling one or two bar loops, but RZA started making four-bar loops. "Nobody was doing that," he says. "So it was the EPS that turned me onto that, and I fell in love with the EPS. I can't fuck with the SP-1200 no more.

And when he came back and we traded back, Ensoniq had made something called the EPS-16 Plus, and I went and got it."[27] Shortly after moving to Purroy Place, he and Shaquan recorded a song called "Method Man" using that gear. RZA also produced the first version of "C.R.E.A.M." as well as the instrumental for "Wu-Tang Clan Ain't Nothin' to Fuck With" during this period. Later, when Ensoniq introduced the ASR-10, RZA says, "That's when I became a master producer. The whole first 100 Wu songs was made on an ASR-10."[28]

Since the ASR was a keyboard sampler, one of its features was being able to trigger the same sample on different keys, thus altering the pitch of the sound. If you held a key down, the whole sample would play through, but playing the sound on different touch-sensitive keys allowed you to create new phrases that sounded nothing like the original sample. RZA became a master of this technique of "playing" samples, which has since become a staple of hip-hop production.

Not long afterward, RZA, his wife and newborn, brothers Divine and Born, sister Shurrie, and Ghost, whom she was seeing, all moved into a two-bedroom apartment at 234 Morningstar Road in Staten Island. With a semistable address, he incorporated his company, Wu-Tang Productions, in September 1992. With his lawyer's help, he also drafted contracts for the friends he intended to sign.[29]

Individually, he approached Shaquan, Deck, Raekwon, and U-God—all of whom were still involved in the crack game. "RZA played a major role in like shifting my brain, 'cause I kept goin' in and out of the can," says U-God. "RZA was like, 'Yo, man, what you doin'? You buggin' out dog.' He said, 'We gettin' ready to rock this Wu stuff.' I was like 20% focused and the rest of me, 80%, was in the streets."[30] RZA's pitch was simple: give me a year of your life, and I'm going to take us to the top, and we'll never have to sell drugs again. Then, one night in late September, he invited them all over to Morningstar Road for the first group meeting.

"It's almost like he did a Gotti move, like he brought all the families to the table," as Raekwon tells it. "So, he made a call one day. He called specific dudes, like I want him, him, and him. Next thing, yunno, everyone came in the studio. It wasn't even great energy in the room, it's just we here for him."[31] Raekwon recognized all the familiar faces in attendance from growing up in the neighborhood, and he was cool with all of them except one. The long-running feud between Park Hill and Stapleton aside, Raekwon says, "Yo, I don't really fuck with Ghost like that. He's a crook, you know what I mean? We tell it how it is. But that didn't mean that he wasn't talented, you know what I mean, and he wasn't a man of respect."[32] Ghost, who had served time for robbery at age fifteen, had a rep on the streets for "yappin'" brothers, or relieving them of all their cash and possessions, and he clearly had a bad history with Raekwon and Power.

RZA admits, "Wu-Tang started with tension. Some of the guys were not as close to each other as they have become. Ghostface and Raekwon are considered to be Batman and Robin, but they were enemies in the neighborhood. Ghost was my man and Rae was my man. There's another guy, Oli 'Power' Grant, who runs Wu-wear—him and Rae were partners and Ghost was the enemy. I'm talking about mortal enemies. But they were always real tight with me."[33] Though the origins of their beef are murky, the situation deteriorated to a point where Power and Rae sprayed Ghost's apartment with automatic gunfire in retaliation for something that he had done.[34] That's how never-ending conflicts were perpetuated in these parts. With these foes now facing each other from across the room, they had a chance to squash their beef and move forward together for a common cause, and they did. But Power came strapped, just in case.

"We just wanted to rep Staten Island 'cause we felt like every other borough was shittin' on us," says Rae. "Anything to get out of the hood and escape that life that we was down for—all of us—and we just said, 'Yo, you know what? We trust your hand 'cause you already made a record—not that it sold anything, just the fact you was able to do it.' So, we trusted his [RZA's] hand on everything he wanted to do. He was a pure brother, yunno, he was about knowledge, and all that played a role in us giving him the opportunity to drive the bus."[35]

According to RZA, "A democracy would not work; it had to be a dictatorship. But it had to be an agreed-upon dictatorship, not by force. I told them, 'I have a vision and I see it. If you give me five years, we're gonna be the number one crew in the country.'"[36] After knowing him for most of their lives and witnessing his passion and commitment to his music, it didn't take much convincing for the others to fall in line behind him.

To celebrate and strategize, the next night, they met at Perkins Restaurant on Hylan Boulevard in Staten Island. As Deck recalls, "We went out to a restaurant, sit down and eat, we got some champagne, and that's the idea right there. 'Yo, we gonna make this joint. We gonna press it up. It's gonna take everybody to put they money up. Niggas got to be for real. If niggas don't want it, get the fuck out right now, you know what I'm sayin'?' And it was real. It was like a family thing." RZA told everyone to bring one hundred dollars the next night so they could pay for studio time at Firehouse Studio in Brooklyn, where he had booked a session. "Everybody was with it. Threw up the toast, bow, it was done," says Deck.

The following day, Genius was playing a game of chess with Jamel Irief (a.k.a. Elgin Turner, a.k.a. Masta Killa), twenty-one, a new acquaintance from East New York, Brooklyn. They had met through a mutual friend, Darkim Shabazz (a.k.a. Derek Harris, a.k.a. True Master), at one of the Five-Percenter street parliaments where members got together to build with one another. An avid chess player, Irief had reawakened Genius's love of the game, and now the two played almost daily. But he had no inkling about his friend's former record deal or involvement in music. "Me and GZA when we met we just clicked right off the top, you know what I mean," says Masta Killa. "And it was actually everything other than music, yunno, it was chess, it was Mathematics, building, you know what I mean?"[37]

At the time, Irief, a high school dropout and former hustler, was trying to get his shit together. He had recently enrolled in a program where he could get his high school diploma and bachelor's degree in one shot. "One particular night I was going to night school, and me and GZA was together," says Irief. "And he was like, 'Hey, man, why don't you come to the studio tonight, you know what I mean? We got some things goin' down.' And I was like nah, yunno, I'm tryin' to do this school thing."[38] Having already missed two sessions, another absence would get him kicked out of the program, and he would have to start from scratch. "'You sure you don't want to come to the studio?' I'm tellin' you, 'Nah, I gotta go to school.' So, I went to school, he went to the studio," says Irief.[39]

The following day, they met for their usual chess game. Irief recalls, "As we're playin' chess, he's like, 'I want you to check out what we did in the studio last night,' and he puts on the tape. And on the tape is 'Protect Ya Neck.' Now when

I heard 'Protect Ya Neck,' I knew I was never going back to school again."[40]

But Rome wasn't built in a day, and "Protect Ya Neck" wasn't recorded in one night. It actually took several sessions to record Wu-Tang Clan's first self-released single and its B side, "Tearz." On the first night, engineer Ethan Ryman had to transfer the sounds from RZA's Ensoniq EPS-16 Plus keyboard workstation to sixteen-track one-inch tape and then bring each track up on a channel of the Peavey mixing board where it was EQ'ed. Then they recorded the first four MCs, which was the incomplete version Irief heard. The following night, RZA recorded himself and the remaining three MCs. Finally, with no one but the engineer around, RZA mixed the track, rearranging the order of the MCs' verses, adding the kung fu sound effects on the intro, and even swapping out the entire original beat.

"Protect Ya Neck" had started off as an RZA / Inspectah Deck tag-team track called "Blowin' Up the Spot." According to RZA, "We let everybody get on it, and then stripped the track, and then I rebuilt the track around everybody."[41] Finally coming into his own on production, he explains, "They killed it to the original track that we used, but when I had the chance to deal with the science of making sounds and puttin' the right sound to the right person's voice at the right time—in other words to remix it over—that's when it came out like that."[42]

Considering how high the stakes were, almost everyone had written their verse in advance, except Raekwon. "You know me. I had to write mine on spot. I wasn't prepared," he admits. "But once I heard Deck set it off with 'I smoke on the mic,' that's when everybody start rollin' up their sleeves. And the next time I heard it, it was lit, yunno. Shit was like 'Word!' And I think Deck comin' in first kinda held the momentum of the record because once it came on, everybody felt like 'Yeah, this is where we want to be at.'"[43]

Deck says, "Once I heard the final of that one, I knew to never doubt the RZA when it came to this music shit because the music that was underneath in the final version wasn't the beat we originally rhymed to. We rhymed to something totally different, and we were all in a different order. The original beat was tight, too, and RZA was just like: 'I just need y'all's voices.' We wasn't used to doing songs like that."[44] The resulting mix was, he recalls, "magic. There just wasn't anything like that beat at the time, especially with the karate chops in there."[45]

Though Marley Marl's 1987 smash, "The Symphony," featuring Juice Crew rappers Big Daddy Kane, Masta Ace, Craig G, and Kool G Rap, provided the template for the posse cut, one would be hard-pressed to find many songs with eight MCs rhyming nonstop in rapid succession with no "hook" or catchy, repeatable phrase. Defying the formula of what a rap song was supposed to be, it was, nonetheless, hip-hop boiled down to its pure essence—a ferocious display of lyrical pugilism over savage beats. If it seemed like each MC was trying to outdo the one before him, they were, but, collectively, they sounded like an unstoppable army. Playing by his own rules this time, RZA had returned with a vengeance, and "Protect Ya Neck" was his middle finger to the music industry.

Wu-Tang Clan needed one more element before they had an official product—artwork. RZA had been discussing logo ideas with a friend of GZA's, who used to deejay for him in the Cold Chillin' days, named Allah Mathematics (Ronald Maurice Bean). Born and raised in Jamaica, Queens, Math used to write graffiti as well as deejay, so he was nice with the pen. He was currently living in the Fortieth projects and working as a carpenter on a construction site. The rough concepts they had discussed included a phoenix, a hand holding a severed head (which was deemed too graphic), a sword, and a heavy tome like the Bible. After sending the masters to Disc Makers in New Jersey, RZA ordered an initial pressing of two thousand copies, but he didn't know they would be ready so quickly. He called Math one night and said he needed something by the next day.

Math recalls, "Got off work, got a 40 ounce of OE [Olde English 800], a Philly [blunt], sat on the floor and came up with what I came up with."[46] The next day, RZA, Ghost, Divine, and Power showed up at his jobsite looking like they were about to pull a heist—hoods up and Timberlands on their feet. Math fetched his black book, in which he sketched, and they went down to RZA's MPV to check it out. Everyone passed the book around to see what he had come up with. The sketch showed a thick book with a sword underneath it. On the book's cover was an almost bat-like figure whose outstretched wings resembled a *W* with "Wu-Tang Clan" emblazoned across it. "Yeah, this is it," everyone agreed. RZA, who paid Math $400, which he said was half of his rent money at the time, made the deal of the century that day.

Promotion of the record started from the streets up. Just as he had put together a top-notch creative team of MCs, who were all friends and family, RZA assembled a management team to help with the business side, which included his brother Divine, who had always supported his music; Power, Divine's friend, who invested a shoebox full of cash into the effort; John "Mook" Gibbons, his cousin and godbrother, who was currently driving a bus for NY Transit; and Michael "Lask" McDonald, the only industry veteran, who had experience in marketing. These guys would assist in getting the record out to mom-and-pop record shops along the East Coast—from Boston to Philly, Baltimore, DC, and even North Carolina—as well as to deejays around the country.

McDonald tapped his old friend at Polygram, Sincere Thompson, to service copies of the "Protect Ya Neck" twelve-inch to record pools nationwide via that company's mail room. Meanwhile, RZA had his friend from Staten Island, Schott "Free" Jacobs, who was interning at Dallas Austin's Rowdy Records, do the same thing. The Clan gave new meaning to the term *guerilla marketing*. Sometimes members just walked the record up to radio stations themselves like they did one night at Columbia University's WKCR 89.9 FM, where Stretch Armstrong (Adrian Bartos) and Robert "Bobbito" Garcia hosted a popular underground hip-hop show on Thursdays from one to five in the morning.

Garcia was by himself that night when RZA, Ghost, and three other unidentified guys barged into the station, somehow evading two security doors, and accosted him to play a white label with absolutely no information on it. "They weren't being nice," Garcia recalls.[47] But after auditioning the record and thinking it was incredible, he gave "Protect Ya Neck" its world premiere in December 1992. That broadcast sent the initial tremors through the underground, contributing to the record's slow-building buzz, but it was still no substitute for a spin on commercial radio.

Finally, in early January 1993, GZA was able to get a copy of the record to Kid Capri, his former labelmate at Cold Chillin', who also had a weekly show on WBLS 107.5 FM. "When Kid Capri played it, we was at RZA sister house, all of us," Deck recalls, "and Kid Capri promised us, 'Yo, I'ma play it for you man. I got choo."[48] Ghost adds, "I remember that day. Kid Capri played it and it was on. Rae, he jumped to the fuckin' ceiling."[49] Says Deck, "When it came on the radio, for a minute I felt like a star. I felt like Big Daddy Kane and all the cats that I was listening to coming up. You really felt like you made it, yunno?"[50] Although he may have felt like the Wu-Tang Clan had finally arrived, this epic ride was just blasting off.

PART 2

BRING DA RUCKUS

CHAPTER 8

ENTER THE WU-TANG

Steve Rifkind's thirty-first birthday is one that neither he nor history will ever forget. On that momentous occasion, March 2, 1993, he happened to be in Manhattan, sizing up his new office on the thirty-sixth floor of the BMG building at 1540 Broadway. Never mind that it was no bigger than a prison cell, barely fitting a desk and two chairs—Rifkind could not have been happier after entering into a new joint venture between his LA-based independent Loud Records and RCA, one of the five big majors. His roster already included a handful of artists—Chicago's Tung Twista, known for a lightning-fast delivery that got him into the *Guinness Book of World Records*, and the groups Madkap and Tha Alkaholiks from LA—who had collectively sold a few hundred thousand units. But he realized that putting his label on the map meant conquering New York, the heart of the rap universe. One of his employees, Zaakir Muhammad, a.k.a. Soup, a future member of the rap group Jurassic 5, tipped him off to an independently released single called "Protect Ya Neck" that was doing big numbers on SoundScan, the new retail tracking system for record sales based on scanning barcodes. Rifkind finally heard it when his A&R guy, Trevor Williams, passed him the twelve-inch, which he had received from

Lansing, Michigan, DJ Jason Staten, one of the first college jocks nationwide to chart the single. Blown away by its rawness and sheer energy, he had spent the last couple of months trying to track down producer Prince Rakeem, whose name appeared on the center label next to a phone number, 718-876-5053. Unfortunately, RZA could not afford an answering machine at the time. But, somehow, he knew of Rifkind's whereabouts that day.[1]

While the label boss was having a meeting with E-Swift (Eric Brooks), DJ and producer for Tha Alkaholiks, who also happened to be in town, the elusive figure of RZA suddenly appeared hunched in the doorway. *Peace! Yo, you Steve Rifkin'? Prince Rakeem, yo.* Cradling a boom box, he pressed play, cranking up "Protect Ya Neck," as Inspectah Deck burst into the room to deliver the opening verses: "I smoke on the mic like Smokin' Joe Frazier." Following Deck, Raekwon came in and spat his bars, and so on, until a revolving cast of six MCs had performed their parts and disappeared. As if on cue, some unidentified guy, whom Rifkind had never seen before or since, popped his head in, saying, "That's that shit!" Momentarily stunned by the whole surreal scene, Rifkind and E-Swift looked at each other, speechless. While the boss was pondering what to do, E-Swift quickly blurted out, "Don't let 'em get out of this building without signing them!"[2] Four days later, on the Jewish holiday of Purim, the day of deliverance, the deal was done, and Wu-Tang Clan joined the roster of Loud Records.

On face value, they may have seemed like strange bedfellows: a hard-core rap group from the streets of New York signed to a fairly new LA-based independent with no hits, distributed by a major with little stake in Black music. But, on the contrary, this union represented a rare alignment of the planets as they negotiated an unprecedented deal. Unlike the typical exploitative arrangement sanctioned by the music industry since its inception, both parties came to the table as equals. Dependent on each other, they acted in true partnership, doing whatever it took to guarantee their mutual success.

Behind his vacuous blue eyes and long blond locks, Rifkind, who looked like an extra on *Baywatch*, was no pushover. Hailing from the suburbs of Merrick, Long Island, he was actually a smashmouth New Yorker with a strong pedigree in the music business. His grandfather, a retired boxer nicknamed One Punch Harry, had managed nightclubs for Jewish gangster and music impresario Morris "Mo" Levy in the forties. In the midfifties, his dad, Jules, started one of the first interracial partnerships in the music business when he launched an artist management company with popular New York radio personality Tommy "Dr. Jive" Smalls, representing some of the top Black talent in the country. As Jules rose within the industry, he had a reputation for hiring Black executives and earning the respect of Black performers with whom he dealt. Steve grew up in that musical environment, meeting legends like James Brown when he was only seven years old. In 1979, the elder Rifkind also had the distinction of releasing the first-ever rap record, "King Tim III (Personality Jock)," on his Spring Records label (distributed by Polygram), which beat "Rapper's Delight" to radio by a good five months. In addition to that seminal release, he was responsible for other early rap records like Jimmy Spicer's 1983 hit "Money (Dollar Bill Y'all)."[3]

In fact, young Steve cut his teeth in the music business at Spring, where the first record he helped promote was "King Tim III." At nineteen, he secured his own client, Telestar

Records, who released a twelve-inch by the rapper Spyder-D called "Smerphies Dance" (1982). Through his father, who called New York radio personality Frankie Crocker a friend, Rifkind pulled off a major coup, getting that record played on WBLS, the city's top Black station. Picking up more clients as a result, he started to enjoy more independence from his father, with whom he often clashed. While promotion was his bread and butter, in the summer of 1986, Rifkind left for LA to take on a gig he couldn't pass up—comanaging the popular R&B boy band New Edition.

That gig propelled him into the upper echelons of the music biz, where he got a taste of how the other half lives. But growing tired of it by 1988, he turned back to promotion work to support himself in LA. There, he targeted a fledgling independent label called Delicious Vinyl, offering to promote records to both retail and Black radio. Once again, through his industry connections, he played a significant role in getting videos for Delicious Vinyl artists Tone Lōc ("Wild Thing") and Young MC ("Bust a Move") added to MTV.

With all the conventional bases covered—radio, retail, and video—Rifkind started looking for alternative ways to push records. Working with a group of independent promoters in LA, he saw how they hit the streets distributing promotional product to barbershops, nightclubs, swap meets, and even gang hangouts. So he hired an assistant, Fabian "Fade" Duvernay, and started developing his own "street team" of rap fanatics and college deejays around the country.[4]

According to author Dan Charnas, "For Steve Rifkind, the whole concept reminded him of what his father used to do at Spring Records. Jules Rifkind pioneered the idea of hiring professional basketball players—who really had nothing to do in those days when they traveled but sit in their hotel rooms—to carry records to cities far and wide. Jules put a few of the New York Knickerbockers on his payroll including Earl 'The Pearl' Monroe. To Steve, deputizing college students and hustling scenesters in locales across the country didn't seem like a strange concept at all."[5] But instead of paying them with schwag—free T-shirts, posters, and so forth—as others were doing, he actually kept them on retainer at one hundred dollars a week.

The timing could not have been more perfect, as many major labels were just dipping a toe into the rap scene but hadn't the faintest idea how to promote it. Rifkind started offering independent promotional services through his newly formed company, SRC (Steve Rifkind Company), and the majors bit. Interscope Records, founded by Jimmy Iovine and Ted Field in 1990, even kept him on retainer at $15,000 per month to hype up pop rappers Gerardo (of "Rico Suave" fame), Marky Mark (who first hit with "Good Vibrations"), and a recently signed Tupac Shakur. Business was so good he had to bring in his former high school buddy from Merrick, Rich Isaacson, a frustrated corporate lawyer who hated his job, to help him run the business.[6]

As his network slowly expanded in the early nineties, Rifkind's army of eyes and ears on the street unearthed all kinds of hidden talent, prompting him to start a label of his own. Early success only fueled his hunger for more, and he especially wanted to make a big score in his hometown. Finally able to secure a distribution deal with RCA—orchestrated, once again, through his father's connections—he was locked and loaded and swinging for the fences. Signing the Clan would be his grand slam. Following their impromptu performance in his office, Rifkind was pumped, saying, "There were nine guys in a group that could spit their asses off.

When I saw them, I thought they could be as big as the Rolling Stones."[7]

Commercial radio skewed heavily toward West Coast rap artists like Dr. Dre, whose *The Chronic* (Death Row / Interscope, 1992) was as big in New York as anywhere else. But the birthplace of hip-hop was also ensconced in its own creative bubble, well fed by the flourishing local scene. A hip-hop fan in the Rotten Apple, for example, was living "phat" off the sounds of Boogie Down Productions, Ultramagnetic MCs, A Tribe Called Quest, Jungle Brothers, De La Soul, Black Sheep, Chi-Ali, Das EFX, EPMD, Redman, Gang Starr, Jeru the Damaja, Group Home, Boot Camp Clik, Smif-N-Wesson, Pete Rock & C.L. Smooth, Nas, Diamond D, Showbiz and AG, Fat Joe, Lord Finesse, Brand Nubian, Grand Puba, and Kool G Rap & DJ Polo, all of whom released records between 1992 and 1993. In New York's insular rap scene, many of these artists already knew each other and cliqued together in crews such as the Flavor Unit, the Native Tongues, Diggin' in the Crates, the Gang Starr Foundation, and the Hit Squad. In fact, new artists were usually introduced to the industry through their crews, establishing an informal vetting process that turned proven talent into A&Rs. But this system also made it that much tougher for unknown artists with no prior affiliations to penetrate that sphere.

According to Raekwon, "We was big fans of EPMD, they whole movement [the Hit Squad, which included Das EFX, Redman, and K-Solo]. They was the real New York before we was the real New York, so we wanted to emulate that. Yunno, for your Redman we got a Method Man. For Parrish Smith and Eric Sermon, you got Rae and Ghost, yunno, that's how we would compare."[8] In fact, "Protect Ya Neck" was the Clan's answer to the EPMD posse cut "Headbanger," featuring the whole Hit Squad. But despite their huge popularity—especially among a hard-core street audience—EPMD represented the plight of many New York rappers: at most, they were gold-selling artists who couldn't compete sales-wise with the platinum-selling Dre.

For all his murderous tales of slangin' and gangbangin' in tha hood, Dre was truly killing it with a clean, smooth sound that set the standard for rap production at the time. After sampling so much of George Clinton's P-Funk catalog, he finally hired studio musicians like Colin Wolfe, who played the sinister bassline on hits like "Deep Cover," to create a new brand of G-funk or gangsta-funk. Dre also rediscovered the Minimoog, an analog synthesizer first introduced in 1970, attempting to channel the Mothership's classically trained keyboard maestro Bernie Worrell with those downright sinister-sounding high-end riffs that lace *The Chronic* and its follow-up, Snoop Dogg's *Doggystyle* (Death Row / Interscope, 1993). Before fabricated rivalries and bicoastal beefs, New York, like the rest of the country, was listening to it and loving it, even though that sound didn't represent the basement boom bap aesthetic that they favored.

It's no secret that the music business is one of the most corrupt, crooked, and exploitative industries to ever exist. Throw race into the mix, and it gets that much worse. That's why it takes a gangster to succeed. Historically, artists—especially Blacks—have been the pawns in the game, holding very little leverage against the white label executives who call all the shots. The Wu-Tang deal with Loud, however, was unprecedented in that it changed this traditional balance of power. Knowing that one record deal would not come close to feeding the nine individual artists in the group, RZA was adamant that he be able to sign each member to a solo deal as well, directly challenging established music industry practice.

Considered boilerplate or standard in major label contracts, the leaving-member clause stipulated that a label that signed a group had exclusive rights to sign any leaving member of that group. After "Protect Ya Neck" started blowing up, none of the major labels that called RZA for a meeting were willing to waive this clause, except Loud. Rifkind says he was amenable to the idea because, following his experience with New Edition, "I always thought the group would be bigger than the solo artist."[9] The only reason he was able to convince the top brass at RCA to see eye to eye with him was because they didn't have much faith that what they referred to as the "Chinese rap group"[10] would sell many records.

So Wu-Tang became the first rap group in history whose individual members were eligible to sign with other labels. The compromise Rifkind reached with RZA allowed Loud to have first dibs to match any competing offers for Wu-Tang solo artists. RZA also secured the guarantee of complete creative control over the album, another unprecedented accommodation. In exchange for these two significant concessions, he rolled the dice, agreeing to settle for a relatively paltry advance of $60,000. In doing so, however, "Wu-Tang not only kept the right to determine the destinies of its members individually, but—fatefully—they also retained their brand: their name, their merchandising, and their publishing. Never before had hip-hop artists negotiated the kind of autonomy that RZA did."[11] Of course, another visionary artist, George Clinton, had pulled off a similar coup in the seventies when he got his bands, Parliament and Funkadelic, which were, ostensibly, made up of the same musicians, signed to Casablanca and Westbound, respectively. But RZA was about to take this concept to the next level.

Even before the Loud deal was clinched, he signed ODB to Elektra and Method Man to Def Jam. By February 1993, when "Protect" became a "Sure Shot" single in *The Source*, the premiere hip-hop publication at the time, Genius scored a deal at Geffen Records. For RZA, everything was proceeding as planned. "So, what happened is now you have major labels who are in competition with each other now working for the same cause without being aware of it," he says. "And now hip-hop is getting a chance to get a new breed of energy that was lacking. Before Wu-Tang, you couldn't find many MCs that was really straight from the projects—ex-felons who would never have got a job, life would be over. Seven out of nine of us are high school dropouts and basically the ones that society would write off as dead or in jail by twenty-five. So, we was able to beat that statistic, bring the real people into the music industry, the people that was feeling it [hip-hop] and living it, you know what I mean, and changed the game."[12]

There was no question that the rest of the Clan was on the same page. In an early interview, GZA said, "Clan represents family, man. Clan means family. We all a family. But we spreading out. Don't think that because he has a solo deal and I have a solo deal that we all just separating and breaking up. It's not that type of thing, man. We just expanding because the talent is so great. It's like we have mad talent in this, yunno, and we just got to spread out."[13]

Dirty added, "We got a master plan for y'all, man. See we tryin' to get all our people in the door. I ain't even gonna tell you. I'ma just show you, man."[14]

In the fall of 1992, shortly after recording their debut single, the Clan took the initiative to shoot a video for "Protect Ya Neck." Before everyone had HD video at their fingertips, this proved a highly ambitious undertaking that required a significant investment of time, money, and manpower. Credit their DIY spirit, youthful exuberance, and naïveté for even taking on such a daunting task. Obviously, before Loud entered the picture, the Clan wasn't trying to spend money they didn't have, so they ended up getting exactly what they paid for—a gritty, low-budget visual rendition of a song that was just as grimy.

Former manager Melquan Smith introduced RZA to aspiring screenwriter and director Kurt Anthony, a Columbia, South Carolina, native who studied film at San Francisco State and had moved to New York in 1989 to get involved with theater. Having made several short student films, he was initially hesitant to get involved, aware of the time, money, and effort it took to shoot on film. But, according to Anthony, "RZA offered me a deal saying if I were to make the video, he would pay me back on the next series of videos once they signed a production deal and had money to do other videos, you know? So, I said, 'OK, I will throw my money into the video.'" It was a calculated risk on his part, considering "they wasn't known. Nobody had no idea who they were," he says. But with the promise of future paid work, he ended up kicking in $2,500 out of his own pocket, adding to RZA's initial investment of $3,000.

Even on such a bare-bones budget in 1992, they were able to rent a 16-mm Arriflex camera, a basic lighting rig, cables, a bulky generator for power, and a truck to haul it all around. Anthony also bought about twenty rolls of the fastest film,

Kodak 400, which was more forgiving in low light, choosing black-and-white stock, he says, "to make it look more hard and raw." His greatest challenge, however, was recruiting free labor, for which he depended on film students from NYU's Tisch School of the Arts. Most could only commit themselves to a day, so there was high turnover among the crew, and the intimidation factor didn't help. "The Wu-Tang Clan was a little taken aback that I had some of these white kids on the shoot and I didn't have any Black filmmakers," says Anthony. "When we was shooting over at the Navy Yard, they put such terror into two white boys I was working with." Both eventually ended up fleeing the scene in panic.

Despite such challenges, the shoot proceeded slowly over three weeks. The first four days were spent filming at Park Hill, where individual group members performed their verses in the entryways and rooftops of buildings and on fire escapes—usually with their whole extended crew behind them. The following week they shot at the Brooklyn Navy Yard and 135th and 5th Avenue near Harlem River Drive. For variety, Anthony shot some color footage on VHS. In need of another main location, the Clan zeroed in on the band shell at East River Park, a decaying amphitheater that doubled as a notorious hangout for junkies and the homeless. It also happened to be a popular spot for rap videos, as EPMD shot 1992's "Headbanger" there. Going even further back, the band shell provided the backdrop for the memorable performance scene in Charlie Ahearn's *Wild Style* (1983), the first hip-hop movie.

For this part of the shoot, an NYU film grad from Finland, Osmo Walden, then twenty-six, responded to Anthony's call for a camera assistant. He arrived early in the morning at an already chaotic set. "There was a really aggressive atmosphere," he recalls. "Obviously the Wu-Tang Clan guys there were taking it really seriously, but their friends were, you know, using drugs and smoking and showing guns and stuff like that in the background." He probably felt even more self-conscious being only one of two white people on the set—along with the DP or cinematographer—among the Clan and their rowdy crew of twenty.

When filming started, things got even more hectic, as someone tossed a brick toward the camera. According to Walden, "After the brick was thrown, the DP said that he has an important call to make and that he will be back in a few minutes because during that time, there were no cell phones, so he had to go to a phone booth. So, I said, 'OK,' and the director also said, 'OK,' and then he just walked away, and we were waiting for him. Then after half an hour or something like that, we realized that he's never going to show up. I think he was kind of scared of the whole shoot. Well, I don't think—I know he was really scared."

The DP's disappearance didn't do anything for the morale on the set. Anthony was at a loss for words, and Walden says, "They [the Clan] were really confused and kind of like depressed. I mean obviously you don't have any, like, insurance, so, you know, they're going to lose the opportunity to shoot or money or whatever." That's when he felt all eyes on him. "They were like, 'Can you shoot?'" says Walden. "Fortunately, I can film. I even been in a school. 'Well, let's fuckin' film then!'" came the general response.

As the evening progressed, ongoing tension with the group forced Anthony to go AWOL at one point, leaving Walden single-handedly holding down the shoot. He says, "I was filming and setting up the lights, pulling cables. There were drug syringes on the ground. Dudes got more and more fucked up and the whole situation was heated. Suddenly in the middle of everything the lights turned off, because the generator they got there broke down. In the pitch-dark I heard a shout, 'Fuck, there is a saboteur in here!'" As it turned out, the generator was out of gas and just needed refilling.

They continued shooting at an incredibly slow pace. At this point, an extremely nervous, tired, and paranoid Walden was reaching the end of his rope. Despite being an unpaid assistant, he decided to make an executive decision. "I thought that, fuck, you know, if we are doing shot by shot these things that it's going to take forever," he says. "And then I said to the Wu-Tang Clan guys and the director Kurt Anthony, I lied to them, and I said to them that, 'Hey listen, I have just one roll of film left. Let's do it so that I will put the lights around you and make a long shot.'" Barely able to judge the depth of field in the camera's viewfinder and having issues framing in darkness, Walden nonetheless captured a four-minute-long handheld shot of the performance that became the video's centerpiece. "I said, 'That's it.' That was it. Then they relaxed," he says. "One of the Wu-Tang guys came to say to me that he really owes me a favor—that I saved their day and their video, and that one day, whenever I need some help, I can call them, and they will return the favor. Well, I still haven't called." Later, he says, he ran into Anthony, who was looking for a phone booth to call for help because he felt his life was in danger. But that was all in a day's work when dealing with the Wu-Tang Clan.

According to Anthony, "I wasn't afraid on the shoot or nothing, but I did have to argue and fight my way through the whole shoot. And I got a number of threats constantly even after I had shot the video about when the film was going to be edited and why it's taking so long." Initially, he started editing the video with RZA at a studio on Broadway and Ninth Street near Astor Place, before the Clan got impatient with him and demanded he turn over all the footage. "I wish I would have gave him the online stage without the time code, but the situation was that they was rushing me to give them the tape, you know, they was threatening me, and I like don't know why they wanted it at that point so soon," says Anthony. Finally, RZA and company were able to stitch together a motley video that mixed formats (film and VHS) and alternated between color and black-and-white, even displaying the time code on some of the shots. Though RZA reneged on their verbal agreement to bring him more paid work and they butted heads throughout the process, Anthony has no regrets about working with the Wu and says, "I was glad to see, at least, my name on the video."

RZA brought the "finished" product to "Uncle" Ralph McDaniels, who, since 1983, had produced a popular music video show on New York's public TV station WNYC called *Video Music Box*. After viewing the roughly hewn production, McDaniels agreed to broadcast it when it was done, but RZA assured him that the video was good to go as is. Uncle Ralph ended up running with it because he had never seen anything like it. The Killa Bees were on a roll, mounting a double-pronged attack through the New York airwaves before they even had a deal.

Yoram Vazan, the owner of Firehouse Studio, had almost forgotten that RZA still owed him money from the "Protect Ya Neck" session, which cost about $1,000. "He was short $200, and really was paying with some singles and some quarters, and I said, 'Man, don't worry about it, you know, forget it. You know the $200 is no big deal,'" Vazan recalls. But after clinching the deals with Loud and the other labels, "RZA calls me up and says, 'Yoram, we're gonna pay you back. We got four or five albums, yunno, we're coming to your studio.' So, they were there for like six months, every night," he says.

An Israeli émigré, Vazan was yet another random character who played a pivotal role in the birth of the Clan. He had come to the States in December 1980 after completing his compulsory service in the Israeli Air Force, where he even stayed on an extra year to study electronics. After arriving in New York, he promptly enrolled in the one-year engineering program at the Institute for Audio Research. But upon graduating and working at a Manhattan studio, he decided to go back to Israel for a year. When he returned to New York in 1984, he started teaching at the Institute.

In November 1986, Vazan opened his first studio, Such a Sound, in Boerum Hill, Brooklyn, with Israeli partner Shlomo Sonnenfeld. The studio was a converted one-thousand-square-foot loft in which one bedroom served as the control room, the walk-in closet was a vocal booth, and the living room was the live room. Vazan slept in the other bedroom. "I bought an Akai 900 sampler, an SP-12 [drum machine], and an Atari computer," he says, "and that started our hip-hop career." After placing an ad in the *Village Voice*, they started getting their first customers, the rap group Audio Two and a producer named King of Chill.

Though the Robinson brothers—Kirk, a.k.a. Milk Dee, and his deejay Nat, a.k.a. Gizmo—of Audio Two were originally from Brooklyn, by the time their twelve-inch "Make It Funky" / "Top Billin'" (First Priority Records, 1987) came out, they were living right around the corner from Park Hill in Staten Island. When the B side, "Top Billin," became a certified hit, many aspiring artists probably looked at the label and saw where it was produced—including Gang Starr, the duo of rapper Guru and producer extraordinaire DJ Premier, who crafted their breakout debut, *Step in the Arena* (1990), at Such a Sound along with female rapper MC Lyte, a labelmate of Audio Two's. "The main word got around by, yunno, word of mouth," says Vazan. "This is a dope studio. This studio sounds great. It's a great vibe. It's not too expensive."

Halfway through 1988, however, Vazan and his partner split. Sonnenfeld ended up keeping most of the equipment, and Vazan kept the space, since he also lived there. Since the building, located at 17 Dean Street, sat across the street from Brooklyn's Station Number Three, he decided to rename it Firehouse. He also outfitted the studio with new equipment, including a British-made Allen & Heath console. In 1990, Melquan Smith started bringing Genius and then-Prince Rakeem there to work on early demos. In 1991, Das EFX, a new duo discovered by EPMD at a talent show in Virginia, recorded their platinum debut, *Dead Serious* (East-West / Atlantic, 1992), at Firehouse. Not long afterward, in October 1992, the Clan recorded "Protect Ya Neck."

By 1993, however, Vazan couldn't turn down an opportunity to move to Manhattan. "The main reason is rent. Rent went down dramatically in Manhattan, which was amazing," he says. "It was twelve hundred dollars [per month]; that was only fifty bucks more than I was paying in Brooklyn. So, I went with an acoustic designer. We looked at the place, we took measurements, and I said, 'OK, I'm going for it. I'm moving to Manhattan.'" Using his cousin, a skilled contractor, Vazan had the new space built in only five weeks. Then, with the help of his engineers, he packed up all the equipment and had it moved and wired up within a week. By early 1993, the new Firehouse Studio at 150 West Twenty-Eighth Street in Manhattan was up and running just in time to launch the Wu revolution.

Despite its name, Jack the Rapper's Family Affair, one of the longest-running Black music conventions, had really nothing to do with rap. Joseph Deighton Gibson (a.k.a. Jack the Rapper), a pioneering radio deejay from Chicago who became a familiar voice on the airwaves at WERD-AM in Atlanta, America's first Black-owned and Black-operated radio station, started the gathering in 1977 to celebrate the richness and diversity of Black music. A star of the civil rights era who was responsible for putting Rev. Martin Luther King Jr. on the radio, Gibson sought to elevate his community and create a venue dedicated to Black entertainment, making the Family Affair the place to be for Black artists and executives.

Over the years, top-tier talent such as Prince, Mariah Carey, Luther Vandross, and New Kids on the Block all headlined the event. Nation of Islam leader Louis Farrakhan even addressed the convention in 1980 in a speech that was later sampled by Public Enemy for their song "Terminator X to the Edge of Panic." Rappers had been attending since the mideighties, but as rap started to blow up in the nineties, they all but took over. At 1993's Family Affair, held between August 12 and 15 in Atlanta, a large contingent from Suge Knight's Death Row Records roamed the lobbies, covering the walls with stickers and posters in support of the much-hyped newcomer Snoop Dogg, who was performing. Meanwhile, Puff Daddy, as he was then known, was throwing pool parties to introduce his new label, Bad Boy, and showing off its marquee artist, the Notorious B.I.G. The infamous Bad Boy / Death Row beef had yet to materialize, as Death Row was then preoccupied with another nemesis, Luther "Uncle Luke" Campbell and his Luke Records, who had released a diss record called "Cowards of Compton." Meanwhile, a care-free Tupac Shakur, still years away from signing with Death Row, was enjoying himself at the OutKast barbecue.

At one of the music showcases, an unnamed rap group from the early eighties was performing when a guy in a stocking mask suddenly took the stage in the middle of their set. According to an eyewitness, photographer Daniel Hastings, "They're like, 'What the fuck, son? We're doin' a set here.' Yo, the man in the stocking mask goes and just snatches the microphone from this dude and pushes him to the side. And then all these dudes with masks just come on stage, and they push everybody out. They fuckin' take the soundman off and get in the booth and do whatever they got to do. And then they start chanting, 'Wu-Tang Clan ain't nothing to fuck with! Wu-Tang Clan ain't nothin' to fuck with.'"[15] After that performance, he says, "That place went bananas, bro; everybody just started jumping around, man, screaming Wu-Tang! I was jumping around."[16]

No casual observer, Hastings had actually been contracted by RCA art director Jackie Murphy to shoot the Wu-Tang album cover. He had previously worked with her on the cover for another RCA group, Rumpletilskinz, and, in the interim, had also shot KRS-ONE's *Return of the Boom Bap* (1993) album. After introducing himself to RZA following that memorable performance, he agreed to powwow with the Abbott back in New York to discuss cover concepts.

Days later, Hastings came down to Firehouse in Manhattan. Even though the place was only a few months old, it had received the Wu treatment. "This place had holes in the walls, wires coming out of the walls, chicken wings on the floor, blunt wraps all over the place, empty 40s all over," says Hastings. "But I talked to the RZA and I'll never forget it, he told me, 'Hey, man, you see this sweatshirt I got on? I've been wearing this shit for like three days. But I'm goin' to blow up because I got beats. And I'm gonna be an empire.'"[17] Whether displaying cockiness or faith or large helpings of both, he clearly knew what lay on the horizon. The two discussed the album and its kung fu themes, and RZA said he wanted to use some kind of monastery as a backdrop. After all, they were representing Shaolin.

Jackie Murphy delivered big-time, finding a dilapidated and abandoned synagogue on Norfolk Street in the Lower East Side. Today, after serious renovation, it has survived as the Angel Orensanz Center, but when it was originally built in 1849, it had the distinction of being the largest synagogue in the country. The building's Gothic Revival architecture, along with years of neglect, gave it that perfect well-worn, mystical look they were after for the cover shoot.

Because Rifkind was traveling and no marketing people from Loud were around to provide direction, Hastings had a tremendous amount of creative control over the actual shoot. He had an artist blow up the Wu-Tang logo, carve it out of foam core, and paint it gold to use as a prop. He also used a fairly complex lighting setup involving tungsten lights, candles, and strobes. But when the Clan showed up, there were only six of them—RZA, GZA, ODB, Inspectah Deck, Ghostface, and Raekwon—as well as RZA's brother Divine and manager Mook. U-God was locked up following another parole violation, and Meth had been arrested that morning in Park Hill for refusing to throw away his blunt when confronted by the cops. Hastings had planned to show their faces but says, "Since not all of them were there we had to use the stocking masks," an inspiration that hit him on the spot. Though the group was initially hesitant about not being depicted on their album cover, he adds, "RZA liked the idea, so we went and did it. But if I hadn't gone to Jack the Rapper, I wouldn't have come up with the idea."[18]

So he dressed everyone up in black hoodies and stocking masks. The group had brought some Wu logo stickers, which they stuck on the hoodies to create a uniform look. Hastings smudged the camera lens with a little Vaseline for effect and took the shot that would become the cover of *Enter the Wu-Tang: 36 Chambers.* On it, a band of faceless ninjas seem to be creeping menacingly forward after performing some kind of ritualistic séance. "When they [the group] saw what I created they were like, 'What the fuck is this? This looks amazing,'"[19] says Hastings. Millions more would eventually agree.

In the midst of all the frenzied activity of 1993—shows, promotional tours, photo shoots, conventions—the Clan's top priority was to deliver an album to Loud, and they were working as fast as they could. By now, Firehouse employed a stable of engineers—including Ethan Ryman, Dennis Mitchell, Blaise Dupuy, Nolan "Dr. No" Moffitte, and newcomer Carlos Bess—to keep up with the amount of work coming through the studio. Ryman, the senior engineer, who had also worked on "Protect Ya Neck," became RZA's go-to person behind the boards. He says, "We became pretty efficient at getting things down quickly. We got along well, and I felt like the roughness of his sound and the roughness of my skills was a good match. He was happy anyway."[20]

He adds, "When we started recording *Enter the Wu-Tang,* the whole group was usually there for every session; sometimes it felt like their whole neighborhood was in the studio. Every now and then RZA and I would have to clear the room so we could get to the equipment. I remember feeling there was a very forceful energy with them. They were not playing around. They would bark orders at each other, not just saying something matter-of-factly but saying things with a tone of underlying 'or else'—like everything was super important. It was badass and I started doing it too. It was like nobody wanted to show any weakness."[21]

When Ryman wasn't available, RZA preferred working with Carlos Bess. Bess, forty-nine, a Puerto Rican from the Upper West Side, grew up with hip-hop and started writing graffiti as a teenager. Around the same time, he started playing drums, which was his entry into the recording studio. Fellow graf writer Mark Williams (a.k.a. BEAM), who also happened to be a musician and producer, took Bess under his wing and had him program drums for him whenever he did a session. That was how he first ended up in Firehouse, when they were located in Brooklyn. Years later, Bess came across an ad in the *Village Voice* classifieds looking for engineers for a new studio in Manhattan. When he called up the number, he discovered it was the same Firehouse. Despite having no formal training or experience as an engineer, he asked Vazan for a job and was told to come down the next day and train. Within a week, he was assisting on sessions and doing whatever work needed to be done around the studio.

One night when Ryman called in sick, Bess got his big break. Vazan asked him if he wanted to do the Wu-Tang session, and he jumped on it. He had obviously seen the guys around the studio, but this would be his first time working with them. That memorable session happened to be for the last song they recorded for the album, "Da Mystery of Chessboxin.'" "That whole night, you know, everyone came through. I mean there was about a good sixty people in the session that night; they were cheering each other on," says Bess, adding, "It was a great vibe, man. It wasn't, yunno, chaotic."

They started working at about six in the evening. First, RZA had him bring up the track from two-inch tape, while he went and wrote some lyrics. Doing what is known as a pre-mix, Bess EQ'ed each individual sound on the Peavey twenty-four-track console and had the beat to his liking by the time RZA returned. Then RZA did some mutes and drops using the computer automation to create a basic arrangement for the track. The microphone, an AKG C414 EB, was already set up in the vocal booth, so they were ready when the MCs came trickling in after seven.

U-God was first in the vocal booth—not surprising since this would be only his second appearance on *36 Chambers* after spitting a quick four bars on "Protect Ya Neck." Having spent the last year in and out of jail on parole violations, he had missed most of the recording of the album. In fact, since this would be his first full verse, he was going to make it count, so he came prepared with a rhyme written in advance.

The Inspectah was on deck. "Deck came in, you know, he did a warmup, and then he just did his take, you know. And then once he finished his verse, RZA came back, and he did some little drops and refinements," says Bess. Meanwhile, Raekwon had been in the studio, checking out the other guys and scribbling furiously on a pad. Bess says, "I remember Rae was writing his verse. He took some time to write his verse, and he went in and did a few [takes]. I think he managed to go through it after a few takes."

Traffic started to pick up, and Method Man arrived about fifteen minutes later with a large entourage that included Shyheim Franklin (a.k.a. the Rugged Child), RZA's former neighbor at Stapleton, who scored his first record deal with Virgin at the age of thirteen. Like Pig-Pen from the *Peanuts* comic strip, a cloud of smoke seemed to perpetually envelop

Meth, but at this point, everyone in the room was puffing on their own blunt. Heads nodded in unison to the beat, and the energy continued to rise, reaching a crescendo with the arrival of Ol' Dirty Bastard shortly afterward.

"Oh, my goodness. He lit up that room like a Christmas tree," Bess recalls. "I mean, everyone was turned up. ODB just came into the room, and he was giving pounds to everybody. RZA was like, 'Hey, listen to this.' We played the song to him, and he goes, 'Yo, yo, I'm goin' right in. Boom.'" But since Meth had already written a hook for the track and was next up, they had to physically remove Dirty from the vocal booth. "RZA was just like, 'Yo, everybody go in there. Shyheim, everybody go in there, "In the front, in the back, Killa Bees on attack."' We did that," says Bess.

After Meth and company nailed the hook in one take, "that's when ODB said, 'Fuck that, I'm going in.' And he went in, and he did it in one take. He did the yelling and walked out for like about ten minutes and then he did the verse," says Bess. Dirty's part started with a long yodel that began during the hook, which they recorded first, before Bess punched him in to do his verse. Satisfied with his performance, ODB didn't stick around much longer, and Meth followed him out. With their respective entourages gone, things quieted down for a minute. Then Jamel Irief (a.k.a. Masta Killa) showed up around the same time as Ghostface, who, like Raekwon, wrote his verse on the spot.

After missing the "Protect Ya Neck" session, Irief started hanging around the Clan and contributing to the effort in any way he could. He gave haircuts to the guys before shows and even drove the van to their early gigs. Meanwhile, he looked, listened, and observed, all the while getting a crash course in lyricism from the eight other MCs in the group.

As RZA explains, "He got his name because Masta Killa is the guy who wasn't part of Shaolin. He came to Shaolin and went through all the training in *36 Chambers* and became Masta Killa. He saw us as his teachers."[22] At age twenty-four, Masta Killa wrote his first rhyme ever, and, even more surprisingly, it was good enough to make the cut, helping him secure a permanent spot with the crew.

But Ghostface laid his verse first. After writing, he went into the booth and did about three different takes, listening to each carefully. "He does his takes very fast, but he's meticulous about which takes he wants to use," says Bess, adding, "After Ghost finished his verse, Masta Killa came in. He choked it, man. He killed it. Put the icing on the cake." Once all the verses were recorded, 4th Disciple, RZA's old friend from Steubenville, who had been hanging around all night and, in fact, for most of the recording of the album, laid down the scratches. Finally, at about two in the morning, they put the track to bed.

"RZA heard the DAT [digital audio tape] that night, and he was like, 'Wow, this is it.' It wasn't mastered yet, and he's like, 'This is great. This is good to go.' There was no recalls," says Bess. "The only recall we did was we needed to do the clean version, you know? And that wasn't the only record I did. I pretty much did a lot of recalls for the album. There was no special edits and none of that. The only edit that was done in post-production was [adding], 'A game of chess is like a sword fight.' That was done in postproduction. That was the only thing. But the actual song was done from beginning to end the way you hear it."

The final step in the recording process was mastering. According to Chris Gehringer, fifty-eight, who mastered the Wu-Tang album at Sterling Sound in Manhattan, "It's about making the album sound good, sequencing it, putting every-thing together, doing final edits and really just tweaking it—adjusting the levels between each song." Usually the art-ist does not even attend the mastering session, but one day, Gehringer, who had worked on everything from Agnostic Front and GG Allin to MC Shan and Main Source, was con-fronted by RZA, Raekwon, Deck, Ghostface, and one of their managers.

He recalls, "I had never heard of them, yunno. Got the DAT, put it in, and it was one of those things where I was lis-tening and grooving on it, and by the time I got to the third track, I was like, 'Yo, this shit is crazy.' I was lovin' it—just the sounds and everything." Still, he admits that sonically, "it wasn't the best sounding record. It was a lot of work. I just wanted the stuff to jump out of the speakers, whatever it takes, whether its adding compression or whatever." The guys, who had seemed a little standoffish at first, lightened up when they realized that Gehringer was in their corner. "We're not audiophile guys; we're grimy niggas from Staten Island," they joked.[23]

Though the album was already sequenced, complete with skits, the kung fu movie snippets had to be added during mastering. "We literally took a VHS machine and copied [the kung fu samples] RZA wanted off the VHS machine and onto a DAT player and edited those pieces in," says Gehringer. "This was back in the days of pre-audio and computer work-stations, so we were using digital editors that couldn't cross-fade more than half a second and they had a lot of those skits that they had to slide in. It was probably more work putting that part of the album together than anything else."[24]

He basically had to take apart the whole album to work on each individual song and then put it back together again, a process he estimates took six to seven hours. "RZA would kinda tell me the vibe of the record and what he wanted, but he liked what I was doing," Gehringer recalls. "After he took the record home and listened to it and came back in, he was like, 'I love it. I love what you did to it.'" But the execs at RCA—not so much.

November 9, 1993. Webster Hall, New York City. Wu-Tang was performing that night to celebrate the release of *Enter the Wu-Tang: 36 Chambers*, and the New York hip-hop community had turned out en masse to raise a toast. This writer was among the throngs of industry people, media, and artists clogging the streets while waiting in line to go through the metal detectors and fill the cavernous room above. Like me, they probably passed a bespectacled ODB, forty ounces of OE in hand, who was holding court on the corner with some of his people, braids twisting out of his head like Medusa's snakes.

Inside, it was straight-up sardines, meaning you had to be extra careful not to spill a drink or step on anyone's immaculate Timberlands. Kung fu movies screened silently on the wall behind the stage. Despite Webster Hall's no-smoking policy, a cumulus cloud of blunt smoke already hung thick— hardly surprising, since this gathering was a who's who of hip-hop. Q-Tip was politicking with Busta Rhymes. Guru from Gang Starr was there, as well as Brand Nubian and the ubiquitous Grandmaster Caz, an old-school emissary from the Bronx. Whenever you had so many artists under one roof and they were there to see who was on stage, you knew you were in for a special night—even in New York, where big things happen all the time. The excitement was palpable, and nobody quite knew what to expect.

When the Clan and their minions finally took the stage like an army of outcasts who had been trapped in the dungeon for years, they unleashed all the pent-up energy of a people denied access all their lives. Ripping through a medley of songs, including "Wu-Tang Clan Ain't Nothing to Fuck With," "Bring the Ruckus," and, of course, "Protect Ya Neck," they set off seismic tremors as floorboards buckled, and heads nodded like a Hasidic prayer meeting. The energy was intense, and everyone in that room knew, maybe not on a conscious level but deep down, that they were witnessing something transformational to the art of hip-hop.

* * *

RZA's entire existence seemed geared up for the making of *Enter the Wu-Tang: 36 Chambers.* Ever since "Rapper's Delight" had ignited his ten-year-old imagination, showing him the possibilities of making a living from his passion, he had dedicated himself to this cause like a Little Leaguer with pro aspirations. After signing his first record deal at twenty-one, the future looked promising, but he had also seen how fast everything could crash and burn. Only a pure vision, an iron will, and perhaps a little luck had allowed him to claw his way back from adversity and failure. Now, at twenty-three, he was finally poised to make good on his dreams and produce the album he had always wanted to make.

"There were no DVDs in those days," RZA explains, "so my idea was that people would get these one-hour audio movies. I did the whole thing with a movie concept. The Wu albums gave you visions. Some people listen to music and want to dance. You listen to my shit and you're seeing it and hearing it."[25] For RZA, hip-hop wasn't simply the five elements of MCing, deejaying, beatboxing, break dancing, and graffiti, but a way of life that encompassed all the influences of his youth—street fashion, video games, comics, Five-Percenter philosophy, and, of course, kung fu movies.

Indeed, an instantly recognizable feature of the album, which sets it apart from other releases, was its clever use of kung fu movie snippets to underscore the themes and topics the group explored in their rhymes. On *Enter the Wu-Tang*, the first words we hear are the dubbed English dialogue from *Shaolin vs. Wu-Tang*: "Shaolin shadow boxing and the Wu-Tang sword style. If what you say is true, the Shaolin and the Wu-Tang could be dangerous. Do you think your Wu-Tang sword can defeat me?" That line is answered by "*En garde*, I'll let you try my Wu-Tang Style" from a different film, *Ten Tigers from Kwangtung* (1979), as you hear the rasp of a steel blade being drawn, establishing the battle motif that frames much of the album. Even before this unconventional introduction ends, the subsonic boom of a kick drum drops as RZA angrily screams the hook—throwing in his favorite expletive for good measure.

"Bring da Ruckus," the album opener, sets the perfect mood with its skeletal beat, eerie atmospherics, and, of course, movie dialogue and medley of Foley effects—the punching, chopping, and kicking sounds—that listeners had never before heard on a rap record. RZA originally used those sound effects as a creative way to edit out curses, but they take on a life of their own, becoming part of Wu-Tang's signature sound.[26] Meanwhile, the movie dialogue, for those in the know, inspires a sense of nostalgia, another recurring theme on this album.

On the original version of this beat, produced in 1991, the inclusion of an unidentified blues riff with piano and bass line totally changes the vibe of the song, making it less menacing and hostile. But according to engineer Ethan Ryman, the label was unable to clear that sample, so it had to be removed, which proved to be a lucky break.[27] Instead of replacing it with another loop, RZA just lets the track breathe, adding even more spooky atmospherics like the processed two-second guitar riff from the Dramatics' "In the Rain," a 1971 hit that sold over a million copies. Here it becomes just another weird piece of sonic detritus that floats in and out of the mix like ear candy, another of RZA's fixations as well as a hallmark of his production style.

Like a superhero relating his origin story, he explains, "As a nine-year-old I had this strange abscess in my head, and I lost my vision for a time. A part of my head just grew and got full of mucus or septic pus or whatever. It lasted about 30 days, but as soon as the pus cleared, I found my hearing was off the hook! While my eyes had been fucked, I'd developed this super-hearing. Now when I'm in the studio I'll find everyone's listening to one part of a track and I'll be zooming in on some other sound altogether."[28] Lacing the mix with these random sounds and noises adds an almost three-dimensional texture to his otherwise basic productions.

"Ruckus" utilizes one of hip-hop's favorite drum breaks— from Melvin Bliss's "Synthetic Substitution" (Sunburst, 1973)—which was actually played by drummer Bernard Purdie. First sampled by Ultramagnetic MCs in their 1986 hit "Ego Trippin'," the popular break has since been used in eight hundred other songs, according to the website WhoSampled.com. RZA employs it as the bedrock for two other songs on *36 Chambers*, but on "Ruckus," he flips the sample with the curious addition of finger snaps, doubling the snare hit, making it sound that much sharper. Layering sounds is a typical hip-hop production technique—especially when it comes to drums—but RZA, once again, takes this process to the next level.

"I take sounds and noises that are not totally related and make them into a [single] phrase," he explains. "On 'Bring the Ruckus' you'll hear a garbage can mixed with finger snaps and a piano in a whole different key. Then you have the distorted bass, which is really the only thing that is in sync. You'll have all this going on, then I sampled a CD skipping and used that for my horns, 'D-D-D-D-D-D.' I didn't have a horn, so I did that."[29] These layers of sound, taken from different sources, contribute to the griminess of the mix.

Above this off-kilter, alien soundscape, we get our first introduction to the Wu-Tang MCs. Originally, Raekwon opens the demo version of the track but with a performance that is clearly not his best. Consequently, on the album version, Ghostface takes the lead-off spot, spitting fire: "Ghostface catch the blast of hype verse / My Glock burst, leave in hearse I did worse." Rae follows with a brand-new verse before Inspectah Deck and then GZA get a piece of the action—each MC sounding angrier than the last. But RZA gets the prize for most pissed off, screaming the hook, "Bring the muthafuckin ruckus," which is nothing less than a declaration of war.

After such an intense opening, an interlude of fight sounds from *Shaolin vs. Wu-Tang* allows for a quick reset before the vibe changes up with "Shame on a Nigga," a more conventional cut. It's powered by the dazzling horn fanfare from Syl Johnson's 1967 single "Different Strokes" (Twilight Records), which appeared on the popular *Ultimate Breaks and Beats* series for hip-hop deejays. The only reason the blues and soul singer and producer from Mississippi is not a household name is that he was on the same label as Al Green—Memphis's Hi

Records. RZA is a huge fan of Johnson's, and his sample clearance fee helped the veteran artist buy a new house, jumpstarting a renewed interest in his back catalog as well.

In fact, while most nineties hip-hop producers were mining funk and jazz staples for samples, RZA stakes his claim to sixties soul and R&B. He says, "Listen to my records carefully and you can tell my big hero is Willie Mitchell, the man who produced Al Green and all that Hi Records stuff. That whole era is my inspiration: Thom Bell's work with the Delfonics, David Porter and Isaac Hayes when they was at Stax. Quincy Jones' legendary production jobs."[30]

Another favorite artist that RZA samples on "Shame on a Nigga" is Thelonious Monk, the bebop innovator known for incorporating dissonance into his unorthodox style of piano playing. For this song, he takes two different parts from Monk's version of "Black and Tan Fantasy" (1956), originally a Duke Ellington composition. A spiritual progenitor of RZA, Monk is an artist the young producer returns to time and again for inspiration, whether lifting a catchy phrase or hitting the keys himself. In fact, RZA spent years searching for the 1988 Monk documentary *Straight No Chaser*, directed by Charlotte Zwerin, and the pianist's influence on him is unmistakeable. The piano, in general, became RZA's preferred compositional tool on this album, largely because he saw Monk destroy all conventions—thus confirming his own approach to hip-hop.

Though Raekwon and Method Man contribute verses, the track serves primarily as a vehicle for show stealer Ol' Dirty Bastard, who drops the hook as well as some memorable zingers. "Blau, how ya like me now," he says, reprising LL Cool J's line from "Mama Said Knock You Out" (1990). We also get a taste of his unconventional flow as he warbles his way through "warriors come out and play," a reference to the 1979 movie about a Bronx gang war, *The Warriors*.

As the track fades on Monk's piano, the extended intro of "Clan in the Front" begins. RZA loops the first four bars of the New Birth's "Honeybee" (RCA/Victor, 1971), whose bass line and kick accompany a buzzing bee sound effect. When sped up, it's a fittingly ominous backdrop for him to proclaim, "Up from the 36 Chambers . . . Wu-Tang Killa Bees, we on the swarm." A roll call of the principal members along with extended Wu-Tang family follows, sounding as if it could go on forever, until another swish of a sword introduces GZA, who launches into one of the only two solo tracks on the album (along with "Method Man").

As the elder MC of the Clan, who either taught the others directly or by example, it's only right that Genius has a chance to shine on his own. With a tone like a drill sergeant, he spits, "No response while I bomb that ass / You ain't shit, your whack ass town had you gassed / Egos is something the Wu-Tang crush / Souped up niggas on the stage get rushed." Musically, RZA keeps it simple and familiar, going back to the "Synthetic Substitution" break beat and another tinkle on the ivories from Monk's "Ba-Lue Bolivar Ba-lues-Are," first recorded in 1956. A stealthy keyboard snippet from the Jackson 5's "The Love You Save" (1970) creeps in almost imperceptibly as a textural element.

After the first three songs flow in fairly quick succession, RZA slows down the pace with what would become one of the Clan's patented skits. While he certainly didn't invent skits, which were employed to great comic effect by such producers as Prince Paul and Dr. Dre, he imbues them with a certain ghetto gothic quality. But the dark realism is tempered with strategic bursts of humor, as exemplified by the

"Killa Tape" skit that precedes "Wu-Tang 7th Chamber." In this comedic slice of life—apparently, a real tape-recorded conversation—Rae accuses Meth of stealing his copy of *The Killer*, a 1989 action thriller by Hong Kong director John Woo. Meth nonchalantly ducks any responsibility, saying the tape disappeared when "niggas came over for 40s and blunts." Then Ghostface barges in and ruins everyone's day by informing them that "Shameek from 220 just got busted in his head two times." The gravity of his statement dissolves into comedy once again when someone asks, "Is he dead?" Ghost goes off on the heckler, talking about "all types of blood all over the place," before rallying the troops to go retaliate against the "niggas in the black Land [Cruiser]" who perpetrated the hit. Instead of sounding gratuitous, this dramatization actually plays out an all-too-familiar scenario of street life, shining a light on the chilling consequences of Black-on-Black violence. A warbling one-bar loop of "Oooh" from the Charmels' "As Long as I've Got You" underscores the dialogue, teasing the use of that same song later in "C.R.E.A.M."

Explaining the inspiration behind this aural cinema vérité, Raekwon says, "That's the organics of what we wanted to do at the time. We wanted y'all to feel our personalities and see how we would act on a normal level. The movie *The Killer* was out right then on DVD or whatever and, yo, we watched that shit every day, like [while] makin' records."[31]

The skit gives way to the sound of someone banging on a metal door with a baseball bat—actually the furious slap of a snare drum recorded in the elevator shaft of Firehouse Studio. As it segues into a drum break from Lonnie Liston Smith's "Spinning Wheel" (1970)—the same one, incidentally, used in A Tribe Called Quest's "Can I Kick It" (1990)—the sampled voice of Robin Williams shouts, "Good morning, Vietnam!"

from the 1987 movie of the same name. This is the setup for "Wu-Tang 7th Chamber," a track driven by a simple piano melody—possibly played by RZA, since there was no sample cleared—and a guitar lick from Otis Redding's "Down in the Valley" (1965). As one of the few album cuts besides "Protect Ya Neck" and "Da Mystery of Chessboxin'" to feature the majority of the group, it clocks in at just over six minutes, which was long for a rap song, considering radio played nothing more than two and a half minutes. In fact, most of the songs on *36 Chambers* are over four minutes, showing RZA's utter disregard for any music industry standards.

On a track where group members were basically battling each other for bars, you can actually hear the grit and tenacity in their voices as each attempts to outdo the previous MC. Such "friendly" intrasquad competition serves as the group's form of quality control. As RZA explains, "The input that we have to each other's lyrics is that we don't allow somebody to come weak. We will sit there and criticize each other so the criticism is what makes us all strong with the lyrics."[32] Since all the MCs on "Wu-Tang 7th Chamber" drop memorable verses, it's up to the listener to debate whose is the best. For those who loved Lucky Charms cereal growing up, however, GZA smothers the competition with "I came down with phat tracks that combine and interlock / Like gettin' smashed with a cinder block / Pow! Now it's all over / Niggas seeing pink hearts, yellow moons, orange stars and green clovers."

Following on the heels of this raucous, up-tempo track, "Can It Be All So Simple" offers a more laid-back vibe, perfect for further introspection. RZA digs into his bag of soul sides and comes up with Gladys Knight's rendition of Barbra Streisand's "The Way We Were" (1974), which he uses for its spoken-word intro: "Hey, you know, everybody's talking about the good ole days," as well as the line that becomes the song's hook. This track introduces the dynamic duo of Raekwon and Ghostface, who display an effortless, natural chemistry as they take a trip down memory lane.

While childhood is generally considered a time of innocence and carefree living, we actually find out that life was not so simple for these two children of the ghetto. Rae raps, "Ignorant and mad young, wanted to be the one / 'Til I got, 'Blau, blau, blau,' felt one / Yeah my pops was a fiend since 16 / shootin' that 'that's that shit' in his bloodstream." In just a few lines, we find out that he was shot as a teenager and that his father was a heroin addict—hardly good ole days. Ghost, meanwhile, contrasts his current situation in life—"bustin' shots" and "runnin' up in spots and makin' shit hot" (i.e., armed robbery)—with his fantasy of owning yachts, gold records, and "enough land to go and plant my own sess [marijuana] crops." Their revelations amount to some of the most poignant expressions in rap—especially coming from two hard rocks from the projects. Incidentally, both exhibit the classic symptoms of PTSD, the result of a life growing up in such a harsh and unforgiving environment.

RZA, who tailor-makes his music for his MCs, provides the ideal musical accompaniment, choosing as his main loop the bass "whomp" of Labi Siffre's "I Got The . . . " (1975)—a sample also subsequently used in Eminem's "My Name Is" (1998). To this steady bounce, he adds soothing subsonic bass tones contrasted against a high-pitched melodic line, Gladys Knight's voice, and his usual ear candy floating in and out of the mix. The cumulative effect is both spooky and sentimental, with far more substance and emotion than you'd expect from your average rap song.

As the track fades, RZA, already demonstrating his mastery of branding, includes part of an actual radio interview with Method Man and Raekwon in which they give a short description of each member of the group. When the interviewer asks them about their ultimate goal, Meth simply replies, "Domination, baby," adding, "We tryin' to make a business of this, man. . . . We tryin' to make our own shit so when our children, our seeds, grow up they got somethin' fo' themselves." Almost prophetically, Rae chimes in, "Longevity! We ain't tryin' to hop in and hop out right quick, know what I'm saying? We out for the gusto, and we gonna keep it raw, know what I'm sayin'?" Conspicuously absent is any mention of money or fame, the usual aspirations for new artists breaking into the industry. From jump, then, it was obvious that Wu-Tang operated differently from most crews.

"Da Mystery of Chessboxin'," named after the film from which Ghostface Killah took his nom de plume, falls squarely in the middle of the selection. By now these movie snippets have become an integral part of the album's landscape, and RZA picks a choice line: "A game of chess is like a sword fight, you must think first before you move," from *Shaolin vs. Wu-Tang*, to introduce this joint. He also borrows a line from one of his all-time favorite films, *Five Deadly Venoms*, "Toad style is immensely strong and immune to nearly any weapon." "Chessboxin'" most notably features the sole appearance by Masta Killa on the album. What's even more surprising, considering the complexity of his verse, is that this rhyme is the first one he ever wrote.

After missing out on "Protect Ya Neck," Masta Killa explains, "When it came down to 'Mystery of Chessboxin,' later on, this is when I decided to take the art form of rhyming a little bit more serious. I started striving to construct my own rhymes. Now let me write something down on paper and see if I really got the talent to do this, OK. So, I wrote down some thoughts that I had, and I took them to GZA on paper. Gave him the paper, 'What choo think about this?' He read it and said, 'You wrote this?' I said, 'Yeah, I wrote that.' He said, 'Wow, if you can learn to say that, you got a job.'"[33]

> Homicide's illegal and death is the penalty
> What justifies the homicide, when he dies in his own iniquity?
> It's the master of the Mantis Rapture comin' at ya
> We have an APB on an MC Killer,
> Looks like the work of a master,
> Evidence indicates that his stature,
> Merciless like a terrorist hard to capture.
> *from Masta Killa on "Da Mystery of Chessboxin'"*

The most humble, low-key member of the Clan adds, "They didn't really need another ninth member. I mean those eight MCs of Wu-Tang was far more than enough to be successful. They didn't need me, you know what I mean, but RZA bein' who he is, and the musical coordinator of everything left this particular track for whoever's gonna make this last shot to be a part of this project. Here's your chance. Now many other MCs threw their darts that night, yunno. My particular dart, I guess he judged it and said this was the one that was gonna make it because, like I said, there was other MCs there who threw darts that night, but I guess this one fit the criteria of what he was lookin' for and, boom, the rest is history."[34]

Killah Priest (Walter Reed), a student of GZA's who eventually went on to a prolific solo career, appearing on many Wu-Tang projects, is one of the other MCs in question. But according to RZA, "Killah Priest is a different type of dude than Masta Killa, and so I don't think he was going to be a Wu-Tang Clan member. And Masta Killa and GZA were so bonded. And Masta Killa was so unique and honorable. 'Da Mystery of Chessboxin'" became his official stamp."[35]

Masta Killa doesn't have the only standout performance on "Chessboxin.'" U-God, Deck, Rae, Dirty, and Ghost all contribute solid verses, and Method Man, who was becoming the hook master, comes up with "My people are you with me where ya at? / In the front, in the back killa bees on attack," delivered in his gravelly basso. Dirty yodels for the first time, previewing what was to become a trademark of his singing/rapping style, and U-God, too, adds his first proper verse to the album after his quick four bars on "Protect Ya Neck." In order to keep the focus on the vocal performances, RZA intentionally keeps the music stripped down, using only the popular old-school drum break from "Tramp" (1967) by Otis Redding and Carla Thomas, a filtered bass line, and harpsichord. He also has someone chanting "boo-ha" in the background, which he fades in and out of the mix.

The onslaught continues on "Wu-Tang Clan Ain't Nothin' to Fuck With," a high-energy, sample-heavy cut and one of the highlights of the album. RZA also uses these samples most creatively. Take the "Underdog Theme," composed by W. Watts Biggers, from the popular Saturday-morning cartoon that ran from 1964 to 1973. He snatches the first five seconds in his ASR-10 sampler; slows it down dramatically; and then cuts, splices, and reassembles different parts to create a haunting harmony that sounds like a chorus singing, "Wuuu." For drums, he jacks another popular old-school break by the Lafayette Afro Rock Band, "Hihache" (Musidisc, 1973)—most notably used on Biz Markie's "Nobody

Beats the Biz" (Prism Records, 1987)—enhancing it with finger snaps and a snare hit from "Papa Was Too" (Atlantic, 1966) by Joe Tex. He also uses a rain sound effect from the Dramatics' "In the Rain" and the words "tiger style" from the Shaw Brothers' *Executioners of Shaolin* (1977).

Though Deck and Meth drop verses on this track, lyrically, this is RZA's show as he screams the chorus, spits some intricate lines, and then includes another lengthy shout-out thanking everyone from the five boroughs down to the radio station at Morgan State University, an HBCU in Baltimore. In his verse, he raps, "I be tossin', enforcin', my style is awesome / I'm causin' more family feud than Richard Dawson / And the survey says, 'You're dead!' / Fatal flying guillotine chops off your fuckin' head!" Once again, he takes fellow children of the seventies back to their youth, referencing the British host of the popular TV game show *Family Feud* that began its lengthy run in 1976. Dawson asked questions based on audience polls, and to check on a contestant's answer, he announced, "Survey says." The other, more obscure reference to a fatal flying guillotine alludes to the bizarre weapon used to remotely cut off people's heads in the 1977 kung fu movie of the same title.

Never one to be overshadowed, however, Meth drops some fire of his own, interpolating the popular Broadway standard "Tomorrow," originally sung by Andrea McArdle in *Annie*, as he says, "The Meth will come out tomorrow / Styles, conditions, bizarro, bizarro / Flow with more afro than Rollo / Comin' to a fork in the road which way to go / Just follow." Meth, the pop-culture maven, reels off a reference to *Sanford and Son*, the seventies sitcom starring comedian Redd Foxx and set in a Watts junkyard. Rollo, a recurring character played by actor Nathaniel Taylor, sometimes appears wearing an afro and dashiki to show his African pride. Such references not only inspire nostalgia but also forge a kind of schoolyard bond with the group, who, it turns out, were watching the same shows as you.

The next track, "C.R.E.A.M.," one of the album's power-houses, distills everything that people like about the group into a four-minute song. First of all, take the title's acronym, which stands for "Cash Rules Everything Around Me." What better way to describe the capitalist curse under which we all live? We are all slaves to the almighty dollar, and instead of celebrating this system of economic slavery—and its natural outgrowth, materialism, in which much rap revels—Raekwon and Inspectah Deck reflect on how growing up in poverty has affected their lives.

They recorded the track, originally titled "Lifestyles of the Mega-Rich," around 1989, when both MCs were still deep in the street life.[36] In fact, Deck says that when he wrote his verse, "I was standing in front of the building with crack in my sock, man. I used to carry a notepad on me and shit, and just jot down some shit." Initially they had been free-styling on the track when RZA told them to paint a picture and come with a story. "RZA originally recorded like maybe three verses a piece from me and Chef," says Deck, "and the song was like extremely too long, but RZA kept it. And what we did, when we did the album, I took the first eight bars of the first verse and the last eight bars of the second verse and put it together and made a 16. That's the 16 y'all hear."[37]

A man with a dream with plans to make cream
Which failed; I went to jail at the age of fifteen
A young buck sellin' drugs and such, who never had much
Tryin' to get a clutch of what I could not touch.
from Inspectah Deck's verse on "C.R.E.A.M."

Meanwhile, Raekwon says he ended up rewriting his original verse for the track. "I had wrote it, and somethin' told me, 'Yo, let your niggas hear your verse first,'" he says, so he took it to Power. "He was like, 'It's aiight, but it's missing somethin.'" Trusting Power's opinion, Rae went home and worked on it. "I wrote 'C.R.E.A.M.' sittin' by the stove like, yo, this nigga's gonna make me write this shit again?" he says. "And the first words came, 'I grew up on the crime side,' and once I wrote that, it took me back to my reality of where I was at, where I was livin', and I just started givin' y'all facts, yunno? Boom. 'My mom's bounced on old man,' I never had a father. I grew up with 80 percent of niggas who ain't have no father, so I knew that was something everyone would be able to relate to."[38]

> But it was just a dream for a teen who was fiend
> Started smoking woolies at 16
> And runnin' up in gates and doin' hits for high stakes
> Makin' my way on fire escapes.
>
> *from Raekwon's verse on "C.R.E.A.M."*

"Woolies" is slang for a blunt filled with crack and marijuana. "Smokin' cracks and weed back in the day, that was our glory times, yunno. We did that because it was expensive, yunno, until people started losing their lives or getting strung out," says Raekwon. "All that shit is like real shit. Fire escape action, know what I mean? Divin' in my mom's window [when the cops were chasing]."[39]

In addition to standout verses by Deck and Rae, this track has one of the most memorable hooks in hip-hop, courtesy of Method Man. Often used by Five Percenters, backronyms became popular among the Wu and their affiliates too. As

Meth explains, "My boy Rader Ruckus, he took 'cream' [and broke it down to], 'cash rules everything around me.' That was the flyest shit I ever heard in my life, so, that just popped in my head, and, OK, let's put some other words to it."

As a child, Meth often hung out with his friend Hassan Johnson, who went on to play drug dealer Wee-Bey Brice on *The Wire*. Meth remembers Johnson's father playing a hot twelve-inch that was out at the time called "Money (Dollar Bill Y'all)," by Jimmy Spicer. An early rap hit produced by Russell Simmons and Larry Smith, the song was, coincidentally, released by Jules Rifkind's Spring Records in '83. On the hook, Spicer chanted, "Dolla bill y'all, dolla bill y'all / dolla, dolla, dolla, dolla dollar bill y'all," which Meth partially borrowed as a homage to hip-hop's roots.

The final piece of the equation is the track itself. "C.R.E.A.M." is driven by a forgotten seven-inch of vintage soul by the Charmels called "As Long as I Got You" (Volt, 1967). Originally known as the Dixiebelles and later the Tonettes, the group, which consisted of Barbara McCoy (lead), Mary Hunt (soprano), Mildred Pratchett (alto), and Eula Jean Rivers (baritone), only recorded four singles for Stax between 1966 and 1968. None were hits—including "As Long as I've Got You," written by the talented team of Isaac Hayes and David Porter—and the group was dropped by the label in 1969. RZA resurrects the opening piano line as his main loop, augmented by snippets of the Charmels' vocal performances to make a truly haunting, poignant, and powerful composition. Never before has a rap song offered so much introspection and raw emotion—along with a catchy hook.

When the single for "C.R.E.A.M." was released, it proved to be a tipping point for the Clan, sealing the group's popularity.

"When we dropped 'C.R.E.A.M.,' that's when we knew it wasn't gonna be the same no more," says U-God. "Right after we did Arsenio Hall, we knew we was takin' off. We started seeing sales triple and quadruple, and it just kept going and going. And we was like, 'Wow, OK.' And that's when we knew we made it through the threshold."[40]

In his memoir, he wrote, "The realism on 'C.R.E.A.M.' is what resonates with so many people all over the world. People everywhere know that sentiment of being slaves to the dollar. Cash is king, and we are its lowly subjects. That's pretty much the case in every nation around the world, the desperation to put your life and your freedom on the line to make a couple dollars. Whether you're working, stripping, hustling, or slinging, whether you're a business owner or homeless, cash rules everything around us."[41] While striking a serious chord, the Clan hit paydirt with that one.

Though U-God does not even appear on the next skit, "Torture," in which Meth and Rae jokingly come up with horrific ways to terrorize each other, his influence is certainly felt. "Yes, I am the inventor of the game 'Torture,'" he admits. "It was just a game we made up 'cause we was bored. We ain't have nothin' better to do on the block, just sit there and wait for [crack] sales to come in, so we made up this little game, yunno. And the game was to think of the most heinous thing that you could do to a mu'fucka, but funny. Keep it funny, though, know what I'm sayin'?"[42]

As far as the album sequence goes, RZA places all the songs that had been previously released as singles or B sides in the last third of the record. These include "Protect Ya Neck" and its original B side, "After the Laughter Comes Tears," now renamed "Tearz," and "Method Man," the B side of Loud's release of "Protect Ya Neck." Even though "Protect" had been the one to crack it open for them, Method Man's solo showcase is the song that has "hit" written all over it. Steve Rifkind recalls, "I was in New York during the summer of 1993 and the 'Method Man' song came on in a club I was at, and motherfuckers were running to the dance floor. They were losing their minds over that song."[43] In reality, however, the track was already a couple of years old by the time *36 Chambers* was released, and several labels, including Cold Chillin', had already heard and passed on it.

To create the musical arrangement, RZA slows down the drum break from "Sport" off the popular *Hustler's Convention* album. Channeling Monk, he plays a simple piano melody and bass line. That's pretty much all the accompaniment Meth needs to let loose his barrage of pop-culture allusions. In the course of the rhyme, he references his preferred peanut butters (Skippy, Jif, and Peter Pan), Saran Wrap, Dr. Seuss ("green eggs and ham"), Fat Albert, White Owl cigars, Humpty Hump, and a popular seventies ad campaign for Tootsie Rolls. He also interpolates many well-known songs, including the Rolling Stones' "Get Off of My Cloud" (1965); "Pat-a-cake, Pat-a-cake, Baker's Man," a folk ditty from 1698; Captain Sky's "Super Sporm," a rap from 1978; *I Taught I Taw a Putty Tat*, from Merry Melodies (1947); "Chim Chim Cheree" (1964) from *Mary Poppins*; and, of course, Hall & Oates's "The Method of Modern Love" (1985), which he uses to spell out his alias. Meth does it with such effortless style and charisma, it's no wonder he is the group's breakout star.

Following up this stellar performance comes "Protect Ya Neck," the independently released street single that set everything off. Even though it supposedly sold ten thousand copies in its first few months of release in 1993, the song was actually a slow burner that didn't pick up steam nationally until around the summer. But by then, it was everywhere. RZA tacks on an actual radio request for the song to introduce it on the album.

After two high-energy selections, RZA, once again, changes up the vibe with "Tearz," a remix of the first song he and Ghost ever recorded, "After the Laughter Comes Tears." The track takes its title and main loop from another obscure soul sapphire unearthed by RZA, "After Laughter (Comes Tears)," Wendy Rene's first single for Stax. The 1964 release became a local hit but failed to chart nationally. Mary Frierson, who changed her name to Wendy Rene when she signed to Stax at age sixteen, had a very short-lived career there, so this amazing record might have been lost to history if not for the RZA.

It's a record meant for sampling, as the organ intro used as the main loop—incidentally played by Booker T. Jones of Stax house band Booker T. & the MG's—plays solo before Rene sings the chorus, which RZA uses as the hook. He pins these elements to a shuffling drum loop from "The Boogie Back" (Polydor, 1974) by Roy Ayers, giving Ghostface and himself a plaintive soundtrack to tell some gloomy tales. They start off the song with another skit documenting their day-to-day reality as an argument on the street leads to the death of someone close to them. After the hook plays, RZA launches into a fictional tale about his little brother getting shot while going to the store for his mother. He raps, "I ran frantically, then dropped down to his feet / I saw the blood all over the hot concrete / I picked him up, then I held him by his head / His eyes shut, that's when I knew he was." According to RZA, "That was an exaggerated story, based on stuff that was happening to me and to everybody at the time. It was therapeutic to put it on a record like that. There was a lot of [bad] things going on when I wrote that rhyme."[44] Ghost follows with a story about a promiscuous guy who succumbs to HIV. Both verses speak volumes about the world in which these guys are living. Music seems to be their only way to cope.

Not wanting to end the album on a somber tone, RZA recycles "Wu-Tang 7th Chamber Part II" as a remix. Using the same vocal performances, he adds a sampled GZA chorus from "Clan in the Front" as an intro. But he scraps the whole backing track, replacing it with a gargantuan drum break sampled from the live playing of engineer Carlos Bess and a cavernous keyboard bass line that rattles the speakers. He accentuates the vocal performances with a horn blast or organ stab for a little variation.

At one of the early Wu-Tang sessions he worked, Bess had given RZA a DAT of drum breaks that he had recorded with his partner, Ralph Vargas, for an upcoming vinyl release on the independent JBR Records. RZA eagerly used some of those breaks on several early Wu projects but learned that nothing is free in the music business. Later on, JBR approached him, negotiating a $30,000 fee for their use.[45]

The track concludes with another part of the radio interview with Method Man and Raekwon, in which the interviewer asks them how they would describe their style. The answer, another piece of sampled dialogue from *Shaolin vs. Wu-Tang*, is "It's our secret! Never teach the Wu-Tang." A final reprise of "You best protect ya neck!" quickly echoes and fades out, bringing RZA's first aural cinema to its conclusion at just over the one-hour mark.

Although the streets immediately embraced *Enter the Wu-Tang: 36 Chambers*, which sold thirty thousand units in the first week alone, the album was a slow burner, peaking at only number forty-one on the Billboard 200 chart. Contrast those figures to A Tribe Called Quest's highly anticipated third platter, *Midnight Marauders*, released on the same day, November 9, 1993. Though Tribe was probably at the height of their popularity, *Marauders* reached number eight on the Billboard 200 and went gold within two months, shipping five hundred thousand units by January 1994. By the following January, that record was certified platinum, with one million units sold. In the interim, however, Wu-Tang had actually surpassed Tribe, selling over two million copies in the US alone.

The early critical reception shows the divided reactions to *36 Chambers*. Obviously, *The Source* review, most relevant to the hip-hop community, set the tone for the streets. In it, regular reviewer Da Ghetto Communicator hits the mark when he says, "This album is a throwback to the days of 1986–7 when rap was filled with honesty, greatness, and skill. . . . While their depictions are graphic and extreme, the Wu are not studio savages looking for a gimmick. They are a clan of strong brothers who have banded together to survive in a world hell-bent on consuming them."[46] He ends the 4.5 out of 5 mic review with "This record is harsh, but so is the world which we live in. For B-boys 'n girls who come from the core of the hard, this is the hip-hop album you've been waiting for."[47] Hip-hop aficionados would agree that this review is spot-on.

Rolling Stone, the grand dame of the music press, didn't even review the album until months later in April 1994, assigning it to former intern Touré Neblett, an Emory dropout who went by his first name. He approached the album with a definite bias, saying, "Wu-Tang make underground rap: low on hype and production values, high on the idea that indigence is an integral part of blackness," a statement that in itself was way off the mark.[48] Demonstrating an almost comical class consciousness, he adds, "It's as though the artists feel that it's not enough to rhyme like have-nots and look like have-nots. They've got to sound like have-nots, too."[49] Though he seems to like the album, later on in the review, when commenting on the "Torture" skit, he curiously labels the group "homoerotic"—another completely off-base observation from a guy who went on to become a mainstream cultural critic.

The bottom line is that as well-regarded as *Enter the Wu-Tang: 36 Chambers* is today, on its release, it proved to be a challenging record that everyone had an opinion about. But like hip-hop itself, its popularity emerged from a groundswell of support from the streets, from the culture, and from people just like the Clan, who recognized that they finally had a voice. Rifkind sums it up, saying, "That album will go down in history as one of the best albums ever made, hip-hop or otherwise. They proved, more than anything, that you could sell a shitload of records without tons of radio play."[50] But in the big picture, *36 Chambers* was just the beginning—the first salvo in the Wu revolution. After planting their flag, Wu-Tang set the stage for the next five solo albums to follow, heralding the arrival of a movement as deep and impactful as hip-hop itself.

CHAPTER 9

METHOD MAN / TICAL

The first time Method Man saw his self-titled video on TV, he says, "I was eating white rice with ketchup on it. No food in the house. I think it was Thanksgiving too. I was feeling bad like, 'Damn, this shit is not popping.' This fucking rap shit is weak."[1] Despite having a song that dominated New York's Hot 97's playlist for months—accompanied by a highly requested video on *Video Music Box*—it was easy to be disgruntled when you were living like a Viking in an apartment with no heat or hot water.[2] Meanwhile, the Clan's debut had sold thirty thousand copies in its first week alone. Though Meth had already signed with Def Jam, corporate checks were cut by ax, not chainsaw, so while waiting on that paper, he was just living day to day, trying to keep his weight up. On top of all that, *The Source* had just come out to Staten Island for their first real coverage of the Clan.

"Our first interview we did with *The Source*, where we took the pictures with the Columbia suits on, nigga, I was makin' [crack] sales between them shots like, 'How many you want?' Know what I'm sayin'," says Meth. "This is real. Real life, real rap, no filters, no nothing, man. We like bummy ass niggas tryin' to fuckin' do somethin' right. And it got to the point where I didn't care if we was makin' money on the road because I was not on that block—whatever gets me off the block."[3] The transition from the illegal life was obviously not an easy one to negotiate. However, he's quick to add, "The funny thing is being on the road for months, I missed the block so much I wanted to go back."[4]

Even before *36 Chambers* dropped, the group stayed on the road. In addition to promoting the album, shows were a financial necessity, providing them with a meager income— sometimes only one hundred dollars a night, split nine ways. Following the record's release, however, touring ratcheted up into high gear, and the Clan only returned to town to shoot videos and do laundry. In fact, taking advantage of the usual holiday downtime at the end of the year, they shot "Mystery of Chessboxin'" and "C.R.E.A.M.," as well as reshooting "Method Man" for MTV, since the network complained about the prevalence of guns and blunts in the original version.

While the original had cost them $5,000, RZA made a deal with director Gerald "Gee-Bee" Barclay—who was part of the huge influx of Liberians to Park Hill in the eighties due to civil war at home and had attended school with members of the group—to reshoot "Method Man" and do a video for "Chessboxin'" for $35,000. Meanwhile, he arranged for Ralph McDaniels of *Video Music Box* to direct the video for "C.R.E.A.M."[5] With their name ringing bells and a label behind them, the bottom line may have increased slightly, but these videos were still low budget by any standard. Regardless, both Barclay and McDaniels managed to turn in memorable visual accompaniments to the music that helped define the Wu-Tang aesthetic. "Chessboxin'" featured human chess pieces battling on a life-sized board, and "C.R.E.A.M.," shot in Park Hill, made Raekwon's limited edition Snow Beach Polo parka an instant collector's item.

After initially hearing "Protect Ya Neck," Tracey Waples, an A&R rep at hip-hop's premier label, Def Jam, zeroed in on Method Man's nascent star power. She came out to Staten Island to hear more, reporting back to her boss, Russell Simmons, that she wanted to sign him. As Meth recalls, "We all went to sit down with Russell and Tracey Waples at some little restaurant. It was mad bougie [bourgeoisie] in that bitch. Their offer was about 250 grand and shit [for the group]. So, RZA's like, 'I'll give you one muthafucka.' They went for it."[6] At age twenty-three, Meth, the youngest member of the Clan, officially signed to Def Jam on August 19, 1993, for $180,000—three times what the whole group had received from Loud.

Here he was, however, months later, still mired in poverty, watching the video for a song he says he didn't even like. "I liked it at first," he begrudgingly admits. "But then the way the thing got so much love, I was buggin'." Even his Wu brothers teased him, calling Meth "the Michael Jackson of rap." While certainly a ham, he was also very much a team player, so it felt awkward to get singled out like that. If his initial acceptance of newfound fame was less than enthusiastic, it was at least understandable. "I haven't changed one bit," he asserted shortly before his record dropped, "but people are changing their ways around me."

Regardless, Meth's solo launch was all part of the master plan. According to Raekwon, "We felt that ["Method Man"] was the most commercial but still authentic shit that made sense to drop it, you know what I mean? And Meth is your fly, light-skin nigga, so we already see the girls start lovin' him. But we always knew it was *Tical* to go first because he was our get busy nigga, our Redman."[7] While "Protect Ya Neck" had been the battering ram that broke down the door, it was "Method Man," the B side to Loud's release, that kept the buzz alive during the recording of *36 Chambers*. It made perfect sense that Meth would have the first opportunity to represent as a solo artist. But that was only made possible because Ol' Dirty Bastard, who had scored a solo deal with Elektra first, took so long to deliver his album.

According to Meth, *Tical* was made under less-than-ideal conditions. "There was a lot of turmoil and stuff goin' on," he recalls. "I had to record on the fly. We were on the road, a road trip to LA, and a lot of music got lost in the flood, so he [RZA] had to redo a lot of stuff, and some of the beats didn't make it."[8] After the shows, when everyone else headed back to the hotel, Meth and RZA had studio time booked at the nearest local spot. He says, "I always felt like my album was real pieced together [because] I recorded in San Francisco, Texas, LA, everywhere. I was recording in some of the weirdest spots. Some of these places had mice and shit and coat hangers with a stocking cap wrapped around it for fucking popper stoppers. When we in the studio recording, on some days, like when we did 'Stimulation,' I couldn't record the way I wanted to because my voice was damn near gone from performing that night."[9]

The flood he referenced occurred at RZA's new address at 9 Michelle Court in Mariner's Harbor, Staten Island, where he moved with his wife and baby after securing the Loud deal. The split-level condo came equipped with a basement, which naturally became his music studio. According to RZA, "As soon as we had finished *36 Chambers*, I already had Inspectah Deck's album, Method Man's album prepared. Because back in those days we had floppy disks and I would make all the beats—Method Man's session, Deck's session, and I was ready to go. Here comes the flood that wiped away about 160 floppy disks. Because I didn't think there'd be a flood I had [the disks] on the floor, under the keyboard. Wu-Tang was out doing some shows in Cleveland, whatever. We came back—water's up this high, washed that all away. Back to the drawing board."[10]

Along with such random accidents, more serious concerns were popping off at home. Though touring allowed a momentary respite from their physical environment, the ghetto cast a long shadow. On Sunday, March 13, 1994, Dontae Hawkins, U-God's two-year-old son, was playing with his babysitter in the project courtyard when he got caught in the crossfire between two rival gunmen. One of the perpetrators actually picked up the toddler, using him as a human shield, resulting in gunshot wounds to Dontae's kidney, pancreas, and hand. Lucky to have survived, he had to undergo years of grueling physical therapy as a result. If that incident wasn't bad enough, tragedy struck again the following night, when Wu-Tang affiliate Two-Cent (Erron Lewis) was killed by an unidentified assailant on Park Hill Avenue.[11] In an environment ruled by poverty and crime, human life seemingly had no value.

On the opposite side of the country, when Wu-Tang Clan should have been celebrating the gold certification of 36 Chambers, which had shipped five hundred thousand units in only five months, they were instead thanking their lucky stars following a close call with the cops. After returning from a trip to the mall, Meth, Raekwon, Ghost, and their Loud rep, Bill "Bigga B" Operin, were riding in a minivan when they noticed the cops on their tail. "I look back, I see like three cop cars and they're radioing for backup. They got shotguns and stuff pointed at us, yunno, and they all made us get out of the car one by one," says Meth.[12] Misinterpreting their directions, however, Ghost exited on the passenger side. "That's when they all clicked they guns on us," says Meth. "Now I'm thinking, is they gonna kill us, or what did I do? They got us on the ground with our faces down on this hot concrete."[13] After cuffing them, the officers kept them immobilized with a foot on their backs while others searched the van. Meth says they were never read their rights but were taken directly to the station for questioning. Only after being released forty-five minutes later without charges were they told that they fit the description of four Black males wanted for a robbery in the area. However, SFPD never issued an apology for such an egregious violation of their civil rights.

Following a command performance of their newly released single, "C.R.E.A.M.," which included fake bills raining down from the rafters and ODB shouting, "The Black man is *God*" multiple times on national TV, RZA, Meth, and Dirty related this all-too-familiar story to host Arsenio Hall, appearing on his show on April 12. Commenting on the incident, RZA said, "It's just another case, you know what I'm sayin', how the police be treatin' all of us, really, whether you successful or unsuccessful. If you got this tone of skin, they gonna kind a really bring it on you. It's the same thing everybody else be goin' through, it's just it happened to us and made us realize that all that gold record and all that whatever, whatever, it don't really save you from the brutality or from the shit you gotta go through out here."[14]

To further compound their pain, on that very same night in Park Hill, Ernest "Kase" Sayon, another friend of the Clan's, was choked to death at the hands of Officer Donald Brown after a routine stop in a case that mirrored the murder of Eric Garner by cops twenty years later. According to the report of medical examiner Dr. Charles S. Hirsch, "The cause of Mr. Sayon's death is asphyxia by compression of chest and neck while rear-handcuffed and prone on the ground immediately following a struggle in which he sustained blunt impacts to his head and trunk."[15] Yet, inexplicably, no charges were ever filed against Officer Brown—incidentally, a Black officer who had grown up in the area and was not well liked.[16]

As America has witnessed countless examples of police violence toward Blacks captured on video—most recently in the case of George Floyd in Minneapolis in 2020—there can be absolutely no question of an implicit bias against an entire community. The refusal to indict and convict cops, consistent in both the cases of Sayon and Garner, also points to a broken justice system mired in institutional racism. While cell-phone evidence of such incidents is commonplace today, rappers have been bearing witness to the police brutality in their communities since the art form started. RZA was correct in noting that no amount of money and fame could insulate them from the harsh realities they faced every day for the crime of being Black.

Unlike *36 Chambers*, a very focused, calculated effort to which the whole Clan contributed over a period of many months while working out of a single studio, *Tical* was constructed under completely different circumstances. Recorded mostly on the road, under pressure, with all of life's changes and other distractions happening concurrently, the album is largely a collaboration between RZA and Meth. Relying less on simple piano melodies or slabs of vintage soul, RZA makes a conscious decision to not repeat himself. Though embracing a more standard album format with fewer skits and less kung fu dialogue, he also pushes more boundaries production-wise, crafting a much deeper, darker sound characterized by minor chords and subsonic bass tones. For someone who's tasted commercial success, he seems to head in the opposite direction that one is expected to go. But RZA is actually beholden to higher ideals here—bringing hip-hop back to its underground roots.

The music not only complements but accentuates the darkness in Meth's volatile state of mind. "The hunger was there because I really wanted to get that shit done," he says. "I was the nigga on the outside looking in, so I was comfortable. I knew that they didn't know what to expect from me, so anything that I put out was gonna work for me because I felt that it would. I had that energy and aura about me at that time, I had the upper hand. I didn't have to live up to a first album because there wasn't one. Everything would be fresh and new."[17]

At the same time, he took this opportunity very seriously, saying, "Yunno, it's like we're the voice of a million people from the same environment, the same struggle we from that just can't be heard 'cause they don't have the outlet. Now when you got that on your shoulders, everything that come outta your mouth gotta be jewels. 'Cause it's like these people are watching. So, you may broaden your shit and get a bigger audience, but make sure your mentality stay direct or on the straight and narrow 'cause a lot of people could easily be led in the wrong direction, and hard to be led in the right. Yunno, that's why a lot of this hip-hop shit is just copycats—a lot of copycats get over. Let's just stop this, all right. We just gonna start pointing the finger anyway at all the fake hip-hop shit."[18]

Fans of real hip-hop responded. Released on November 15, 1994, almost exactly a year after the Wu-Tang debut, *Tical* reached number four on the Billboard 200 and number one on the Top R&B / Hip-Hop Albums. Only a couple of months later, the album was certified gold, and on July 13, 1995, it reached platinum, shipping over one million units. Following the plan precisely, Meth did exactly what he was supposed to do: blow up.

* * *

Tical opens with its title track, and probably one of the creepiest, most theatrical introductions to a rap album ever. A somber flute melody plays, punctuated by the sound of distant thunder. "You've been lucky. I wish I got you last time," says a voice from the movie *Ten Tigers from Kwangtung*, which RZA recycles from the Wu-Tang debut, using the exact line: "*En garde*, I'll let you try my Wu-Tang style," along with those familiar fighting sounds. Underscoring this dialogue are frantic strings, origin unknown. "From the tip-top," says Method Man as an orchestral crescendo from the *Ten Tigers* score by Eddie H. Wang heightens the tension before the beat finally drops. For those first forty-five seconds, however, you are removed from time and place, propelled into a Wu-Tang wormhole.

What kind of rapper would begin their album with "Promenade" from *Pictures at an Exhibition* (1874), a well-known classical piece by Russian composer Modest Mussorgsky? Avid viewers of eighties kung fu films on VHS would recognize that opening flute solo as the theme music for World-Northal, a distributor of arthouse films that became a major player in the kung fu craze. Their logo appeared before the opening credits of films they distributed, accompanied by that classical composition.[19] Obviously, where RZA was concerned, anything was fair fodder for his ASR—even corporate logo music, which he figured would fly below the radar of the sample detectives.

Meth finally appears, speaking in falsetto as he alternately repeats the hook, "What's that shit they be smokin'? . . . Tical . . . Tical. Pass it over here . . . Tical . . . Tical," pulling you deeper into his realm. By this time, Wu-Tang had already introduced their Staten Island slang for weed. According to Meth, "It started off as 'method,' then we started saying 'methical,' know what I'm sayin'. Then niggas started using 'tical' all over the place like, 'We goin' to the store, tical. We goin' to get lifted, tical. Let's go up in the stairwell and get lifted, tical.'" Though Meth derives his stage name from the herb he loves to smoke, on this song, he is actually talking about (and under the influence of) something else entirely.

PCP (phencyclidine), commonly known on the street as angel dust, is a mind-altering substance originally introduced as an anesthetic in the fifties but currently classified as a schedule II drug, along with cocaine and opium derivatives like heroin and fentanyl. "Dust is a powerful drug. I was dusted when I did ['Tical']," says Meth. "I was gone! I just wanted that to be known."[20] In lower amounts, dust mimics the effects of alcohol inebriation—slurred speech, unsteady gait, loss of balance—but higher doses can lead to hallucinations, distorted perception of sound, seizures, and even violent behavior. The problem with such an illegal and unregulated street drug is that you have absolutely no idea how much is too much until you see alien spaceships landing on your rooftop. Meth's confession makes perfect sense considering the track itself sounds dusted, with its spooky keys and a growling, languorous four-note bass line. His uninhibited performance takes it over the edge with lines like "I'ma grow like a rash on your nasty ass / In a whip with no brakes and I'm hittin' the gas."

This narcotic opener plunges right into the next joint, "Biscuits," one of the many slang terms for guns, which does not even appear in the song's hook. Instead, this track plays more like a ferocious freestyle, with Meth mixing mama jokes and other insults with graphic threats like "Let me pull that brain out your ass with a hanger." A master at adapting popular tunes and lyrics into his own idiom, he "samples" an old country standard, "Just an Echo in the Valley" (1932) by Harry Woods, Jimmy Campbell, and Reg Connelly, changing the words slightly: "Just an echo, yoo-hoo / We be livin' in the valley, yoo-hoo / It may be difficult to bring back sweet memories of you." While American icon Bing Crosby made the song famous, Meth probably heard the awkward character Alfalfa sing it on *Little Rascals*, a Depression-era children's show whose popular reruns aired throughout the seventies.

"Biscuits" is one of two tracks where Meth's basso is almost lost in the mix, drowning in the impossibly low-end tones from the Novation Bass Station that dominate. Aside from another crushing drum loop from Carlos Bess's *Funky Drummer Breaks* series, the only other recognizable sample on the track comes from "Angel" by James Clarke and Brian Bennett. The 1974 album *Suspended Woodwind* on which it appears bears the imprint of KPM, a label highly regarded for their film and TV soundtrack music. RZA samples only a few notes of keyboard into his ASR-10, speeding it up dramatically and then replaying it on the keys of his sampler to create the melodic riff that drives the track. He juxtaposes this loop with an operatic wail, which has also been sampled and sped up—most likely the voice of singer Blue Raspberry, who makes her debut later on.

The sound of a car skidding and crashing opens up "Bring the Pain," the album's first single, which reached number forty-five on the Billboard Hot 100 as well as the top spot on the Hot Dance chart. Far from being his latest material, however, this track was one of the first ones RZA ever made with the SP-1200 drum machine back in 1991.[21] A fairly simple construction based off a loop from "I'm Your Mechanical Man" (Mercury, 1974) by Jerry Butler, this track showcases the creativity of RZA's sampling. Catching a snippet of Butler's vocal, where he is singing "Oooooh" over the drum, bass, and conga groove, he creates a two-bar loop out of it. RZA's penchant for incorporating vocal riffs into his palette of sounds quickly became a trademark of his production style. He knows how to pick 'em, too, because Butler, who had performed in the church choir with Curtis Mayfield as a youth, went on to become the lead singer of Mayfield's group, the Impressions, before going on to a very successful solo career.

Joining Meth on the track is Booster, making his first and only appearance on a Wu-Tang project as he sings/chants the lyrics of popular Jamaican artist Ninjaman, also known as the "Don Gorgon." In patois, he says, "Now you listen to the Gorgon / And a Gorgon sound a reign / And if you jump and come test me / Me ah go lick out dem brain," quoting verbatim from the song "Don't Test the High Power" (VP Records, 1991). The lyrics translate to him bragging that he's the best, and if you want to challenge him, he'll blow your brains out. Meth underscores this threat, which he actually calls a "promise," engaging in a friendly game of "Torture" as the track fades.

When asked about this track's seemingly sadistic title, Meth explained, "What's real in this world really? Pain. You can't hide pain. Once it hits you, you're struck."[22] Thus he raps in the refrain, "Is it real, son, is it really real son? / Let me know it's real son, if it's really real." By measure of his dark lyrics, Meth has obviously seen his share of suffering, but using music as an outlet for expression actually serves as therapy to help ease that pain.

Beginning in the early nineties, activists such as Tipper Gore, C. Delores Tucker, and singer Dionne Warwick launched a well-publicized campaign against violent and misogynistic lyrics, which may as well have been a crusade against rap itself (though "Cop Killer" by Ice T's heavy-metal band Body Count was also singled out). Meth's response was, "Basically, what C. Delores Tucker and them need to do is instead of analyzing the lyrics for all the curse words and the nasty stuff in there, try to figure out why they comin' with these lyrics like this. What have they seen in they life, they time, that at such a young age eighteen, nineteen, twenty, twenty-one that they got lyrics like this?"[23] Touché, Meth.

Between the huge reaction to "Bring the Pain" and the next track, "All I Need," whose remix, featuring R&B chanteuse Mary J. Blige, soared to the top of the Hot Rap, Dance, and R&B charts as well as reaching number three on the Billboard Hot 100, Meth had an unlikely platinum debut on his hands. Typically, an album this raw, dark, and unconventional might appeal to only hard-core heads, but obviously, Meth's natural charm and charisma took him much further. On "All I Need," he pushes street concerns to the side, writing a heartfelt ode to his girlfriend, Tamika, whom he married in 1999. At the same time, he reveals the softer side of a guy adept at flipping a razor blade around his mouth and hiding it under his tongue.

Meth made the song during a three-week swing out to the West Coast while they were staying in San Francisco. "Being out on the road so long, I was missing my girl, so I used my money and flew her out," says Meth. "Me and RZA had joining rooms. So, he's in there making the beat and I swear on everything I love I wrote that record right there while she was laying next to me, asleep in the bed."[24] The ladies didn't even have to hear that romantic tale to appreciate the tenderness, vulnerability, and sincerity in Meth's voice as he says, "Even when the skies were gray / You would rub me on my back and say 'Baby, it'll be OK.'"

Unlike the majority of his productions, RZA bases this track off a well-known hit, "You're All I Need to Get By," by Marvin Gaye and Tammi Terrell. Produced by the all-star production duo of Nick Ashford and Valerie Simpson for the Tamla label, that song sat at the top spot of the Billboard Hot R&B Singles chart for five weeks, one of the longest runs for a number one in 1968. It's hardly surprising, then, that a whole new generation started grooving to the remixes—with versions by RZA and Puff Daddy—that added Mary J. Blige to sing Terrell's part. Even the *New York Times* hailed it as "The Great Summer Love Song of 1995," and the "Razor Sharp Remix" ended up winning a Grammy for Best Rap Performance by a Duo or Group in 1996.

"At first there were nothing but grimy niggas at my shows. Once that record dropped, it was blond hair and silver outfits all in the front! There were a bunch of little Mary J. Bliges running all through the damn party," Meth recalls. "Then we got the Grammy. That was cool. Mary got a few after that but I got that one. I am very proud of that award. It was Mary's first too, so I can always say I was her first."[25] A welcome windfall, the Grammy obviously helped supersize Meth's expanding fan base.

After briefly exposing his heart, Meth returns to bringing the ruckus with "What the Bloodclot!?!," a title that acknowledges the era's strong Jamaican influence. Ever since the late eighties, when KRS-ONE started using a faux patois accent on tracks like "9 mm Go Bang" and lifting the simple piano ditty from the island's 1986 smash hit "Boops" for "The Bridge Is Over," both from his groundbreaking debut *Criminal Minded* (B-Boy, 1987), the long-lost cousins of rap and ragamuffin (Jamaican dance-hall music) started reacquainting themselves. The sudden cachet of the Caribbean sound might have had something to do with its association with the Jamaican posses, strong men in the crack trade. By the early nineties, rap/reggae fusion peaked with the popularity of Jamaican artists like Shabba Ranks and Super Cat and, of course, rappers like KRS, Jamalski, Busta Rhymes, Wise Intelligent of Poor Righteous Teachers, and Fu-Schnickens. Influenced by the West Indian culture around the way—courtesy of Dusty and the dreads—Meth touches it too.

A crude reference to the female menses, "blood clot" is a common cuss word in Jamaica, but used in this context, it means, "What the fuck!" The title apparently describes Method Man's mood when he came up with it, as he recalls, "I remember when I wrote 'What the Blood Clot,' I was on an airplane. We argued about some shit. I forget what, but I knew I was just mad at niggas. That whole verse I was just shooting at everybody on my team [*Laughs*]. I was mad as shit."[26] After RZA sets off the track with some shout-outs, proclaiming, "Shaolin is runnin' this shit son," Meth gets busy right out the box: "All I hear is gunshots, Can I touch something? What the blood clot! / Niggas want tical, make it happen / You know my fuckin' style, fuck the rappin' / We can take it back to '85 if you want to start acting like you live."

Rekindling memories of the crack era, which put a low premium on human life, he slices and dices his way through the track, alternatively boasting and antagonizing would-be opponents. This song is one of two in which he memorializes his friend Kase, who was murdered by the cops. He winds it up with a long shout-out: "To my brothers in the belly of the beast." Rader Ruckus, his partner in crime from the days up in 6-B, when they were cooking crack by candlelight, tops the list, but Meth ends with, "A big major shout-out to my old dad, who just got home on work release." It's hard to take for granted the number of friends he has behind bars, but then again, considering the nature of his prerap hustle, it's a miracle he didn't end up there too.

RZA keeps the beat stripped down and ominous, using a popular sample—"Blind Alley" (Stax, 1972) by the Emotions, which Big Daddy Kane borrowed for his 1988 hit "Ain't No Half Steppin'"—but in a very unconventional way. Instead of going for any of the obvious samples in the song's intro, he takes only the first bar, looping a small section of keyboard with drums and bass and slowing it down dramatically. That's basically the whole track, enhanced with hi-hats and tambourines and, of course, that subsonic bass boom that is omnipresent on the album.

The first cameo from a member of the Clan other than RZA occurs only six tracks deep, when Meth battles Raekwon in "Meth vs. Chef." This is one of those joints that sounds like it could have been an outtake from *36 Chambers*, but it was actually recorded toward the latter stages of *Tical* when RZA and Meth, back from tour, settled into the legendary Chung King Studios on Centre Street in Chinatown to mix the album. Dubbed the "Chung King House of Metal" by Def Jam's Rick Rubin, who did a lot of work there, as well as "the Abbey Road of Hip-Hop" by owner John King, the studio served as the production home for Def Jam artists for the label's first four years and counts Run-DMC, Beastie Boys, and LL Cool J among its early clients.[27]

Battling is an integral part of the Wu-Tang ethos. Sparring with each other on the mic has always been a means by which Clan members maintain their skills, like steel sharpening steel. It's also a way to settle disputes—especially regarding who gets to rhyme on which track. According to Raekwon, "Me and Meth loved the beat. For the world to really know, me and Meth always go back and forth. We like to argue, fuss, and fight with one another, so everybody in the Clan they kinda get a kick out of us two geekin' and lunchin' on each other every time. But, yeah, when we did that song we definitely was on some battling shit."[28] From his perspective, Meth says, "I guess that song was a precursor for things to come because we used to always bump heads and we disagreed on a lot of shit so we would argue with each other. He felt shit should be one way and I felt shit should be another way. It's crazy, way after 'Meth vs. Chef' he became the one I argued with the most."[29] It should also be noted, however, that while most families squabble, a true measure of Meth's respect for his "nemesis" Raekwon was naming his firstborn son after him. Now, that's love.

Kicking off the song are fighting sounds from the film *Ten Tigers from Kwangtung* along with a line from the *36th Chamber of Shaolin*: "You are worthy of a general. If you want to fight, fight with me, one to one, man to man," both serving to connect back to the Wu-Tang debut. RZA reprises the frantic string loop that opened the album, later developing it into a whole track on Raekwon's solo debut. Meanwhile, Lounge Lo, one of Meth's buddies (and Cappadonna's brother), steps up as ring announcer, introducing the verbal joust. To maintain focus on the MCs, RZA, once again, keeps the track simple, using the well-known drum break from "Papa Was Too" (1966) by Joe Tex, supplemented by his own programming. He also creates a simple melody out of no less than three sounds layered on top of each other, another innovation for which he would become known.

But one of the producer's greatest contributions to hip-hop production is the use of pure noise in a musical context. Once again, he did not introduce this concept—Marley Marl really pioneered it in the mideighties, and the Bomb Squad, Public Enemy's production team of the Shocklee brothers (Hank and Keith) and Eric "Vietnam" Saddler, later took it into the stratosphere. But, like the best punk rockers, RZA exploited noise as a crucial part of his sonic arsenal. "The cool thing about music, in my opinion, is that everything has a musical connotation," he says. "Whether it's the flapping wings of a butterfly, or the running sound of water, or the crackling of fire. Even the noise of a subway train passing over at four a.m. It all has a musical connotation. So, when a sampler came out, I made it my business to sample those kinds of sounds."[30] Like a disciple of John Cage, he adds, "Any noise can be manipulated to music. I'm a big kung fu movie fan, so I would pull sounds from kung fu movies. I think once you are aware of the beauty of music, you could find it almost anywhere."[31]

Imagine RZA watching *Master of the Flying Guillotine* (1976), a Shaw Brothers classic written and directed by Jimmy Wang Yu. As the blind monk displays his mastery of this bizarre helmetlike weapon attached to a chain, which can decapitate someone from a distance, foreboding industrial sounds play behind the opening credits. RZA samples this unconventional piece, which happens to be the track "Super 16" (1973) by the krautrock band Neu! Hailing from Düsseldorf, Germany, Neu! was formed in 1971 by drummer Klaus Dinger and guitarist Michael Rother after they left Kraftwerk, another seminal krautrock outfit. That band had been responsible for "Trans-Europe Express," one of the elements sampled in Afrika Bambaataa's electro-smash "Planet Rock" (Tommy Boy, 1982). Incidentally, Neu!'s unofficial third member, Conny Plank, was an experimental producer whose cutting-edge work provided a precursor to techno and electronic music. RZA uses a mechanical-sounding smack from "Super 16," drenched in reverb and delay, as his snare for "Sub Crazy," one of the darkest and most boldly experimental tracks on *Tical*.

At its most basic, hip-hop depends on a beat, but RZA dispenses with the usual drums this time around, generating rhythmic propulsion from a combination of sub-bass tones and that sampled hit. He also taps a more conventional drum loop from "Love Potion-Cheeba-Cheeba" (1973) by the Mighty Tom Cats but only brings it in sporadically, leaving you drowning in a sea of bass—ergo, "Sub Crazy." (Incidentally, the Mighty Tom Cats, who also recorded as the Harlem Underground Band, released several singles on Paul Winley Records, a doo-wop label started in 1956 that put out some of the first rap records, including the *Super Disco Brake's* series and Bambaataa's 1980 "Zulu Nation Throw Down.") RZA and coproducer 4th Disciple lace the pulsing, subterranean beat with the whistling sound of a bomb dropping and the eerie, processed wailing of singer Blue Raspberry, creating the soundtrack to your worst trip.

On top of this disorienting, alien soundscape, Meth drops some of his most ferocious rhymes of the album: "Creepin' niggas in the dark, triggers with no heart / Rippin' ass apart, I be swimmin' with the sharks now / Stay out my water or its manslaughter / Kid you oughta start reachin' for that nickel plate auto[matic]." It's as if the streets have prepared him for this cutthroat industry he's in, and he's ready to bite back—no doubt with the newly acquired jewel-encrusted fangs that he shows off on the album cover. Later, the smoked-out master of metaphors raps, "The ism [weed] helps to stimulate my pugilism / I bust rhymes like jism / Impregnate the rhythm with the wisdom." In an already strong and consistent album, "Sub Crazy" is a stroke of brilliance, taking listeners to the nether regions of hip-hop.

RZA and Meth don't leave us hanging after such a break-out performance, following it up with "Release Yo' Delf," an anthemic banger that became the album's second single. It's also a proper introduction to Blue Raspberry, a frequent early Wu collaborator, who sings an interpolation of Gloria Gaynor's disco sensation "I Will Survive" (Polydor, 1978). The original, penned by Freddie Perren, sold fourteen million copies worldwide on its way to becoming an anthem of the era. Meth must have had fun rewriting the hook for Blue, who sings, "When I first stepped on the scene, niggas was petrified / Jet back to the lab, like they were being chased by Homicide / My rap flow does you right, Tical / And it will never steer you wrong / And all you bitch ass niggas in the industry, your careers won't be lasting long." Hearing those words sung by a glossy female voice sounds pretty gangster to begin with—almost a subversion of R&B—but when she starts flaunting her full vocal range, you realize that Wu-Tang's first female collaborator is no joke.

Originally from Pleasantville, New Jersey, Candi Lindsey (a.k.a. Blue Raspberry) first met the Clan on April 22, 1993, while working at urban radio's IMPACT Music Convention held at the Bally Casino in Atlantic City. After completing a shift as a valet parking cashier, she was walking through the casino floor with her cousin when "Somebody Loves You Baby" by Patti LaBelle started playing on the PA. "I was just singing [along], and these guys in bandanas were standing by one of the pillars," she recalls. "They said, 'Yo, do that again.'"[32] The bandana-clad brothers—none other than members of Wu-Tang Clan—left Candi a copy of "Protect Ya Neck" on a white-label cassette. Later, she met RZA, impressing him with her powerful pipes. Vowing to put her on when the group blew up, he made good on his word. With a newly minted name courtesy of Killah Priest, who said she reminded him of that unique flavor of Slurpee, she made her debut on *Tical*, featuring prominently on three tracks: "Release Yo' Delf," "Mr. Sandman," and "Stimulation."

On "Release," RZA supplies a pumping groove for her and Meth to really let loose. He recycles the same simple boom-bap that he used on "Wu-Tang 7th Chamber"—"Make It Funky" from Carlos Bess's *Funky Drummer Vol. 1*—speeding it up slightly and embellishing it with extra hi-hats. He pairs the beat with the triumphant horn riff from Herb Alpert's "Treasure of San Miguel," released on Alpert's own A&M label in 1967. Rounding it out with a relentless bass, he creates a fist-pumping, head-banging anthem fit for any titleholder to enter the ring.

Once again, Meth rises to the occasion, delivering a knockout blow with verses like "Serial killer style from the isle of Stat / My peoples are you with me where ya at? / Shit's getting' deep in here, I mean like thick / Niggas lookin' all in my face like they want dick / Shit's about to hit the fan, hit the floor / It's all I can stands, and I can't stands no more." After ratcheting up the tension, he ends with a wink to *Popeye the Sailor Man*. At one point, he even sounds like Ol' Dirty hitting some shrill notes during the bridge, but he returns to his usual McGruff voice, chanting "We keep it movin'" toward the end of his vocal workout.

As the track fades, we launch directly into "P.L.O. Style," one of two songs featuring Wu-Tang affiliate Carlton Fisk, a member of Meth's crew. The first lines he delivers, "Oh, what a tangled web we weave, when first we practice to deceive," sounds vaguely Shakespearian, but it's actually from the epic poem "Marmion: A Tale of Flodden Field," written by Sir Walter Scott in 1808. Talk about your obscure lyrical references. Fisk goes on to say, "The street life is the only life I know, I live by the code, style—it's mad P.L.O. / Iranian thoughts and cover like an Arabian / Grab the nigga on the spot and put a nine to his cranium," explaining the song's title—sort of.

Once again, count on Wu-Tang to pull another obscure reference out of the bag—this one of a geopolitical nature. The Palestine Liberation Organization, or PLO, started in 1964 as a means of resisting the Israeli forces who were occupying their land, making them second-class citizens in their own country. Equipped and heavily funded by the US to the tune of billions, Israel waged asymmetric warfare against the Palestinians. The PLO countered with the only tactics available to them—suicide bombings—classifying them as a terrorist organization by the US until 1991. Shortly before the release of Meth's album, the PLO renounced violence and acknowledged Israel's right to exist in exchange for their recognition as the sole representative of the Palestinian people. But their reputation for being a bunch of badasses who resisted the occupation and fought for their human rights persisted. So "P.L.O. Style" does not refer to the black-and-white checkered *kaffiyeh* scarves worn by Palestinians, which later became fashionable in hip-hop; instead, Meth and his crew were making an analogy between their struggle and the rebel tactics of the PLO. Today, Black Lives Matter has defined that struggle in even clearer terms, openly allying themselves with the plight of the Palestinian people, but, as usual, Wu-Tang were ahead of the curve.

The song's hook, "P.L.O. Style, Buddha monks with the Owls," actually comes from Meth's verse from "Wu-Tang 7th Chamber." Meth also has a hand in coproducing this track, a steady head nodder with only one identifiable sample, a slowed-down horn riff from "Look What You've Done for Me" (Hi Records, 1972), by Al Green. RZA adds texture to the track with his usual ear candy in the form of random squeaks, whistles, and a flourish of harp—all of which are best appreciated with headphones.

Asked about his style of rhyming, Meth responds, "I don't know, I just say everything that everybody like to hear, know what I'm sayin'? I take it back, I mean way back to days when you waking up early in the morning, Saturday morning, and watching cartoons, right, all that. People recognize when they hear stuff like that, and when you say some stuff people are familiar with, it becomes fun for them."[33] Here, Meth zeroes in on one of the main reasons people relate to him— his pop-culture references and love of nostalgia.

A classic example appears on the next track, "I Get My Thang in Action," whose title interpolates a line from "Verb: That's What's Happening" by Zachary Sanders, part of the extremely popular *Schoolhouse Rock* series that singer/songwriter Bob Dorough started in 1973. These catchy animated shorts appeared on ABC on Saturday mornings, teaching kids about math, grammar, and even civics to a very funky soundtrack. RZA doesn't sample any of the music but rather a short section of the intro of Bo Diddley's "Hit or Miss" (Chess, 1974), the same bouncy loop that drives the 1989 posse-cut "Buddy" by De La Soul, featuring Jungle Brothers and A Tribe Called Quest. He spruces it up with the addition of the snare fills that begin MC Shan's seminal hit "The Bridge," produced by Marley Marl in 1986.

Curiously, while Meth raps, a Dolomite impersonator drops ad-libs in the background before stepping in for the outro. "I taught the boy everything he know," he begins, riffing through a short monologue that sounds like the real Rudy Ray Moore, down to his parting advice: "If you can't get yourself a ten, the least you can do is fuck two fives." As is sometimes the case on Wu-Tang projects, no one is credited for this performance, but a good guess might be ODB, who was certainly around for the making of Meth's album.

The obligatory posse cut, "Mr. Sandman," follows, taking some weight off Meth and bringing in the bench, which includes Inspectah Deck, Carlton Fisk, and Streetlife, another Wu affiliate making his debut splashdown. The song's title comes from the Chordettes' 1954 hit of the same name, which Blue Raspberry interpolates in the hook, but that is not the only lyrical sampling going on. Meth drops Lovin' Spoonful's 1966 hit "Hot Time, Summer in the City" to kick off his verse, and Fisk returns with another obscure but well-known reference when he quotes, "What evil lurks in the hearts of men," the popular tag line from the 1930s serialized radio show *The Shadow*, written by Walter B. Gibson.

RZA also joins in on the mic, and you can hear the angst and hunger in his voice as he screams, "Lyrical shots from the Glock / Bust bullet holes on the charts / I want the number one spot." Then Deck, probably the Clan's most underrated MC, ups the ante with "Hazardous thoughts to cut the mic's life support short / Brains get stained like tablecloths when I let off / Powerful poetry pushed past the point of no return / Leaving mics with third-degree burns." Maintaining the energy, Streetlife picks up with "Yo, watch me bang that headpiece son there's no survival / My flow lights up the block like I'm homicidal / Murder, underground beef for the burger / P.L.O., criminal thoughts you never heard of." He ends with a shout-out to his murdered comrade: "Don't sleep, niggas tend to forget, however / Peep this, my nigga Kase lives forever." Finally, Fisk, batting cleanup, brings everyone home with some graphic street cinema, which sees him breaking down the door and dodging shots as he interrupts a drug deal. Dislocating one guy's shoulder, he takes the other hostage and then makes it look like they killed each other as he flees the crime scene. Fisk and Streetlife hint at the enormous talent lurking within the Wu-Tang fold.

The album goes out with a boom on "Stimulation," featuring RZA, Meth, and Blue Raspberry. The well-known drum break from Manzel's "Midnight Theme" (Fraternity, 1979) provides the track's foundation, but RZA loops only a short section of drummer Steve Garner's crisp eight-bar intro. The beat marries perfectly with arranger Don Costa's lush strings that open "Snowbound" (Roulette, 1963) sung by Sarah Vaughan, the celebrated jazz singer who had a career spanning almost fifty years. Once again, RZA displays his amazing taste for obscure classics, choosing to sample a release that critics considered an "overlooked gem"[34] of her extensive catalog.

RZA's use of the sample evokes that feeling of nostalgia, consistent with the overall vibe of *Tical*. The bass, as usual, is booming, sometimes obscuring Meth's gravelly baritone, which was already hoarse from performing the night he recorded the track. But Blue Raspberry's overpowering vocal cuts right through as she delivers the hook, "Let's come together for the Stimulation / Methical hit 'em with the Stimulation." For ear candy, RZA employs a sample of Wendy

Rene's scatting from "After Laughter (Comes Tears)" in the background, as well as some disembodied saxophone and harp. It's curious today to hear Meth saying, "The Wu-Tang saga continues," before the track fades out, as if he knew what kind of future lay ahead for the Clan. But that casual toss-off would become a stock phrase on subsequent Wu-Tang solo projects, gaining more gravity as they started to dominate hip-hop in the nineties.

A lean, mean album, clocking in at just over forty-four minutes, even with its bonus track—the uninspired "Method Man" remix—*Tical* proves that the Wu-Tang magic is not some first-time fluke. RZA crafts a record that sounds completely different from *Enter the Wu-Tang* while retaining some of its choicer elements—namely, the dirtiness and darkness. Meth, meanwhile, shows he can largely carry an album on his own, fulfilling his promise as the bankable star of the group. On the shoulders of his success, the next man would launch, and so on, and the Clan would grow together, as was the plan all along. So far, so good.

It's no mistake that the "Method Man" remix ends with the same piece of dialogue that ends the Wu-Tang album: "It's our secret. Never teach the Wu-Tang," from the movie *Shaolin vs. Wu Tang*. Aside from providing continuity and further brand development, it's RZA's way of reveling in the mystique of his creation, which he knows has powerful attraction. With a wink and an evil grin, he's also letting everyone know that even though this is Method Man's gothic hip-hop horror show, Wu-Tang is lurking in the shadows, ready to strike again when you least expect.

CHAPTER 10

OL' DIRTY BASTARD / RETURN TO THE 36 CHAMBERS: THE DIRTY VERSION

It was Oscar Levant, the American composer and pianist whose star resides on the Hollywood Walk of Fame, who said, "There is a fine line between genius and insanity. I have erased this line." Known as much for his quick wit as for his openness about his neuroses, Levant eventually became addicted to prescription drugs and was committed to mental institutions more than once before succumbing to a heart attack at age sixty-five. But his words survive as an aphorism today, befitting other brilliant but tortured minds, including the character known as Ol' Dirty Bastard.

ODB was, simultaneously, larger than life and deeply authentic and real. Explaining his alter ego in a rare moment of self-reflection, Russell Jones said, "Dirty is just the negative side of me, know what I'm sayin'? The pressure that built up inside me. Then when somebody get on my nerves, it gots to come out."[1] The rapper previously known as Ason Unique was given his somewhat dubious nom de guerre by his cousin RZA because he reminded him of a character from the kung fu film *Ol' Dirty & the Bastard* (1981), played by Yuen Siu-tien (Simon Yuen). The perpetually red-faced

Beggar So, an endearing old codger who had mastered the art of drunken boxing, hilariously dispatching opponents with his tipsy technique, appeared as a recurring protagonist in three earlier films: *Drunken Master* (1978) with Jackie Chan, *Story of Drunken Master* (1979), and *Dance of the Drunk Mantis* (1979). For Ason, who, of course, loved beer as much as battling MCs, the alias fit as perfectly as his fingers around the waist of a forty-ounce. Sure, the name Ol' Dirty Bastard sounded bizarre—especially in an art form known for self-aggrandizement—but that was the whole point. Ason Unique already knew he brought a certain style and energy that hip-hop had never seen before, and in ODB, he found the perfect vehicle to blaze his own trail.

He even customized the meaning behind his new moniker. "Old" referred to his love for the soul and R&B music of the sixties and seventies he had grown up listening to—artists such as James Brown, Marvin Gaye, Millie Jackson, and Gladys Knight. "Dirty" was a description of his raw, uncut style that came straight from the gutter, uncensored and unapologetic. "Bastard" signified that there was "no father to his style," as Method Man explained to an interviewer during one of the interludes on *36 Chambers*. Long before Drake started singing and rapping his way up the charts, ODB had already been there, leaving a trail of muddy paw prints to follow. His warbling vibrato combined with the guttural, almost inhuman sounds he hocked up from deep inside his esophagus was not even considered singing by someone like his mother, who had a real voice. But for the midnineties hip-hop audience, Ol' Dirty Bastard was a character so brand spanking new, raw, and original, he might have just flown in on a UFO.

With a marble-mouthed delivery, not always bothering to rhyme, heavy use of onomatopoeia, or breaking into song or spoken non sequiturs in the middle of a track, it wasn't just his unorthodox style that set him apart but also his magnetic personality. Upbeat and always on stage, he was the Energizer Bunny of the Clan, rallying the troops, as he kept it moving to the beat of a different drummer. *Uninhibited* was an understatement when applied to Dirty, who was wild, reckless, outspoken, and free. Even before he found fame, he seemed headed in that direction. Dirty was the guy who, at age eleven, told his mother that he would never work for anyone. While he eventually made good on his word, he also surrendered to the temptations of the sex, drugs, and rock 'n' roll lifestyle. He was plagued by the pressure to always perform as the larger-than-life character of his own creation, and it all proved to be too much for Dirty. He crossed that line between genius and insanity, heading toward a train wreck of an ending, but not before making the people of Earth feel his presence.

A&R man Dante Ross, a veteran of Def Jam and Tommy Boy, had the good instinct to sign the rapper after hearing him spit only a freestyle on the radio. After moving on to Elektra Records, he assembled a formidable roster that included Leaders of the New School (and their soon-to-be solo star, Busta Rhymes), Brand Nubian (and their breakaway member, Grand Puba), and Pete Rock & CL Smooth—all giants of their era despite record sales that fell short of gold or platinum. Dirty had the distinct honor of being the first member of the Clan to get a solo deal, even before the group signed with Loud.

It all happened during the wee hours of January 28, 1993, when Ross was tuned in to the *Stretch and Bobbito Show* on Columbia University's WKCR 89.9 FM. He heard Dirty singing "Tommy" by the Who before dropping his verse from the song that would become one of his hits, "Brooklyn Zoo."[2] Matty C (Capoluongo) from *The Source*, the first journalist to cover the independent release of "Protect Ya Neck," had already informed him that the individual members of the Clan were up for grabs, so without delay, Ross hopped a cab down to the station. The first person he ran into was RZA, who recognized him, saying, "I know you from the God Melquan. You knew me at Tommy Boy when I was wack."[3] After exchanging dap and sharing a laugh, Ross got right down to business, saying he was interested in signing Method Man and Dirty. He left his business card, telling RZA to come down to the office the next day, a Friday. RZA, Inspectah Deck, Dirty, and Power all showed up at Elektra four days later, on Monday. Ross said he wanted to make Meth and Dirty into the next Run-DMC, but RZA had other plans. He was going to shop Meth to Def Jam, but he offered to keep Dirty at Elektra, "with the Gods," referring to fellow Five Percenters Brand Nubian and Grand Puba. "And he [RZA] gave me a cassette tape, and I signed him [ODB] shortly thereafter," says Ross, "and the rest is history."[4]

Despite being the first Clansman to score a deal, Dirty didn't deliver an album for almost two years. Chalk it up to the hive of activity surrounding the Killa Bees, who were touring constantly, as well as Dirty's own lax work ethic. As his homeboy Buddha Monk (Ellery Chambers), who was in the studio with him every step of the way, says, "He had fun making his album, and he took his time doing it. It couldn't have gone any other way, or we just wouldn't have come out with the same album."[5] Such an approach suited Dirty's personality as well as his ultimate goals. According to Monk, "Everybody in Wu-Tang wanted to make money to take care of their kids, and everybody in Wu-Tang wanted to make good music. But for Dirty, if he wasn't enjoying himself, he didn't want to do it. So, when Dirty showed up at the studio, he usually showed up with three or four girls—anybody from old girlfriends to groupies he met in front of the building."[6]

Though Dirty's weakness for women goes back to before puberty, his entry into the music industry introduced him to a new vice—cocaine. Prior to that, malt liquor—specifically Olde English 800—had been enough to lubricate the wheels of creativity and ignite his wacky sensibilities. "Me and Dirty is known for 'firewater'—we call alcohol 'firewater.' That's our energy," Buddha Monk explained. "It sets a flame of energy out of you that comes forth on the mic. It's all the anger, all the frustration of our families or whatever we're going through. We don't take it out on people, we bring that out on the mic."[7]

Unfortunately, "firewater" was the last thing someone with Shinnecock Indian ancestry, like Dirty, should have been indulging in. (His great-grandfather Chief Wickham Cuffie was supposedly one of the last to speak the tribe's native language.) ODB eschewed weed, saying it made him paranoid. But blow was what the big boys fucked with, and for him, following in the footsteps of some of his idols—entertainers turned addicts such as Richard Pryor, Rick James, and Sly Stone—proved to be far too easy.

John King, owner of the legendary Chung King Studios, confirms an incident that occurred during the making of Dirty's album that has since become music industry lore. "One of my favorite stories is when ODB and I were sitting in the office, and we might have been snorting something, and we were drinking champagne," he says, "and LL [Cool J] was supposed to come in and be on the session that day, and he didn't come in, and ODB just got up, walked over, and pulled

LL's [gold] record off the wall and pissed on it."[8] Behind the eyebrow-raising humor, however, lay the harsh reality that cocaine was one hell of a drug, responsible for making Dirty go that extra mile. Coupled with his volatile behavior and his appetite for excess, it eventually proved to be his undoing.

Dirty's addiction and self-destructive behavior was hardly a secret either. RZA, eulogizing his cousin at the rapper's funeral in 2004, apologized for bestowing that name upon him, saying, "I ask for forgiveness for that. I say forgiveness because a man don't make a name. It's like sometimes the name makes you. Sometimes your attributes become a reflection of yourself."[9] The sad contradiction about Dirty was that the same outrageous, over-the-top behavior that fans loved him for would also prove to be the anchor around his neck.

In the early days of ODB's career, however, anyone confusing his genius for insanity would have been greatly mistaken. Dirty knew exactly what he was doing, for example, when he engineered one of the most memorable publicity stunts in recent history, which involved the cover of his album. Ross, who enjoyed a close relationship with Dirty, says he came to his office one day with an idea: "Yo, I got crazy thoughts! I got crazy thoughts, yo! I got my album [cover] thoughts."[10] The rapper pulled out a public-assistance ID with his picture on it—actually his wife's card, on which he had pasted his mugshot—and asked Ross if they could use that as the album cover. As far as the A&R man was concerned, it was a great idea, and one that had precedence. The English pop-reggae group UB40 took their name from the British unemployment benefits card that doubled as the cover of their first album, *Signing Off* (Graduate Records, 1980). Though Ross would have to run it by the suits upstairs, he thought it could work.

After taking the card to the art department and blowing it up to album-cover size on a color copier, he showed it to his colleagues, who loved it. The suits eventually signed off as well.

On March 30, 1995, just two days after the album dropped, Dirty had the bright idea of inviting MTV News to accompany him and his family as they went to pick up their $375 allotment of food stamps at a local check-cashing spot in Brooklyn. Riding in a limousine with his wife and three young children, Dirty sipped on a cocktail from the wet bar as he spoke about the virtues of "free money." Despite having received a $45,000 advance from Elektra for his expenses, as well as royalties from *36 Chambers*, he had not yet filed last year's taxes, so he was still technically eligible for government benefits—until, of course, the segment aired.

On-air personality Kurt Loder had his crafty cronies in the editing room cut in footage of a Bill Clinton speech from June 14, 1994, where he says, "We have to repair the damaged bond between our people and their government manifesting in the way the welfare system works. We have to end welfare as we know it." They juxtaposed this clip with ODB saying, "I think it's terrible. You know how hard it is for people to live without nothing? You owe me forty acres and a mule, anyway, for real."[11] Amplifying the controversy, Loder actually posed the $100,000 question out loud: "Is ODB a welfare cheat?" as if willfully trying to get him in trouble. While MTV was certainly not out to do the rapper any favors, that one widely seen clip thrust Dirty into the public consciousness, and as they say in the business, no publicity is bad publicity. Dirty first saw it himself while on tour in Germany and actually felt bad enough to call Ross to see how he could make amends— probably the last time he cared about the consequences of his actions. But the damage was already done. While confirming to polite society the rot in the system, Dirty also reinforced an ugly stereotype. In the eighties, Reagan had singled out poor Black women for allegedly gaming the system with the racist trope "welfare queen," but in the nineties, ODB usurped the crown for himself.

Ironically, the reckless stunt probably helped sell a lot of records too—especially in the hood, where folks were more sympathetic to Dirty's schtick and actually understood where he was coming from. From his point of view, he was expressing solidarity with his community and showing that there was no shame in receiving government aid. At the same time, in his own mischievous way, he was testing the limits of how far he could go in challenging authority. He came off as Robin Hood in the hood, where they already knew him as the superstar who would stop his BMW at a random intersection and hand out dollar bills to all the kids and adults. Ultimately, the MTV debacle worked out to his advantage, putting him on the radar of R&B diva Mariah Carey, who enlisted his services for the remix of her single "Fantasy" (Sony, 1995). After that song shot to the top of Billboard's Hot 100, staying there for eight consecutive weeks, with a video in heavy rotation, even more people knew the name Ol' Dirty Bastard.

But few knew him well, and those who did say he was greatly misunderstood. According to Ross, "He was brilliant. Before substances took real control of him, he was one of the most creative minds. He really understood himself as an artist. And in all of his madness, he gets portrayed as a buffoon sometimes, and I think that's like—it's easier to think of him as a buffoon than someone who was really creative and understood himself as an artist. And I think that's the tragedy of his demise—one of them—that his artistry gets lost 'cause that first record is incredible."[12]

Even Dirty was aware of that gap between perception and reality, as he told an interviewer, "People know of me as being crazy and wild, but they don't really know of me. So, that's why I put in my album all sorts of pieces and particles of me, so people can really see a full understanding of me—an understanding that I got some shit for you, I got some shit for her, I got some shit for him."[13] That description pretty much went to the heart of an album that was as diverse, dynamic, wacky, and bold as the guy who made it.

* * *

While *The 36th Chamber of Shaolin* is regarded as one of the all-time greatest martial arts movies, *Return to the 36th Chamber* (1980), its sequel, is a bit of an oddity. Despite the return of director Lau Kar-leung and his star Gordon Liu, as well as an almost identical plot hinging on themes of overcoming oppression and attaining mastery through practice and discipline, the film has a more comedic slant. Perhaps that's why ODB decided to call his own album *Return to the 36 Chambers: The Dirty Version*—for the obvious Wu-Tang allusion coupled with the humorous streak that laces the album. If any single entity embodied the witty, unpredictable talent and natural game, it's the one-man army Ason, the charismatic heart and soul of the Clan.

Return to the 36 Chambers, an unwieldly beast of an album that flaunts so many conventions, breaks rules, takes risks, and qualifies as much as performance art as a genre recording, is the equivalent of Dirty beating his chest and howling like Tarzan. To call it a concept album would be misleading because there is no concept—it's all over the place like his ADD. In fact, the record plays more like an eclectic mixtape that takes you on all kinds of unpredictable twists and turns.

But within the madness, there's some kind of strange coherence, and, believe it or not, it's Dirty, himself, modeling how to be completely at ease and let it all hang out while riding the lightning. If we could all be so free and not take life so seriously.

Dirty displays absolutely no shame and no filters, mining his own experiences as a matter of course. "Where I come from, in my neighborhood, my people know me, you know what I'm sayin'?" he told an early interviewer. "See, if I try to come any different, they ain't gonna respect me no more. You know, if you come from that neighborhood, they'll say you could get out the neighborhood, but you can never take the neighborhood out the people."[14] ODB lives by these words and offers his whole life to his art—especially the nasty bits.

Take the totally gonzo yet entertaining intro, clocking in at 4:47, which only Dirty would make us sit through. Assuming the role of master of ceremony under his legal name, Russell Jones, he proceeds to hype up his alter ego as "somethin' crazy, he's somethin' insane." But when he says, "Tonight you're going to see somethin' that you never seen before; somethin' that nobody in the history of rap ever set they self to do," believe it's no idle boast.

He abruptly switches gears, confessing, "I'm happy to be living. A nigga tried to shoot me down and shit," referring to an attempted robbery that occurred just months earlier on Kingston Avenue in Bed-Stuy. Though he got shot in the back, the bullet miraculously missed his spine, piercing his spleen before exiting. Even more incredibly, he was able to drive himself to the hospital to get his wounds treated.

After mentioning this very real brush with death, Dirty makes another startling confession—this time of the highly personal kind—volunteering that he contracted gonorrhea, not once but twice. What most people would never, ever publicly disclose, Dirt Dawg seems to wear as a badge of honor, even reveling in it. A paragon of anti–political correctness, he jokingly admits to killing the "bitch" who gave him the STD before dedicating a bawdy Blowfly song to her—"First Time Ever You Sucked My Dick" (a risqué takeoff of Roberta Flack's "First Time Ever I Saw Your Face")—from the comic's 1975 album *Zodiac*. For the first time, we are treated to Dirty singing a cappella, and, except for the lewd, cringeworthy lyrics, he doesn't sound half bad.

Later on, in "Goin' Down," he takes authenticity to the nth degree, bringing his wife into the vocal booth to re-create a vicious argument they had regarding groupies. As the beat cuts out in the middle of the track, Icelene says, "Fuck that bullshit, Unique. You my motherfuckin' husband. I ain't got no fuckin' time for these bitches callin' my motherfuckin' house with that bullshit," while Dirty drowns her out with a rousing rendition of "Over the Rainbow," a childhood classic from *The Wizard of Oz* (1939). The track plays like his own personal episode of Jerry Springer, showing that whether he is being shameless, provocative, or simply real, ODB likes to give it to you raw.

He says as much on the first proper track, "Shimmy Shimmy Ya," crooning "Ooh, baby, I like it raw" on the hook. Most took it as a paean to sex without a condom—especially considering Dirty's propensity for picking up STDs. But he challenged this assumption, since being raw and unfiltered was a way of life. The label, however, knew that commercial radio would balk at airing the single unless Dirty changed the lyrics, something that was obviously out of the question for him. But in a rare act of compromise—one of the few he made during his entire career—he recorded a safe-sex disclaimer to be played before the track.

That simple concession allowed this song, the album's second single, to become one of its biggest hits—thanks in part to a Hype Williams video that had Dirty wilding out on the dance floor in a re-creation of the *Soul Train* set from the seventies. Like the hit "Method Man," it's a dated track, recorded before ODB even had a deal, as well as a very simple construction featuring only drums, bass, and piano. The drum loop is based off two bass notes and a snare shuffle from "I Like It" (Stax, 1969) by the Emotions. Channeling Thelonious Monk, whom he's sampled enough times, RZA plays the catchy piano melody on a cheap keyboard called the Dr. Synth (Boss DS-330), his first synth, purchased for $200, which he also used for bass lines.[15] In fact, the booming two-note bass stab probably comes from this nifty little gadget as well.

RZA's ear for detail is evident in the vocal samples he chooses to embellish this track. The first is a scratchy snippet of Richard Pryor saying, "Fuck you, you can't even sing" from "Have Your Ass Home by 11:00" (off the 1974 Stax LP *That Nigger's Crazy*). No doubt Dirty was accustomed to such criticism. In a nod to hip-hop nostalgia, RZA also inserts the line "I like the way you talk" from "D'ya Like Scratchin'" (Island, 1983), by Sex Pistols' impresario Malcolm McLaren and World's Famous Supreme Team. The team—consisting of See Divine the Mastermind and Just Allah the Superstar, two Five Percenters who had a radio show on WHBI in Newark, New Jersey—first gained acclaim after appearing on McLaren's early rap hit "Buffalo Gals" (Island, 1982).

Dirty's approach is the complete opposite, however, as he inexplicably repeats the same verse twice, separated by a verse played backward. But RZA, who knows his cousin better than most anyone, gives him the latitude to do that because they have been collaborators since they were kids. He doesn't attempt to impose artificial structure but, instead, rides the chaos, always confident that Dirty will deliver. This time, his catchy hook, "Shimmy shimmy ya, shimmy yam, shimmy yay / Give me the mic so I can take it away / Off on a natural charge, bon voyage / Yeah from the home of the Dodger Brooklyn squad," is all he needs to win the day.

Some tracks, like the next one, "Baby C'mon," don't even bother with hooks—or even editing—as Dirty starts by asking, "Are you taping, baby?" But it's the inclusion of such details, whether accidents or imperfections, that add a sense of spontaneity and looseness to the mix. The track begins with a staggered bass line and snare hit played at different pitches, giving the impression of a warm-up, prompting Dirty to start riffing on the phrase "Oh yeah" before an explosion and the sound of breaking glass introduce his verse. He emerges from the smoke rhyming haphazardly, as if he's making it up as he goes along, his wild cadence and flow precariously clinging to the track like an extreme roller-coaster ride. Once again, authenticity seems to be a main concern as he says, "If I wasn't really raw, standing here on the floor / You'd be like, boo, he ain't hardcore." Taking a cue from Jamaican dub producer Lee "Scratch" Perry, RZA throws some delay on Dirty's voice toward the end of the track, making it echo out over the instrumental.

"Brooklyn Zoo," the album's biggest single, arrives next with another simple piano ditty that has RZA written all over it. However, this track is True Master's sole contribution to the album, with an assist from ODB. True Master (Derek Harris), who became one of the earliest Wu affiliates after meeting RZA and GZA at a music convention in 1989, must have had some serious pull with the Abbott to get a song on Dirty's album, but he more than earns his keep with this banger. The now-familiar piano line that drives the track is actually a sample from an obscure reggae seven-inch by Bobby Ellis & the Desmond Miles Seven called "Step Softly" (Crystal Records, 1967) that True Master chops up and replays over a simple boom-bap beat.

Dirty attacks the track, turning it into a battle anthem as he jacks part of his verse from "Protect Ya Neck" for the hook, "Shame on you, when you step up to, Ol' Dirty Bastard, Brooklyn Zoo." He also busts some of his best lines yet: "Ason, I keep planets in orbit, while I keep coming with deeper and more shit / Enough to make you break and shake your ass / As I create rhymes as good as Tastykake make." The track would become an anthem, representing not only a whole borough and a reemerging East Coast but also Dirty's immediate crew, which included his cousins Merdoc, Raison the Zu Keeper, 12 O'Clock, and Shorty Shitstain and best friend, Buddha Monk, all of whom appear later on.

The last of the piano-based tracks, "Hippa to da Hoppa," which sounds like it's from the same era as "Shimmy Shimmy Ya," closes out the first part of the album. Once again, RZA uses the Dr. Synth to play his own piano melody while sampling a couple of other sounds—a bluesy guitar lick and an organ wail—from "Hip Hug-Her" (Stax, 1967) by Booker T. & the MG's. For the beat, he borrows a popular break beat, "It's a New Day" (GSF, 1973) by Skull Snaps, but truncates it at one bar to sound slightly different. Like the three preceding tracks, this one is also swimming in bass. Its sheer simplicity allows Dirty's stream of consciousness to spread out and fill every nook and cranny. Clearly, his rhymes have of an ad-libbed feel to them, and when he says, "Ah shit, here I go once again, rhymes get shitty from the time that I spend," he suggests, perhaps, that the less time he spends writing them, the better.

In fact, according to Method Man, who was around a lot during the making of *Return*, "The majority of the verses on that album are old RZA rhymes and GZA rhymes. Dirty took all their shit and made it his own, and GZA ain't say shit. Most of [Dirty's verses] was GZA's shit. I remember GZA and ODB got in an argument one night and GZA was like, 'Nigga most of that shit on your fucking album is mines anyway!'"[16] That would explain a lot—especially why Dirty uses the same verse from "Damage," a tag-team duet with GZA, on "Brooklyn Zoo II (Tiger Crane)," on which Ghostface appears. It also goes to show how the Clan freely shared material with each other. GZA even admits that the rhymes Dirty borrowed for his album were written during his high school years and that he had already outgrown them, so it was never an issue.

Up to now, the album's been all Dirty until the next track, "Raw Hide," an amazing collaboration featuring the first cameos by other members of the Clan. RZA cooks up one of his fattest beats for the occasion, setting it up with a clip from the 1980 kung fu film *Two on the Road* (a.k.a. *Fearless Dragons*): "Dragon fist, horse fist. Freeze, bastard! I didn't know who you were." Besides the drums, a short section of "CB#1" from *Funky Drummer Vol. 1* (JBR, 1993) by Carlos Bess, there are very few recognizable samples on this track, which ranks as one of the most experimental of the producer's oeuvre. In fact, eschewing the usual boom bap, the track's rhythmic foundation is provided by a diabolical chord progression laced with a thundering kick. Dirty spits pure fire on his second verse, saying:

Yeah, gotta come back to attack
Killin' niggas who said they got stacks, 'cause I don't give a
    fuck

[inhales] I wanna see blood, whether it's period blood
Or bustin' your fuckin face some blood!!
I'm goin' out my fuckin' mind!
Every time I get around devils [heavy breathing]
Let me calm down, you niggas better start runnin'
'Cause I'm comin', I'm dope like fuckin' heroin

Even the printed words cannot convey the powerful timbre of his voice as it fluctuates from high-pitched to growling or how he uses breath to underscore his emotions. While "spitting" has become a common euphemism for rapping, you can literally feel Dirty's spray in your eye.

Method Man and Raekwon don't let the team down either. Meth pulls another pop-culture reference out of his magic hat, interpolating the theme song from the popular sixties TV series *Rawhide*, written by Frankie Laine, for the hook, "Move 'em in, move 'em in, move 'em out, move 'em out, stick it up, [whip sound] rawhide!" When Rae raps, "Yo, check the bulletproof fly shit, strong like Thai stick / Then I'll remain to tear your frame while I freaks it / Like some fly new sneaks and shit / Now eat my shit, bitch tried to creep and got hit," the sheer intensity of his delivery and its internal rhymes slices through the track like surgical steel. Dirty returns for some shout-outs and ad-libs, putting the perfect exclamation point on the track as he says, "See this ain't somethin' new that's just gonna come out of nowhere / No! This is somethin' old! And dirty! / And dirty!"

Dirty's not shy about putting the whole family to work. While re-creating an argument with his wife on "Goin' Down," he also uses his toddlers on the intro of the next track, "Damage," getting them to repeat his name along with that of "the Genius," who shares the mic. The duo takes it back to the days of All in Together Now, trading battle rhymes that Dirty, wittingly or not, recycles on "Brooklyn Zoo, Part II." RZA and Dirty similarly reunite for a duet on the album's last track, "Cuttin' Headz," another euphemism for battling on the mic, which originally appeared on a Wu-Tang demo tape from 1992.

But the middle of the album plays host to more experimental fare, such as the highly entertaining "Don't U Know." The track starts off with a hilarious exchange between a groupie, who is enthralled with Dirty, and another girl, who can't possibly understand what her friend sees in that "bummy motherfucker." Dirty responds with a story rhyme that's a throwback to GZA's high school days. It starts off routinely enough before devolving into a crazy sexual fantasy involving the teacher, who is conducting a class on oral sex, using Dirty as her volunteer. With a rhyme style straight out of *Hustler's Convention*, he raps, "I tried to run, she yelled out freeze / Pulled down my drawers, dropped to her knees / Ripped off my drawers as if she had claws / Broke the rules that defied sex laws." His performance is straight out of Ghetto Masterpiece Theatre, and you can't imagine Genius delivering those lines any better. All the while, a Lyn Collins loop in the background is screaming, "Don't you know that, I know," taken from her version of "Ain't No Sunshine" (People, 1972).

"Don't U Know" is also notable for the introduction of Wu affiliate Killah Priest, who barely missed his shot at being on the Wu-Tang debut after being beaten out by Masta Killa's verse on "Da Mystery of Chessboxin'." Here, he drops an intricate story rhyme about going on a date with a girl until her angry father shows up. Brooklyn Zoo member Shorty Shitstain also makes a cameo—not rhyming but more testimonial—simply declaring his preference for a "nasty bitch" who is willing to do anything. Despite its recycled rhymes, the way Dirty conceptualizes the whole track and puts it together with these added elements serves as further proof of his demented genius.

He follows that one-off with "The Stomp," a coproduction with RZA. According to Buddha Monk, who witnessed the genesis of the song, Dirty laid the foundation for the beat with a snippet of sound from the 1991 movie *A Rage in Harlem*, which he looped using the ASR-10 that RZA had loaned him.[17] Still, this song is really nothing more than a bass line and a snare hit, leaving plenty of space for Dirty's usual antics. He sings, slurps, raps, and sings some more, even interpolating the lyrics of the traditional folk song called "Long Legged Sailor" when he says, "Have you ever, ever, ever, in your long-legged life, had a bald-headed bitch for your bald-headed wife." It's one of those random non sequiturs for which Dirty is famous.

He tops that performance on the intro to the next track, "Goin' Down," where he re-creates an old game that pulls you back into the deep recesses of childhood. "Remember when we used to say who could do this the longest," he says, slowly exhaling to produce a clicking sound from his larynx. After running out of breath, he giggles and does it again, this time not only sustaining the sound but segueing into an operatic wail that begins the song. It's cleverly nostalgic but, at the same time, so head-scratchingly bizarre. It should come as no surprise, then, when he breaks into "Over the Rainbow" later in the song—more nostalgia, since most people remember seeing *The Wizard of Oz* when they were children. One of Dirty's great gifts, in fact, as noted by his cousin RZA, was that "he was able to bring his childhood to his adulthood and share that with the world."[18]

Part of the ability of keeping that inner child alive involves not taking oneself too seriously, a trait Dirty displays in spades in "Drunk Game (Sweet Sugar Pie)." This track sounds totally out of place on this album yet, somehow, fits right in. According to engineer Ethan Ryman, the song's coproducer, he was working on this cheesy Casio keyboard-style R&B track for a completely different project when Dirty heard it and had to have it. Over syrupy chords and canned percussion, the rapper sings and croons R&B style, revealing a smoother side that's been hidden up to now. But you're not sure if it's straight parody or if he's really enjoying it—especially when he starts paying tribute to all the singers who have influenced him, including Diana Ross, Michael Jackson, the Temptations, and, last but not least, his mother, Cherry Jones.

Dirty's been hogging the mic for most of this show, but during the last third of the album, we start seeing more cameos by the Clan and their affiliates, including Sunz of Man and Brooklyn Zoo. "Snakes" begins with a snippet of dialogue from the film *Five Deadly Venoms* (1978) that talks about the "snake style," a not-so-subtle reminder that this is a Wu-Tang production. RZA crafts another banger reusing a familiar Joe Tex break—from "Papa Was Too" (Atlantic, 1966)—as well as the vocal hook from "I'll Never Do You Wrong" (Dial, 1968), also by Joe Tex. In order to make the hook fit the tempo of the track, he speeds it up, making it sound like a chipmunk voice—an innovation that would become a part of his signature style until other producers like Kanye West and Just Blaze jumped on the bandwagon and ran with it.

Once again, Killah Priest sets it off with another powerful story rhyme, detailing episodes of casual violence in the ghetto. RZA stays on message with a rhyme about various snakes in the hood, including "a Five Percenter, who all he knew was one to ten / He loved the Gods with his heart, but his brain was filled with sin / And when he came through niggas be lookin' out / Hopin' he gets shot or tooken out or locked the fuck up in Brooklyn House." He could have been talking about the infamous Supreme Team of South Jamaica, Queens, a notorious drug gang whose members all claimed righteous names and spoke in a code based on Supreme Mathematics while committing the most heinous crimes. Next up, Masta Killa delivers another solid performance, telling the story of a Jamaican rudeboy named Trigga who comes to America and gets involved with the drug game.

Then, out of the blue, Dirty cuts in with his rendition of Jim Croce's "Bad, Bad Leroy Brown" (ABC, 1973) before ad-libbing some of the craziest twelve bars on the record. "Fuck my name, who I be," he says. "Fuck the game, it's all about the moneyyyy! / [some inhuman noise] / Sometimes I get high with the Meth then I turn to the Killah Priest / When it comes TWELVE O'CLOCK!! I turn into the demon beast." He proceeds to snarl and growl for effect as RZA screams, "Who's the baddest!?! Who's the baddest!?!" Poor Buddha Monk, in his rapping debut, has to follow this mayhem with a few rushed verses that seem like an afterthought on a track that is already saturated. Still, Dirty returns with a declaration of "I don't need to rhyme no more, niggas know!" before he shouts out all the Wu-Tang members, somehow omitting Masta Killa.

Clocking in at 7:20, "Brooklyn Zoo Part II (Tiger Crane)," Dirty's duet with Ghost, featuring his recycled rhymes from "Damage," ranks as another album oddity. It begins with Dirty spouting random ad-libs in the vocal booth, like "All types of shit, yo, let that shit ride," before belting out the opening line of "Blue Moon." Though the popular ballad, written by Richard Rodgers and Lorenz Hart, dates back to 1934, Dirty was probably more familiar with the Marcels doo-wop version from 1961—or, for that matter, Sha Na Na's seventies redux. Then, for no apparent reason, Dirty feels compelled to explain, "I just want all y'all to know the reason why I curse is because my momma and my daddy, they grew up cursin'. So, please respect my style, please!" He must have been well lubricated with firewater in that vocal booth because after botching his first attempt at a verse, he runs through it again with a completely different cadence, keeping the whole performance, warts and all. That leaves the floor open for Ghost's sixteen-bar romp to the finish, which, despite his abstract wordplay, sounds so precise in contrast.

Instead of concluding, however, the track abruptly switches to a snippet of "Damage," as if the needle just skipped. The listener soon realizes that a mini album recap is underway, as clips from "Baby C'mon," "Brooklyn Zoo," "Drunk Game," and "The Stomp" also play before the original beat returns with Dirty ad-libbing and then chanting the hook to "Brooklyn Zoo." While it all seems so haphazard and zany, there is actually a method to Dirty's madness, as he is setting up the next track, "Protect Ya Neck II (the Zoo)," a posse cut featuring Brooklyn Zoo and Sunz of Man. He uses actual audio from a live show where he is introducing the group to begin the track.

It's pretty audacious to title anything after the original hit single that started everything off for the Clan, but "Protect Ya Neck II (The Zoo)" ranks as a worthy sequel. Not only does the track feature seven MCs ripping up the mic in quick succession, but RZA delivers a slamming backbeat to match, one of his illest productions to date. Isolating a single guitar note from "Groovin'" (Hi Records, 1968) by Willie Mitchell, he replays the sample on different keys to create his own riff—an innovation he didn't pioneer but firmly put his stamp on. For the drums, he loops a small section of Otis Redding's "Hard to Handle" (Atco, 1967), which, incidentally, was the same song Marley Marl sampled for his legendary posse cut "The Symphony" (Cold Chillin', 1988).

Dirt plays master of ceremonies on this one, setting off the track with one of his usual confrontational ad-libs. "Whether you're from Brooklyn, Queens, or Manhattan, I don't give a fuck where you be, motherfucker! Where you reside," he says before launching into his shortest verse on the whole album: "Sort ya stack out / This one's the blackout / Three fifty-seven to your mouth, blaowww!" Without missing a beat, Buddha Monk jumps in with four bars of his own, followed in quick succession by Prodigal Sunn (Lamar Ruff) of Sunz of Man and Zu Keeper and Merdoc, both members of Brooklyn Zoo. The lyrical beatdown never stops as Killah Priest drops another solid performance, passing off to 12 O'Clock (David Turner), Dirty's cousin. Then Dirt man pops his head in real quick, saying, "Hut one, hut two, hut three, what! / Ol' Dirty Bastard live and uncut / Shame on a nigga who tried to run game" before the high-pitched Shorty Shitstain returns with his first proper verse on the album.

Proving that he will not be outdone—especially by his own peeps—Dirty follows with an actual verse: "Roll and stroll with the party scene / Niggas want to know me as Mr. Clean / Wza-wza-wza-wza Wu-Tang, flip the script and / Test my skills, nigga, you trippin." Finally, another cousin, 60 Second Assassin (Frederick Cuffie Jr.) from Sunz of Man brings it home, and as his deadly alias suggests, he doesn't even need a whole minute to slay you with his rhymes. The logistics of incorporating so many MCs and their varied styles on a single track must have been challenging, but these guys make it sound so organic and natural, ending the album on a high point.

"Protect II" is the last new track, followed by an older RZA/ODB duet from 1992, "Cuttin' Headz." Despite its less-than-optimal sound quality, this throwback joint shows how much these MCs have improved their craft in such a short time as they bounce tag-team rhymes off each other. Beat-wise, RZA recycles Melvin Bliss's classic hip-hop break "Synthetic Substitution," as well as the same Monk piano riff from "Ba-Lue Bolivar Ba-Lues-Are" that appears in "Clan in the Front," though he loops a different portion.

While the album's running time already extends just short of an hour (59:04), two bonus tracks are tacked onto the CD version. The RZA-produced "Dirty Dancin'" featuring Method Man is a keeper—if only for Meth's verse. While Dirty continues his ill, stream of consciousness, sometimes-nonsensical ad-libbing, Meth takes it to the bank with lines like "Crazy, lurkin' in the shadows, I'm shady / Shysty, get your weight up, don't take me lightly / Blasted, dirty to the grain I be stained with the madness / It's the Meth-Tical with the Bastard."

Despite their contrasting approaches, the chemistry between these two MCs works amazingly well, and we get a little taste of what would have happened if Dante Ross had his way and signed both rappers. This track segues perfectly into "Harlem World," the actual album closer, with clunky production courtesy of Big Dore. It's almost as if Dirty doesn't want his show to end, as he sings and rants for over six minutes in what amounts to another extended ad-libbed comedy routine. But recalling the album's crazy, never-ending intro, this final excursion brings the listener full circle.

When *Return to the 36 Chambers: The Dirty Version* finally crawled out of Dirt's garage on March 28, 1995—four months after the release of *Tical*—it peaked at number two on the Billboard Top Hip-Hop and R&B albums and number seven on the Billboard 200, selling eighty-one thousand copies in its first week. Three months later, in June, it went gold on its way to a Grammy nomination for Best Rap Album in 1996. For Russell Jones, it was a boyhood dream finally fulfilled.

RZA and Dirty had been working toward this moment since the days of wearing Pro-Keds and Lee jeans, and the chemistry they developed over the years directly contributed to the album's success. Describing it as "the freest moment of expression"[19] in the group's catalog, even RZA, the control freak, took a hands-off approach, letting Dirty do exactly what he wanted to do and at his own pace. He also allowed Dante Ross and engineer Jack Hersca to handle the daily business of Dirty, while he busied himself with the other upcoming solo Wu-Tang projects. But Dirty practically had first dibs on RZA's entire catalog of beats and knew exactly which ones he wanted to rock with—the dirtiest ones he could find, of course. Following Meth's dark, offbeat odyssey, Dirty plunged even deeper down the rabbit hole when everyone expected Wu-Tang to make a more commercial pivot in order to capitalize on their newfound success. But stubbornly, like the group he repped to the fullest, Dirty did it his way, and instead of pandering to the masses, he made them come to him.

In this respect, *Return to the 36 Chambers* works as a worthy adjunct to *Enter the Wu-Tang*. What stands out about Dirty's first solo release is the originality, creativity, innovation, and sheer chutzpah he displays throughout. While ascending to icon status in death, he was pretty much an unknown entity when the album dropped, which makes its impact all the more impressive. Cappadonna sums it up best when he says, "What made it [the album] such a breath of fresh air was Dirty's willingness to boldly go where a lot of people are afraid to go. Dirty would break all the barriers of what's allowed and what's not. That record was saying, 'Just be yourself. Go ahead and be hood, if that's who you are, without being ignorant about it. You don't have to be accepted by anybody, but yourself."[20] Dirty was just living out his name, and people loved him for that.

CHAPTER 11

RAEKWON / ONLY BUILT 4 CUBAN LINX

Even though the gods were smiling down upon him, Steve Rifkind was pissed off. As if having a hot label wasn't enough, by the summer of 1994, features in *Billboard* and the front page of the *LA Times* were touting the work of his street promotions company, SRC, a name now inextricably tied to the term *street team*, which his lawyers were in the process of trademarking. Expanding operations, he hired Schott "Free" Jacobs, a former rapper himself who, in turn, lured Matty C from *The Source* to become Loud's first New York employees. A Staten Island native, Jacobs already had ties to the Clan. In a masterful stroke, revealing his chess-born strategy of thinking many moves ahead, RZA had asked him to connect with Rifkind so they could have an inside man at the label to look out for their interests. When the two met, Jacobs discovered he had attended the University of Maryland with Rifkind's brother, Jon, and since connections matter, a job offer was in the pocket. The new A&R department's first signing was the Queensbridge duo Mobb Deep, who had previously recorded the album *Juvenile Hell* (4th & Broadway / Island, 1993) when they were only teenagers. Loud was beginning to look like the label for second chances. But the fact that Rifkind couldn't hold on to Method Man or ODB irked him to no end.

According to Jacobs, "The [Wu-Tang] deal was structured so that Loud got to keep two artists. At me and Matty C's request, we kept Deck and Rae. I figure if we had Rae, we had Ghost." Actually, Loud had first dibs on all the members of the Clan—provided they could secure the advance money from RCA to beat out any competing offers. Already upset about losing two of the breakout stars of the Clan, Rifkind was hedging his bets on Raekwon, who had clocked the most rhyme time on 36 Chambers. Unfortunately for him, this path led through the notoriously frugal Carol Fenelon, RCA's chief attorney, who was considered a pit bull at the negotiation table. Thinking she might be swayed by RZA, Rifkind's partner, Rich Isaacson, set up a meeting involving Fenelon; Rifkind; Rifkind's lawyer and cousin, Jamie Roberts; and RZA, Divine, and their lawyer, Tim Mandelbaum. Unfortunately, the talks, which convened in the RCA conference room on the thirty-sixth floor, did not proceed well, as Fenelon refused to budge from her best offer, even though the company came in only $20,000 under what RZA wanted. "Get yourself another nigger. I'm out of here," he reportedly said before rolling out with his team.[1] With the Wu-Tang album already surpassing gold and Method Man's first single for Def Jam, "All I Need," saturating the airwaves, he was confident in the strength of his position and was not about to be nickel-and-dimed by some corporate stooges.

No sooner had RZA left the room than the blood rushed to Rifkind's face. Even though, technically, his interests were aligned with RCA's—to offer the artist the least amount possible—he was not your average record company executive, and Wu-Tang was not a regular group. Perhaps some of their street mentality had rubbed off on him because, as a ferocious argument ensued, Rifkind completely blacked out, picking up a chair and heaving it across the table at Fenelon as if he were Hulk Hogan. Barely missing her, it crashed through the window, plummeting to the street below, where, miraculously, no one was harmed. The terrified attorney fled the conference room, screaming for building security. Rifkind was promptly arrested and escorted out in handcuffs.

The incident required the intervention of Strauss Zelnick, head of BMG North America, who tried to appease Fenelon by promoting her to head of business affairs at Arista. To Rifkind, he offered some free words of wisdom: "Be a businessman, not a gangster."[2] Zelnick was also instrumental in getting Raekwon's deal finally done, greased by the release of Meth's album, which sold over 120,000 copies in its first week alone. "You dealing with thirsty niggas," says Raekwon. "We was thirsty, but we wasn't starving, know what I'm sayin', where we ready to sell our soul for anything." And they didn't. Confident that his stock was soaring, RZA asked for more money than before because he knew he could. According to Rae, "I caught half a mil, you know what I mean?"—thanks, in part, to a gangsta move by his label boss.

While RZA's master plan always included solo albums for all the individual members of the Clan, Rae was initially hesitant when his turn came around. "At first it was like, yo, I questioned it because I always was a team player," he says. "But overall, when I had the opportunity to do a solo thing, I had to figure out what chamber did I really want to be in, yunno. See, if you look at Wu-Tang Clan, it's like it's all based on style, yunno, everything is based on different styles, but I didn't have a crazy style then, yunno, so I didn't really consider myself a hundred percent that kind of Wu-Tang member."[3] Perhaps that's why he chose Ghostface, his partner in rhyme on "Can It Be All So Simple," to guest star on the album with him.

Though initially enemies in the hood, Rae and Ghost were cut from the same cloth and had more in common than they even realized. Both were raised in poverty by single mothers and eventually gravitated toward the illegal life of the streets to sustain themselves. It was superficial divisions—namely, the long-standing Park Hill / Stapleton rivalry—that had kept them apart. But with a common denominator in RZA, who had known Raekwon as far back as second grade and was roommates with Ghost for two years, they were able to set aside past differences and become the dynamic duo we know today—a powerful example of reconciliation and transformation.

"Like when me and him [Ghost] started clicking is based on RZA because we both loved RZA the same," Raekwon explains. "We get into the studio, and it's like we never really had an issue, but we would laugh about a lot of shit we would talk about in the neighborhood. We would laugh about it, and that would help build our relationship because we both knew where we was from. We been through so much of the same shit that it was easy for us to really relate. So, just the chemistry alone, it's magical shit, B, and Riz brought it all to the table."[4]

Ghost agrees, saying of Raekwon, "That's my brother. That chemistry, we like peanut butter and jelly, man, we go together, man. Like rice and beans, whatever, you know, man, eggs and turkey bacon, nigga, this is me and Rae. It's us, you know, our chemistry. When the Father put us together, yunno, we didn't know what we was getting into, but it happened, you know what I mean, and people love it like that."[5] Ghost even claims Raekwon as his favorite rapper, adding, "I never have to question his lyrical content, and he would never question me. But we would sit here and listen to the track together and know exactly how to throw shots at it, and, yunno, you don't really get that with dudes that you don't fully grow up with from a kid, but with me and him, we had a mean chemistry and still do."[6]

While Ghost raps on all but three tracks on Rae's album, every other member of the Clan makes an appearance as well, making it a truly family affair. Says Rae, "I didn't never take it like it was a solo project 'cause every project that we was makin' at that time, it was always a Wu-Tang album to us. It was just his chamber, his chamber, his chamber. And that particular chamber was something that they knew was my style, and I needed everybody to support that, and I don't think it would have been the same if everybody wasn't on it."[7]

Unlike Meth, who had to write and record his album on the fly during the group's endless stint on the road, or Dirty, who was too busy enjoying himself, Rae and Ghost leisurely chose the beats they wanted to write to and then skipped town to the tropics. RZA had suggested Jamaica or the Bahamas, but they ended up going to Barbados, sharing a private villa at a luxury resort called the Fairmont Royal Pavilion in St. James. "I remember us being up all night, like we'll start rhymin' like twelve o'clock in the afternoon, like just writin' shit, listen to about four or five beats. But a lot of times we got busy like at night when it was like, you know, the ocean is looking black, you got the windows open. The breeze is coming in," Rae recalls. "We may take a little breather and listen to some old-school shit. Some R&B shit, like we soulful niggas. So, that really was like the vitamin to a lot of our shit. Because you know, when you put yourself in a great state of mind, when you listen to good music, when you getting ready to go tap into something that you're really passionate about, you ready."[8]

Unfortunately, hospitality at the luxury resort was not up to par. Management advised Ghost that his camouflage cargo shorts did not meet the property's dress code, and other guests complained about the racket they were making at odd hours. For their part, Rae and Ghost resented the treatment of the all-Black staff and how even generous tipping couldn't put smiles on their faces. After about a week, they got tired of dealing with the bullshit and simply left, retreating to the Pelican Hotel, one of the art-deco establishments that line Ocean Drive in Miami Beach. Here, they finished writing while gazing out across the vast blue expanse, though they never went in for a dip. Returning to New York, they had eight songs and completed the rest of the album in RZA's basement.

As much as the Clan was breathing new life into the music industry, the industry, flush with cash at the time, was changing them as well. Today, Cristal, the flagship champagne of manufacturer Louis Roederer, is a name most associated with rappers like Jay-Z or 50 Cent, but back in 1995, nobody from the streets had ever heard of it—and for good reason. The premium brand, originally created for Czar Alexander II of Russia in 1876, was essentially private stock for the moneyed classes. While most wine and champagne bottles were made of green glass to help prevent oxidation, the czar, wary of assassination attempts, wanted to see exactly what he was drinking, so he commissioned a Flemish glassmaker to design Cristal's trademark clear bottle.

Raekwon first developed a taste for the expensive bubbly, which retails for around $300 a bottle, during a label dinner with Steve Rifkind. With someone else footing the bill, he was on a mission to sample the priciest sip in the house, so, naturally, he ordered Dom Pérignon by Moet & Chandon. When they didn't have it, Rifkind told the waiter to bring the next best thing. "They came out with Cristal," says Raekwon. "Me and Ghost liked the bottle and the name on the bottle was Louis Roederer. I was like, 'I'm Lou Diamond, Louie Roederer.' Me and Ghost is loving how fruity the bottle looked. It cost more than the muthafuckin' other, so we was like, 'Cristal, nigga! That's our new shit!'"[9]

Their upscale taste in beverages was not the only trend that Rae and Ghostface unleashed on *Only Built 4 Cuban Linx* (Loud, 1995), their salvo in the Wu revolution that was slowly changing hip-hop. Adopting Mafia-style aliases for the album—Rae assumed the identity of Lex Diamonds after the Irish American gangster Jack "Legs" Diamond, while Ghost became Tony Starks—they opened the floodgates for rappers with alter egos, including Nas Escobar or Notorious B.I.G. calling himself the Black Frank White, after Christopher Walken's drug kingpin in *The King of New York* (1990). They also spun a whole dictionary of slang out of their intricate rhymes, taking storytelling to new levels of detail and description. While their subject matter—crime and the street life—had provided ripe fodder for rap since the days of Schoolly D, KRS-ONE, and especially Kool G Rap's gritty mobster chronicles of the eighties, Rae and Ghost actually lived the life that fueled their rhymes and weren't shy to admit it.

Though his style, at this point, may have been a work in progress, Raekwon says, "What I did bring to the table was the reality side of the streets, yunno, the mess, the poverty, all a that. And it was just somethin' at the time I was just livin' it, yunno, so I just came in and started writing according to that lifestyle. And it was more just lookin' out my window, but then also givin' y'all visions of things I been around and seen, you know what I mean? It's just growin' up in the hood, and that's what I wrote on paper."[10]

While plenty of rap traffics in this same subject matter, what really set Rae and Ghost apart and what they perfected on this album was the art of the story rhyme. "I love to write stories," says Rae. "My story raps mention states, cities, describes people, describes cars, and the colors of the whole fucking scene. That's my lane. I'm an MC. I want to go beyond the depths of making a rhyme. I want to create visions. I mean, I like being flashy and all that, but I think storytelling is my department. I'm good at putting films in your ear, kid."[11] Coupled with RZA's cinematic beats, *Only Built 4 Cuban Linx* (OB4CL) changed the game, once again, exceeding the high bar set by *Enter the Wu-Tang* and elevating the concept album to new heights.

At the same time, it took rap back to the gritty streets from where it came. Take the title itself, which, according to Rae, came to him before they even started working on the album. It originated from a Ghostface freestyle in which he says, "Only built for Cuban Link niggas who pull stings / Sportin' big pieces of ice carved in rings," which they performed on BET's *Rap City*.[12] "The chain we used to rock back in the days was Cuban links," says Ghost. "So, Rae came up with the theory, like a Cuban link is one of the roughest chains to break. Only built for Cuban Linx—real niggas, strong niggas."[13] Indeed, Cuban link chains boast an interlocking, usually diamond-cut pattern, making them thicker and more masculine than the delicate Franco or Figaro chains typically designed for women. While Rae wanted to call the album

"Only Built 4 Cuban Linx Niggaz," the label persuaded him to drop the last word—no doubt for marketing's sake (though it's not like the N-word doesn't show up prominently all over the album). While this title may have been somewhat cryptic to many, it didn't matter because Raekwon was so gangsta that even his album had an alias—*The Purple Tape*.

Rae wanted to set his product apart from every other album out there, so he turned to the streets for some marketing inspiration. Crack dealers often packaged their product in small vials with a colored top to distinguish their "brand" from that of their rivals. Common colors included green, red, and blue tops. According to Rae, "I made the tape purple because I wanted it to be away from everybody else's, yunno? Back on the block, that was our way of separatin' ourselves from other people, whatever, so, yunno, I kind of kept that same logic, and I said, if this was my product in the street, I gotta make sure it's different from everybody else's."[14] Unable to get his first choice of money green, his favorite color, he was left to pick from yellow, red, or purple. "I already knew Redman had a red tape out back in the day, [*Dare Iz a Darkside* (Def Jam, 1994)], so, I was like, 'Hmm, I can't do red,'" says Rae, "and purple was just lookin' at me, so, I was like, everybody might think I'm a little funny guy with the purple—yunno, this is me thinking myself—and I'm like nah, nah, and I just looked up what purple meant. It's royalty—it's perfect, so, I'll take it. And next thing you know that's how it was born."[15]

It's hilarious that people remember the color of the packaging more than the actual album cover itself, which features an iconic shot by photographer Danny Hastings, who did the *Enter the Wu-Tang* cover as well. On it, a menacing Raekwon, freshly cut and wearing a $600 black-and-white checkered designer silk shirt, blows a perfectly curled plume of blunt smoke out of pursed lips, while Ghost stands behind him, face partially obscured by his shadow, thrusting his hands like twin pistols around Rae in what resembles a classic B-boy stance from back in the day.

The purple tape dropped on August 1, 1995, when people still had tape decks in their cars—believe it or not. If you lived in New York, that was the sound of the summer, cascading out of SUVs and boomboxes across the five boroughs like water from a jacked fire hydrant. In perfect alignment with RZA's astral chart, it arrived five months after Dirty's album, which had come out four months after Meth, ensuring that the revolution was in progress, and Wu-Tang product was steadily taking over the market. More than 130,000 copies flew off shelves in the first week, and the album hit gold sales of 500,000 only two months later. But even more than numbers, *OB4CL* represented hip-hop at its finest—heavy beats and hard rhymes with a healthy dose of street swagger—putting New York front and center once again. The most fully realized Wu-Tang solo project yet, it cemented the Clan's status as a serious contender who were here to stay.

* * *

The maximum capacity for a CD back then was seventy-four minutes, and Raekwon pushes the limit, using up 73:35 for this eighteen-track opus, a metaphor for his whole approach to the album as well. Cinematic in scope, it begins and ends with extended spoken-word pieces. RZA encouraged his crew to buy portable DAT (digital audio tape) players to capture spontaneous inspiration, and Rae and Ghost put theirs to good use with homemade skits that reflected their state of mind. In "Striving for Perfection," the album's intro, they have a conversation that establishes the album's loose plot, which follows two seasoned criminals who vow to take down one more big score before getting out of the game entirely. "A couple of times, you may throw a lick in the street and then you up. And the next thing you know, a couple of months, you down," Raekwon explains. "So, when you been on both sides, where you had it and you lost it, it's like it really doesn't mean nothing to you no more, but to try to get it and keep it now. So, it was all about holding on to something that's gonna be strong and [in] my eyes [that] was always about being legit. I wanted to be legit and get out of the street."[16] The album, metaphorically speaking, represents the big caper, and pulling it off will deliver them from the street life.

"I'm hangin' this shit up if this shit don't work right here, God. I got shot at. My mom's windows got shot the fuck up, man," says Ghost, referring to an actual incident dramatized in the Hulu series *Wu-Tang: An American Saga*. What he doesn't say is that Raekwon and Power were the ones responsible, spraying his Stapleton apartment with bullets in retaliation for something Ghost had done to them. Who would have ever imagined that these two mortal enemies would one day become BFFs, writing an album together at a luxury resort? This confessional sounds all the more earnest set to the plaintive opening theme of *The Killer*, composed by Lowell Lo. John Woo's classic 1989 Hong Kong action film starring Chow Yun Fat, in fact, serves as the conceptual framework for *OB4CL*.

RZA's choice of movie works for several reasons. First of all, it involves two characters who are natural enemies—a professional assassin and the cop on his trail—like two dudes from rival projects. One thing these men share, however, is a strong sense of morality and honor, adding complexity to their characters and making them much more sympathetic. The assassin, for example, played by Chow Yun Fat, looks after a nightclub singer, whom he accidentally blinded with the muzzle flash from his gun during his last mission. After being double-crossed by a client and stepping into an ambush, he also takes the time to rescue a little girl caught in the cross fire. The cop, too, displays unusual empathy when he realizes that the assassin is actually an honorable man trying to escape his questionable past. He ends up joining forces with Fat's character against the criminal organization that wants the assassin dead. Much deeper than the violent, bloody gangster movie its trailer touts, *The Killer* mirrors a sentimental streak that runs through *OB4CL*. Fittingly, RZA uses plenty of dialogue from the movie to underscore the album's themes, but, of course, he doesn't bother clearing it.

"I met John Woo that same year," he says. "He sent me a letter. He was honored that we did it. I felt confident we could settle anything that came up. You can usually settle that shit. It's part of the budget, man. But John Woo didn't want nothing, never no money for that. We actually became friends. He took me and Ghost to lunch and dinner so many times. He gave me a lot of mentoring in film."[17] For the gracious Woo, the hype and attention the album received reflected back on his critically acclaimed film, no doubt helping to expedite his transition from Hong Kong to Hollywood.

After the big motivational speech that kicks off the album and paints them as brothers in the struggle, we are suddenly thrust into a night scene (complete with crickets) where they have just pulled off a caper and are divvying up the loot, albeit unfairly, as in "one for you, two for me." According to Raekwon, "That was just one of them tracks where we felt like we just got finished robbing a bank, and we got home and broke that money up."[18] As the title, "Knuckleheadz," suggests, they are playing the role of ignorant street thugs who act impetuously and settle everything with violence—hardly a stretch, since this is where their crime saga begins. "We were once straight knuckleheads waiting for opportunities to come so we could get that coin," Rae admits.[19]

Fittingly, U-God, another stone-cold hustler, joins him and Ghost on the track, making his sole contribution to the album. As with *36 Chambers*, on which he appears only twice because he was still caught up in the system due to parole violations, U-God had just returned from the pen two days earlier when he dropped his verse. "I came back home and got on Rae and Ghost's album," he says, "but I ain't get a chance to do my vocals over. When I did that, I got locked up again."[20] So much for a knucklehead wanting respect. But that at least explains his subpar vocal performance and probably why he still made the cut too. On his first piece of music on the album, RZA keeps it simple with his usual boom bap, composed of layered kicks and snares and a bowel-shaking bass line over which he plays a simple but catchy piano ditty. For atmosphere, he laces this street cinema with the sound of sirens and gunshots.

Next up, "Knowledge God," one of Rae's three solo appearances, starts off with some prominent nasal sounds, which certainly sound like the obvious—especially considering the album's subject matter. "But that wasn't like we was sniffin' coke in the studio or no shit," says Rae. "The sniffing at the start of the song just happened. That was part of the take. When I did it, it wasn't like we knew that was gonna be part of the track."[21] A prime example of randomness and the unplanned in the creative process, RZA's inclusion of this sound makes it an important component of the track.

"We could have really been getting skied up, going to get this nigga after that," says Rae. "So, it matched perfectly."[22]

As the sniffing gives way to poignant strings, a sample of composer Stanley Black's "Meadowland" from the album *Russia* (London Records, 1965), Rae gets nostalgic, saying, "You know we had the baddest motherfuckin' unit back in the days, kid." He goes on to name-check "wild ass niggas" like "Su, Tyrese, Size," who, for all we know, are either dead or in jail, before launching into his rhymes. In the first verse, he's talking on the phone to a friend in jail, whom he vows to look out for upon his upcoming release: "Chill pa, the God'll be a star when you come home / Light bones, and let you rock my 3G stone." He also fills him in about the crack game, lamenting the high price of a kilo of coke, which has forced him into taking serious measures: "Keys, 24 a brick / Colombians be on some bullshit / That's why Papi got hit."

Then he drops the hook, ending with the line, "What's today's Mathematics, son? Knowledge God." This question-and-answer form of interaction illustrates how Five Percenters identified and communicated with their own. According to Supreme Mathematics, the numeral 1 means knowledge while 7 stands for God. So "Knowledge God" would be the 17th— along with a full breakdown of the significance of those words to that particular day.

In the second verse, however, he breaks from this conversational format with a story. "Hit a store owner named Mike Lavona / Italiano, slanted eye, banging a fat Milano / Sellin' coke right out the bottle," says Raekwon, referring to a character that he knew in real life. A Milano, the chocolate-filled vanilla cookie, incidentally, refers to a person of mixed race. "I was talking about going to hit up a real nigga, a store owner like Mike Lavona—them niggas that be havin' money in the hood and they be trying to stay out of the way of the tough guys," he says. "But at the same time, he still hold his ground because he got business out here in these streets. He's thinking, 'I'm not going to be intimidated by y'all young boys, but at the same time I know some of y'all young boys might be schemin'.' That's where that character comes from."[23] Unfortunately, for guys like Mike, their involvement in the streets eventually catches up to them, as he winds up getting shot sixteen times in the song. While Raekwon drops the hook again along with some ad-libs and shout-outs, RZA allows the instrumental to play out, something he does more on this album than on the previous two solo efforts.

In addition, while Meth and Dirty's albums included a substantial amount of material he already had in the vaults, RZA is creating new stuff rapidly and learning on the fly, coming into his own as a producer on *OB4CL*, the first album he also tracked, engineered, and mixed mostly on his own. "Our music, it's not popular music being done over and over. It's new music being invented," he said around the time of the making of this record. "So I think right now, Wu-Tang is inventing the sound of the future." To be sure, if anyone merely considered the Clan a blast of nostalgia or throwback to the golden era of hip-hop, tracks like "Criminology" set the record straight.

"That record right there was definitely one of the records where we were like, 'Yo, we dare anybody to get in our way right now.' Me and Ghost were just bloodthirsty wolves right there," says Raekwon of the second single off the album, which hit the streets on June 26, 1995.[24] In fact, "Criminology" sums up the album's concept better than any single track and could have easily filled in as the album's title as well. According to Ghost, "This whole world is based on criminology, man. Yo,

I'm tellin' you, the richest niggas did crime before, man, to get where they at now, so, yo, it's a part of life, man. Some live through it, some don't; some get caught up in it, and some strive for more, you know what I mean, so, it's in everybody's blood."

If anyone had prior doubts about Ghost, his verse on "Criminology" cements his rep as a dart master, spouting lines like "First of all son, peep the arson / Many brothers I be sparking, and busting mad light inside the dark / Call me dough snatcher, just the brother for the rapture / I hang glide holdin' on strong hard to capture / Extravagant, RZA bake the track and its militant / Then I react like a convict and start killing shit." His delivery alone displays pure ferocity as he attacks the track like a lion pouncing on his prey. He also sets the bar pretty high for his partner, who, nevertheless, meets the challenge with rhymes like "AK's black, bust back like 70 Macs / I'm all that, street niggaz knowing my steez black / Ron G, you know he coincide with me, see / marvelous menace to society." At the time, Ron G was a popular mixtape deejay whose coveted cassettes were only available from the bootleggers on 125th Street in Harlem, so Rae was proclaiming that his product was underground, authentic, and exclusive. While the casual listener might catch the reference to the Hughes brothers' 1993 hood drama *Menace II Society*, unless you were a New York hip-hop head, the mention of Ron G was typical of many of Raekwon's obscure references.

Along with some of the hardest lyrical content and slang, the sound of "Criminology" was something hip-hop had never before heard. "I remember coming to the studio, and that shit was just blasting, yunno," Rae recalls. "*Ding, ding, ding*! I'm like, 'Oh, shit! RZA, you did it with this one!'"[25] While the break jacks the entire opening riff of Black Ivory's

"I Keep Asking You Questions," from the LP *Don't Turn Around* (Today, 1972), the song's main loop, an echoing xylophone phrase, comes from just a single note of the Sweet Inspirations' "Why Marry" (Stax, 1968). Listening to the original, it strains credulity to believe that RZA is able to excavate such a loop, but he doesn't. Using the ASR-10, he samples only a small piece, replaying it on the keyboard to create a totally new melody distinct from the original. While he has always experimented with this method of playing samples, *OB4CL* marks the first time he makes it the centerpiece of his production style.

Speaking of which, the "Criminology" video sparked a new look for Ghost. Says Raekwon, "I told Ghost, 'I need you to be Vincent "the Chin" Gigante right now. Don't have no muthafuckin' gear on, all I need you in is a mean robe.'"[26] In the annals of the Mafia, Vinnie "the Chin" was a former professional boxer turned Mob enforcer who worked his way up to become head of the Genovese crime family between 1981 and 2005. During those years, he evaded the law by feigning insanity, wandering the streets of Greenwich Village in slippers and a robe, mumbling to himself. "That record made Tone [Ghost] be like, 'Yo, I ain't wearing no more clothes no more, just Wallabees and robes and shit,'" Rae adds. "Not like me, I want all the ice. That's why they call me Lex Diamonds 'cause I always love diamonds and big shit and sparkling shit, yunno, that was that character at that time. Yunno, it was almost bein' like a drug dealer / superhero / real nigga / reinvented Rakim nigga, you know what I mean? That was me comin' to that life again, the Caesar [haircut], yunno, the silks and all that shit."[27]

With blazing verses from Rae and Ghost over a banging beat from RZA, the track was almost there but needed something to take it over the edge. "I remember sittin' down, and we told RZA we need something in the beginning to light this shit up," says Rae. "And at that time, we was lookin' at *Scarface*, so we went to that. Fuck that, we gonna put a skit on here—you know we was into skits."[28] Since Al Pacino's *Scarface* had ascended to the holy grail of crime films among hip-hop circles, it's an appropriate choice, and RZA picks the part where Pacino as Tony Montana declares war on his Colombian connect Sosa before repeatedly slamming the speakerphone as if it were Sosa's head. "We was like, 'That's it!' and then the beat just came, and that's when me and Ghost was like, 'Yunno what? Now we gonna go to another level with niggas'," Rae recalls.[29] Forget Polo, which, like gold, was so eighties. Rae dedicated the track to gritty New York shitty and "all my Tommy Hil', ice-rockin' niggas," elevating another overrated American clothing manufacturer, Tommy Hilfiger, in the process and turning diamonds into a thug's best friend.

It's hard to believe that the next track, "Incarcerated Scarfaces," was never meant for this album, since it's got Rae's vibe written all over it and fits into the overall selection so well. According to RZA, however, "I wasn't making that beat for Rae. I was finished with Rae. I was making it for GZA probably. He was next. But then Rae heard that beat, grabbed his pen and paper and started writing."[30] As Rae recalls, "I came in RZA's basement one night and he just had that shit poppin', and I looked around the room and nobody was there. I was like, 'I want this shit! This is me!'"[31] Most of the time, that's how things operated inside the Wu-Tang camp—first come, first served—but Rae also has a reputation for being greedy for beats. "I wrote my rhyme in maybe fifteen minutes—the whole three verses. I was just flying. It was just coming to me 'cause that's how I get it in sometimes. If something really yokes me up like this—the beat—then I'm ready to get on it."[32] RZA remembers it taking more like two hours, but even that would be record time for completing an entire song.

A completely solo effort on the mic, Rae even wrote the hook, where he says, "Now yo, yo, what up, yo, time is running out / It's for real though, let's connect, politic, ditto / We could trade places get lifted in the staircases / Word up, peace incarcerated Scarfaces." Says Rae, "I wrote that song right there for all my niggas that was locked up. I happened to just be thinking about it. I think one of my man's had just went away for a long time. I wanted to have something on the album to represent the niggas that's inside the belly of the beast. You got a lot of cats also that wear that scar on their face."[33]

RZA keeps the beat simple but deadly, using the drum break from the Detroit Emeralds' "You're Getting a Little Too Smart" (Westbound, 1973) and a guitar strum from Koko Taylor's "Wang Dang Doodle" (Checker, 1966), augmented by some keyboard lines of his own. The cherry on top is an intro from *The Killer*: "He looks determined without being ruthless / Something heroic in his manner / There's a courage about him, doesn't look like a killer," which we assume applies to Rae. Then the punchline drops: "You don't trust me, huh? Well, you know why. We're not supposed to trust people in our profession."

Though RZA's productions still rely mostly on samples, he's also increasingly hitting the keys himself, gaining more confidence as a musician capable of creating his own riffs. Examples of his budding musicianship are evident throughout the album, including the next track, "Rainy Dayz," where he lays down some melancholy chords over a simple rim-shot beat, "CB#5," courtesy of Carlos Bess from the *Funky Drummer Vol. 1* LP (JBR, 1993). The real star of this track, however, is singer Blue Raspberry, making her first appearance on the album singing the hook, "It's raining, he's changing / My man is going insane." The inspiration for that line came from the Barbra Streisand and Donna Summer duet "No More Tears (Enough Is Enough)" (Columbia, 1979) in which they sing, "It's raining, it's pouring, my love life is boring me to tears." Blue Raspberry's voice also adorns the song throughout, as she riffs and ad-libs in an impressive display of her vocal range.

"That one specifically, we wrote by the water. Had the good villa right off the ocean and shit. Three, four in the morning, wind is blowing, curtains is blowing and we really got a chance to put it down," says Raekwon. "We just basically gave you some action on how niggas in the hood think—how a nigga lady think. We was like, this is gonna be perfect for the struggling girl who can't understand her man and he a thorough nigga."[34] Here, the word *thorough* is Raekwon's slang equivalent to what the Mafia would call a "made man"—basically an officially recognized thug who gets respect on the streets.

He and Ghost also open up about their inner lives, offering some poignant insights. Ghost says, "Waitin' on these royalties take too long / It's like waitin' on babies, it makes me want to slay thee / But that's ungodly, so, yo, God, pardon me / I need it real quick, the dough flow like penmanship." He expresses his frustration at being caught in limbo between the street life and legitimacy. Meanwhile, Rae says, "I puff what's only right, leave the poison alone / Projects, infested with rats, cats, and crack homes / Half of us will try to make it, the other half'll try to take it." Making a statement about the environment that produced him, he speaks of the jealousy of some of his fellow ghetto dwellers, who, like crabs in a barrel, don't like to see their neighbors doing well.

"This is one of my favorite tracks, if not my favorite track," says RZA. "This was too emotional and too real for me. Too close to my personal situation. This was the life we was living, just talking and rapping and hoping. Record royalties take too long to come. We had a platinum album, but we waiting on the check to come fast like babies wanting they food."[35] It's quite evident how RZA feels about one of the album's stand-outs because of the amount of detail he invests.

The intro starts out with Blue Raspberry singing a cap-pella: "It's a mystery inside, of how I'm going to get mine / I'm thinking 'bout so many ways / Of how to conquer these rainy days." He then cuts in some dialogue from a scene from *The Killer*, where the cop first confronts Jenny, the night-club singer who was accidentally blinded by the assassin he is chasing. "You sang beautifully just now," he says. "I sang for him, and he isn't here," she responds before Ghost drops some ad-libs as he prepares to jump into his rhyme. After both MCs' verses, the track seems to end, but the instrumen-tal starts up again amid the sound of rain and a reprise of Blue Raspberry. "Rainy Dayz" is a hauntingly beautiful track that combines elements of R&B—specifically Blue's voice—with hard-core hip-hop in ways that had never before been imagined. They pull it off beautifully, however, creating a template for more of this kind of R&B fusion.

Wu-Tang has always been known as a self-referential group, not afraid to recycle beats, rhymes, and concepts within the family, and the track "Guillotine (Swordz)," fea-turing Inspectah Deck, Ghost, and GZA, provides a prime example. Originally a short interlude from *Tical*, used in the intro to "Meth vs. Chef," Raekwon liked the beat so much that he practically demanded that RZA make it a full song for his album. It proves to be a savvy move because, down to its opening dialogue from the martial arts film *Shaolin vs. Lama* (1983), the track brings your attention back to the group, connecting to the saga that *36 Chambers* began. Inspectah Deck, a master of the internal rhyme, sets it off, as he so often does: "First to criticize, but now they have become / Mentally paralyzed from the hits that I devise / Now I testify, the best is I / Rebel INS, your highness, blessed to electrify / With voltage of an eel, truth that I reveal."

While GZA had scored a deal with Geffen by then and was busy working on his album, Deck, one of the most consistent and underrated MCs in the group, who Loud planned to sign, suffered a setback when RZA lost most of the beats for his album in a flood. That unfortunate calamity helped push back his release date indefinitely, while other factors kept him in a state of limbo until his debut, *Uncontrolled Substance* (Loud/Relativity), finally saw light much later in October 1999. Until then, his stock continued to rise with scorching verses on other Clan solo albums.

Following right on the heels of "Guillotine" is a remix of "Can It Be All So Simple," the song from *36 Chambers* that originally showcased the chemistry between Rae and Ghost. Remixes were "a thing" at the time, and while most simply swapped out the original music, RZA does the opposite, keeping the Gladys Knight sample that powers the track and only slightly embellishing the beat while letting the MCs rewrite their verses. They also add an intro skit in which Rae informs Ghost of an unidentified dude selling crack in front of his building. As Ghost accosts the stranger, he gets shot in the confrontation that ensues, mirroring an incident that happened to him in real life when he got shot in the neck in Steubenville, Ohio. Dipping into his personal files, Ghost rhymes:

> I doze off, catch a flashback on how I got trapped
> And got licked like Papsy in a mob flick, I got hit
> Stumbling, holding my neck to the God's rest
> Open flesh, burgundy blood covered my Guess
> Emergency trauma, black teen headed for surgery
> Can it be an out of state nigga tried to murder me?

A lot of rappers employ gun talk as a means of pumping themselves up and showing how tough they are, but Ghost is one of the few MCs to ever speak about being on the receiving end of a bullet—and he still comes off tough because he survived.

Nine tracks into the album, we are treated to an intermission of sorts with another extended spoken-word piece called "Shark Niggas (Biters)." To call it a skit would be inaccurate because it's really just an unrehearsed exchange between Rae and Ghost caught on portable DAT. Coming from an era in hip-hop in which there was an unspoken rule against "biting," or copying someone else's lyrics, style, or even music, Ghost makes a valid point: "Be original." Gassed up on the Ballantine Ale, however, he goes a step further. Without naming names, he mentions that "people" bit off Nas's album cover for his groundbreaking debut *Illmatic* (Sony, 1994), which depicts the seven-year-old afroed rapper superimposed over an image of the Queensbridge Houses where he grew up. The Notorious B.I.G.'s album cover for his debut, *Ready to Die* (Bad Boy / Arista, 1994), released only five months later, depicts the artist as a toddler in diapers, also sporting a 'fro. It doesn't take Sherlock Holmes to figure out who Ghost is pointing the finger at.

In hindsight, however, he explains, "I was 25, yo, goin' in. At that time, I had a bunch of goons around me. We didn't give a fuck. What was said, was said sideways, like a sideways dart. We didn't give a fuck how a nigga took it."[36] Though a chorus of oohs and aahs from the sidelines initially greeted this dis, such a confrontation on wax was nothing new to rap and usually helped sell records. For his part, Biggie had already collaborated with Method Man on "The What" on his album, and his love for the Clan was well documented. Two years later in LA, when Ghost met Biggie face-to-face, they squashed any beef. "We shook hands on some peace shit, but that was all 'cause they was on their way leavin' out," says Ghost. "A day or two later, niggas aired him out. I felt bad like, 'Damn, the niggas aired out one of my New York niggas.'"[37]

A true slang originator, Raekwon's obsession with diamonds spawned a new slang, "ice," which appears in no less than three song titles on *OB4CL*, including "Ice Water," "Glaciers of Ice," and "Ice Cream." "Ice Water," which comes next, serves as our official introduction to Cappadonna, a.k.a. "Cappachino," a longtime homey from the hood who goes back to the days of rhyme battles at Park Villas and smoked-out ciphers in project staircases, when he was known as Original. Cappa, who took his current name from Staten Island war hero Father Vincent R. Capodanno, the "Grunt Padre," used to be the envy of Park Hill—a sharp-dressed neighborhood star whom everyone looked up to. He showed people like Deck, U-God, and even Raekwon how to rhyme. Unfortunately, serious jail time took him out of commission. He happened to be minding his business one day in front of his building when another guy, named Boo-Yay, was running from the cops and ditched a package of crack rocks at Cap's feet.[38] He caught the rap for it even though it wasn't his. But Cappa managed to keep his darts sharp during his lockdown. After standout performances on *OB4CL* and Ghost's album *Ironman*, he eventually signed to RZA's Razor Sharp label and released his own solo album, *The Pillage* (Razor Sharp / Epic, 1998) before eventually joining the group as an official member.

He makes his name on tracks like "Ice Water," where he spits powerful bars like "Sipping on a Moet, laid up, Rae-Gambino / Mastermind the plan, Tony Starks, Cappachino / Developed while your head be swelling up off of the Nation / Blinded by the ice while I release the confrontation." Like Ghost, Cappa's rhymes could be so abstract and obtuse that they were like deciphering riddles. But he has a way with flipping words and a flow and delivery that perfectly complements his partners on the track. Big Un, an associate of Ghost's who is currently incarcerated, also makes an uncredited appearance dropping some ad-libs. According to RZA, "He's in jail for life, a thorough ass nigga, a real street nigga. We let him do the talking between the second and third verses. He confirmed Ghost and Rae's association with the streets."[39]

Sonically, RZA outdoes himself once again, taking us into an entirely new chamber of production. Instead of sampling a piece of music or even an instrument, he takes a monosyllable, the word *I*, sung by Delores Hall on "Where Do We Go from Here?" (RCA, 1973), pitching it down to sound like a man's voice. He loops that over a double kick and snare section of the drum loop, "S.C.R." by Carlos Bess from *Funky Drummer Vol. 1*, augmenting it with his own percussion to create those signature chunky rhythms. The overall result sounds like something far beyond the sum of its simple parts, taking hip-hop into unfamiliar territory. While the whole Wu-Tang aesthetic centered around a respect and nostalgia for the "golden era" of 1986–1988, they were also moving the art form full-steam ahead to the future. Tracks like "Ice Water" helped quench the thirst of fans for real hip-hop during that hot summer of 1995.

According to Ghost, "We tried to make every song, every song like a fuckin' hit. That's what made that *Cuban Linx* shit a real classic, too. Each song is so dope—that's how we planned that shit to be. Nothing less. Not just an album cut. We don't want an album cut, we want singles on every song, and that's what it was."[40] Such high standards of quality control even applied to the B sides of singles. When "Criminology" was released as a single, for example, its B side was "Glaciers of Ice," the next track in the album sequence. The sonic assault of "Glaciers," one of the most experimental tracks in RZA's oeuvre, destroys any preconceived notions of what a hip-hop song is.

The track begins innocently enough with another long skit—this one really a monologue from Ghost about dyeing Clarks Wallabees. "We was in the car one day, driving around with the DAT machine with a microphone, and we just started talking shit about how we're gonna do it this summer with the Clarks," says Ghost. "The dyeing was something I was doing already. I'm an inventor. Niggas can't fuck with me when it comes to style."[41] Rae adds, "We had bumped into a Chinese nigga who could dye shit. That was Ghost's man. And we was just runnin' back and forth to that nigga every time. We was into shoes hard. We wanted to wear Clarks because the shits was comfortable and nobody in the game was fuckin' with 'em."[42]

The fellas had Dusty Fats and his posse of West Indian hustlers, who had once ruled over the neighborhood, to thank for this choice of footwear. Clarks' classic brand of English shoes, especially the all-suede and crepe rubber sole Wallabees, were a status symbol in the former British colonies of the Caribbean—not to mention comfortable and stylish. At the time, however, they only came in basic solid earth tones, but Ghost planned to change that. "I'ma rock niggas this summer," he gushes on the album, referring to his "blue and cream" dyed Clarks, which he planned to make in even more colors.

As the track segues in under the intro, we are immediately thrust into a house of horrors with suspenseful strings and what sounds like a harpsichord. That sample is actually a few seconds of a guitar strum, which RZA utilizes to ill effect, once again playing it on his sampler's keyboard to create a phrase that sounds nothing like the original. He picks a fairly obscure source to sample from as well, "Heartbreaker" from the album *Volumen 2* (Arena, 1970), by the Chilean psychedelic rock band Aguaturbia. The drum programming is his own, a variation on that basic double kick and snare pattern—boom, boom, bap—that lay at the foundation of many of his tracks. But we see a definite style emerging in his productions, in which one element in the track, whether it be the main loop or something else, seems slightly off-kilter due to the absence of quantization to keep things tightly on beat. "Glaciers of Ice" provides a case in point, as the strings and guitar combine to create a chaotic element that would be completely unhinged if not for the steady beat. RZA also turns it up a notch with the freestyle wailing of Blue Raspberry.

"One night, I was just at the studio and I was playing around on the microphone singing Patti LaBelle's 'Over the Rainbow,' with no music, no nothing," the singer recalls.

"And when I got to the end like, 'Why then, oh, why c-a-a-n't I,' RZA recorded it. And that's where he put it, in 'Glaciers of Ice.'"[43] It's uncanny how much Blue's soaring vocal matches the power of LaBelle's original. She also interpolates another vocal riff from "Sing a Simple Song" (Telefunken, 1975) by Please, which RZA slides into the mix behind the hook.

Raekwon sets it off with some of his best lines on the album: "Stand on the block, Reebok, gun cocked / Avalanche rock, getting paid off mass murderer's services / Chef break 'em, watch the alley cats bake 'em / Po-nine made 'em, drop grenades and take 'em / Quick fast we reflect like the sky be blue true / Wu-Tang saga continue." That last line plays off what Meth says on his album, becoming a catchphrase on future Wu-Tang releases to express the continuity of the movement.

He's followed by Masta Killa, right off the bench in his first appearance on the album, displaying deadly skills. Not much is known about Masta Killa at the time other than that he's got a bad temper. A background player with an intense gaze, he acquired somewhat of a rep after assaulting journalist Cheo Coker because he didn't like the artwork that accompanied Coker's article about the Clan in *Rappages*. Offering some keen insights into his mentality, Killa raps, "Thoughts roll down the shaft of the brain / Mental gives the signal to the physical / Whirlwind kicks and hits from every angle / Violent temperaments left continents dented." The moral of the story: never underestimate the quiet ones. A cousin of ODB, 60 Second Assassin, provides the final element of this masterful production as he harmonizes—not raps—the closing stanzas of the song: "It's been a long time, since the Father left in '69," referencing the death of Five-Percenter founder Clarence 13X. "It's been a long time, since Wu-Tang had the chance to shine." Backed by the sounds of an evil harpsichord, it all sounds rather baroque.

Ghost isn't kidding about their "all killer, no filler" approach to this album because sometimes it seems like the onslaught never stops. Before you can catch your breath, they drop another classic, like the next track, "Verbal Intercourse," featuring the first guest outside the Wu-Tang family, Nas (Nasir bin Olu Dara Jones). Following his classic debut, *Illmatic* (Sony, 1994), the young Queensbridge rapper became the toast of New York, drawing comparisons as the next Rakim. A childhood friend of Havoc of Mobb Deep, he also made a guest appearance on their Loud debut, *The Infamous* (Loud/RCA, 1995), sharing the mic with Havoc, Prodigy, and their labelmate Raekwon on "Eye for an Eye (Your Beef Is Mine)." That collaboration sparked a friendship between him and Raekwon, two street soldiers with a lot in common. "Rae would come out to Queensbridge, I would go to Staten Island," says Nas. "We'd just ride and hang out all night. We didn't call each other to work. We would call each other to hang out."[44]

One night, after getting smoked out and hanging at a local Chinese restaurant in Park Hill, they wound up at RZA's studio. Of course, the Abbott had beats on the grill, and Nas auditioned a few different verses to see what fit. Putting on his A&R cap, Raekwon listened intently until he heard something he liked. When Nas said, "Through the lights, cameras, and action, glamor, glitter, and gold / I unfold the scroll, plant seeds to stampede the globe / When I'm deceased, by then the Beast arise like yeast / To conquer peace, leaving savages to roam in the streets," Rae sent him into the vocal booth. "After that one, I threw my dart in ten minutes, just because I was so happy that he did something great as far as within our camp. It really made me feel good," says Rae, sounding like a proud big brother.[45]

The track employs the same staggered rim-shot beat from "CB#5" by Carlos Bess that RZA used on "Rainy Dayz." For the main loop, he goes back to one of his main sources of inspiration, the Stax/Volt label, whose production team of Isaac Hayes and David Porter churned out some serious soul and R&B classics in the sixties and seventies. RZA samples the intro to "If You Think (You May as Well Do It)" (Volt, 1972) by the female vocal trio the Emotions, catching some of their vocal performance, "I want to love you, but what if he wants me," in the slowed-down loop.

Following this spate of features, the focus switches back to Rae and Ghost, with a solo contribution from each. "Wisdom Body" gives Ghost a chance to spread out from his usual street raps, as he turns his attention to another favorite topic of his—women. Originally titled "Fly Bitch Shit" and featuring an introduction from Dick Williams playing "Pretty Toney" in *The Mack* (1973), the track finds our hero scoping out a desirable female and delivering his pitch. "Peace, excuse me, allow to introduce myself / Yo, I'm the man, and honey, you've been rated top shelf / Yo, what's your name, hon? Hair wrapped up in a bun / Your eyes sparkle just like glass in the sun," he says over a loop that RZA jacks wholesale from BJ Thomas, appropriately titled "I'm Going to Make You Love Me" (Scepter, 1969).

While this certainly doesn't sound like the Ghost we've known up to now, it's his way of cannily revealing another side of his personality, which he further develops on his solo effort, *Ironman*. Ghost remembers being well-lubricated with Ballantine when he recorded that track, so he did several passes and had to punch in several times because he was slurring his words. But you'd hardly notice from the final result. "That's the thing about these albums we made earlier," he says. "We used to keep a lot of the fuck-ups. That's what made it raw. Everything ain't always gotta be perfect."[46]

Rae's second solo performance on the album immediately follows—"Spot Rusherz," which happens to be RZA's least favorite track. "I wasn't really feeling the beat," he says. "It's one of those things where he [Raekwon] came in and aired it out, and to me, it saved the beat. I still don't like the beat. I still wanted to get it off the album."[47] But according to Rae, "I love that fucking beat. I love to write stories and that beat was perfect for a caper. Yeah, RZA fought me for it, and didn't want it on there, but I insisted. I mean RZA's the type of nigga who wants authentic material. Anything that's too clean was wack to him back then. But for me, I think I sound good over clean beats sometimes. I love to tell stories, and that's what *Cuban Linx* is—a bunch of good stories within a story itself."[48] In his rhyme, Rae drops more fashion references than an issue of *Vogue*, name-checking Polo, Hilfiger, Donna Karan, Perry Ellis, and Claiborne. But he also gets his Raymond Chandler on with lines like "Heard the key in the lock, cocked the Glock / Turn the lights out, dip behind the couch / Kion, gag his mouth / Infra-red at his head when he entered." Crime rhymes, in fact, became his bread and butter, defining his style throughout his prolific career.

While RZA lobbied to get "Spot Rusherz" off the album, Raekwon was not feeling the next track, "Ice Cream," which became the third single. "I hated 'Ice Cream,'" he admits. "That's crazy, right? It's funny 'cause I loved the beat. The only thing I didn't like about the record, I felt like it was too soft for *Cuban Linx*. When I tell you everybody fought with me, even Ghost was like, 'Nah, G, this is it.' And I was like, 'Nah, it's too soft. We need everything hard! Gutter!'"[49] In addition to being the most radio-friendly track on the album, it was also the Clan's only outreach to the ladies.

After producing the beat one night using the drum break from Rufus Thomas's "The Breakdown (Part II)" (Stax, 1971), and a tiny section of a guitar riff from Earl Klugh's "A Time for Love" (Liberty, 1980), RZA was struck by an inspiration. When Meth came over, he says, "I told him I got a crazy idea on this one. I wanna use girl's breasts as imaginary ice cream cones. I came up with the idea to make T-shirts to go with it. 'Meth, you gonna do the hook.' It was the first song besides 'You're All I Need to Get By' that we pressured him into."[50] RZA even supplied him with the flavors he wanted to use— french vanilla, chocolate, and butter pecan.

Then the unplanned happened yet again. U-God went to fetch Cappadonna, who had only recently returned from prison. Currently working as a security guard at Park Hill, Cappadonna had not been to RZA's new basement studio yet. When he arrived, RZA played him the track, to which he had already added Rae and Ghost's verses. "Oh, that's dope right there," Cappa recalls saying. "So I was joking around with RZA really, and I was like, 'Yo, let me drop a verse on that right there.' And he was like, 'Aight.' [I said] No, just fuckin' with you!"[51] While Cappa might have been only half serious, RZA wasn't, challenging the former neighborhood star to step up and get busy. Cappa says, "I wrote it right there on the spot. Took me about ten minutes. I did the 'Black chocolate girl wonder' verse, and boom! Next thing you know, Meth came in about fifteen minutes later. And RZA was like, 'Yo, you got a hook for this?' And Meth did his little ten, fifteen minutes. And I'm lookin' at him like, 'What the fuck?'"[52]

Meth, the hook master, comes up with a classic: "Watch these rap niggas get all up in your guts / French vanilla, butter pecan, chocolate deluxe / Even caramel sundaes is getting touched / And scooped in my ice cream truck, Wu tears it up." Meanwhile, Cappa makes his Wu-Tang debut, rhyming, "Ice cream, you got me falling out like a cripple / I love you like I love my dick size / Ooh, baby, I miss you, your sweet tender touches / Take pulls off the Dutches / Orgasm in my mind-state, masturbate in your clutches." The summer of 1995 couldn't get any hotter.

"Then, next thing you know, RZA called me like a week or two later and was like, 'Yo, this gonna be a single,'" says Cappa. "I was like, 'Yo, that's what's up. Do your thing, know what I'm saying?' He was like, 'Nah, you gotta be on, you gotta get down with this shit.' I was like, 'Nah, I'm good.'"[53] Following his prison stint, he was simply trying to get his life in order, and rapping seemed a thing of the past. He even threatened not to show up for the video. "But, boom, I did that video, boom, next thing you know, a month later, he was hittin' me with a production deal. So, that's when I received my first check for like sixty grand," he says.[54]

But the story doesn't end there. Cappa beelined to the nearest bank to cash the check. While waiting for the teller to bring him his money, he was checking his pockets, figuring out where he was going to stash such a large sum of cash. Instead, she returned with the phone, saying that someone wanted to talk to him. "I'm like, 'Fuck is you talkin' 'bout? I didn't call nobody here, I don't want to talk to nobody,'" he says. "Already I'm vexed right now 'cause it's like y'all about to do it to me. I just want mine, yo. I'm about to turn this bank out. Word up."[55] The guy on the other end of the line was RZA's brother Divine, who had just issued the check. He informed Cappa that he had to open up a bank account to access his money. "Yeah, that's the ignorance that [I] came in with, know what I'm saying," says Cappa. "But that's how they do. The system is geared where they gotta hold your money for you. Yeah, you ain't the dude you thought you was 'cause those niggas hold everybody money."[56] As to what he did when he finally got his hands on his cash, Cappa says, "It was sky's the limit after that. After that, it was like, yo, I was eatin' whole boxes of Captain Crunch, the whole gallon of milk, and all 'a that shit. Just wildin."[57]

As *OB4CL* draws to a close, one of the last new songs, "Wu Gambinos," featuring Method Man, RZA, Masta Killa, and Ghost, gives the crew a chance to showcase the alter egos they had assumed for the album. Some aliases are inspired by the 1984 gangster epic *Once upon a Time in America*, directed by Sergio Leone, of spaghetti western fame, that follows the lives of childhood friends David "Noodles" Aaronson (played by Robert De Niro) and Maximilian "Max" Bercovicz (played by James Woods), who both grow up in poverty and enter a life of crime. Rae bestows those names on Masta Killa and GZA, respectively, since they reminded him of those characters and hung out together. Other nicknames—like Johnny Blaze for Meth and Tony Starks for Ghost—are inspired by comic books. Deck's alias, Rollie Fingers, comes from the major league pitcher with the trademark handlebar mustache but describes the Inspectah's proficiency in rolling blunts. Golden Arms, of course, derives from the 1979 Shaw Brothers film *Kid with the Golden Arm*, which applies to U-God, and RZA simply resurrects his old deejay name, Bobby Steels, which is also an allusion to Black Panther cofounder Bobby Seale. As for the song's title, Meth explains, "Raekwon always had that mobster mentality—always liked to watch gangster movies and read Mob books and stuff like that. Plus, Staten Island is known for mobsters."[58] Long before reality shows like *Mob Wives* exploited that connection, real-life Mafia dons such as Paul Castellano made his home—nicknamed the White House— in the tony Todt Hill section where Meth lives today.

Providing a soundtrack that would not be out of place in a Mafia movie, RZA samples a melancholy piano melody from "If" on Henry Mancini and Doc Severinsen's *Brass on Ivory* LP (RCA, 1971). He pins it to the shuffling rhythm from "I Like It," courtesy of the Emotions, that he's used before. Another snippet from *The Killer* introduces the track in which the assassin is offered a job for $1.5 million, signifying that this is the big one.

According to Masta Killa, everyone was in the studio together when they recorded this cut. "And it was a beautiful thing to see," he says. "Wu-Gambinos. You see Meth come in; he lays his verse. You see Deck come in; he lays his verse. RZA is there; he lays his verse. It's inspiring to just see other MCs come through, and not just MCs. This is your brother. This is your family. It's like the Jackson 5 and shit. They all in one room—it's going to be magical."[59]

Meth adds, "We were high, hanging out. It was always a relaxed atmosphere because we were so used to being there [in RZA's basement], sleeping on the floors and all that. So, it was like being home, writing rhymes in your own house. You went from the floor to the booth. It took three hours tops just to put the vocals on it."[60]

RZA steps into the vocal booth for the first time on the album, cramming syllables as he raps at lightning speed: "The grand exquisite imperial wizard or is it / The RZArector come to pay your ass a visit / Local biochemical, universal giant, the black general / Licking shots at Davy Crockett on the bicentennial." With all his focus on production, he wants to prove that his darts are still sharp and handles the job in his inimitable style.

The album's last cut is actually the first song they recorded for *OB4CL*, "Heaven and Hell," which appears on the soundtrack for the underrated film *Fresh* (1994), a crack-era drama directed by Boaz Yakin. Powered by a soulful Syl Johnson loop from "Could I Be Falling in Love" (Hi, 1974), it's one of the rare occasions where RZA jacks an obvious sample that's good enough to stand on its own. Rae counts it as one of his favorite tracks on the album, and though he wrote most of the lyrics, he gives Ghost some verses to say. The song actually starts with the hook, which Rae recalls from an earlier time. "That was a hook that me and Cappa made up way back in the day before we were even thinking about becoming stars," says Rae. "And I just remembered the hook for this beat. And I called it 'Heaven and Hell' because we want to be in heaven but we're living in hell."[61]

He breaks it down further, explaining, "Heaven is something once you make it, hell is what you go through. So, I was just telling a real nigga story 'cause shit like that really take place on the block."[62] Blue Raspberry returns to sing the hook, "What do you believe in, heaven or hell / We don't believe in heaven 'cause we're living in hell," which appears only once toward the end, while Ghost delivers an extended shout-out, remembering fallen soldiers from the hood like Two Cent and his physical brother Devon, who succumbed to a battle with muscular dystrophy. It sounds like a fitting end to an epic album, but Raekwon isn't quite finished yet.

The cherry on top, a CD bonus track, features another extended spoken-word piece called "North Star (Jewels)," set to the music from Barry White's "Mellow Mood (Pt. 1)" (20th Century Fox, 1974), which serves as the world's introduction to Popa Wu. "When I heard that beat, I pictured a little kid witnessing some street action, sitting right in the middle of a shoot-out," says Rae. "So I came up with a story from Barry White's 'Mellow Mood (Pt. 1)' line and arranged all that. Popa Wu was perfect to deliver that motivational type speech from an older brother's point of view. I mean, everything we learn, we learn from the older brothers anyways. That was the kind of vibe and message I was trying to get at in order to end the album."[63]

According to RZA, "Everybody had dibs and dabs of street knowledge, knowledge of self, and I brought him [Popa Wu] in to be a mentor to these men like, I love them and you the only person I know that have the intelligence to keep them in sync with knowledge. It's very poisonous unless they got proper guidance. He was the smartest man I'd ever met at a certain time in my life. After two years they turned him into a Wu-Tang member."[64] While Popa Wu reminisces with Raekwon, fortifying him for the struggle ahead, ODB quietly makes his sole appearance on the album, harmonizing in the background.

When the music finally fades out, you feel like you've been on a whirlwind journey through the underbelly of society. Holding PhDs from the school of hard knocks, Rae and Ghost offer a perspective on the street life as it's never been seen before—up close and personal. In the process, they influence many of their peers as well as a whole new generation coming up. But, predictably, the $600 silk shirts, bling-bling, and bottles of Cristal are soon appropriated by a new kind of rapper, more enthralled by the good life and all its material trappings than by representing their own reality. These "playas" start bringing rap back to the clubs and eventually the strip clubs. It's the usual cycle, as mainstream and underground, pop and hard-core battle for the soul of hip-hop. But for a brief moment in 1995, all bets were off. Between Meth, ODB, and Raekwon, Wu-Tang was running this shit.

CHAPTER 12

GZA / LIQUID SWORDS

An underappreciated element of the Clan's success is the group's internal dynamic—how they relate to each other—and, more importantly, how nine distinct personalities were able to come together in the first place and survive all these years in the cutthroat environs of the music industry. It all comes down to a single word—*respect*—the kind forged through familiarity and over time. There's a very telling moment on the "intermission" of *Enter the Wu-Tang: 36 Chambers* when an interviewer asks Method Man and Raekwon to describe the other MCs in the group. When they get to the Clan's senior member, Rae gushingly blurts, "The GZA, the Genius, he's just the backbone of the whole shit," before Meth grabs the ball, interjecting, "He's the head. Let's put it that way. We formed like Voltron, and GZA happened to be the head."

You see the reverence toward him from other members of the group as well, including Inspectah Deck, who says, "Genius is one of the illest niggas I ever heard on the mic, know what I'm sayin', as far as pound-for-pound lyrics—fuck a track. And I'm talkin' about Rakim, KRS—I'm classifying him with niggas like that." Like an older brother teaching by example, "he taught me how to form my shit in sentences," says Deck. RZA, undisputed architect of the Clan, backs him up, saying, "Rakim, Kool G Rap, Kane—I've listened to them since day one. I've met them and they're exceptional MCs, I mean exceptional MCs. But to my personal taste, none of them could touch the GZA. I knew it in my heart way back before the Wu-Tang, and I strived to be like him, not like them."[1]

So while fans endlessly debate who's the best MC among Wu-Tang's all-star lineup, among group members, that issue's already settled. It's hardly surprising considering that GZA is the only MC in the Clan who can trace his MC pedigree directly back to the Bronx originators who first lit that fire in his belly. Honing his craft since the age of eleven, he is also first among his peers to get a major label record deal, years before Wu-Tang even existed. No doubt, as a result of his experience and standing, the veteran rhymer is also featured on one of the only two solo tracks on *36 Chambers*, "Clan in the Front." After the buzz and hype of that album brought the major labels flocking, GZA became the third member of the group to get a solo deal, signing with Geffen.

On face value, this boutique imprint, started by industry veteran David Geffen in 1980 and distributed by the Universal Music Group, seemed an odd choice. While their initial signings include disco diva Donna Summer and John Lennon and Yoko One, Geffen made their name with such big-haired eighties rock groups as White Snake, Tesla, and, of course, Guns N' Roses. As indie or alternative rock ascended in the nineties, their subsidiary David Geffen Company (DGC) owned a big piece of the action, signing Sonic Youth, Nirvana, Weezer, and Beck. As far back as 1988, they had even attempted to enter the rap market, putting in the highest offer for De La Soul, but the group decided against being the token rap act on a label filled with mostly white rock artists.

But change happens quickly in the industry. By 1993, Geffen had lured a young A&R assistant, Wendy Goldstein, from the competition. One of the few female A&R people in the business, the no-bullshit native New Yorker had just made her mark signing the white ragamuffin sensation from Toronto, Snow, to East-West / Atlantic. His breakout 1992 hit, "Informer," produced by Queensbridge's MC Shan, spent seven weeks on the top spot of the Billboard Hot 100. Geffen doubled Goldstein's salary and put her in charge of their New York office on Fifty-Seventh and Broadway.

They were not sorry. Two weeks into the job, she signed the Roots, a live hip-hop band from Philly whose buzz was slowly spreading outside the City of Brotherly Love. Def Jam's Lyor Cohen had passed on signing them, and after finding out that Goldstein had bit, he called her to declare that there was no future for a hip-hop band. (So much for mansplaining.) A couple of weeks after that, Tim Mandelbaum, RZA's lawyer, called her up to pitch GZA. "You have a rock label, and we have a rock star," she recalls him saying. Considering the Clan's total domination of the day, he wasn't a hard sell, so around May/June 1993, GZA signed to Geffen for $500,000.

From the veteran MC's perspective, his journey from a label synonymous with hip-hop to one with only two Black artists made complete sense. "I was signed to Cold Chillin' before, and it was distributed through a major, which was Warner Bros.," he says. "That deal didn't quite work out for me due to lack of promotion and support from Cold Chillin' because they were into other acts on the label that were quite bigger acts as far as popularity and record sales. I didn't really stand a chance being on that label."[2] Genius also came to Cold Chillin' at the end of an era, when the label was on the downslide. With a fresh start at Geffen, he says, "I was getting all the push from them. I was probably one of the first rappers to be signed to the label; I was getting so much support because of the popularity from Wu-Tang."[3] In an industry not known for second chances, both he and RZA had seemingly beaten the odds. On top of that, they had done it on their own terms and finally felt like they were in a position to control their own destiny.

"We in our own world with this shit, man. We not tryin' to be industrialized anymore by mu'fuckas who run this shit," GZA explains, puffing on a blunt in the driver's seat of his parked Jeep Grand Cherokee, whose color matches his hunter-green parka. Conducting his first interview in advance of the release of his sophomore effort, *Liquid Swords* (Geffen, 1995), he opts for the crisp fall air down on Broadway instead of Geffen's plush conference room in the sky. "If we allow them to come amongst us and do trading, we gonna trade, but it's like we comin' with our own shit now. That's the new industry," he says, as if stating fact.

A battle rapper since the days he started rhyming, he frames everything in the context of combat. "Once you wounded in a war, you gonna become more wise if you survive through that struggle. Then you become more determined to break through," he explains. "See, we had to leave. Me and RZA had to go back and get the family. We couldn't do it alone, yunno. We made attempts to fuck with these labels, but it wasn't connecting right. We had to go back and grab all our peeps—couldn't do it without them, know what I'm saying? So when you see brothers come together—especially from the hood—and put something together like that, man, and then all do they own little thing individually, and build corporations, man, that feed people, and get people jobs, man, that's positive, yunno."

GZA strikes the figure of a wise general laying down his strategy for success. Revealing their special sauce, he says, "It took quite a few things, man. It took trust, it took love, it took a lot of discipline. It took humbleness, yunno, learning how to humble yourself to your brother, you know what I'm saying, and observe him and then speak your mind instead of arguing all the time. But we were determined, and we were thirsty, and we were hungry, and we had to eat, and we just applied the knowledge we had, man." Even though the other members of the group looked up to him, the mark of a true leader is being humble enough to give credit where it is deserved, and he says, "RZA came with the master plan, and yunno, we all came together, man, and we worked on this project, and then it worked itself, really, 'cause it was too powerful. It was too strong. When you heard it, it was like, 'Who the fuck is these niggas,' know what I'm saying? It was like a fucking meteorite hittin' the fucking Earth or something."

Invoking Supreme Mathematics, which is practically part of his DNA, he sums it up by saying, "So, it took all those things to build that, man. It took knowledge, it took wisdom, it took understanding, it took culture, it took freedom of self, it took power, it took refinement. It took equality. It took the power of God. It took building, and it also took destroying, 'cause we had to build things and then destroy the things that were trying to destroy us, yunno. And then it took the nature of borning things—making it complete—'cause born means to bring into existence. We had to make it complete, like renew the cycle. That's what we call going from knowledge to born and back to knowledge."

One of the deepest thinkers in the group, GZA, who clearly earned the title of "The Genius," sometimes blurs the line between entertainer and philosopher. For him, an interview seems less an opportunity to promote product than to speak his mind. Through herbal vapors, he expounds on such topics as the Illuminati (before it became somewhat of a cliché in hip-hop); programming people through subliminal messaging, as in the John Carpenter film *They Live* (1988); virtual reality, which had just arrived on the scene; and population control ("It's too crowded out here, it's too many people, they're trying to exterminate people, they're doin' it already, man."). Like his fellow brothers in rhyme, he demonstrates a degree of intelligence and sensitivity to what's going on around him that shreds stereotypes. But, somehow, no matter how far he strays, he always manages to bring the focus back to MCing.

"All you gotta do is teach. Teach and open up muthafuckas," he says of his mission in that booming voice you hear on records. A late bloomer, he didn't always speak with so much bass and didn't even like the way he sounded as a teen coming up. But having matured as an artist, he's using his platform to inform and uplift. He can't resist conspiratorially adding, "The average muthafuckin' household don't know, man. Soon as they see that shit on television, 'This is not a test, this is the Emergency Broadcast System. Please report to so and so.' They packin', they gone. How many muthafuckas gonna be analyzin', be like, 'It's on!' 'Cause you know you been seeing all your life, 'This is a test.' Now what about when you see, 'This is not a test.' Then what?"

After churning out four completely distinctive back-to-back masterpieces from his basement, RZA was not only on a roll but wholly in his element by the time it came to making *Liquid Swords*. At his home in Staten Island, he built up his studio, or "lab" as he liked to call it—naturally named 36 Chambers—partially to save on recording expenses but, ultimately, for convenience sake, because that was how he had always operated. During those many months making the first round of solo albums, that was where you could usually find him, relentlessly at work, honing his chops as both a producer and engineer.

"I like making albums in one creative force," says RZA. "You got to be in sync with that shit; you got to come and spend months with me in the zone. Raekwon and Ghost, we spent months in that basement eating turkey burgers. Me and GZA played hundreds of games of chess before we made the songs for *Liquid Swords*."[4] Needless to say, the two had also practically grown up together, along with Dirty, pursuing music as their lifelong dream, which was now slowly unfolding in real time. If Rae and Ghost could establish such an amazing chemistry in their comparatively brief time rhyming together, imagine what these two cousins, collaborators since childhood, might conjure.

Any pressure to perform, therefore, was replaced with "a lot of excitement," according to GZA, who calls making the album "just a great, fun moment for me at the time."[5] While there would, no doubt, be comparisons to the other Wu solo releases, that did nothing to sway his approach to the record. "I didn't have to try to do anything different. It was going to be different regardless. My goal was to make great songs and tell great stories and use metaphors as ways of explaining what I was doing,"[6] he says, adding, "I keep it visual regardless of what I'm talking about. And it's always been that way for me as far as rhyming, and I've never changed it—I can't."[7]

GZA had the added luxury of taking his time and simply focusing on his craft because he knew he was in the capable hands of the RZA.

"I mean Raekwon and Ghostface can step in and record a song in about 45 minutes," he says. "I, on the other hand, would often go back and finish rhymes that I started. I would say I pieced things together [more] slowly then. Songs generally take me two to three days to write. Sometimes I take different sentences and put them together."[8] As any good writer knows, the goal is to get your point across in the simplest and most direct way possible. To that end, GZA says, "I'm always trying to make it tighter and tighter, draft and draft, then re-draft and re-draft over and over. I change sentences; I change words until I feel it's right."[9]

While the passage of time and pounds of weed make it virtually impossible for him to remember individual sessions, he lays out the writing and recording process as follows:

I'll come through in the evening and he'll [RZA] put the beat on. We'll be talking and I'll be writing. He's doing other things. He may have a few other Clan members in there. We're smoking weed and drinking forties here and there. Every now and then I would get tired after writing about four lines. It may take me about six hours to get four lines on paper because I'm such a perfectionist with it also. And then, about four, five, six hours, I'm napping, and then I'm up at two in the morning. I may get another four lines off in three hours and then I'm napping. And then RZA is up and he's in the city handling meetings and stuff and he comes back in the evening. The beat is still running. "What you got now?" "I got 12 [lines]." "Damn, Just, You ain't got that rhyme ready yet?" A lot of days were spent like that—days with the beat just playing for maybe 35 hours straight.[10]

Thankfully for him, the album consists of a lean twelve tracks (with a CD bonus track by Killah Priest). Relaxed and definitely well rested while working on it, GZA adds, "It was a great feeling because we were in our own space; we were on our own time. I didn't have to get up. The session wasn't over. We didn't have to leave. Everything was in-house and the timing was right. I wasn't really rushed to do a song."[11] As someone known for his complex verses, he had the added advantage of having people like Method Man, Ol' Dirty, and U-God around to write hooks, as well as the support of the rest of the Clan on certain tracks. Such a division of labor not only helped take some of the weight off him but also made the project more of a group effort, in much the same way as OB4CL.

MCing was not the only skill GZA picked up at an early age. When he was only nine, an older cousin taught him how to play the game of chess. But after losing two matches, he lost interest and didn't play again until he reached his twenties. Credit Masta Killa for reviving his interest in the game and making chess part of his daily routine. "One day I was play-ing a game of chess with Masta Killa, and the game was over, and he won the game, of course—when I first started playing again with him, he was beating me a lot," says GZA. "But the pieces were still on the board, so I just started drawing the pieces and sketching them out."[12] At first, he sketched them as they were—frozen in checkmate—but then he started adding weapons in their hands. "I get this vision of the board, and then I drew this whole thing out," he continues. "Imagine if this was war right here. I thought about 'Chessboxin.' I said we could use that for the cover of 'Chessboxin.' Then I was like, nah, it shouldn't be a single cover, it's bigger than that, and I just held that, but that was three years before *Liquid Swords*."[13]

While the group adopted GZA's concept of warring factions on a chessboard for the "Da Mystery of Chessboxin'" video, he kept his drawing in the stash for later use. Then, when the time was right, GZA commissioned comic-book artist Denys Cowan to turn his illustration into album-cover art. The superhero-inspired piece depicts a guy about to get his head taken off by a sword-wielding ninja in a GZA hoody. In the background, another assailant is downed by a flying guillotine, a bizarre weapon introduced in the 1975 martial arts film of the same name. Included in the album's inside artwork is a black-and-white drawing—based on GZA's original—of chess pieces fighting on the board, drawn by Mathematics, who is also responsible for both the Wu-Tang and GZA logos. Unlike his first album, *Words from the Genius*, which shows the artist on the cover wearing a gold lamé robe, the only photo of GZA on *Liquid Swords* is a grainy black-and-white photo of him playing chess in a black hoodie.

The album's title, according to GZA, "is a concept of being lyrically sharp, flowing like liquid metal—mercury—you know? It comes from the flick, *Legend of the Liquid Sword* [1993] where people would get their head cut off, but it would still be on their shoulders. No one else would notice, because the sword was so sharp. Wu-Tang is a sword style, and this here in the sharpest."[14] Curiously, however, no dialogue or other material was taken from this film, perhaps because it was more comedic.

As the Wu revolution gathered momentum, fans were beginning to expect more from a Clan production. After

Cuban Linx, it was no longer possible to have simply fat tracks and dope lyrics—an album needed skits as well as an overarching framework that made the record more than just a collection of random songs. Of course, RZA's modus operandi all along had been to raise the standards of hip-hop, and he was proceeding with his plan. Unfortunately, he had been juggling so many projects that, by the time *Liquid Swords* was finished and mixed, it sounded like a tight collection of songs but lacked the conceptual cohesion of previous releases.

RZA only realized this deficiency when he came to the mastering session at Sterling Sound in Manhattan. The final step in the recording process, mastering, involved EQ'ing all the finished material to sound consistent when played next to one another and then placing them in the correct sequence for the album master, which was used to manufacture LPs, CDs, and cassettes. Mastering involved highly technical work— basically twirling knobs and dials—that an engineer usually completed on his own without anyone else present. In this instance, however, not only were GZA and RZA in attendance, but they were joined by Masta Killa, Killah Priest, Dreddy Kruger, another one of GZA's friends, and this writer. Halfway through the session, RZA sent one of the studio assistants to the Deuce to buy a movie. The guy returned with a VHS copy of the brutally violent and bloody film *Shogun Assassin* (1980).

Among fans of Chinese kung fu, the film is considered a cult classic—even though it's made from pieces of two other Japanese films, *Lone Wolf and Cub: Sword of Vengeance* (1972) and *Lone Wolf and Cub: Baby Cart at the River Styx* (1972), both directed by Kenji Misumi. The *Lone Wolf and Cub* series, which actually started out in the seventies as a popular manga (comic), written by Kazuo Koike and drawn by Goseki Kojima, follows a disgraced executioner-cum-renegade assassin and his son on their adventures in feudal Japan. Because he has defied the shogun who rules the land, the Lone Wolf, Ogami, played by Tomisaburô Wakayama, has no shortage of enemies he must dispatch in order to keep his little cub, Daigoro (played by Akihiro Tomikawa), safe.

David Weisman, a Warhol protégé, acquired the rights to Misumi's films and, with partner Robert Houston, repackaged them into a single story, using the first twelve minutes of the first film and most of the second. In addition, they dubbed the movie into English, adding the obligatory cheesy synthesizer score, since it was the eighties. Though the stout, sleepy-eyed Lone Wolf doesn't immediately strike you as a highly efficient killer, actor Wakayama's real-life martial arts skills precluded the use of stunt doubles. Regardless, it's his specially forged blade, or *katana*, that does most of the heavy work, severing limbs and heads and turning opponents into spurting fountains of blood, which initially led to the film being banned in Britain.

Even in a pinch, trust RZA to pick the ideal movie to provide the interstitial glue for GZA's album. "Instead of using kung fu to introduce his stuff I used Japanese samurai because GZA's style is like one fuckin' slice and you're dead," he says.[15] After obtaining the movie, mastering engineer Tom Coyne pulled out the VHS player so they could patch it up to his system and sample snippets of dialogue. In the process of doing so, however, they ended up watching the entire film, which ran about ninety minutes. As they sprawled out on the couch and floor, the only thing missing was the popcorn. It may have been a scene from RZA's basement if they weren't paying $350 per hour for the mastering suite. Genius, who was seeing the film for the first time that night, says, "I loved it immediately and thought it fit with the album well."[16]

After the feature ended and RZA had taken what he could, he still wasn't satisfied, so he decided to stage an impromptu skit right then and there. Using some ambient street sounds that GZA and Killah Priest had recorded earlier on portable DAT and this writer, who up to that point had been a fly on the wall, simply observing, he improvised the skit of a drug deal gone bad that opens "Killah Hills 10304." This was probably the first and last time that a mastering facility had been used for such purposes. Though all these spontaneous, last-minute machinations added time and trouble, it's impossible to imagine the finished album without them. In the same breath, however, they didn't come without a cost. The final bill for that marathon mastering session, according to Goldstein, came to a whopping $15,000.

* * *

Liquid Swords, the song and the album, opens with an extended monologue from *Shogun Assassin*, in which the young Daigoro, voiced by Gibran Evans, introduces his father as "the greatest samurai in the empire," who "cut off the heads of 131 lords" over the dark, moody film score by W. Michael Lewis and Mark Lindsay. Metaphorically speaking, this description refers to none other than GZA himself. The intro begins with a bluesy Willie Mitchell loop taken from the song "Mercy, Mercy, Mercy" (Hi, 1968), over which RZA gets appropriately nostalgic, saying, "We gonna take y'all back to the source." Instantly, it's replaced by the infectious rhythm guitar riff from "Groovin'" (Hi, 1968), again courtesy of Willie Mitchell, as GZA joins RZA on the hook: "When the MCs came to live out their name and to perform / Some had to smoke cocaine and act insane before Pete rocked it on."

Harmonized in the style that old-school rappers copped from the doo-wop era, this hook is adapted from an All in Together Now routine from 1984 that went, "When the MCs came / To live out their name / Some rocked the rhymes that was all the same / And when I elevated and mastered time / They were stimulated from the high-powered rhyme / They was shocked, 'cause they knew they were rocked / Like the sucker MCs from off my block."[17] RZA's intro makes total sense now, since it's his idea to revamp this old hook for a new tune.

From the moment GZA digs into his first verse, "Fake niggas get flipped in mic fights / I swing swords and cut clowns / Shit is too swift to bite, you record and write it down," it's obvious he's opening with one of his bread-and-butter battle raps. However, he describes it as "braggadocious," saying, "It isn't meant to stand for anything. I'm talking about my skills and how I'm better than the rest."[18] It's also one of the few songs he completed fairly quickly as the track never alternates from its bouncy rhythm—save for a couple of dropouts, during which GZA improvises—allowing him to plow through two long verses.

As the song fades, we hear another snippet from *Shogun Assassin*—the part where the Shogun challenges Lone Wolf to a duel with his son—fused with dialogue from the 1979 kung fu film *The Dragon, the Hero* ("I see you're using an old style"). They provide the intro to one of the album's highlights, "Duel of the Iron Mic," also one of GZA's personal favorites. "I like how I delivered on this one, and I love RZA's beat," he says.[19] The main loop, a mellow piano section originally from David Porter's "I'm Afraid the Masquerade Is Over" (Stax, 1971), sounds downright menacing in RZA's hands. A much more obvious loop from that same song, incidentally, provides the basis for Notorious B.I.G.'s "Who Shot Ya."

GZA, meanwhile, matches the intensity of the track with some graphic metaphors: "Picture bloodbaths in elevator shafts / Like these murderous rhymes tight from genuine craft / Check the print, it's where veterans spark the lettering / Slow moving MCs is waiting for the editing." Once again, like Rakim, he displays a propensity for rhyming about rhyming itself. Later on, in the same verse, he shows just how tight his metaphor game is, saying, "I ain't particular, I bang like vehicular homicide / And July 4th in Bed-Stuy / Where money don't grow on trees and there's thievin' MCs who cut throats to rake leaves / They can't breathe, blood splash, rushing fast / like running rivers, I be that whiskey in your liver." GZA compares his impact on the mic to being fatally struck by a car, and having grown up in Bed-Stuy, he conjures raucous Fourth of July celebrations where gunshots fired in the air accompanied the sound of illegal fireworks. He likens MCs who "bite" or steal lyrics to hired assassins, and in that last line, he's comparing himself to hard liquor, which causes diseases like cirrhosis of the liver. All of this detailed imagery unfolds in a few precise lines.

Named after the 1971 Shaw Brothers kung fu classic *Duel of the Iron Fist*, the track also features standout verses by Masta Killa and Inspectah Deck and a short but effective hook by ODB in his sole appearance on the album. "Duel of the Iron Mic / It's the fifty-two fatal strikes," says Dirty, referring to the "52 Hand Blocks," a style of hand-to-hand combat developed in prisons and also known as "jailhouse rock." Mr. Consistency, Masta Killa, continues his killing spree with lines like "Damaging lyrical launcher / Lunge at the youthful offender that injure / Any contender, testing the murderous Master, could lead to disaster / Dynamite thoughts explode through your barrier." Obviously benefitting by his close association with GZA, his sensei, Masta Killa's skills are advancing by leaps and bounds. Deck, of course, always holds his own, rapping, "No peace, yo, the police mad corrupt / You get bagged up depending if you're passing the cut / Plus shorty's not a shorty no more, he's living heartless / Regardless of the charges, claims to be the hardest / Individual critical thoughts, criminal minded / Blinded by illusion, finding it confusing." With tight performances like these, it's no wonder GZA feels no pressure making this album.

"Living in the World Today" is another straight-up lyrical beatdown that continues GZA's self-referential style of MCing. This time he's talking about the Wu-Tang phenomenon itself when he says, "If you're living in the world today / You be hearing the slang that the Wu-Tang say / Niggas that front we don't have 'em / So we blast 'em, alright, well, okay." Once again, GZA reaches into the old-school files, flipping a vintage hook by a crew of Bronx rappers who used to say, "If you listen to me rap today, you be hearing the sounds that my crew will say. And we know you wish you can write them, well don't bite them, well okay."[20] By changing the words around, GZA stays true to that era's unwritten rule of not "biting" or copying someone else directly. RZA and Method Man also appear on the track, adding heft to the hook, while Meth and GZA go back and forth, line for line, on the bridge, mimicking the tag-team rhyming of classic Run-DMC.

Often less is more when it comes to production, as RZA illustrates here. Over a programmed drum-machine beat and booming four-note bass line, he adds only a tiny flourish of strings from "I'm His Wife (You're Just a Friend)" (Sound Stage 7, 1977) by Ann Sexton, slowing it down to create the main loop. For the break, he speeds up the horn fanfare from "In the Hole" (Stax, 1969) by the Bar-Kays, calling it a day. With MCs like GZA and Meth in the mix, he knows he doesn't always have to reach into his bag of tricks.

After three straight songs about MCing, GZA changes up the subject matter with "Gold," a truly epic track both lyrically and sonically. "The whole song is talking about hustling and stuff, but I don't say it plainly," he says.[21] Still, it doesn't take a slang interpreter to appreciate verses like "I'm in the park setting up a deal over blunt fire / Bum nigga sleeping on the bench, they had him wired / Peeped my convo, the address of my condo / And how I changed a nigga name to John Doe." With writing worthy of an Emmy, GZA offers up a whole new perspective on street crime, avoiding the typical clichés about the drug game that too much rap traffics in—an approach he develops even further on "Killah Hills 10304." While painting vivid pictures, he also strives to engage all the senses with lines like "His Glock clicks like high-heeled shoes on parquet floors."

RZA's production on this track, like several other songs on the album, boasts a definite rock feel. It's not simply the snippets of electric guitar he samples but the Marshall stack hugeness of his sound. For the main loop, a rousing orchestral choir, he returns to Stanley Black's "Meadowlands" (London, 1965), which he also used on Raekwon's album. Other credited samples, like "Aries" (Capitol, 1972) by Cannonball Adderley & Nat Adderley Sextet, are used so skillfully that one cannot even discern what sounds he borrowed from it. For the drum loop, however, RZA revisits one of his favorite sources, using "The Hoody Beat" from *Funky Drummer, Vol. 2* (JBR, 1994) by Carlos Bess and Ralph Vargas.

"Normally, when I hear a beat, I already know where to go with it. I can picture the track and just vibe off it," says

GZA. "As soon as I heard the beat to 'Cold World' I knew it would be another inner-city story."[22] RZA's melancholy track brings the subject matter to life. Using as unlikely a source as Frank Zappa's Mothers of Invention, he employs a short keyboard phrase from their song "Plastic People" (Verve, 1967) to create the languid, four-note melody that drives the song. Meanwhile, a single processed guitar note from "In the Rain" (Volt, 1971) by the Dramatics adds a little variation. But this is one of the few tracks built around the hook, an interpolation of Stevie Wonder's "Rocket Love" (Motown, 1980), as sung by GZA's cousin Life.

According to GZA, "He was singing the hook, 'Took me riding in your rocket, gave me a star, but a half mile from heaven, you dropped me back down to this cold, cold world.' RZA was the one who told Life to change the words and use it as a hook."[23] What he came up with was an incisive commentary about life in the hood: "Babies crying, brothers dying, and brothers getting knocked / Shit is deep on the block and you got me locked down / In this cold, cold world." Life also borrows some lyrics from the Debarge song "Love Me in a Special Way" (Gordy, 1983) for the bridge, where he sings, "You know you had me / With your sensuous charm / But you looked so alarmed / As I walked on by."

Inspectah Deck also makes his second appearance on the album with another standout performance. "My hood stays tense, loyalty puts strength in my team / 'Cause niggas' main concern is the cream," he says. "Some niggas in the jet-black Galant / Shot up the Chinese restaurant for this kid named Lamont / I thought he was dead but instead he missed the kid / And hit a twelve-year-old girl in the head, and then fled." Rapping about real issues, Deck might have ripped these rhymes from the headlines.

RZA opens the next track, "Labels," with a little warning to rappers trying to get rich off a record deal. "All these labels be tryin' to lure us in like spiders into the web," he says, but "if you don't read the label, you might get poisoned." One of the hardest and most minimal beats on the album, the song sees him getting deeper into his rock chamber. In fact, aside from the beat—a simple double kick, snare, and tambourine—he uses only a one-note sampled guitar riff and a vocal wail to create a headbanging backdrop for GZA's rhymes. All two seconds of the sped-up vocal sample comes from Thelma Houston's "Don't Leave Me This Way" (Motown, 1976), and unless you hear both songs back to back, you would never guess the sound's source.

RZA, obviously tired of paying so much for samples, is getting pretty crafty with their usage. It's even surprising that he has to pay for this one—though clearing it in advance was obviously preferable to settling later in a lawsuit as people like Biz Markie painfully learned through experience. In 1991, he used Gilbert O'Sullivan's 1972 hit "Alone Again" without permission and had his album pulled from the shelves as a result, providing fair warning for other producers. By the midnineties, when sampling was at its peak, a big business had sprung up in sample clearances because lawyers were always on the lookout for further sources of revenue.

Lyrically, "Labels" plays like a word game in which GZA crams every record label he can think of into a loose narrative. Obviously, his whole negative experience with Cold Chillin' had something to do with this song, but what really sparked the idea was taking a peek into the rhyme book of Wu-Tang affiliate Timbo King and seeing the line "Fuck Tommy, he ain't my boy."[24] From that single phrase, he crafts the opening couplet, "Tommy ain't my motherfuckin' boy / When you fake moves on a nigga you employ," obviously referring to RZA's treatment by the label. In another couplet, he strikes back at his old label, saying, "And Ruff up the motherfuckin' house 'cause I smother / You Cold Chillin' motherfuckers, I still Warn-er Brother." And, of course, he's got to big up his new digs while throwing some shade at P. Diddy: "Now who's the Bad Boy character, not from Arista / But firing weapons released on Geffen." He ends with a shout-out to his cousins, "Dirty, like that bastard" and "RZA razor RZA razor sharp," while declaring, "another Wu banger" as the beat rocks on.

Side two charges out the gate with another powerful posse cut, "4th Chamber," featuring Ghostface, Killah Priest, and RZA. The track is introduced by another snippet from *Shogun Assassin*—the scene in which Lone Wolf asks his toddler to choose between a sword and a ball in order to determine his destiny. He, of course, chooses the sword, following his father down the path to hell. "It's not even a GZA song to me—it's a Wu-Tang song," says GZA. "And Ghost's verse is incredible to me. He delivered so well."[25] So well, in fact, that GZA, who didn't have a rhyme in mind for the track, opted to go last. Compared to his concise sentences, loaded with visual flair, Ghost's abstract, stream-of-consciousness flow sometimes leaves you pondering the meaning of his inscrutable word salads. "Ironman be sippin' rum out of Stanley Cups, unflammable / Noriega aiming nozzles, stay windy in Chicago / Spine tingles, mind boggles, Kangols in rainbow colors," he spits with a cadence and acrobatic flow that somehow makes everything work.

Killah Priest follows with a short but classic verse, which begins, "I judge wisely, as if nothing ever surprise me / Lounging between two pillars of ivory / I'm lively, my dome piece is like building stones in Greece / Our poems are deep, from ancient thrones I speak." Though never an official member, Priest carves out his own niche within the Clan with rhymes full of ancient imagery and biblical allusion. As one of GZA's longtime "students," he also gets some solo shine on the album's bonus track, "B.I.B.L.E," which helped him secure his own deal with Geffen, who released *Heavy Mental* in 1998.

After filling in on plenty of intros, interludes, and hooks on this album, RZA finally unleashes his first verse, and it's a doozy. "The year is 2002, the battle's filled with the Wu / Six million devils just died from the bubonic flu / Or the Ebola virus, under the reign of King Cyrus / You can see the weakness of a man right through his iris." As far removed from bragging or materialism as you can get, RZA's rhymes rip the status quo to smithereens. For what rapper would even know about the devastating Athenian plague that occurred in the fifth century BCE when Cyrus the Great ruled the Persian empire? Such hidden jewels reflect the wide and diverse array of information he absorbs and injects back into his rhymes.

Sonically, too, RZA shreds all standards of production, sampling and replaying shards of sound instead of recognizable loops. Here he uses some guitar fuzz from the soundtrack of *Dharmatma*, a 1975 Hindi thriller; revisits Willie Mitchell's "Groovin'" for an organ stab and guitar lick; and even takes some of the synthesized sounds from the *Shogun Assassin* soundtrack to create an otherworldly aural pastiche. The cumulative effect sounds like a rock song, but at the same time, it doesn't—exactly what RZA was talking about when he said that Wu-Tang was creating new music that hadn't been done before. On this album, in particular, he shows and proves.

Though Method Man is usually the go-to guy for hooks, on "Shadowboxin'," he returns for two solid verses, while 4th

Disciple scratches in the hook, "Allow me to demonstrate the skill of Shaolin: the special technique of Shadowboxing," from *Shaolin vs. Lama* (1983). The main loop establishes the laid-back vibe of this track, sampling the intro of Ann Peebles's "Trouble, Heartaches, and Sadness" (Hi, 1972), where she sings, "Whoa, old man trouble." RZA catches a section of the drum, bass, and organ groove—including "Whoa"—speeding up the loop to make it sound like the "chipmunk voice."

Meth wastes no time diving into his first verse: "I break it down to the bone-gristle / Ill speaking Scud missile, heat seeking / Johnny Blazin', nightmares like Wes Craven / Niggas gunning, my third eye seen it coming, before it happen." But his delivery is laid-back—not the usual Meth in motion. GZA follows, chiming in about one of his favorites subjects, sucker MCs: "Check these nonvisual niggas with tapes and a portrait / Flood the seminar, trying to orbit this corporate / Industry, but what them niggas can't see / Must break through, like the Wu, unexpectedly." He is referring to the New Music Seminar, an annual music convention in New York started in 1980 by Tom Silverman of Tommy Boy and heavily tilted toward rap and dance music. Aspiring artists flocked there, demos in hand, in hopes of making contacts with labels and getting a record deal. GZA obviously considers this a futile pursuit compared to the Wu's underground tactics.

Moving deeper into the selection, we arrive at "Hell's Wind Staff / Killah Hills 10304," another one of GZA's personal favorites. "It's a very special song as far as the album's concerned because it's long as hell and has no hook," he says. "It's uptempo and straight through."[26] It also puts RZA's budding musicianship on display, as he plays all the classical-sounding melodies on a red Nord Lead Virtual Analog keyboard, a new toy he acquired during the making of this album. "Hell's Wind Staff," named after the 1979 Hong Kong martial arts film, is a title the Wu has used more than once—it's also a track on *Wu-Tang Forever* (1997)—but here, it probably refers to the memorable skit where RZA meets drug dealer Mr. Grieco, played by this writer, and they attempt to transact a deal. RZA ends up accusing Grieco's partner Don Rodriguez of selling him out. "Do you believe him?" says Grieco before the voice-over of GZA, like a narrator in a film, cuts in, saying, "Life of a drug dealer," incidentally, also the title of a track on his first album, *Words from the Genius*.

But "Killah Hills 10304," a nod to Park Hill's zip code, is unlike any other song about the drug trade ever made. "What made me write that song," GZA says, "was because I wanted to show these cats that talk all this gangsta stuff that this is the real level of getting it."[27] Going far beyond the corner hustlers, he was talking about international kingpins: "These were more sophisticated cats. Some of it came from a documentary I saw on the infamous Pablo Escobar. He was sending judges intimate photos of their wives and things like that. I think this is my first real Mafioso track. It's like a dense short film."[28]

Indeed, the imagery in the first couplet, "Restaurants on a stakeout, so order the food for takeout / Chaos outside Sparks steakhouse," refers to the real-life gangland assassination of Mob boss Paul Castellano outside Sparks Steakhouse in midtown Manhattan in 1985. That brazen daytime hit allowed John Gotti to consolidate power and take over leadership of the Gambino crime family. GZA delivers further Oscar-worthy flavor when he says:

There's no need for us to spray up the scene
I use less men, more powerful shit for my team

Like my man Mohammed from Afghanistan, grew up in Iran
The nigga runs a neighborhood news stand
A wild Middle Eastern, bomb specialist
Initiated at eleven to be a terrorist
He set bombs in bottles of champagne
and when niggas popped the cork, niggas lost half their
    brains.

At a time when the Cristal craze unleashed by Raekwon and
Ghost had rappers buying up the bar, these lines seem like
another implicit threat to sucker MCs. Conceptually, from
the skit through the verses, "Killah Hills 10304" could be the
album's standout in much the same way as "Rainy Dayz" is
for *OB4CL*.

Speaking of Raekwon, he finally appears, along with
U-God and Ghost, on the next track, "Investigative Reports,"
a stripped-down affair that plays like an episode of *True
Crime*. Over one of RZA's trademark shuffling beats and a
loop derived from the opening strings of Three Dog Night's
"I'd Be So Happy" (Dunhill, 1974), he reminisces about his
past: "Way of life got me thinking, plus I'm analyzing young
/ Youths on roofs, you know, three-time felony brutes / Roll
together, tropical trees puff, whatever / Yo we could go run
up on kids for leathers." RZA spices up the simple production
with excerpts from a TV news report about the historic Battle
of Brooklyn that occurred during the War of Independence.
U-God, finally out of the slammer for the last time, delivers the hook, a roll call of his surroundings: "Crack patients,
dime smokers / Vial carriers, mocha tokers / Burnt buildings,
brothers building / Save the children, investigative reports!"

The last new track on the album, "Swordsman," is one of
GZA's few solo appearances. It's also one of the only tracks

that requires no sample clearances, demonstrating RZA's skill for disguising his sources or, really, using such a small part of something and replaying it himself so it bears no similarity to the original. The hard, pounding beat, awash with atmospheric sounds and buzzing guitar riffs, is just the kind that GZA likes. In his verse, he talks about being raised in a religion (Christianity) that taught him superstition before eventually gaining knowledge of self and becoming a Five Percenter, or a God. As the first member of the Clan to be indoctrinated in the ways of the Nation of Gods and Earths, it's actually surprising that this is the only track on the album where he explicitly shares some of that wisdom, saying, "So look, listen, observe, respect this jewel / Drawed up, detect and reflect this / Light I shine because my power is refined / Through the truth, which manifest through eternal minds."

Apparently, Wu-Tang albums never really end with a bang but rather with a track that's been out for the longest time. Just as "Heaven and Hell" from the *Fresh* (1994) soundtrack closes out *OB4CL*, the final selection on *Liquid Swords*, "I Gotcha Back," comes from that same film. That makes the track sound somewhat dated—even though it's only a little more than a year old. It might even be older than that because RZA recycles the same snippet of the Charmels' "As Long as I've Got You" that he used on *Enter the 36 Chambers*. But such an observation is less critique and more a confirmation of the fact that the producer's skills are increasing at an exponential rate during his long stint in the basement working on these back-to-back solo albums. In the period between 1994 and 1995 alone, RZA produced albums by Meth, ODB, Raekwon, and GZA, managing to make each sound distinct and tailored to the artist whose name was on the cover but also part of that Wu-Tang sound that is revolutionizing hip-hop.

"I Gotcha Back" does have an interesting story behind it, however, as GZA wrote it for one of his young nephews, who appears in the video for the song, which he directed. "When I said, 'My lifestyle was so far from well / Could've wrote a book called Age Twelve and Going Through Hell,' it's for my nephew, who was twelve at the time, and whose father, my brother, had been locked up since '88, so he wasn't around for my nephew when times were rough," says GZA.[29] There's a scene in the video where some young thugs are busting off shots for fun, and in a sad case of life imitating art, GZA's nephew ended up serving eight years for doing the very same thing. Even as an artist, he can't escape the never-ending cycle of crime and incarceration in the hood.

True to GZA's style, *Liquid Swords* remains the tightest and most concise of the first round of solo albums, clocking in at 50:49. The CD version, however, includes a bonus track by Killah Priest, "B.I.B.L.E (Basic Instructions Before Leaving Earth)," produced by RZA's main protégé, 4th Disciple. Over a fairly obvious loop from "Our Love Has Died" (Westbound, 1972) by the Ohio Players, Priest breaks things down to the nitty-gritty, showing the hypocrisy and lies in which organized religion traffics. Like Raekwon giving Ghost his own solo track on *OB4CL*, Priest's solo appearance on GZA's album is testament to the Clan's brotherhood and solidarity as they actively worked to infiltrate the industry.

Upon its release, *Liquid Swords* shot to number two on the Billboard Hot R&B / Hip-Hop Singles while peaking at number nine on Billboard's 200 chart, racking up critical accolades as well—a further step toward the Clan's bid for total domination. "My plan was to get the industry to work for me," says RZA. "To have Def Jam, which was in competition with Loud Records, who was in competition with Elektra Records and Geffen Records to all work for the sound of Wu-Tang, work for hip-hop, and eventually work together, because, yunno, they don't work together. For some reason it's all about who got the bigger balls. And one year they all did work together. The first year they all worked together on a campaign was in 1995. All four major labels combined and formed the Wu-Tang family tree [a promotional Christmas display featuring *36 Chambers* and the four solo releases] and put it in all the retail stores across the country, and each label doubled their sales as a result."[30] The plan was working because they were working the plan, each member falling in line and playing their position while RZA pulled the strings. The result was the creation of a formidable catalog, unprecedented in the annals of hip-hop.

Wu-Tang Clan *(Al Pereira)*

Wu-Tang Clan *(Al Pereira)*

The RZA *(David Corio)*

The GZA *(Al Pereira)*

Ol' Dirty Bastard *(Al Pereira)*

Method Man *(Al Pereira)*

Ghostface Killah *(Ernie Paniccioli)*

Raekwon the Chef (L) with Popa Wu (R) *(Ernie Paniccioli)*

Inspectah Deck *(Ernie Paniccioli)*

U-God (*Al Pereira*)

Masta Killa *(Alice Arnold)*

Cappadonna *(Eddie Otchere)*

DJ Allah Mathematics *(Eddie Otchere)*

U-God, Masta Killa, Ghostface, Inspectah Deck, and Raekwon of Wu-Tang Clan
(Alice Arnold)

Gravediggaz (clockwise from top): The Gatekeeper (Frutkwan), the Undertaker (Prince Paul), Grym Reaper (Poetic), the RZA-rector (RZA) *(David Corio)*

The author with Method Man on the roof of Def Jam,
November 1994 *(Christian Lantry)*

Method Man and ODB at the Source Awards, 1994 *(Al Pereira)*

Divine (Mitchell Diggs), RZA, and Method Man *(Ernie Paniccioli)*

Ghostface, John "Mook" Gibbons (manager), and Raekwon *(Ernie Paniccioli)*

RZA as Bobby Digital *(Eddie Otchere)*

ODB at his last performance with the Clan, at Manhattan Center, November 2000 *(Ernie Paniccioli)*

ODB mural at the corner of Franklin and Putnam Avenues in Bed-Stuy, Brooklyn *(Al Pereira)*

Wu-Tang Clan District sign, Staten Island *(Al Pereira)*

CHAPTER 13

GHOSTFACE KILLAH / IRONMAN

One of the initial attractions to the Clan was the aura of mystery surrounding the group, who seemingly emerged out of nowhere to hijack the music industry like a band of guerillas toppling a corrupt government. After losing the stocking masks that concealed their faces on the cover of *Enter the Wu-Tang*, the only member who chose to remain incognito was Ghostface Killah. According to the word on the streets, he was dodging the law or, perhaps, a contract on his life— most probably a convenient urban legend that only bolstered the Wu-Tang mystique. Of course, Ghost, who claims the singular honor of spitting the first verse on the group's full-length debut, did eventually reveal his mug—along with a plethora of talent and charisma—rising to the role of best supporting actor on *OB4CL*, where he commandeered the chamber of ghetto enforcer. Here was a guy, according to Method Man, who took a bullet to the neck and shoulder during an attempted robbery and ended up shooting the assailant with his own gun.[1]

But Ghost kept that one in the pocket because real bad boys move in silence, so they say, also rarely showing emotion. So it came as quite a shock when this same tough guy penned a real tearjerker, "All That I Got Is You," a touching tribute to his mother that also documents the struggles he faced growing up. A bundle of contradictions cloaked in a mystery, with a personality as complex as calculus, Ghost is that guy you just can't pigeonhole. Maybe that's why he's constantly able to reinvent himself. Defying expectations, he has proven his durability as the most consistent and prolific solo artist within the Clan—all a part of his enduring mystique. But when first thrust into the spotlight, he was as reluctant as Raekwon. It wasn't easy becoming *Ironman*.

Despite dominating 1994–1995 with four successful solo albums that raised the flag of a rap dynasty, the group was also experiencing growing pains. "We fucked up in '96, to tell the truth—sort of," says RZA. "We wasn't sure what we wanted to do, know what I mean? Should we drop [a] Wu [album]? It was a fucked-up year. Cops raided the studio, Deck got locked up. It's a lot of shit happened. It was beef in the streets—all kinds of shit. Ninety-six was a bugged-out year."

Before getting bagged up, Inspectah Deck, who signed to Loud for $650,000, simply off "the hype and hysteria of Wu-Tang," as he describes it, got caught up in the shuffle of label politics.[2] When it came time to schedule a release date for his album, not only was Loud too busy throwing their full weight behind Raekwon, but they had also signed the smoking-hot three-hundred-pound sensation Big Pun, a protégé of Fat Joe. To complicate matters, Loud's distribution deal was migrating from BMG to Sony. "Then RZA had a flood in his apartment," says Deck. "Lost my whole first album. My first album wasn't even the album that you hear as *Uncontrolled Substance*. It was a totally different album."[3] An earlier flood, which had struck after the making of *Tical*, didn't significantly delay the release of ODB's album, since he took his time anyway. This second calamity, however, helped totally derail Deck. Along with his detention and other legal issues (trying to leave the label), these setbacks ensured that his album would not see light until the end of 1999. With 36 Chambers also out of commission, another outcome of the flood was that Ghost's album had to be recorded elsewhere, at a local spot called Mystic Recordings Studios located at 26 Bay Street in Staten Island's commercial district. As RZA said, it was a bugged-out year but not entirely unsalvageable.

In the midst of shopping Ghost to Epic Street, a sublabel of Sony that had released music by Compton's MC Eiht and original East Coast gangsta Kool G Rap, he negotiated a label deal for himself at Sony. Unlike the independent Wu-Tang Records, through which he had released "Protect Ya Neck," Razor Sharp, his new imprint, had corporate coffers and promotional might behind it—not to mention shiny new offices in the heart of Greenwich Village. Following the buzz on the streets, RZA's first signing, naturally, was Cappadonna, hot off his appearance on *OB4CL*—though his long player, *The Pillage* (Razor Sharp / Epic Street), would not come out until March 1998. Cappa wasn't even officially a member of the group at the time, and vaulting ahead of U-God and Masta Killa, two Clansmen who were still patiently awaiting their turns, was bound to create some tension within the group, as U-God admitted later in his memoir.

All these behind-the-scenes industry machinations meant that Ghost would be the only Clansman to release an album during the transitional year of 1996, which saw a changing of the guard in rap. As Tupac was dropping his last living testament, *All Eyez on Me* (Death Row / Interscope), Jay-Z was just getting his hustle on with *Reasonable Doubt* (Rock-a-Fella / Priority). Meanwhile, the Jiggy era, personified by P. Diddy and his Bad Boy label, was about to take off. While Wu-Tang had sparked an East Coast underground renaissance, inspiring other artists such as Nas, Mobb Deep, Busta Rhymes, Redman, the Fugees, A Tribe Called Quest, De La Soul, Jeru the Damaja, Heltah Skeltah, Originoo Gunn Clappaz, and M.O.P., all of whom released albums that year, they were also threatened to be eclipsed by it. The future of the Wu-Tang saga rested squarely on the shoulders of one Ghostface Killah, a.k.a. Tony Starks, a.k.a. Ironman, a man who was himself in a state of flux.

"I was ready but there was a lot of things going on," he says. "To me, *Ironman* was kind of dark for me. I wasn't looking for it to be dark like that. That's why I say it could have been better."[4] At age twenty-six and finally pulling in a legitimate paycheck, Ghost still had one foot in the streets. "I remember one time doing the album, I even had the Delfonics with me," he says. "I had got into a shootout, and they was with me. I was in one car and they were in a van in back of me watching it all go down."[5] During that time, several of the goons he was running with got locked up for long bids. On top of that, Ghost was plagued by medical issues. "I was pissing all day, losing weight, dry-mouthed and dizzy with blurred vision," he says. "I didn't know what that shit was."[6] Turns out his blood sugar level was off the charts, and he was diagnosed with type 2 diabetes, which was further complicated by drinking forties and smoking weed. Living on the razor's edge, it was a hell of a time to be working on your first album, but only someone as strong as Tony Starks could rise to the challenge.

"I'm not a big comic book fan," says Ghost, the member of the Clan most associated with a Marvel superhero. "Everybody thought it was that, but it was just that me and Rae was choppin' one time. I had this shirt and we was slang masters. Our slang was just off the meat rack, so, once I put that shirt on, I just came with Tony Starks, like 'This shirt is Tony Starks right here.'"[7] No doubt the fictional Anthony Edward Stark's reputation as a wealthy and powerful businessman, playboy, and gifted scientist who invents and dons the Ironman suit gave Ghost a worthy role model to aspire to, but unlike Meth and RZA, who were serious comic book nerds and collectors, he was no fanboy. In fact, he adds an extra *s* at the end of Stark to distinguish himself from his fictional namesake. "So that's what it was," says Ghost. "It wasn't like, 'Oh, shit!' Like I was just a comic book fanatic, and then I took the name and ran with it. Nah it wasn't like that."[8]

When it came time to christen the album, Ghost originally wanted to name it *Supreme Clientele*, the title of his second album, but RZA convinced him otherwise. "Back then we were deciding if I should name [the LP] *Ironman* or *Supreme Clientele*," he says. "RZA convinced me with *Ironman* because of [my nickname] Tony Starks. If not, *Ironman* would've been named *Supreme* and *Supreme* would have been *Ironman*."[9] In a nod to one of the memorable skits on *Cuban Linx*, in which the entrepreneurial Ghost shares his idea for dyeing Clarks Wallabies in different colors like "blue and cream," he is depicted on the cover of *Ironman* with his partners in rhyme, Rae and Cappadonna, sorting through a pile of colored Wallabies. It's as if he's saying, 'Remember that great idea I had a while back? Well, boom! There it is." That's Ghost in a nutshell—his word is his bond, and he always comes through with the goods.

Following his breakout performance on *OB4CL*, people kind of knew what to expect from Ghostface, but at the same time, they didn't. The first inkling of what his album might sound like came from the single "Winter Warz," released in January as part of the soundtrack for the Wayans brothers' film *Don't Be a Menace to South Central While Drinking Your Juice in the Hood* (1996), a spoof of all the hood flicks that hit theaters in the early nineties like the second coming of blaxploitation. This up-tempo banger, in which he raps alongside Raekwon, U-God, Masta Killa, and Cappadonna, could have just as well been a Wu-Tang track. In April, "Motherless Child," another soundtrack contribution—from the film *Sunset Park* (1996)—dropped, sounding like a reprise of *Cuban Linx*, as Rae and Ghost tag-teamed on another crime story. It wasn't until the third single, "All That I Got Is You," was released on September 22, 1996, that people got a true measure of Ghost as a solo artist, which was not at all what they expected.

Instead of the grimy crimey, spinning tales of bullet-ridden capers and drug deals gone awry, the rapper wrote a plaintive ballad in praise of his mother, Diane, telling of all the struggles he endured growing up in poverty. From the mysterious "now you see him, now you don't" character he had cultivated up to now, a vulnerable Ghost laid himself open like an almanac, revealing a surprising amount of personal information and details.

His father left him when he was only six years old. He grew up living in a three-bedroom apartment with fifteen other family members, sleeping four to a bed. The other unwelcome denizens were roaches, who infiltrated everything, including the cereal box. He had to pick them out before he ate breakfast and share a single spoon with his siblings and cousins. They also shared each other's pants when it came time to go to school. Sugar water was a popular drink in his household—most likely contributing to his diabetes later on. They also ate a lot of grits and, in the summer, took advantage of the free-lunch program. He shopped with food stamps and sometimes had to borrow food from neighbors, since his family was so broke. When they ran out of toilet paper, his mother told him to use newspaper. Two of his younger brothers were born with muscular dystrophy, and he was tasked with helping take care of them. After running through this depressing inventory of his childhood memories, he admits that throughout the struggle there was always love: "But I remember this, moms would lick her fingertips / To wipe the cold out of my eyes before school with her spit." The weepy backing track, a loop of the Jackson 5's "Maybe Tomorrow," perfectly complements his words, as does the hook, "All that I got is you, and I'm so thankful I made it through," sung by Mary J. Blige. "I hold on to times I had to struggle," says Ghost. "That's the science of going through hell and having to come out right—because everybody gots to go through hell to come out right."[10]

An odd choice for a single, the track caught everyone off guard—especially hard rocks fiending for more gutter fare. "See, that's the first song that we ever made that made people cry," says Ghost. "I mean, big people, big brothers with muscles cry, like 'Yo, G, I dropped a tear like, yunno.' It was a picture that I painted, which I been through and saw. That's what made 'em cry, yunno. That's how come they could identify— whether you went through it or not—'cause the picture is so clear, like you seen it on the news."[11] Thus, in one fell swoop, Ghost demolished everyone's preconceived notions about him, showing and proving that he was far from a one-dimensional MC. At the same time, he was able to regain that crucial element of surprise that his Clan had utilized so well to their advantage. A few weeks later, he dropped the fourth single, "Daytona 500," a fast-paced lyrical assault featuring Raekwon, Cappadonna, and Staten Island's own Force MDs, set to the popular old-school break from Bob James's "Nautilus" (CTI, 1974). One could already tell that *Ironman* was going to be a hell of a ride.

RZA can't claim to be the only movie buff in the Clan. In addition to being a slang originator, Ghost was an avid fan of movies growing up and the first to catch an inspiration after seeing a VHS tape of *Shaolin vs. Wu-Tang*. It's not surprising, then, how influential films were to *Ironman*, just as in prior Wu-Tang releases. While the sixteen-track album used snippets from such popular Hollywood crime dramas as *The Usual Suspects* (1995) and *Carlito's Way* (1993), kung fu films like *The Mystery of Chess Boxing* (1979), and Japanese anime such as *Crying Freeman* (1986–1988), by far the most sampling came from Black films virtually unknown to mainstream audiences, including *J.D.'s Revenge* (1976), *Cornbread Earl and Me* (1975), and, most notably, *The Education of Sonny Carson* (1974).

Hitting squarely during the latter part of the blaxploitation era, when other Black films such as *Cooley High* (1975) and *Let's Do It Again* (1975) found eager audiences, *The Education of Sonny Carson*, based on the real-life biography of the Brooklyn social activist, somehow slipped through the cracks. Directed by Michael Campus right after he made *The Mack* (1973), a cultural touchstone starring Max Julien and Richard Pryor, the film followed Carson, a young honor student sent to jail for stealing, who becomes involved in a street gang. The gang life presented a catch-22, affording him camaraderie and protection from the harsh elements of the streets while also propelling him further into a life of violence and crime. After robbing a deliveryman to buy flowers for a fallen comrade who died during a gang fight, he was sent to prison at age sixteen, becoming the youngest inmate at Sing Sing. After serving his time, he finally reemerged from behind bars to find redemption as an activist and civic leader.

Says Campus, "When Sonny came to me with this picture, what he wanted to say and what I embraced, and I totally believe with all my heart and soul, is that we are wasting young black lives. It's true today and it was true back then. These kids never had a chance. They never had an opportunity. They're 10, 12, 14-year-old kids. They are not going to be Shaq, Michael Jordan, or even Barry Bonds," adding, "You must change what's happening with young black kids, young black males."[12] Incidentally, Carson was able to make a difference in the life of his own son Lumumba, who became the rapper known as Professor X of the Afrocentric group X-Clan.

Using real gang members as actors and shooting on location in Bed-Stuy, Brooklyn, the film presented a kind of vérité missing from similar examples of the genre, as it depicted the brutal beatings Sonny (played by Rony Clanton) received at the hands of police as well as during his initiation into the Lords. It easily connected the dots between poverty, drug use, crime, and depression, detailing their impact on the African American community, who have been enduring such conditions for generations. Campus summed up the film by saying, "It tells the story of the kids who really suffered."[13]

One of those kids was a young Dennis Coles. First incarcerated at the age of fifteen for stealing, he obviously saw a lot of himself in Sonny. The fact that Ghost used that film to frame the songs on *Ironman* was testament to its impact on him. The cipher was completed when the attention he brought to this hidden gem allowed it to finally climb out of obscurity and be acknowledged as a crucial and poignant document of society in crisis—as timely and relevant today as it was forty-five years ago.

* * *

Ironman begins with a lengthy exchange from the film in which a young Sonny, played by Thomas Hicks, confronts a Brooklyn street gang, the Lords, to deliver a message from their leader, whom Sonny had met in jail during his three-month incarceration for stealing. When the precocious youth suggests hanging out with the gang, he is instantly rebuffed and insulted, but, instead of backing down, he taunts them, saying, "Kiss my ass, motherfucker." Shorty then challenges the main man Smokey, the acting leader, to go mano a mano with him, saying, "I'll put trademarks around your fuckin' eyes," a provocation one might attribute to a young Ghost as well. Instantly, the blaring horns from Al Green's "Gotta Find a New World" (Hi, 1969) announce the start of "Iron Maiden," an adrenaline rush of a song featuring Ghost and his sidekicks Raekwon and Cappadonna.

Even though this album reunites the powerful trio from *OB4CL*, which was released only a little more than a year earlier, it already sounds totally different. Perhaps it's that old soul sound to which Ghost has always been partial—RZA's biscuits and gravy too. Here, he leans heavily on Al Green, bringing him back on the break—a two-note phrase with strings, rim-shot, and bass from "Strong as Death (Sweet as Love)" (London, 1975). He also uses Green a couple of songs later on "260," a wholesale rip-off of the first four bars of "You Ought to Be with Me" (Hi, 1973).

For *Ironman*'s sonic motif, RZA digs deep in his crates of sixties and seventies soul and R&B, using artists such as Johnny Mathis, Otis Redding, Jimmy Ruffin, the Persuaders, the Undisputed Truth, the Jackson 5, and Teddy Pendergrass. In addition, he employs both the Force MDs, a well-known rap/R&B act from Staten Island known for their doo-wop style of harmonizing, and the Delfonics, one of the groups that defined the sound of Philadelphia soul, to bring some of that nostalgia to life. Lyrically, Ghost dominates, sharing the spotlight with Rae, who appears on all but four of the sixteen tracks, and Cappa, who leaves his indelible darts on five tracks. The rest of the Clan, aside from GZA and ODB, rally around to make this album another family affair, as Ghost takes only four solo turns on the mic.

After Rae sets things off on "Iron Maiden," another clip from *The Education of Sonny Carson* introduces Ghost's verse. Wolfe, the leader of the Tomahawks gang—admirably played by real gang member Derrick "Champ" Ford—addresses his membership before a huge gang rumble in the park, saying, "Just let me get mines first. Then after I get mines, y'all can do what you want to do." In the background, someone else shouts, "Fuck 'em up bad." In the Wu-Tang lexicon, real fighting is usually equated with lyrical pugilism, but everyone knows Ghost is down for whatever.

At the Def Jam Christmas party a couple of months after his record hit the streets, for example, he sees rapper Wish Bone of the group Bone Thugs-N-Harmony (signed to Eazy-E's Ruthless Records) walking through Manhattan's packed Terminal club with a bodyguard and aggressively confronts him. He ends up hurling a bottle of champagne at the rapper, accidentally hitting someone else, and starting a huge melee in the club. Immediately afterward, Ghost is spotted in the parking garage, changing out of his yellow Helly Hansen out-fit and donning a black "ninja suit" with four others, whose intentions we can only surmise.[14] So don't test the kid, and never underestimate him, either.

Even so, some of his non sequiturs will leave you scratch-ing your head, like "Fuck Benadryl, the violin in 'Knowledge God' sounded ill," he says, reminding you of Rae's classic album. He also pulls obscure pop-culture references out of his sleeve. When he raps, "Me and my girl'll run like Luke and Laura," only hard-core viewers of the ABC soap opera *General Hospital* would know what he's talking about— instantly transported back to the summer of 1980 when the show's darlings, played by Tony Geary and Genie Francis, were running from the law like Bonnie and Clyde. The action had daytime viewers on the edge of their seats, and, obvi-ously, a ten-year-old Dennis Coles too.

Fresh off his breakout performance on "Winter Warz," Cappa picks up where he left off on *Cuban Linx*, shredding the third verse with lines like "Every evening, I have a by myself meeting / Thinking who's gonna be the next to catch a beat-ing / From my mental slanging, bitching rap twist the point of warfare / I brutalize, all competition catch hell here." On fire at the time, Cappa earns every dollar of that Razor Sharp deal. After Rae performs the hook, "Iron Maiden" closes with another snippet of dialogue from the same prerumble scene in *The Education of Sonny Carson*, when Wolfe says, "The way I wanna get 'em, I want 'em got. I want 'em layin' out, 'cause niggas need to be got. He need to be taken off of here." The similarities between Ghost and this jive-talkin' street tough are obvious, and he uses his voice again to open "260."

But first he runs through his first solo track on the album, "Wildflower," a scathing diss of a girlfriend who cheated on him while he was away on tour. Fittingly, he opens this one up with dialogue from the bizarre thriller *J.D.'s Revenge* (American International Pictures, 1976). After being hypnotized at a show, New Orleans cab driver Isaac "Ike" Hendrix (played by Glynn Turman) is mysteriously possessed by the spirit of an old-time pimp/hustler known as J.D. Smith, who was wrongfully accused of killing his own sister and was eventually murdered. Suffering a series of mental blackouts, Ike increasingly takes on J.D.'s persona.

After picking up a girl named Sheryl (played by Barbara Tasker) at a bar, he goes back to her place. They sample the part where Sheryl reveals the following morning, "That was the best fucking I ever had" as Ike gets dressed. Then, hearing someone enter the apartment, she freaks out, realizing that her boyfriend has arrived. Still channeling J.D., Ike calmly tells her, "You better go talk to him" before eventually slashing the guy to death with a straight razor. Once again, Ghost chooses the ideal intro for a song about infidelity.

Setting off the track is Jamie Summers, a recent Razor Sharp signee and the perfect foil to Ironman. She takes her name from Jaime Sommers, a character played by actor Lindsay Wagner, a guest star on the popular seventies TV series *The Six Million Dollar Man* who eventually ended up with her own spinoff, *The Bionic Woman*. The rapper Jamie Summers makes her major-label debut with the opening couplet, "I'm mind shocking, body-rocking, earth shaking, money making / Sitting high / lookin' fly / sippin' on the best wine," offering Ghost a ripe target.

He goes right for the jugular: "Yo bitch I fucked your friend, yeah you stank ho," showing he knows a thing or two about revenge. He then launches into a litany of insults, calling her a "crab bitch, chickenhead ho, eating heroes / I'm the first nigga that had you watching flicks by De Niro / You gained crazy points, baby, just being with God / Taught you how to eat the right foods, fast, and don't eat lard." But his attempts to "civilize" her according to the Five-Percent tradition prove unsuccessful. In addition to spewing venom, he also talks about the intimacy they shared ("I fucked you while you was bleedin', held you down in malls / Sexually you worshipped my d-dick like a cross") and also about the pain he feels as a result of being cheated on ("I got jerked, gave away my pussy, that shit hurt / It feel like somebody died or shot your old Earth"). In short, Ghost grapples with the emotions of someone whose heart has been broken, to which most anyone can relate. Exposing his own vulnerability, he wins, once again, with the element of surprise.

It doesn't hurt, of course, that RZA provides another banger crafted out of a few simple elements—a skill he has, by now, mastered. After programming a kick/snare beat, he plays, then samples some simple chords on a lap steel, a type of guitar played horizontally, using a metal bar pressed against the strings. Treating himself to a new piece of equipment becomes a tradition for him on every new project, and the lap steel is what he's experimenting with at the time. His constant learning and reinvention of his sound makes him one of the most compelling producers in an era already awash with talent. The only sample he pays for on this track is the flourish of strings that opens up Johnny Mathis's "Someone" (Fontana, 1958).

After getting a solo turn on *OB4CL*, Ghost returns the courtesy to Raekwon on "The Faster Blade," a one-verse stream-of-consciousness soliloquy in which Rae talks about his favorite subject, the streets. "Ay, yo, movin' on these niggas like they old soul bro / You know how we go, shift 'em out like *perico*," he says, throwing out the Jamaican slang for freebase cocaine. He's talking about the competition on the corners and how he and his crew are superior. RZA backs him up with one of his trademark shuffling beats, sampled from "El Rey y Yo" (EMI Odeon Chile, 1970) by the obscure Chilean pop band Los Angeles Negros. He embellishes it with two different xylophone parts from the intro to "Can't Get No Further and Do No Better" by the Persuaders, an R&B band formed in New York in 1969, who had a huge hit with "Thin Line Between Love and Hate" (1971).

Four songs deep into *Ironman*, we are finally rewarded with the first Rae and Ghost crime caper, which fans had come to expect, on "260." It starts with Wolfe's rousing monologue from *The Education of Sonny Carson*. Then, backed by the first few bars of Al Green's "You Ought to Be with Me" (Hi, 1973), complete with horn fanfare and the singer riffing, "Yeah," Ghost has the perfect soulful groove on which to perform his verbal gymnastics. "Yo, kicked down the door in the spot, 260 / 2L, I heard they had O's for sale / I heard the same shit, money drive a burgundy whip / Keep a low fade, license plates engraved 'PAID,'" he says, referencing the song's title, a building in Park Hill. Turns out some out-of-town cat from New Jerusalem—Five-Percenter slang for New Jersey—is moving in on their turf, selling ounces of blow. Since anyone from outside the projects is referred to as an alien or "UFO" and, therefore, not to be trusted, Ghost says, "We gotta get him, dun, aliens is snatching our bread / UFOs moving in with bigger plans than Feds, yo."

Rae picks up the action in the second verse, saying, "Two hours later, scheming like De Niro in *Casino* / Son better have more coke than Al Pacino," recalling the 1995 Scorsese crime epic and the infamous final scene of *Scarface*. After borrowing two shotguns from an associate, Daddy-O, they're ready to make their move. "We walked in both of us looked like terrorists / Masks on, second floor, yo dun I'll handle this," says Rae. But when they burst into the apartment, they find the guy having sex with a white chick, which doesn't stop Rae from shooting him in the neck. Then he asks, "Where the blow at, *I ain't got shit*, stop fronting," before Ghost completes his line, "Yo Chef, throw the joint in his mouth, money'll stop stunting." Then they alternate, line for line, with Rae delivering the girl's response, "It's in the kitchen in the ceiling," and Ghost finishing it off, "Baby girl kept squealing / Only found a white block of cheese from New Zealand / Ohhh shit! Yo, yo where that shit at yo?" The story ends with them coming up empty-handed, finding no coke.

Ghost's last lines segue perfectly into a scene sampled from *The Usual Suspects* (1995), a heist movie in which a team of thieves pursue a nonexistent shipment of cocaine. After searching the boat on which the product is supposedly transported, team leader Dean Keaton (played by Gabriel Byrne) screams, "There's no coke!" This dialogue, in turn, segues into the sound of a man running and panting before he yells, "Help, please," taken from the Japanese anime *Crying Freeman* (1995). But these pleas are answered by the sound of a gunshot as the beat to "Assassination Day" begins.

One of the hallmarks of a Wu-Tang project is the amount of thought and detail that goes into these transitions between songs and, ultimately, how these albums are so perfectly sequenced that one track flows effortlessly into the next, supporting a larger narrative or concept. As far as using movie snippets to that end, *Ironman* is one of the best examples of this multimedia approach, made possible by Ghost's direct involvement. "It's not always just making the songs, it's about how does the next song come after the next?" he explains. "See, these guys nowadays, they don't do that. The sequencing, that's how I did mainly all my albums. We basically try to keep you here when you put on the CD."[15]

Considering "Assassination Day" ranks as one of the strongest tracks on the album, with masterful contributions by Inspectah Deck, RZA, Raekwon, and Masta Killa, Ghost's absence is conspicuous and somewhat puzzling. But he explains, "On 'Assassination Day' where everybody but me was on it, I couldn't think."[16] After being diagnosed as a diabetic, he often describes his head as being "fogged out," and it's a miracle that his condition didn't affect his performance even more.[17] Thus, while the track seems tailor-made for Ghost, we don't actually miss him here because of superb performances by everyone else.

Deck, once again, sets the bar high with his first stanza: "I move through the Third World, the third eye's my guiding light / Invite the fight, we all die tonight / The life I live's a 25 to life bid / Parole reneged, I stroll the globe fugitive." The Rebel INS comes off as some kind of mystical warrior. Without a solo project of his own, RZA usually takes at least one turn on the mic on his fellow Clansmen's albums, and his verse here ranks as one of his deadliest yet. He raps, "I stopped producer's careers / The weak spot was the ears / Scorpion darts hit the mark, pierce the heart with silver spears." Further on he says, "The mic is in my clutches / Thugs who bring ruckus leave in crutches / Unforgivable snakes face the double-edged swords starts to swivel / Decapitates the head, makes the projects more livable." Though he has evolved into a producer par excellence, you can't sleep on him lyrically either. Rae and Masta Killa come with equally strong, short verses, but Masta Killa's is eminently more quotable, as he compares himself to a shotgun: "Now who's best to describe for what I specialize in / Murderous rhyming, constantly inclining / My mind spits with an enormous kickback / Your brain then absorbs the impact / Disorderly conduct from the crowd is the feedback." Very few MCs were writing rhymes with such powerful imagery in the midnineties, so the Clan practically cornered the market on lyrical skills.

Following this standout performance, which would have been at home on any Wu-Tang album, Ghost dials up the intensity on "Poisonous Darts," his second solo appearance. In Clanspeak, darts are simply rhymes, but add the poison pen of Ghostface, along with his raw energy, and you get a track like this one—a straight lyrical sprint to the finish with no hook. RZA intros the track with a snippet of dialogue from *The Mystery of Chess Boxing* (1979). Unfortunately, this is also his laziest production on the album, in which he utilizes a one-bar string loop and some horns to create a very monotonous backing track with little or no variation. But that doesn't deter Ghost from going in as he drops his opening couplet: "So what the fuck I got to lose ha? Word to God let's get it on / Clap your heels three times, grab the magic wand." Many of his rhymes here are a mixed bag of metaphors and free association, but sometimes he cuts through the abstraction: "Yo, yo, mountains of blow like snow constant cash flow / Rocking a Shaft afro, Tony got mad glow with hoes / Mega powder dripping from they nose / Fucking Jet magazine bitches with wide pussy pose." This track is Ghost being Ghost, and one gets the impression that even if it were a cappella, it would still rock, revealing the true power of his persona.

After Ghost's solo smackdown, we are treated to another posse cut, "Winter Warz," featuring Raekwon, U-God, Masta Killa, and Cappadonna. While this cut was originally meant to be a teaser for Ghost's album, it actually provides a great vehicle for Cappadonna, who flaunts his considerable skills on a runaway verse that only ends when the tape unspools. He begins with the couplet "You heard other raps before but kept waiting / For the Son of Song, I keep dancehalls strong," and then proceeds to conduct a veritable rhyme seminar that goes on and on.

"It was a freestyle at first," admits Cappa of that legendary outburst, "and then I started sayin' it over and over. Eventually I had to write it down and then splash it. It's like I don't even know how long the verse really was or how much I had written down or if I stopped in between 'cause when I got to the studio, it was like, keep going."[18] Masta Killa, who was around that night after having just dropped his own verse, witnessed Cappa in action. "He came right in and that might have been one take," he says. "I mean no punches, he just came right in and just got right in the booth and just went crazy."[19]

For the track, RZA samples the intro to Manzel's "Midnight Theme" (Fraternity, 1979), a drum break he's used several times before, but little else. All the other keyboard and incidental sounds he plays himself, demonstrating the confidence he is gaining in his own musical abilities and his urge to break out of the trap of sampling, which was costing a lot of money in clearances.

Known for his openness to experimentation and trying something different, RZA adds a little variety for the intro of "Box in Hand," which refers to a martial arts training technique in which the student attempts to snatch a box from his master's hand. Instead of relying on the obvious kung fu movie snippet, he employs the Force MDs, who provide guest vocals on "Daytona 500," to sing a short a cappella. Antoine

"TCD" Lundy, an original member of the group who succumbed to Lou Gehrig's disease in 1998, does the honors, interpolating the melody of the Jackson 5's "Never Can Say Goodbye" (Motown, 1971) as he croons, "Wu-Tang will survive, no no no-no no no / Wu-Tang will survive / 'Cause every time they flip a party / You know the party screams and shouts." Perhaps RZA throws that out there to answer the doubters who assumed the worst for the group after the solo successes of its individual members.

But one listen to "Box in Hand," featuring Raekwon and Method Man, is enough to kill the noise. Both Ghost and Rae spit pithy, abstract verses—Rae flaunting his knowledge of Russian-cut VVS diamonds, a grade below flawless, and Ghost, the free-word associater, rapping, "It's like space kid, the whole world is pitch black, granola rap / Dough got smaller famous team, walked up in Fotomat." Meth, in his only appearance on the album, bites off a longer verse, stealing the show with lines like "Do or die, it be I, Meta-physical Man / Holding court from my Wu, indivisible clan."

Musically, this track has an urgency about it, propelled by the up-tempo drums from Les Baxter's "Hogin' Machine" (Sidewalk, 1969). RZA later recycles a guitar riff from that same song for the Ghostface / Jadakiss duo "Run" (2003). Along with composers Martin Denny and Arthur Lyman, Baxter's name is most associated with the development of the easy-listening style known as "exotica," or lounge music, which produced all those records from the fifties and sixties with colorful album covers and tropical motifs. While there are clearly two other prominent samples in the track—a piano riff that serves as the main loop and another tinkling piano that comprises the break—RZA either plays them or feels they are so obscure that he doesn't bother clearing them.

Since it's a given that the Abbott usually handles all the production on a Wu-Tang project, it's always a surprise to see another name popping up on the credits. On the next song, "Fish," the honors go to True Master, the same producer responsible for the hugely popular "Brooklyn Zoo" off ODB's debut. An early affiliate of the Clan, True Master is one of the few producers with a style complementary to RZA's, and on "Fish," he even gives the Abbott a run for his money with one of the standout tracks on the album.

Like RZA, True Master shies away from the obvious samples and loops, taking only snippets of sound, which he weaves into a uniform tapestry. He usually replays his samples as well, completely divorcing them from their original context while lending a musicality to his productions. On "Fish," True Master conducts a seminar on the creativity of sampling, taking the drums from the Amazing Rhythmettes' "A Jackass Gets His Oats" (ABC, 1970) to make a simple beat. He then layers various elements—a guitar strum, an organ wobble, a horn fanfare—from Otis Redding's cover of Sam Cooke's "A Change Is Gonna Come" (Atco, 1965) to create an entirely new melodic phrasing. It's still imbued with that retro sound, however, since sampling picks up the rich analog texture of vintage vinyl as well as its crackle and pop. Comparing the two tracks side by side, one would be hard-pressed to say that sampling is not an art form.

Sounding like an outtake from *Cuban Linx*, the track opens with sampled dialogue from both *Crying Freeman*, the Japanese anime, and *Crime Inc.: Birthright of Gangsters* (Thames TV, 1984), a British TV series dealing with the Mafia crime families and drugs. Then Ghost drops the title of the song in his first line, saying, "We eat fish, tossed salads, to make rap ballads." It evokes another monumental rap song, "Paid in Full" (1987), in which Rakim declares that fish is his favorite dish. But Rakim's rhymes are much easier to decipher than Ghost's, who spits inscrutable mash-ups like "Grey Poupon is Revlon rap, smack pawns, swing like batons." By the end of his verse, however, he's locked into the soulful nostalgia of the music, saying, "Every day is like a video shoot, check this shit / I take it back to Playboy, stash guns in whips / Picture afro picks, shish kabobs and dashikis / Thousands civil marched, raised their fists in early sixties." Whether Ghost realizes that Sam Cooke's original version of "A Change Is Gonna Come," recorded in 1964, was adopted as an anthem for the civil rights movement is unclear, but it makes for a great moment of sonic synchronicity.

Popping in with one of his shortest verses yet, Cappadonna still comes off with lines like "Destination be the cash one, I step past one / Don't make me blast one, I'm cold like Eskimo floe." And, of course, Rae is going to have his say. Combining all his aliases into one, "Lex Louis Rich Liberace," Raekwon brings it home with his usual dense imagery: "Now let's rap a taste, connect dots, aim Glocks, train stop / Figaro fly jeweling, Tri-colored Cubans / Swerving with power Germans in Suburbans." In Rae's lines one can see the abstract influence of his partners.

The trio return for "Camay," another mold-breaking rap song in which Ghost gets a chance to show his romantic side. According to Raekwon, "This right here was strictly for the ladies of the world because we knew that we had started to get a female fan base. We wanted to definitely seal the girls up. It's almost like having a 'Ice Cream' again, but now it's an 'Ice Cream' for Ghost's album."[20] Not only was the song a little something for the ladies, it was also specifically directed, as Ghost reveals in his verse, at older women. Fittingly, RZA goes right to one of the kings of the quiet storm, sampling two vocal parts from Teddy Pendergrass's "Can't We Try" (Philadelphia International, 1980) for the hook. The last words you'd ever expect to begin a Wu-Tang track—"Love was never meant to say goodbye" and "Just another helpless fool in love is what I am"—set the tone for this slow burner, over which the fellas wax poetic about something other than the streets.

Setting it off, Rae approaches a blonde at the bar, breaking the ice by complimenting her watch. After ordering drinks, he finds out who she's here with and asks her what type of fabric she's wearing. "*It's only wool and rayon,*" Rae raps her reply, going on to describe her: "Lipstick crayon / fly Fahrenheit spray on." After a few drinks, however, he blows it and gets impatient, saying, "Fuck negotiating, is you with me, is you waiting?" But she's not that type of girl. "*I don't get down like that* / I don't get down neither / Cuban links skeezer why you acting like a rap teaser," he says, showing his frustration. Unfortunately for him, Rae is definitely not getting laid tonight.

Cappadonna, meanwhile, plays the smooth charmer, innocently asking, "How's life today, your hands are softer than Camay, too / Your hairdo way more class than Halle Berry / Caught visions of me and you riding on the ferry." He's able to sum up her description in one line, "She elegant, pretty eyes, glasses, intelligent." And who would have pegged him as the hopeless romantic, as he ends his verse, "As I grab her hand, sat her politely in the chair / As we stopped to stare at one another, black sister to brother / I'm thinking all the time how she could be my lover."

However, Ghost, a notorious ladies' man, gets the last word. His rhyme, delivered in an easy conversational tone, is as detailed and visual as we've ever seen. He describes the object of his desires as "half Hawaiian with a slight touch of Chinese / Seen you working at a law firm on Fifth Avenue / Three blocks from the Gucci spot is where I trapped you." She's also "quiet and shy" with an "earring" in her left nostril. Cracking jokes with her, Ghost threatens to leave his "wiz" or girlfriend but remains on his best behavior, parting with, "Here take my number let me pull the chair from under / I had fun, plus your backyard speak with thunder." Ghost shows it's not always about the quick conquest as he drops some grown-man rhymes. In an art form known for misogyny, the ladies, no doubt, took note.

RZA constructs a slow, sexy soundtrack for these aural seductions. He jacks the familiar bass line from Southside Movement's "I Been Watching You" (Wand, 1973), pairing it with a stark kick and snare and that ever-so-exquisite tinkling of ivories that opens "Ne Me Quitte Pas (Do Not Leave Me)" (1972) by Belgian singer Jacques Brel. Though not a household name in the States, Brel ranks as the third-highest-selling Belgian chanteur of all time, with twenty-five million records sold. In addition, his songs have been recorded in English by a who's who list of artists, including David Bowie, Ray Charles, Nina Simone, and Frank Sinatra. In light of the track's minimal atmosphere and plodding tempo, RZA adds an off-kilter shaker that fades in and out of the mix to fill up some of the empty space.

Though the Clan may have turned Staten Island into the heart of the hip-hop universe, they are by no means the first to represent the forgotten borough. That honor goes to the Force MCs (later Force MDs), a group formed in 1981, who began performing on the ferry and in Times Square. Starting off as rappers, they were known for their doo-wop style harmonizing, which eventually led them into singing. By the mideighties, they had successfully made the transition to R&B with such hits as "Tears" and the Jimmy Jam / Terry Lewis–penned love song "Tender Love."

"So, we kinda respected them for their legacy and what they did for Staten Island," says Raekwon. "Me and Ghost invited them to come do a track with us. So, they were just chillin' with us getting drunk, high, buggin' out. They heard the beat, and were like, 'Damn, y'all niggas want us on this shit?' We were like, 'Yeah, this one.' So, it was an all-nighter. They were goin' in there trying shit and we were like, 'Again. Nah, yeah, nah, yeah.'"[21]

What they finally come up with for the hook is "All these MCs start realizing / That Ghost got that shit that'll keep you vibing / The Wu is here to bring you Shaolin's finest / But if your skills are weak you better step behind us." And you know it must have been a raucous session, too, because Rae adds, "This was back then when Ghost used to get high, so we were geekin', high. We're drunk, buggin' out. He may have been smoking some dust before he came in, but he got it under control. You know, this is back in his wild crazy days. But, at the end of the day, he was like, 'Nigga, that's my album, we gon' go in on this.'"[22]

"Daytona 500," a title that reflects the frenzied pace of the track, begins with a Force MDs a cappella that interpolates the melody to Michael Jackson's "Lady in My Life" (Epic, 1982), in which they basically shout-out Ghost, Rae, Cappa, RZA, and the rest of the Wu-Tang Killa Beez. Then, like a pack of pit bulls on acid, the MCs chew up the classic old-school break beat "Nautilus" by Bob James, a favorite from the park jam era. RZA simply speeds up the tempo, embellishing it with some additional drum programming—including a pounding kick drum. The dust must have been really good that night, as Ghost drops lines like "In the Philippines, pick herbal beans, bubbling strings / Biochemical cream, we burn kerosene." While his meaning is as elusive as the man himself, the rhythm and cadence of his words fits the track like a glove.

After flexing the abstract linguistics, Ghost and Rae return to a more traditional story format on "Motherless Child," which appeared on the *Sunset Park* film soundtrack. Its title and vocal hook come from O. V. Wright's song of the same name, released on Backbeat Records in 1968. In fact, RZA uses two other songs by the southern blues and soul singer—"Into Something I Can't Shake Loose" (Hi, 1977) and "A Fool Can't See the Light" (Hi, 1989)—for Wright's vocal riffing, which rivals that of James Brown. Beatwise, he samples a section of staccato drums from "Help Yourself" (Tamla/Motown, 1974) by the Undisputed Truth.

Though Rae delivers a brief intro verse, this track is really another Ghost solo mission, as he spins a tale of repercussions. He talks about what happens when a drug dealer who pulls a gun on some dudes at a movie theater runs into the same crew later at the Albee Square Mall in downtown Brooklyn. Unaware that he's being watched, the dealer spends $5,000 on a gold King Tut headpiece chain before they rob him. Ghost, in the role of stick-up kid, says, "Drop the head, don't want to get blood on the Tut / He burped, I shot him, bitch screamed out I'm robbin' him / Had to hit him ten more times, make sure I got him." Then he has to shoot his way out of Albee Square. Far from glorifying violence, however, Ghost is simply relating what happens in the hood on a daily basis, ending the song with "Oh shit, what the fuck? / This shit is horrible."

Making his first appearance since *OB4CL*, Popa Wu returns for the intro to "Black Jesus," dropping some "jewels" of Five-Percent wisdom. His verbose yet entertaining monologue boils down to "all the elements that it took to create you / Everything that's in the universe, God / That created the universe, God, is just within you," a pretty heady thought to begin a rap song. But then again, its title is "Black Jesus," and the track is powered by a dramatic loop from "Riot" (Fantasy, 1975) by the Blackbyrds that sounds like a church choir.

That song, incidentally, is taken from the soundtrack of the film *Cornbread Earl and Me* (1975), appearing at the exact cue when Earl, a popular neighborhood kid who's looking forward to going to college on a basketball scholarship, is ruthlessly shot in the back by police, who mistake him for a burglar. As much as we have seen similar tragedies transpire in recent times, caught on cell phone video, it's obvious that nothing has changed. Black males remain an endangered species in America.

While Rae and Ghost carry on with their usual antics, spouting braggadocio rhymes and abstract street raps (Ghost's most inscrutable couplet is "Ah shit say Starkologist / Starks-ologist, fried fish halibut), the underappreciated U-God clocks in with his second solid verse on this album, proving that he is much more than simply a "four-bar killer." Comparing himself to both uncut cocaine and the Energizer Bunny, he says, "Similar to pure, rhyme blowing out the pore / Battery in the back, keep me charged for the raw / I'm bred type thorough, pistolero gun hero / Renaissance rebel chatter-boxing your barrel." Following his verse, RZA fades out the track on the Blackbyrds sample.

Moving toward the end of the selection, "After the Smoke Is Clear," featuring Raekwon, RZA, and the Delfonics, is one of the few songs that begins without any intro or transition. It's also the one with the fewest samples, as RZA makes the most of his special guest vocalists, who not only sing the hook but also riff and harmonize throughout the track. The only thing borrowed this time are the opening four bars of a drum-and-bass groove from Jimmy Ruffin's "What Becomes of the Brokenhearted" (Soul, 1966).

It must have been quite surreal for Ghost to be working with a group whose music he had fallen asleep to as a child—their first platinum-selling smash, "La-La (Means I Love You)" (Philly Groove Records, 1967), released even before he was born. For the Delfonics, consisting of William Hart, Major Harris, and Frank Washington, it was probably even more surreal to be involved in a shootout in the midst of that collaboration. For RZA, who was advancing as a producer, it must have been a treat working with real professionals instead of just sampling their records. Although they deliver a very simple hook, "After the smoke is done / Wu-Tang, Delfonics number one," their harmonizing lends a very ethereal, nostalgic quality that really distinguishes this track from the rest.

The vibe they establish also blends nicely into "All That I Got Is You," Ghost's heartfelt tribute to his mother, in which he expresses a level of vulnerability seldom seen in the macho world of rap. Ghost finds another perfect clip from *The Education of Sonny Carson* to introduce the track, as Carson's story of being incarcerated at thirteen closely mirrors his own. In it, a fellow inmate, observing how young Sonny is, tells him he should be at home with his mother. In a subtle but implicit indictment of a criminal justice system that disproportionately imprisons Blacks, he says, "Thirteen? Damn, the bastards must be runnin' outta niggas to arrest."

Though Ghost raps solo on the track, he gets a major assist from R&B chanteuse Mary J. Blige, who sings the hook as well as a little freestyle toward the end. Popa Wu also returns with more words of wisdom, boiling down the essence of the song into the following lines: "Because see, that's the child I was / What made me the man I am today / See 'cause if you forget where you come from, heheh / You're never gonna make it where you're goin', aheh." Obviously, Ghost knows what time it is because his lyrics display absolutely no hint of regret or embarrassment about his past struggles but rather pride and gratitude in having made it through. He's not being intentionally sappy or looking for pity but rather showing you the source of his strength.

Up until *Ironman*, the last song on a Wu-Tang project was usually an older cut or a single released before the album came out. "The Soul Controller," however, bucks that trend, going out with one of the strongest and definitely the longest track on the album, clocking in at 6:50. Deviating from the record's retro-soul motif, this song is driven by a sample of classical strings taken from J. S. Bach's Brandenburg Concerto No. 1 in F Major—"Adagio," composed in 1721. RZA juxtaposes this plaintive loop with vocals by the Delfonics, who interpolate Sam Cooke's lyrics from "A Change Is Gonna Come." Though Ghost finishes his third verse around the 3:10 mark, RZA rocks the instrumental and one last round of the hook until 5:19. Unfortunately, this track was subsequently removed from the selection because Sam Cooke's estate does not allow any sampling of his catalog.

Two different movies provide the outro to *Ironman*. First, we hear an extended clip from *Carlito's Way*, the 1993 crime drama that reunited director Brian De Palma with Al Pacino, his star in *Scarface*. It comes from the very end of the movie, when Pacino, playing former hustler Carlito Brigante, lies on a train platform, fatally shot, musing about his fate over a score composed by Patrick Doyle. Then Ghost pulls a double whammy, also including Kevin Spacey's last lines from *The Usual Suspects*: "Greatest trick the devil ever pulled was convincing the world he didn't exist. And like that, he's gone." It's the most apropos ending for a guy who calls himself Ghost.

Of course, in the era of CDs, which could hold up to seventy-four minutes of audio, artists felt compelled to use up as much real estate as possible, so *Ironman* includes a bonus track, "Marvel," which doesn't really hold up to the rest of the album. Judging by its clunky, almost carnivalesque beat and how young Ghost and RZA sound, it appears to be an older track that they tacked on to fill up some space. Though the weakest link on an otherwise powerful album, it hardly dilutes the overall effect of *Ironman*.

Upon its release on October 29, 1996, the album debuted at number two on the Billboard 200 while claiming the top spot on the R&B / Hip-Hop chart. In its opening week, it sold 156,000 copies on its way to going gold at the beginning of the new year. Critically lauded as well, the album's breakout success was a surprise to some who wondered when Wu-Tang's hot streak would end, but not to the group's growing hard-core following, who had high expectations for Ghost, especially after his performance on *OB4CL*. Laying down a royal flush on the first round of solo albums, the Clan had vaulted to the top of the totem, cranking up the anticipation and putting themselves in an ideal position to deliver their long-awaited follow-up to *Enter the Wu-Tang: 36 Chambers* in the new year.

CHAPTER 14

WU-TANG FOREVER

One would assume that everything was copacetic in the Wu-Tang camp when the ball dropped in Times Square to usher in 1997. After all, they had accomplished just about everything they set out to do in RZA's famous "five-year plan" for total domination. After storming the gates with their breakout debut, *Enter the Wu-Tang: 36 Chambers*, the Clan continued the onslaught with five celebrated solo releases, a juggernaut that further solidified their iron-fisted grip on the consciousness of hip-hop. While the rest of the rap world squabbled over turf, Wu-Tang managed to totally transcend regional rivalries. They were too busy carving out their own legacy within the larger movement of hip-hop that was hitting the mainstream like a tsunami. If *Enter the Wu-Tang* had been regarded as a defining moment in the art form, the group's follow-up, *Wu-Tang Forever*, was seen as nothing less than the Second Coming.

From the industry side, Loud Records, who had taken the initial gamble on Wu-Tang, giving them an unprecedented deal, watched patiently as four members of the group they signed went on to make gold- and platinum-selling records for their competitors. But buoyed by the success of Raekwon's album, they were eager for the Clan to reconvene and work their collective magic once again. In fact, Loud had a lot riding on a new Wu album. According to author Dan Charnas, "The execution of their new joint-venture agreement with RCA Records and its parent conglomerate, the Bertelsmann Music Group, depended on their delivery and release of the next Wu-Tang album by June 30, 1997; Strauss Zelnick, the CEO of BMG North America, needed to make his numbers by the end of the company's fiscal year. Rifkind, with the backing of Zelnick, dangled a lucrative advance before the group as an incentive: $4 million payable upon delivery."[1] Compared to the $60,000 Loud had shelled out for *36 Chambers*, this amount represented a significant investment—especially for a young company constantly trying to one-up itself. Though Rifkind had complete faith and confidence in the group, the stakes and expectations couldn't get much higher.

Fans, critics, and industry observers wondered whether the group could reassemble after five of its members had experienced success as solo artists. The music industry was, of course, littered with the remains of groups who suffered the consequences when even one member became a breakout star. In the five years that transpired, Wu-Tang had become a supergroup, and with their stars ascending, they acquired attitudes to match. Critics rightfully contended that coaxing a bunch of rich ghetto celebs to capture lightning in a bottle for a second time would be far different from nine hungry MCs willing to pay for their own studio time. The notoriously fickle hip-hop audience also expected a lot from the Wu, who had consistently raised the bar for rap albums, pushing creativity, originality, and innovation to new heights.

But the greatest pressure came from within the group itself as they sought to defend their crown and maintain their dominance. When you're at the top, there's no place to go but down, and RZA and his crew of alpha males had a serious chip on their collective shoulder. Like the gods of Olympus, they liked the view from on high and were not willing to cede their position for anything. Especially for RZA, who had promised to deliver a number-one album, unfinished business was calling. On the streets, reputation was everything, and with that of his squad on the line, he was going to make this count. Extreme pressure can turn carbon into diamonds, and it was also enough to make the Clan's follow-up to *36 Chambers* one of the biggest albums in the annals of hip-hop.

That kind of stress would be enough to overwhelm anyone, but RZA, who had spent a lifetime on the front lines, was inured to the struggle. Growing up among ten siblings had taught him how to negotiate the chaos and become the eye of the storm. By this time, anyway, having produced six consecutive masterpieces, he was making it look all so easy. Next to what the Clan had been through on the streets, writing rhymes and meeting deadlines was cake. They were a well-oiled machine at this point, ready for combat. At the height of their power, Wu-Tang was calling the shots this time, and they approached the making of a new record like everything else they did—on their own terms.

Their first departure from the norm involved adopting the format of a double album, a novelty in rap at the time. Had they wanted to simply satisfy contractual obligations, they didn't need to make an album with twenty-nine tracks, clocking in at almost two hours. Obviously, they were aiming for epic. Tupac had been the first major artist to go the double-album route with *All Eyez on Me* (Death Row / Interscope) released on February 13, 1996. He, of course, had every incentive to do so, as Suge Knight and Jimmy Iovine of Interscope had put up $1.4 million to bail him out of jail in exchange for a three-record deal. Since Pac was sitting on a lot of unreleased material, a double album would count as two records toward settling that debt. Biggie followed suit with his second album, chillingly titled *Life After Death* (Bad Boy / Arista), released on March 25, 1997, only a couple of weeks after he was murdered. Hitting the streets on June 3, *Wu-Tang Forever* became rap's third major double album, followed by Bone Thugs-N-Harmony's *Art of War*, released on July 29.

But if double-disc sets seemed like somewhat of a trend at the time, the Wu had their own reasons for jumping on the bandwagon. Unlike solo artists like Tupac or Biggie, the Clan had nine MCs, so having more space was almost a necessity. RZA also figured that it had been too long since the last official group release and that by making a double CD, he was satisfying the fans as well as the label, whom he owed a total of five albums. Finally, he was able to bring in more help from his extended family, thereby allowing more Wu affiliates to infiltrate the industry.

Though perfectly capable of producing the entire album himself, RZA had been grooming his protégés, who shared a similar style—the Wu-Elements—to spread their wings. For a fresh take on the Wu-Tang sound, he deployed 4th Disciple, who produced five tracks; True Master of "Brooklyn Zoo" and "Fish" fame, who crafted two bangers; and even Inspectah Deck, who had just started dabbling in production and contributed a hot selection to the album.

RZA traded off production duties for more time on the mic. In fact, on the lyrical side, he and Raekwon made the most appearances on *Forever*, each contributing verses to twelve tracks. Directly behind them were Meth and Ghost, who both rapped on eleven tracks. U-God, who still had something to prove, since he had yet to secure a solo deal, got busy on nine tracks, including one solo performance, while Deck, who was signed to Loud but in limbo as far as his release date, rapped on eight tracks, with a solo performance as well. As for the Brooklyn contingent, both GZA and Masta Killa contributed verses to seven tracks apiece, while ODB appeared on six, one of those being a solo joint. Rounding out the MCs, Cappadonna, fresh off his appearance on *Iron-man*, spit on five cuts, while Streetlife, a veteran from *Tical*, appeared on two. From a practical standpoint, then, a double album made total sense, allowing everyone a chance to shine. But as far as time constraints were concerned, it also proved to be highly ambitious.

Once again, RZA showed his true mettle in the way he approached making this album. Though he had recently purchased the "Wu Mansion," a huge property (7,934 square feet to be exact) in the woods of Millstone Township, New Jersey—complete with recording studio—that also served as a clubhouse for the Clan, he knew his team well enough to realize that there would be too many distractions if they made the album there. Since each Clansman rolled with his own posse/clique/entourage, they brought the projects to the boondocks with animated dice games and the like, and the place could get hectic, as it often did. The only way to isolate and sequester the individuals of the group would be to take them far away in order to vibe with one another and really focus on getting the album done.

With that in mind, RZA headed to LA in early January to scout out studios. He settled on Ameraycan Studios in North Hollywood, owned by singer/songwriter Ray Parker Jr., a veteran of Hamilton Bohannon and Barry White's bands, whose last big hit was the theme song for the movie *Ghostbusters* in 1984. The low-key spot on Lankersham Boulevard, featuring two rooms equipped with sprawling SSL mixing boards, appealed to RZA because it was off the beaten path and they could get twice as much work done. After all, when you have a double album to turn around as quickly as possible, two rooms with two engineers were obviously better than one.

RZA was already in the midst of mixing the second Gravediggaz album in New York with engineer Carlos Bess, who had worked on *36 Chambers*. He asked Bess to come out to LA, where they could finish Gravediggaz in one room and then start working on Wu-Tang. RZA recruited another set of ears in veteran knob-twirler Scott Harding, a.k.a. Scotty Hard, who had mixed the first Gravediggaz album—not to mention records by Ultramagnetic MCs, BDP, Jungle Brothers, and De La Soul, as well as an impressive assortment of rock, jazz, and world music artists. Both engineers joined RZA in LA in mid-January, shortly before the group arrived.

They were initially tasked with building a preproduction studio in RZA's hotel room so that he could work whenever he wanted, which was always. Though he had already created enough music to fill thirty to forty reels of two-inch tape, which each hold about seventeen minutes, he was constantly churning out new beats. RZA's basic setup consisted of an ASR-10, his bread and butter, as well as an MPC1000 drum machine and several keyboards—including a Yamaha V-71, a Nord Lead virtual analog, Roland 2080, and a Novation bass station. Everything was patched into a twenty-four-track Mackie board, and he recorded onto three ADATs, which were basically eight-track tape machines that recorded digitally onto Super-VHS cassettes. He could take these to Ameraycan and dump them onto twenty-four-track two-inch tape. Harding recalls accompanying RZA to the nearest Guitar Center, where they dropped about $10,000 on gear, and then wiring it all up at his hotel room and, later, at his apartment.

The rest of the Clan trickled into town in late January, with Dirty arriving a week after everyone else. The fellas were particularly psyched to see Cappadonna in the mix this time, since he had schooled many of them in the art of rhyming back in the day. With everyone accounted for, they moved into the Oakwood apartments, only about a ten-minute drive from the studio. Functional and suburban but hardly glamorous, these short-term rentals, which came furnished and with kitchenettes, were mainly used by actors and other temporary workers from the various Hollywood Studios in the vicinity, but one of the complex's long-term tenants happened to be the elusive Sly Stone.

Once assembled, it took the group a minute to get settled and down to business. The first track they worked on, "Triumph," had originally been recorded back at the Wu Mansion in New Jersey and, for all intents and purposes, was done. With a lengthy 5:38 running time and no hook, it was the antithesis of a radio-friendly tune but was meant to be the lead-off single from the album. But "Triumph" essentially stuck to the same template as "Protect Ya Neck," their initial breakout single. RZA, in fact, admitted that he always included a track like that on every Wu-Tang album because it would be familiar to the fans. For whatever reason—maybe because this was the first single—they decided to rerecord their verses, which took a whole week. After promptly mixing it, they were able to turn it around for a February 11 release.

Despite its lengthy running time, radio had no choice but to play it, and the Clan was out of the starting block in fine style.

The group eventually fell into a routine that saw them working in the studio six days a week, with a day off on Sunday. The engineers arrived first, at about two in the afternoon, and brought up tracks from the reels per RZA's instructions. After they set up a premix of the day's selections, group members started trickling in at about four. In the era before cell phones, they somehow managed to get the long-distance code for the studio line and spent this time making free calls to their people back in New York. Then, in each room, different beats looped endlessly into the a.m., allowing the MCs to wander between them and write at their own pace. The Clan often tossed around lyrical ideas and concepts of songs with one another in the lounge and also argued about who would set it off or go next. When they were ready to record their verses, they stepped into the booth and got busy. Despite the internal competition, it was all very relaxed and communal. While anyone could drop a verse on any given track, RZA reserved the right to make the final cuts.

The Abbott was everywhere, popping in to check on the progress in both rooms while spending the bulk of his days making beats in his room. He was always around when it came time to mix a track, either programming the drops with automation or doing them live with the mute button. In his absence, he didn't leave many specific instructions for his engineers other than making sure that the vocals were upfront and popping. Paranoid of bootlegging, to which ODB's album had fallen victim, RZA allowed absolutely no cassettes of finished material to be dubbed, insisting that the engineers take the two-inch reels back with them every night instead of leaving them in the studio vault. This required moving ten to twelve reels, each weighing about twenty pounds, twice daily, for which Bess eventually bought a dolly.

Recording and mixing continued at a steady clip through March and April and into May. Even the murder of Notorious B.I.G. following a *Vibe* party that the Clan had also attended did not impede their progress, although they were clearly shaken up by it. On the day after, as the whole group convened in RZA's apartment for a meeting, not a single one of them brought up the elephant in the room, though their pensive expressions said otherwise. And while scores of other visiting New Yorkers immediately fled LA, they remained behind to continue their work. In May, they finally shot the $800,000 video for "Triumph," directed by Brett Ratner. The final work then shifted to New York, where the album was edited and finally mastered. Despite a late start and endless delays, the Clan managed to deliver ahead of schedule, releasing the highly anticipated *Wu-Tang Forever* on June 3.

The album debuted at the top spot of the Billboard 200, selling a staggering 612,000 copies in its first week alone. Four months later, on October 15, it was certified quadruple platinum by the Recording Industry Association of America after moving two million units (times two CDs) in the US. The expanded nature of a double album practically guaranteed that there would be filler, but not enough to offset the universally positive reception it received from critics and fans alike.

At a lean and mean forty-five minutes, disc one was almost flawless, with standout cuts like "Reunited," "For Heaven's Sake," "Severe Punishment," and "It's Yourz," which saw a much cleaner style of production than RZA's usual grit. Disc two had its high points as well—including "Triumph," "Impossible," "The M.G.M.," and "Heaterz"—but, with a running time of 67:08, it was bloated, including tracks that just couldn't hang with the best material on this side. At the top of his game and feeling self-indulgent, RZA chose not to trim the fat but let it ride to make a grand statement. *Forever* represented a high point for the Clan, fulfilling RZA's five-year plan and cementing their place in hip-hop history. For observers who had followed the evolution of this clique of scrappy underdogs, it was nothing short of poetic justice, testament to the fact that all things are, indeed, possible.

* * *

Speaking of self-indulgent, imagine opening an album of this magnitude with a rambling, six-minute cacophony by two people who aren't even in the group. That's what "Wu Revolution," featuring Popa Wu and Uncle Pete, sounds like— some ill, funked-up sermon from a street corner. While fans are already familiar with group mentor Popa Wu, the Clan's spiritual compass, crazy Uncle Pete sounds like somebody's inebriated relative—and he is. The blood uncle of ODB and Popa Wu's makes his recording debut singing and riffing in the background in a raspy, bluesy voice: "Why do we kill each other? Look at the children. What kind of a future?" Meanwhile, Popa Wu goes off on one of his extended rants, dipping heavily into Five-Percent doctrine as he admonishes listeners to respect women and stay away from alcohol and drugs. Copping a moralistic tone, he preaches about the ongoing mental war between God and the devil. It's hard to take him seriously, however, over the clunky backing track—one of RZA's not ready for prime-time productions. Hardly the most auspicious beginning to an album, the track is fast-forward worthy, and disc one would have been much tighter without it.

Sampled dialogue from *Shaolin Temple* (1976) brings you back to familiar turf: "Shaolin kung fu, to survive, must be now taught to more young men. We must expand, get more people, so the knowledge will spread." The opening blast we've been waiting for, "Reunited," immediately follows, utilizing the unexpected—a live drum loop, courtesy of engineer Carlos Bess, and an incredible performance by violinist Karen Briggs (inexplicably, credited to Miri Ben-Ari), who both solos and riffs. Unlike the dirty sampled drums RZA usually favors, this live beat is crisp, clear, and booming, while the strings lend an almost classical feel, which seems to be the musical motif of this album. The song's memorable chorus, "It's Wu motherfuckers, Wu-Tang motherfuckers," sung by vocalist Ms. Roxy in her first and only appearance on a Wu-Tang project, sounds like a true declaration of victory.

Breaking the seal lyrically on this album, the cousins GZA, ODB, and RZA, joined by Meth, are as sharp as ever. "Reunited, double LP, world excited / Struck a match to the underground, industry ignited," says GZA, encapsulating the Wu-Tang saga into a powerful couplet. Next up is Dirty with probably his longest verse on the album, in which he shouts out, "The Indian that sold Manhattan to the white man / My grandfather, step up and get knocked right the fuck out." Though he's actually talking about his great-grandfather Chief Wickham Cuffie, of eastern Long Island's Shinnecock nation, that tribe had nothing to do with the sale of Manhattan. RZA, meanwhile, raps from higher realms with lines like "Grow like a fetus with no hands and feet to complete us / And we return like Jesus when the whole world need us," working in a clever analogy to the Second Coming. "I think that was supposed to be some RZA and GZA shit, taking it back to when they first started out," says Meth. "But big-head

Meth was in the studio, so I had to get on it."[2] No regrets there, as he brings it home: "Drunk off of cheap wine / Each line be on point when I speak mine / On behalf of my crew, SUUUUUUUUUU, Enter the Wu / 36 more deadly chambers to take you through."

Forever improving and expanding his chops, RZA starts studying classical piano around this time. A knowledge of chords and notes enhances his musicianship, but he still uses samples in very creative ways. The next track, "For Heaven's Sake," showcases a popular technique he pioneers. The song's hook, "Oh baby for heaven's sake," comes from a line from New Orleans singer/songwriter King Floyd's "Don't Leave Me Lonely" (Cotillion, 1971), which RZA speeds up in order to fit the tempo of the track, giving it the effect of a chipmunk voice. The loop's strings almost feel like a piece of classical music, lending a timeless quality to the song.

Deck, the ever-dependable lead-off man, strikes first: "Boom master, with the faster blade, track slasher / Manufacture poems to microphones, bones fracture." Meanwhile, the cool and deadly Masta Killa sounds like he's delivering a royal edict: "Now all pay tribute to this entity / A spark that surges through the undergrowth / Overwhelming the populace from the entry / The Wu-Tang dynasty has emerged." Never one to be outdone, Cappadonna flaunts a stream-of-consciousness flow: "Wu Pirates, sneak inside the club, low eyes / Low down dirty, twelve thirty, night-time crawlers / Off-the-wallers, basketball gun brawlers." Delivering a diversity of styles, these guys make it clear that the days of lyrics and flows are officially back.

This certified banger switches abruptly into "Cash Rules / Scary Hours (Still Don't Nothing Move but the Money)," which brings Meth, Rae, and Ghost together over a spooky production. Sounding like vintage RZA, this joint is actually the first of five produced by 4th Disciple. Here, he flips a Skeeter Davis sample from "The End of the World" (RCA / Victor, 1962), taking two vocal snippets from the line where the teen country sensation asks, "Why does the sun keep on shining?" and turning them into ghostly loops. Not only does he share a similar aesthetic with his mentor, but he's as adept at disguising samples too. He layers these elements over a simple programmed kick and snare, adding a melancholy piano section from what sounds like *The Godfather* theme for gothic effect.

The rhymes revolve around those "scary hours" between dusk and dawn, when the bulk of illicit activity goes down. Wu-Tang is not far removed from those days, as Meth recalls, "I remember sticking fiends at the one-six-ooh / When we was starving, ducking five-oh, paying 'em dues / Times is hard in the slums I'm from, they got us barred in / We warring and case dodging, ripping and robbing." The "one-six-ooh," of course, refers to building 160, Park Hill's legendary drug spot, where Meth not only sold crack but also, apparently, robbed customers when he was desperate. While some rappers glorify their gritty ghetto environment, he paints a picture of being trapped in bleak desperation. Meanwhile, Ghost delivers an electric performance, rapping until he runs out of tape. He name-checks high-end jewelry brands like Ted Rossi one minute, cryptically dissing "Judge Cuffner" the next. Turns out he is talking about Charles Kuffner, the West Brighton judge who revoked ODB's probation on drug charges, sending him back to prison.[3]

As Ghost runs out of real estate, the sound of the two-inch tape slowly rewinding (another inspired idea, used sometimes in dub music) opens "Visions," another heavy hitter showcasing Inspectah Deck's first production work. With its fragments of guitar and organ riding a steady boom-bap beat, this, too, could easily pass for a RZA creation. He's obviously been teaching the troops well. Despite a strong showing all around from Meth, Rae, Ghost, and Masta Killa, Deck also steals the show lyrically with his internal rhymes: "Mind arson, my squadron surround the sound garden / Guns for hire, plus you're under fire, and a target / Sniper in the cipher, I Pied Piper / Move the housing by the thousand / I watch out the Chrysler." In fact, *Forever* would prove to be his breakout moment, as the unsung MC finally receives long-overdue recognition for his impressive skills.

They pick up the tempo on the next track, "As High as Wu-Tang Get," which reunites the duo from "Shadowbox-ing"—GZA and Meth—with Dirty handling the chorus. Not one to mince words, GZA dives right in: "Yo, too many songs, weak rhymes that's mad long / Make it brief, son, half short and twice as strong." That last line, ironically, encapsulates one of the main criticisms of *Forever*. Never a weak rhymer, Meth holds his own, rapping, "The way these rhymes keep comin' at cha splash ya / Get your head piece fractured, with killer cuts / From the Shropshire Slasher, rip shit up." The pop-culture maven and comic book freak even manages to work in a reference to an obscure Looney Tunes villain who first appeared opposite Daffy Duck in the 1956 car-toon *Deduce, You Say*. Aside from a sample of Albert King's "I'll Play the Blues for You" (Stax, 1972), which provides the foundation for the main groove, a live drum loop, played by Carlos Bess, and a bouncy two-note bass line from the Nova-tion is all RZA needs to turn up the heat.

The Abbott understands something about hip-hop pro-duction that few appreciate: keep it simple. Taking a cue from the stark drum-machine workouts of Run-DMC that rescued rap from the disco era, he knows that hip-hop really relies on only two main elements—strong lyrics and hard beats. With more equipment at his disposal—including the brand-new Clavia Ddrum, sent to him by the manufacturer—he programs more of his own beats instead of sampling, and when he does sample drums, they are usually from the live workouts of Bess, whose *Funky Drummer* break-beat series was up to its fourth volume.

"Severe Punishment," which follows, provides a master class in RZA's minimalist approach. Pairing a mechanical Ddrum beat—kick, snare, and hi-hat—with a detuned piano bass line, he evokes the feeling of impending doom. The only samples he uses come from the martial arts film *3 Evil Masters* (1980)—one a vocal snippet to introduce the track ("I despise your killing and raping") and the other for its dramatic horn fanfare that he drops several times during the course of the track.

Seven cuts deep into the album, we've heard from the whole Clan except U-God, who busts out of the gate with some of his best lines, rapping, "Check these hi-hats, sling tings movin' through the rubbish / Party robust, rec room style for you brothers / Time's tickin', erupt misconduct / Enterin' one funk before the drum dry up." Sidelined for so much of the group's early output, U-God has to put in a lot of work to bring himself up to the level of his brothers, but his hunger, as well as his huge improvement on the mic, characterize his contributions on *Forever*.

Among the other MCs on this track—GZA, Masta Killa, and Raekwon—RZA's verse also stands out. He starts out borrowing some of GZA's lines from "Words from the Genius" (Cold Chillin', 1991): "MCs wonder, what's hip-hop thunder / Tell you truth it's just one nation under / A groove, getting' down for the funk of it / Like Fred Sanford and the bitch." Then he gets downright metaphysical, rapping, "Fabulous establishment, metabolism Blackfoot Indian / Cherokee, started out smaller than amphibian / Then grew to a physical body with five meridians / As the pendulum swings close to the millennium two thousand / Wickedness is spread amongst my citizens." Known for stacking syllables, his dense verses also come laced with a lot of information. Here, he pays homage to his part-Cherokee heritage and invokes traditional Chinese medicine, dealing with the pathways in the body where chi energy flows, while indulging in a little premillennial paranoia.

Steamrolling through the perfectly sequenced selection, we arrive at another 4th Disciple production, "Older Gods," featuring Rae, Ghost, and GZA. He's learned well from RZA, rocking a simple piano melody for the main loop and adding some weird off-the-beat industrial sounds as ear candy. Aside from Popa Wu's opening screed, this track is the first to overtly acknowledge the teachings of the Five Percent and its influence on the group. It's also one of the few songs with an actual hook, delivered by Rae and Ghost, who say, "The Older Gods put me on, on how to rock this / Maintain 360 Lord and live prosperous / It only takes a lesson a day, just to analyze life / One time in the respectable mind." After sharing solo albums with each other, Rae and Ghost are so joined at the hip that even GZA sounds like an interloper on this track.

ODB, who has seen limited action so far, pops up on the next track alongside Cappadonna and RZA. He actually has two verses on "Maria," a track "dedicated to all you bitches," as he says in the intro before getting as nasty as he wants to be. In his second verse, he affirms his love for back-door action: "Dirt Dog ain't choosy, pussy move me / Pretty black dick up in the booty, I like it muddy and swampy / By now you find your ass up shitty creeky." Reprising his seductive style in "Camay," Cappadonna takes a slightly different tack:

> I seen you at the five and dime wasting your time
> Oh you shine, I'm looking at your ass from behind
> You walked by smelling like watermelon
> You might make me a felon, my eyeballs swelling
> My nuts start yelling, excuse my prick
> Wanna have a talk with you, I'm sick
> My medicine is can I walk with you.

Such imaginative lines are laugh-out-loud funny. RZA, on the other hand, spins a cautionary story rhyme about the typical project floozy: "Suicidal, she been in more hotels than Bibles / Idol-worshipping bitch wasn't the type to make bridal." Despite RZA's warnings, she ends up giving his friend an STD. "Maria" provides compelling commentary on sexual politics in the hood.

Musically, RZA recycles a drum break from Lee Dorsey's "Get Out of My Life Woman" (Amy, 1966), pairing it with a single organ note and guitar strum from Blood, Sweat & Tears' "I Love You More Than You'll Ever Know" (CBS, 1968). He fleshes it out with some violin parts, which sound like outtakes from "Reunited." The song ends with dialogue from the movie *Four Assassins* (1975) about "the next generation," meant as a prelude to the following track, "A Better Tomorrow."

This title comes from the John Woo movie of the same name—one that the Clan also recycles for the name of their sixth studio album, released on Warner Bros. in 2014. The track represents another departure for the group for its positive messaging delivered over a sentimental, introspective beat, but with the Wu, you learn to expect the unexpected. Producer 4th Disciple catches a piece of Peter Nero's well-known "Love Theme from Romeo and Juliet (A Time for Us)" (Columbia, 1969) that sounds so unrecognizable yet captures the musicality of that orchestral piece.

Over the beat, Inspectah Deck, Masta Killa, U-God, RZA, and Meth team up to spread knowledge and drop some jewels from their own experiences. Deck sums it all up in the hook: "You can't party your life away, drink your life away / Smoke your life away, fuck your life away / Dream your life away, scheme your life away / 'Cause your seeds grow up the same way." In a single track, we witness the transformation of a group of wayward ghetto youth into grown men. Four years after bringing the ruckus, they now espouse responsibility and accountability, which rarely find expression in rap. Coming from them—especially after what they've seen and been through—it doesn't sound preachy but rather good advice from older brothers who know from experience.

"Right now, they ain't gonna hear the hunger. What they gonna hear is the strength, know what I'm sayin'? They gonna hear the power of this shit, for real," RZA explains. "See, most niggas come from the street life, right, knowing the shit is hell; get out of hell; and then keep trying to act like they in hell. We showin' niggas the way out—fuck all that. If you wanna be stupid, be stupid, but we gonna show y'all the way out, without even compromising. We didn't compromise ourselves; we still the same mu'fuckas."

As the song dissolves into the noise of a crowded stadium with chants of "Wu" audible in the background, disc one's final selection, "It's Yourz," commences, conjuring the park jam era with a shuffling break beat courtesy of Gaz's "Sing Sing" (Salsoul, 1978). The only other sample RZA uses are the opening chords of Jean-Pierre Decerf and Marc Saclays's "Look on a Soft Side" (Editions Montparnasse 2000, 1979), which he replays as a stirring melody evocative of church music. Raekwon wastes no time attacking the track with "Machine gun raps, for all my niggas in the back" before RZA and U-God tag-team the hook: "*It's yours!* The world in the palm of your hand / *It's yours!* 23 million of useful land / *It's yours!* The seed and the black woman / *It's yours!* Double LP from Wu-Tang Clan." Like a mantra shouted from the mountaintop, it's the self-realization that Wu-Tang has arrived.

Incidentally, the curious line "23 million of useful land" is the answer to question number seven of the student enrollment section of *Supreme Wisdom Lessons of the Nation of Gods and Earths*, which asks, "How much of the Earth's useful land is used by the original man?" In addition, the song's title—another nod to hip-hop nostalgia—comes from a twelve-inch by T La Rock and Jazzy Jay, produced by Rick Rubin, which made a splash back in 1984 as the inaugural release of the storied label Def Jam.

Demonstrating one of his finer qualities, consistency, Inspectah Deck throws down some of his best verses: "It's only natural, actual facts are thrown at you / The impact will blow trees back and crack statues / Million-dollar rap crews fold, check the sick shit, explicit / I crystallize the rhyme so you can sniff it." Comparing his "lines" to cocaine, Deck is on a tear on this album. He also delivers the goods on "Triumph," which opens disc two, after a spoken-word introduction by RZA and GZA.

While disc two is not a complete washout, its sheer length—sixteen tracks with a running time of 67:08—is problematic. It includes plenty of filler material—tracks like the sappy "Black Shampoo," U-God's solo turn, and "The Second Coming," a straight-up hot mess of an R&B track by Tekitha—that have no place on a Clan album. Not known for their strong closings, Wu-Tang also end *Forever* with a completely unnecessary rant by Raekwon, whose voice we have already heard on twelve tracks. After a string of largely flawless releases, chalk up all these sudden lapses in quality control to a moment of self-indulgence by a group who, after struggling and sacrificing to get to the top, are taking their victory lap—to hell with the haters.

"Triumph," an almost six-minute song with no hook, provides the theme song for this celebration as well as the album's first single. "I just started making this track that I thought would have a classical attitude yet still the soul music and the hip-hop," RZA explains of the song's inception. "So, you hear my drums, it's that constant hip-hop sound, but when you hear me playing the strings, even though it's the same notes, when it comes back around later, it's the same notes an octave higher and played with more amplitude."[4]

The track didn't even have strings when Inspectah Deck first heard it—just that pounding beat with its gargantuan kick drums. The song began in the wee hours at the Wu Mansion in New Jersey, where the entire Clan was crashed out after a typical all-nighter. "I was sleeping, too, but subliminally I heard the beat," Deck recalls. "I hear RZA making the beat. What's that? Oh, shit! I hear the drums—he didn't even have the whole beat yet. So, I'm just listening, I'm like, 'Man, that shit sounds tough.'"[5] Unable to go back to sleep, Deck joined RZA in the studio and started writing to the track.

Using the bulk of a verse that he had spit on Tony Touch's *Power Cypha: 50 MCs Volume 1* mixtape, he added to it.

"Next thing you know, he [RZA] finds these keys," says Deck. "He's doin' that, and I'm just like 'Yo!' know what I mean? That shit sounds ill!"[6] Turning to his turntable for help, RZA discovers a soulful "Ooooooh" from "Just Found Me" (Truth, 1975) by gospel outfit the Rance Allen Group. He samples it into his ASR-10 and plays it over the beat as the wide-eyed MC looks on. "I'm like, this motherfucker is the illest dude I know, man," says Deck. "Yunno, I love Primo, I love Pete Rock, you know what I'm sayin', but the RZA, man, like I watched him doing that shit, and it was amazing to me."[7]

Seeing his producer in action spurred Deck to write one of the greatest verses of his career, which was later recognized as a hip-hop quotable in *The Source*. "I bomb atomically, Socrates's philosophies and hypotheses / Can't define how I be dropping these mockeries / Lyrically perform armed robbery / Flee with the lottery / Possibly they spotted me," he raps. After going into the booth and laying down his verse, Deck goes back to sleep. In the meantime, Method Man, Masta Killa, and U-God hear the track and add their own verses. "Everybody hears it, and they're like, 'This shit is dope! We want to get on it.' That's how the majority of Wu-Tang tracks are made," says Deck.[8]

As "Triumph" is the only track on the album that everyone blesses—including Dirty, who appears for the intro and some ad-libs—competition for bars must have been ferocious. But that's exactly why the lyrical performances on *Forever* are so uniformly strong—they're battling each other in friendly competition. Masta Killa also slings some of his tightest verses: "Light is provided through sparks of energy / From the mind that travels in rhyme form / Giving sight to the blind / The dumb are mostly intrigued by the drum." That last line is a sideways diss to those who don't appreciate clever lyrics.

Originally titled "A Soldier's Story," the reason the song was renamed, according to Meth, is, "basically, we saying we conquered all the he say/she say, the rumors of the group splitting up, East Coast / West Coast beef and all that. We triumphed over it."[9] Always one to tell it like it is, though, he adds, "'Triumph' was like, all the pressure of the name being bigger than the group and everybody smelling themselves and thinking they were bigger than they really was. You can hear all that on 'Triumph.'"[10]

"Impossible" immediately follows, another one of the highlights of disc two. Unlike the celebratory vibe of the latter, however, this track sounds darker and more introspective while still delivering a similar message—namely, that it's "impossible, you can never defeat the Gods," as Tekitha sings in the hook. This time, producer 4th Disciple digs deep down in the crates, using the opening piano of Beethoven's Piano Sonata Number 8, *Pathétique*, first movement, composed in 1799, as his main loop, melding it to some skeletal percussion and two-note bass line. Since no one else was really sampling classical music at this time, tracks like these on *Forever* really stood out.

Not usually one to set off a track, RZA delivers one of his longest verses on the album, which begins, "Fusion of the five elements, to search for the higher intelligence / Women walk around celibate, livin' irrelevant / The most benevolent king, communicatin' through your dreams / Mental pictures been painted, Allah heard and seen." Not content to simply make beats and seal deals, he raps like he's got something to prove. Overall, his performance on *Forever* sets him up nicely for his first solo project, *Bobby Digital in Stereo* (Gee Street / V2, 1998), the following year. Afterward, U-God takes the baton with an equally long and pithy verse, but both MCs are eclipsed by Starks, whose epic bars earn him Verse of the Year in *The Source*. He tells a story rhyme about the death of his friend Jamie, who's been shot and lies on the ground bleeding. Ghost talks to him and tries to keep him conscious until the ambulance arrives, reminiscing about their youth. But Jamie knows he's not going to make it and gives Ghost the charm around his neck that contains a picture of his kids. Jamie's mother finally arrives when the ambulance does, crying and clutching her chest, but she is too late, as her son is pronounced dead at 12:10.

"One of my favorite Wu-Tang joints was 'Impossible' because it was serious. It was serious and it was a story that went on," says Ghost. "But it was just like my mind, my pen was going off like crazy."[11] Ghost caught an inspiration off the "theatrical" beat, which, he says, "touched me, and I like things that touch me, know what I mean, so when I hear that [beat], I could catch a chill 'cause you could just see everything like it was a flick."[12]

After exploding out of the gate with two powerful tracks, disc two then shifts into lower gear. It's not that selections like "Little Ghetto Boys," featuring Rae and Cappa; "The City," an Inspectah Deck solo cut, produced by 4th Disciple; and "The Projects," featuring Rae, Meth, Ghost, and U-God, are clunkers—they just seem as redundant as their titles. After finally reaching the big time, perhaps the Clan is trying to reaffirm their allegiance to the streets, but since authenticity has never been an issue for them, it's an unnecessary exercise. Anyway, most of their material is about little ghetto boys from the projects making their way in the city.

It's also puzzling that RZA, the last person to copy anyone else, would even make a song called "Little Ghetto Boys," based off Donny Hathway's original "Little Ghetto Boy" (Atco, 1972). Dr. Dre had already been there on his blockbuster album *The Chronic* (Death Row / Interscope, 1992), using "Little Ghetto Boy" as one of the cuts that established a newly minted Snoop Doggy Dog. RZA distinguishes his version, however, by sampling the string melody and bass line of O. V. Wright's "Ghetto Child" (Backbeat, 1973) as his main loop and speeding up Hathway's chorus for the hook.

"Deadly Melody" follows as a mock freestyle session powered by a catchy piano melody and another live drum break courtesy of Carlos Bess. A multitude of verses—ten, to be exact—alternate between Masta Killa, U-God, RZA, Meth, GZA, Ghost, and Streetlife, in his first appearance on the album. There's even one verse in which Masta Killa, U-God, and GZA complete each other's lines in quick succession: "Check the 150-millimeter heater / As it blows holes through your fucking speaker / *Making you weaker creeping inches centimeters* / **Fifty-caliber street sweeper** / **Shots from Shaolin that go to Massapequa**." Clearly, it's all about the lyrics, and Bess says he had a hell of a time recording this track, since MCs were ferociously battling for bars, sometimes stacked in the vocal booth together.

In fact, lyrically, there are few weak performances on the album. All the MCs are obviously at the top of their game, and RZA's strategy of having them record the album together ensures that they keep their swords sharp, constantly battling each other in a friendly competition to get on tracks. Consequently, joints like "Bells of War," "Duck Seazon," and "Hellz Wind Staff" don't suffer from their verses but rather lack the usual punch production-wise. When RZA boasts that making beats is getting too easy for him, that statement also implies a lack of inspiration or even burnout, which may not have been exclusive to him.

"By the middle of the album, focus was being lost," says Method Man. "I'm speaking for myself, not my crew. My focus was lost by the middle of the album and my heart just wasn't in it like it used to be. I don't regret anything that I did, but I wish I would've been a little more focused on the shit that really mattered at that point in time."[13] Though one couldn't tell from Meth's performances on the album, certainly working six days a week for several months on end could take its toll. Whatever the case, one can feel the group's loss of focus and energy over the course of disc two.

The highlights of this disc include True Master's dual productions, "The M.G.M." and "Heaterz." The first track gets its title from the well-known Vegas hotel and casino where undefeated (at the time) boxer Julio César Chávez challenged Pernell "Sweet Pea" Whittaker for his WBC welterweight title on September 10, 1993, a memorable and controversial fight that ended in a draw. Though this bout actually transpired at the Alamodome in San Antonio, Texas, Rae and Ghost use the M.G.M. as a backdrop to spin another compelling yarn about being in the audience that night, people watching. They thoroughly immerse you in the environment, name-checking attending celebrities like Deion Sanders and Chanté Moore while alternating lines: "Seventh round, Chavez bleeding from his right ear / Yo, keep your eye on that same nigga from right here / *Popcorn spilling all over Liz Claiborne / Ghost had the fly Gucci mocks with no socks on.*" Not only does this narrative provide a great concept for a song, but they pull it off like pros with the hype backing of True Master. Except for the high-pitched bell before rounds, his samples are so well disguised that he doesn't pay for any clearance fees here. Later, he chops up the Gladys Knight and the Pips' classic "Giving Up" (Soul, 1970) to create the musical foundation for "Heaterz," featuring Rae, Deck, ODB, U-God, and Cappa.

Aside from Wu affiliate Streetlife, Dirty clocks the least amount of time on the album. "As far as Ol' Dirty goes, once we hit Cali you couldn't find that nigga," says Meth. "When we got him in the studio, we tried to throw him in as much shit as we could."[14] This period marks the beginning of Dirty's issues with drugs, when he was becoming difficult to work with. According to Harding, "Dirty was walking around there saying, 'Dirty don't write no rhymes,' 'Dirty ain't takin' no pictures,' 'Dirty ain't doing this, Dirty ain't doing that.'" At one point, he says, the rapper punched a hole in the wall in the lounge because he was being pushed to do something he didn't feel like doing.

When it comes time to record his solo track, he pulls another diva-esque move, complaining about his throat. The studio assistants have to fetch packs of honey and lemon for him from the nearest fast-food joint, while Meth helps him write his rhyme and coaches him on how to deliver it. While recording his verses requires a lot of punch-ins, an animated Dirty goes in and completes "Dog Shit" in a night. A gratuitously filthy track by anyone's standards, he rants about his love of sluts, anal sex, "tossing salad," and defecating on someone's lawn, which sounds like a metaphor for something particularly kinky and vile. However, Dirty has a way of making it all sound hilarious, especially on the hook when he riffs off the word *ho*, yelling, "Hoooooo / Yeah, haaaaay / De haaaaaa / Bitch hooooo." RZA can only follow this crazy performance with some spontaneous stand-up by an unknown comic in the crew that closes out the track. We all know Dirty can do better, but slipping him in between "The M.G.M." and "Duck Seazon" as a bit of comic relief ultimately makes the track work.

While *Forever* might not pack the same asteroid-hitting-Earth impact as *Enter the Wu-Tang*, it represents the Clan at the zenith of their collective power. "The sum of our parts is worth all the organizing," says Method Man. "It's like the Power Rangers where they come together to form that Megazord shit. Them guys are lethal, but when they come together, it's even more incredible. This album will destroy every hip-hop record made in the last 10 years."[15] Realizing the power of the collective and what it took to get here, Meth's claim is no idle boast.

But in the dynamic world of hip-hop, where change is the only constant, kingdoms rise, and kingdoms fall. Dr. Dre's West Coast dynasty was already ceding dominance to Puff Daddy and the Family. Meanwhile, Atlanta's Outkast was leading the charge of the Dirty South, on the rise again thanks to independents like New Orleans's Cash Money Records and Master P's No Limit. After an incredible five-year run, Wu-Tang Clan ruled the world of beats, but the first cracks in the foundation were already testing the unity of the group. Meant as their bid for immortality, *Forever*, ironically, signaled the beginning of the end of the Wu dynasty.

PART 3

THE SAGA CONTINUES

CHAPTER 15

FOR THE CHILDREN

"We had the world in our hands, and we dropped it," RZA remarked of that period immediately following the release of *Wu-Tang Forever*. "I could feel my power was gone. Even when we were recording the album, I realized the Clan was no longer a dictatorship with me telling who to get on what song and what to do."[1] While his carefully deployed strategy to dominate the music industry took five years to pull off, it all began to unravel in less than five months. The thrill and exhaustion of finally reaching the mountaintop and being rewarded with a number-one album clearly obscured deeper fissures within the group. Ironically, the slow and steady decline of the Wu can be traced back to that glorious summer of 1997, which found them soaring to Olympian heights but about to be brought back to earth like Icarus. Two incidents, in particular, precipitated that fall: getting blackballed by New York's Hot 97 after dissing the radio station at their own popular Summer Jam concert and dropping out midway through a huge stadium tour with agit-rockers Rage Against the Machine.

At the beginning of the nineties, WQHT, otherwise known as Hot 97, was a top-forty / dance station struggling to find itself. Lacking a clear identity, it perpetually came in last in the rankings behind New York's other major programmers like WBLS (107.5 FM) and WRKS (98.7 KISS-FM). All of that changed rather quickly, however, with the hiring of program director Steve Smith, a white Long Island native who came to his new position from Power 92 in Phoenix. Though a rock fan himself, Smith deferred to market research that clearly identified rap as the sound that most New York City listeners wanted to hear. A recent new addition, Funkmaster Flex (Aston George Taylor Jr.) already helmed the station's most popular show, *Friday Night Street Jam,* helping break "Protect Ya Neck" and later popularize the "Method Man" single. Smith doubled down on hip-hop by bringing on *Yo! MTV Raps* hosts Ed Lover and André "Dr. Dre" Brown to do the morning show and hiring his boss's assistant as the overnight person. Though Angie Martinez, a Brooklyn Boricua, had absolutely zero experience on the air, she was an "around the way" girl who could talk the talk and relate to her peoples, eventually earning her reputation as the "Voice of New York." Such bold moves paved the way for Hot 97's transition into the place "Where Hip-Hop Lives."[2]

Since the rise of Wu-Tang had practically paralleled that of Hot 97, it was only right that the group headlined the first major concert event sponsored by the station in 1994. Based on a similar annual branding event held by San Francisco's KMEL, that inaugural Summer Jam was a rousing success, also featuring performances by Nas, Gang Starr, A Tribe Called Quest, and Queen Latifah. For the 1997 Summer Jam, held at Meadowlands Arena in New Jersey on June 7, the station wanted to bring the Clan back to head a lineup that included Jay-Z, Mary J. Blige, Bone Thugs-N-Harmony, and Puff Daddy and the Bad Boy Family—featuring Blackstreet, Lil' Kim, 112, Faith Evans, Mase, Foxy Brown, the Lox, and

Aaliyah. The only problem was that the group was already in the middle of a European tour, which they would have to interrupt.

New York's top rap station played hardball, however, demanding that Wu-Tang show up if they wanted to continue hearing their records on Hot 97. To add insult to injury, the group would have to pay for their own flights. Despite the support they had given the Clan over the years, the station's demands seemed totally unreasonable. Tours are scheduled many months in advance, and if the station wanted to secure a headline act, it should not have simply assumed that the hottest hip-hop group in the world would be available at a moment's notice. Under pressure, the Wu took a group vote, deciding it would be in their best interests to return for the gig—better to disappoint some European fans than piss off their hometown radio station. Regardless, the whole episode left a bad taste in their mouths.

Matters only deteriorated when Wu-Tang arrived at Meadowlands Arena that night straight from Newark International. They watched as Puff Daddy and the Family, mobbing the stage in matching baseball jerseys emblazoned with the Bad Boy name, performed a tribute to the late Notorious B.I.G. Puffy asked the capacity crowd to hold their lighters aloft in remembrance of the Brooklyn icon, snuffed out in his prime, and the whole stadium lit up like a Coca-Cola commercial. The Clan, tired and jetlagged, didn't relish following such an emotional outpouring of love—especially for the deceased.

As the Bad Boy fam dispersed, DJ Mathematics rode up on a hydraulic lift that delivered him to the stage, the needles on his turntables skipping badly. The resulting cacophony, carried over the stadium PA, introduced Wu-Tang's set.

Then, Ghost, unable to contain his frustration, jumped up on a speaker and shouted, "Fuck Hot 97. They sabotaged us. Ain't no way in the world we could come behind Biggie Smalls after he fuckin' just died, motherfucker. Fuck that."[3] He proceeded to lead the crowd in chants of "Fuck Hot 97" before the Clan ran through an abbreviated set. They had not even said "Peace," however, before half the crowd was already leaving in order to get a jump on the huge traffic jams that inevitably accompanied the conclusion of Meadowlands events. It was not a good look, but the Clan took it personally.

So despite making good on their promise to come back and perform at Summer Jam 1997 and paying for their own flights, Wu-Tang was banned from Hot 97 for a number of years as a result of Ghost's antics (they were eventually invited back to perform at Summer Jam 2013, for their twentieth anniversary). While the group always sold records regardless of radio play, their exclusion from one of New York's top stations most definitely had a detrimental effect on their career because their music was not represented alongside that of their contemporaries, such as Nas, Mobb Deep, and Biggie. Due to the primacy of the New York market, Hot 97 exerted influence nationwide, and their playlists were adopted by stations in other markets. This ensured a virtual radio blackout for Wu-Tang. In hindsight, Tracy Cloherty, who was Hot 97's program director at the time, says, "I guess it [Biggie's tribute] was such an emotional moment that Wu-Tang didn't want to follow it, and I understand why they would feel that way, but it was something that was never discussed with us and maybe we could have changed things."[4] While hindsight is obviously twenty-twenty, a serious lack of communication was to blame for this debacle—a problem that soon reared its head again.

The Clan returned to Europe to finish their dates there, including the massive Hultsfred Festival in Sweden, where they were the sole hip-hop act in a lineup that included Daft Punk, the Prodigy, Rammstein, and Rage Against the Machine. Perhaps this one-off festival date sparked some ideas all around because, in a very surprise announcement in July, Rage announced that the Clan would be opening up for them on their upcoming North American tour.

Originally formed in LA in 1991, Rage Against the Machine could almost be regarded as rock's analog to the Clan. Not only did they rank as one of the most popular and influential bands of the nineties, but they also maintained a certain indie cred thanks to their revolutionary rhetoric and antiestablishment stance. The band, formed by guitarist Tom Morello, a Harvard grad, whose Kenyan father had strong ties to that country's independence movement (Morello's great-uncle was the first elected president of Kenya, Jomo Kenyatta); and vocalist Zack de la Rocha, whose Mexican grandfather was a member of the revolutionary Zapatista movement, took their name from a de la Rocha lyric. Like the Clan, they released their 1992 eponymous debut (on cassette) themselves before it was picked up by Epic Records and went on to sell over three million copies. Its follow-up, *Evil Empire* (Epic, 1996), also entered the Billboard 200 at the number-one spot before going triple platinum as well.

Known for their incendiary live performances, the band hammered out a reputation for themselves with a relentless touring schedule. They were even invited to open up for U2's Popmart tour during the first part of 1997. No strangers to controversy, they were banned from *Saturday Night Live* after an April 13, 1996, performance where they attempted to hang upside-down American flags—a maritime call of distress—on their amps in protest of host Steve Forbes, a Republican candidate for president. They also famously staged a protest against censorship at a Lollapalooza show in Philadelphia on July 18, 1993, where the band's four members stood silently in the nude with duct tape over their mouths for the duration of their fifteen-minute set. Even though they represented different genres of music and supposedly different audiences, Wu-Tang and Rage could not have been more simpatico as music industry rebels who operated on their own terms. The ever-strategic RZA actually sought them out as touring partners because he knew that even if Wu-Tang made less money in the short term as an opening act, the exposure to new and bigger audiences would help facilitate their push into the mainstream.

It was actually a brilliant move on his part because America's overt racism made stadium tours by rap acts next to impossible. As far back as Run-DMC's Raising Hell tour in 1986, where riots broke out at the 14,500-seat Long Beach Convention Center when members of the Crips and Bloods got into it with each other, insuring rap concerts had become so cost prohibitive that very few promoters were willing to take them on. Even when Hot 97 staged their first Summer Jam at Meadowlands Arena in New Jersey on June 21, 1994, the venue gave them a list of artists who would be prohibited from performing due to security concerns, including Tupac, Snoop Dogg, Dr. Dre, N.W.A, Public Enemy, Masta Ace, LL Cool J, Ice-T, Ice Cube, and Onyx.

Of course, none of this was lost on the woke Morello, who said, "Due to the racist sentiments of concert promoters around the country, Wu-Tang Clan can't go on tour by itself. No one will book them. [But with us] Wu-Tang Clan gets to be up in the mix with 20,000 people every day."[5] In truth,

both groups had something to gain from the arrangement—
bigger venues and more exposure for the Wu and, for Rage,
greater street cred and an affiliation with the rap crew that
everyone wanted to be down with.

Everything started off on the right note. The Clan, just back
from rocking the Hawaiian Islands for the first time, were pos-
itively glowing after the unmitigated outpouring of love from
the fans as well as five-star treatment at hotels and venues. It was
a far cry from the days of cramming into a twelve-passenger
van and crashing in cheap motel rooms. The tour, which kicked
off in West Palm Beach, Florida, at the Coral Sky Amphitheatre
on August 8, was scheduled to work its way around the country, finally winding up in Phoenix, Arizona, on September 20.
Wu-Tang, or some configuration of the group—as individual
members missed different shows—only managed to make sixteen of the twenty-nine shows.

Along the way, they were responsible for inciting a riot
at the Deer Creek Music Center in Noblesville, Indiana,
when they urged the crowd to come closer to the stage and
claim the empty premium seats in the front. In Chicago,
they also allegedly beat up a promoter who falsely claimed
that members of the group would be performing at his after-
party, as well as a Loud Records promotions rep who went
on the radio to advertise that same after-party.[6] Then, after
missing consecutive shows in St. Louis and Kansas City,
Wu-Tang formally dropped out of the tour on September 2,
citing internal conflicts within the group. Upon finding out,
Morello confirmed the news, saying, "It is my understanding, through the twisted labyrinth that is the communication
system of the Wu-Tang Clan, that they're not playing any
more shows on the tour in part because of difficulties they're
having within their own group."[7]

Once again, the complexities of keeping nine different personalities on the same page came into focus. Race, apparently, was foremost in the minds of some group members, who privately questioned why they were playing for predominantly white audiences as opposed to their own. That same provincial, small-minded ghetto thinking that kept people in poverty was trying to sabotage their success when the only color that really mattered was green. "As far as continuing to tour, we have some things we have to settle some amongst ourselves," RZA said. "We had to get together— we better get together—before we present ourselves to the people. We're not going to go out there and present ourselves to the people if we don't got our own acts straight, so we're going to take some time and sit back on that."[8]

Obviously, egos played a major role. According to Buddha Monk, who had the behind-the-scenes perspective, "By 1997 you had a stage full of niggas who were each one a superstar. Each one thinking, 'Shit, if Dirty don't have to show up why the fuck should I have to show up either?' Nine egos were too big to keep under control. Dirty stopped showing up. But this time he wasn't the only one. At one show there was no Dirty, the next no Dirty and Method Man. Then the next there was no Method Man, no GZA, and of course, no Dirty."[9] Perhaps they saw it as no different from cutting school back in the day. But since Wu-Tang was now a big business and the stakes couldn't get any higher, they were ultimately shooting themselves in the foot.

Ignorance and inexperience were contributing factors as well. According to U-God, the trouble started when manager John "Mook" Gibbons started gassing up the group, saying, "Yo, the promoters are low-balling us. We could be getting way more money."[10] Despite making $45,000 a night, a healthy haul for a support act, it probably didn't seem like all that much when split ten ways—especially for a group with a number-one album on the charts. But while they had the foresight to sacrifice a large advance their first time around in exchange for greater autonomy and bigger budgets later on, the group could not make that same mental leap with touring. Not surprisingly, according to U-God, Ghost and Rae led the charge to leave the Rage tour over RZA's insistence that they finish. But after putting it to a group vote, the Abbott was overruled.

"My opinion is that sometimes, deep down, some people have a fear of success," says U-God. "I'll never really understand that, though—isn't that what we're here for?"[11] But at the same time, the transition from being practically invisible and having nothing to suddenly being the center of attention and having the means to acquire everything you ever wanted cannot be an easy one. It's bound to change the way a person thinks of oneself as well as how they are perceived by others. And, of course, there are countless examples of how so-called success, fame, and money have ruined people who were not ready for it. Ironically, the same group who had perfectly crystallized the meaning of capitalism into the phrase "cash rules everything around me" were now discovering Biggie's "Mo Money, Mo Problems" more appropriate to their own situation.

RZA, who had guided them this far, was obviously frustrated. "As you evolve, things around you gotta evolve, people around you gotta evolve," he observed. "If you a person who evolve quick, it's a painful thing and shit. It's also a pleasurable thing, but, yunno, nobody knows what the fuck you talking about. Niggas don't understand." No longer driving the bus, he had to accept that he was just another one of nine generals whose opinions held equal weight. Despite the problems plaguing their summer of discontent, Wu-Tang returned home triumphant with a quadruple-platinum certified album that also garnered a Grammy nomination for Best Rap Album of the Year.

No sooner had the Clan reassembled to produce and promote the new album than they went their separate ways again after completing the job. RZA, U-God, and Deck, who had yet to taste solo success, went off into their own corners to work on albums. Meanwhile, the rest of the crew, expected to deliver overdue sophomore albums, were in absolutely no hurry. Meth and Dirty, the first two Clansmen to score solo deals, should have been feeling the most heat, but Meth was content doing cameos on other artists' songs and making more money. Dirty, who won the worst attendance award during the tour, was just happy to be away from any form of structure, routine, or responsibilities, which he avoided like a prostate exam.

By this time, Popa Wu had opened his own studio, Brooklyn Sounds, in the basement of the famed Billie Holiday Theatre at Restoration Plaza in Bed-Stuy. Here, he started working on his own compilation, *Visions of the 10th Chamber*, featuring a slew of unknown acts affiliated with the Clan, including Da Manchuz, Zu Ninjaz, and Cuffie Crime Family. ODB and his ever-present sidekick Buddha Monk made this studio their temporary base.

One February afternoon, after recording some tracks with his cousin 12 O'Clock, Dirty stopped at a fish market on the busy commercial strip of Fulton Street on his way home. At the time, Arthur Braxton of Virginia Beach, Virginia, was driving his blue 1996 Ford Mustang down Fulton when he accidentally struck a little girl who was crossing the street. The four-year-old, named Maati Lovell, was walking with her twelve-year-old sister when it happened. From the sidewalk, their mother, Maxine, could only scream in horror as she witnessed her child hit the hood of the car before rolling off and disappearing from sight. In minutes, a visibly hostile crowd had gathered around the driver, threatening to mete out vigilante justice.

But when somebody shouted that the child was trapped under the car, Dirty sprang into action. "Come on. We can lift this car!" he shouted, encouraging several bystanders to help him raise the vehicle while someone else slid the frightened child out from underneath. It was only after she was safe in her mother's arms that the little girl started bawling. Maati was taken to Kings County Hospital and treated for first- and second-degree burns, but her story might have ended much worse without Dirty's intervention. The rapper even visited her the next day under an assumed name to make sure she was all right, and none would have been the wiser if Maati's older sister hadn't recognized ODB and later alerted the media. For a guy perpetually portrayed as irresponsible and crazy, Dirty went out of his way to save a child's life and was humble enough not to draw attention to it, showing his true colors.

Speaking of which, with the fortieth annual Grammy Awards only days away, Dirty needed some new vines to wear to the festivities, which were being held at New York's renowned Radio City Music Hall at Rockefeller Center. The National Academy of Recording Arts and Sciences, who administered the awards, had only added the category of Best Rap Album in 1995, the same year *Return to the 36 Chambers: The Dirty Version* had been released. Though that album received a nomination, it lost out to Naughty by Nature's *Poverty's Paradise* (Tommy Boy / Warner Bros., 1995). While Dirty had skipped the ceremony, he was positive that *Wu-Tang Forever* would win the prize this year, and he wanted to make damned sure he looked his best when he went up to claim it. After going shopping in downtown Brooklyn, he bought this fancy burgundy combo with a long coat that would have made him the envy of the Players Ball.

On Grammy night, February 25, 1998, Steve Rifkind, who lived catty-corner to Radio City, was having a little pre-awards cocktail party at his place, which Dirty attended. Rifkind already knew that Wu-Tang had lost, since the award for Best Rap Album was presented earlier in an untelevised ceremony. Of the five contenders that year—Missy Elliot's *Supa Dupa Fly*, *Wyclef Jean Presents the Carnival*, Biggie's *Life After Death*, *Wu-Tang Forever*, and *No Way Out* by Puff Daddy and the Family—Puffy, predictably, came away with the prize as the Grammys traditionally championed pop, usually of the most mediocre variety. It's also almost unfathomable to believe that as late as 1998, when sales of rap records had far eclipsed even that of country music, the presentation of the Best Rap Album award did not make it to prime time.[12] When Dirty found out, he was pissed—mainly because he had spent $1,500 on a new suit and no one was going to see him in it. Of course, that made him more determined to attend—even if Rifkind was staying home to catch it on TV.

Arriving at Radio City, Dirty hooked up with U-God and two members of the raucous Black skinheads of rap, Onyx—Sticky Fingaz and Fredro Starr. Despite being nominated artists, they had nosebleed seats all the way up in the rafters, which irked Dirty even more. During a commercial break, they decided to make their way down to the lobby, which is where Dirty revealed his plan. "Come on stage with me and hold me down," he asked U-God, but his fellow Clansman would have no part of it, replying, "Nah, you gonna get me locked up."[13] U-God turned around for a minute to consult with the guys from Onyx, and when he looked back again, Dirty had disappeared.

On stage, Wyclef Jean of the Fugees and Erykah Badu were just finishing up an acoustic duet of "Gone Til November," a hit from the *Carnival* LP. They were scheduled to present the award for Song of the Year next. After announcing the nominees, Badu said, "And the Grammy goes to . . . " Wyclef mimicked a drumroll: "Brrrrrr . . . Brooklyn!" As if that last magical word were his cue, Dirty's profile appeared on the left-hand side of millions of TV screens worldwide as he planted a wet one on Badu's cheek. Having just announced winners Shawn Colvin and John Leventhal for their song "Sunny Came Home," she appeared as bewildered as the artists, who had made the short walk from backstage to claim their award.

Looking and feeling like a million bucks in his long burgundy coat set off with a white silk fringe scarf, Dirty was just doing what he had done on so many other occasions in the past—grabbing the mic when he wasn't supposed to. At various times in his career, he had suddenly upstaged artists such as Capelton, Akinelye, the Roots, and even Biggie Smalls, who briefly became his hype man at a memorable show in Brooklyn. Dirty's trademark Medusa braids had been tamed into orderly cornrows on his head, while the oval frames he wore bestowed a certain dignified air as he said, "Yo, please calm down. The music and everything. I went and bought me an outfit that costed me a lot of money today, know what I mean, 'cause I figured that Wu-Tang was gonna win. I don't know how y'all see it, but when it comes to the children, Wu-Tang is for the children. We teach the children. Puffy is good, but Wu-Tang is the best, OK. I want you all to know that this is ODB and I love you all. Peace!" Then he bowed his head to scattered applause and turned around and handed the mic to a tuxedoed gentleman with a headset who had just been sent to intercept him before walking off stage on his own recognizance. Aside from the initial bum-rush, he had been completely respectful and succinct and appeared to be 100 percent sober. No harm done, a slightly confused but gracious Shawn Colvin delivered her delayed acceptance speech, and after returning from commercial break, host Kelsey Grammer made light of the incident, joking, "I'd like to thank the gentleman from Wu-Tang for that clarification. Thank you very much, and peace to you as well."

Not only was Dirty's unscheduled appearance the highlight of the Grammys that night, as well as something people talked about for years (inspiring Kanye West's bad behavior in 2009), but his words resonated as a kind of cultural signifier—especially the phrase "Wu-Tang is for the children." It's the last thing you'd expect to come out of the potty mouth of Dirty, the Blowfly of the crew. Though his meaning might not have been readily apparent, in an abstract way, it made perfect sense.

As Five Percenters, or poor righteous teachers, their mission was to educate and spread knowledge, wisdom, and understanding to the youth, who represented the future. Hip-hop, too, could be seen as a youth movement. Just as Kool Herc became the Pied Piper of the Bronx, initially attracting a young following, the Clan, who ushered in a hip-hop renaissance, earned the loyalty of legions of young fans in the process. Even today, almost thirty years into an unprecedented career, they continue to expand their popularity among people who were not even born when the cream of their catalog was released. So Wu-Tang is for the children. "That's a statement that's going to live forever, man," says Cappadonna.[14]

In the immediate aftermath of Dirty's stunt, while being interviewed on air by MTV's Chris Connelly, he apologized for the intrusion, explaining, "Something just jumped into my blood," as U-God sat silently beside him. But he certainly didn't show any remorse, adding that it was the appropriate venue to make such a statement. Afterward, Dirty called his boy Buddha, whom he had promised to bring to the Grammys, to gauge the reaction in the hood. Buddha replied, "Man, I can't walk outside without people saying, 'Yo, Buddha, your boy is off the hook!'"[15] Pleased by the impact he had among his people, he then called Steve Rifkind. "How'd I do?" he asked his label boss. "You did great," said Rifkind. "You hungry?"[16] Dirty returned to Rifkind's place, where he ate a nice home-cooked dinner with the boss and his family before they headed out to BMG's Grammy after-party.

The next day, the rapper appeared on Howard Stern's show on Sirius XM, looking slightly sheepish and more than a little hungover but thrilled to be there as he bestowed the best compliment a bastard could give the shock jock: "Mr. Howard Stern, you are very, very, very, very, very unique. I love your show." A snickering Stern replied, "I like that you find me unique. I was just thinking the same thing about you" before he and cohost Robin Quivers peppered him with questions about the big imbroglio. In contrast to the boldness on display the previous evening, Dirty looked like a shy schoolboy as he spoke softly into the mic, grinning without making much eye contact with the hosts and answering them with one-word replies. At one point, he picked the sleep out of his eye, examining it like a scientist before rejoining the interview. At the same time, however, he was extremely lucid and outspoken, expressing his disappointment that the rap awards were not televised as well as doubling down on the fact that he in no way meant to diss Puff Daddy.

A look of genuine surprise overtook his face when Quivers informed him that it was Erykah Badu whom he had kissed. Then, when they showed him playback of his speech, his face broke out into a toothy, bejeweled smile, quickly succumbing to embarrassed laughter. On further questioning, he also maintained that he was stone-cold sober during the incident. When Stern pointedly asked whether Puff Daddy was pissed off, Dirty revealed that, backstage, Puff's bodyguards had approached him "like the Mafia," asking him to clarify his comments.

It might have had something to do with the fact that some time earlier, Puffy's artist Mase (Mason Betha) had dissed Wu-Tang at a show, and when Mase subsequently crossed paths with Ghostface and his crew, he was rewarded with a broken jaw. Everyone thought Ghost had personally delivered the beatdown until the rapper set the record straight in a lyric: "Yo, I-Cham punched Mase in his face over some bullshit" (from the song "Malcolm" on *Supreme Clientele*), referring to a member of his crew. But Puffy's bodyguards would have been the least of Dirty's problems. Following his Grammy stunt, pretty much everyone in the world became familiar with Ol' Dirty Bastard and knew that his name spelled "trouble." To his detriment, he became like an exotic creature, constantly under the microscope, and that's when the attention he craved became like a noose around his neck, exposing and magnifying all kinds of personal problems.

Despite releasing a plethora of gold and platinum product, neither Wu-Tang Clan nor any of its individual members was ever nominated for a Grammy again—a situation comparable to the Emmys repeatedly overlooking the brilliance of HBO's *The Wire*. It certainly had nothing to do with Dirty's episode or the group's music; the Clan and industry politics just didn't mix. They had already proven that they didn't need radio or the establishment's blessing to sell records. In fact, they were too busy fulfilling their promise to become the new industry, flooding the market with new releases between 1998 and 1999.

Frequent Wu collaborators Killah Priest and Cappadonna set it off with strong solo showings on *Heavy Mental* (Geffen/MCA) and *The Pillage* (Razor Sharp), respectively, both released in March 1998. Wu affiliates Sunz of Man and Killarmy dropped *The Last Shall Be First* and *Dirty Weaponry* on Wu-Tang Records. A compilation of Wu affiliates, *Wu-Tang Killa Bees: The Swarm* (Priority) followed later in July. Then Method Man's *Tical 2000: Judgement Day* (Def Jam) and RZA's *Bobby Digital in Stereo* (Gee Street / V2) appeared days apart in November. GZA followed with *Beneath the Surface* (MCA) on June 29, 1999, while Dirty's *Nigga Please* (Elektra) came out on September 14. Loud finally dropped Inspectah Deck's solo debut, *Uncontrolled Substance* in October—the same month that U-God's *Golden Arms Redemption* (Priority) saw light. The sequel to *OB4CL*, Raekwon's lackluster *Immobilarity* (Loud) capped off this run in November 1999. Masta Killa was the only Clansman not to release a solo effort until 2004's *No Said Date* (Nature Sounds).

Many of these latter releases fell victim to the dreaded "sophomore slump," simply not matching up to the excellence of their predecessor. Aside from RZA's *Bobby Digital*, a decidedly more experimental album that allowed him to stretch out as an MC as well as a musician, the missing element from all these other releases was the guiding hand of the Abbott himself. For the second round of solo albums, he only produced four tracks for Meth, one for GZA, two for Deck, three for Dirty, three for U-God, and none for Raekwon. Part of this was planned, as RZA delegated production duties to members of his Wu Elements squad, including 4th Disciple, True Master, and DJ Mathematics, because there was no way he could handle so much work by himself. But the Clan members wanted to explore other possibilities as well.

In addition to RZA's scaled-back involvement came a lack of participation by the other Clansmen, making this second round sound less like family affairs and more like an effort to create some distance from each other. For a group that had come up together and seen their greatest success as a collective unit, it was, in their own words, hustling backward. To complicate matters, a whole host of third-string Wu affiliates—including GP Wu and Virginia's Wu-Syndicate— was unleashed on the scene, but with no one at the helm providing quality control, the Wu-Tang brand became somewhat tarnished.

Ghost was the only member of the team who defied the sophomore slump and returned with an arguably better album than his awesome debut. Spawning such memorable singles as "Cherchez la Ghost" and "Apollo Kids," *Supreme Clientele* (Epic / Sony / Razor Sharp, 2000) was a critical and commercial success that went gold in a month and saved the Clan's reputation when they needed it most.

The decisive factor lifting *Supreme Clientele* above the rest of the lackluster second-round solo albums was—no surprise—RZA's involvement. Though producing only four tracks, he curated and mixed the entire selection with Ghost, stitching it together with the usual skits and interludes fans had come to expect. Despite having to suspended work on the album while Ghost served four months on Rikers for a 1995 attempted robbery charge at New York's Palladium club, it still came out fresh—maybe because the rapper had reinvented himself once again.

In the fall of 1997, after coming off *Wu-Tang Forever*, his aggravated condition from diabetes brought him to Benin, West Africa, where a bush doctor treated him with natural herbs. In a rural village, with nothing to write to but the sound of cows and chickens, he perfected his free-association word sport. He also experienced a change in attitude. "Fuck all this Tommy Hilfiger, Polo . . . all this shit . . . they don't give a fuck about none of that over there. Everything is the same," Ghostface told *The Source*. "But over here, everybody wanna be better than the next one. . . . They might be fucked up, money-wise, but trust me, them muthafuckas is happy, man. Them niggas in harmony 'cause they got each other."[17] He realized, once again, the importance of family and included appearances by Raekwon, Method Man, Cappadonna, U-God, RZA, GZA, and Masta Killa, along with Wu affiliates Hell Razah and Redman, as well as introducing Chip Banks, Solomon Childs, and Lord Superb. The hype stirred up by *Supreme Clientele* came just in time to ratchet up the anticipation for another group effort, *The W*, which would serve as a bookend for the Wu-Tang decade of the nineties.

Four years between albums was an eternity in hip-hop, as the Clan discovered when they dropped *Wu-Tang Forever*.

For this reason, they made a point of reassembling much sooner to work on *The W* (Loud/Columbia, 2000). Since the comparative isolation of LA had worked for them last time, they returned, RZA sequestering the troops at a rented mansion in the Hollywood Hills that looked like a porn set, complete with swimming pool and grand piano. They stayed there for two months so that they could focus on the job at hand, but they ended up partying their fair share as well and rubbing elbows with the Hollywood elite.

That summer before the album came out, RZA teased, "[This album's] gonna be a B-boy album, cause we strictly hip-hop, man. It's gonna be an album that gonna make you take off your fuckin' gators and put your muthfuckin' Timberlands back on, take off your silk shirt, put your hoodie back on, nah mean, and bring your Glock outside." He expressed his frustration at both radio—"They play some shit that sound like us, but don't play our shit"—as well as the "Jiggy era" that had taken over hip-hop. "All these fake niggas runnin' around, grabbing bitches, flashin' their jewelry, c'mon, man, niggas is mad," he said. "New York is mad about that. My whole hood is mad. My whole hood ain't been off the island in years, just like heated animals in a cage. They waitin' to get the fuck off the island and tear New York up. That's what happened last time before we came out." Clearly, times were changing, and Wu-Tang was struggling to remain relevant in this new era.

When *The W* dropped on November 21, 2000, it debuted at number five on the Billboard 200 and number one on the Top R&B / Hip-Hop Albums. After moving 301,000 units in its first week, it reached platinum about a month later. Critically lauded, it was a strong, concise thirteen-track album, fully produced by RZA—except for the track "Do You Really

(Thang, Thang)," produced by Mathematics—but featuring the most outside cameos of any Wu project to date. Not only were rappers Busta Rhymes, Nas, Snoop Dogg, and Redman invited to contribute, but legendary soul man Isaac Hayes and iconic Jamaican singer Junior Reid also joined the party. ODB, on the other hand, appeared on only one track, "Conditioner," a duet with Snoop, for which he delivered his verse over the phone from jail. While *The W* showed flashes of brilliance—especially on the first side—there was also plenty of mediocre material. But, overall, the Clan's first salvo of the new millennium was probably their last cohesive musical statement as a group.

CHAPTER 16

TEARZ

At the height of their fame and glory they turned on one
another each struggling in vain for ultimate supremacy. In
the passion and death of their struggle the very art that had
raised them to such Olympian heights was lost. The techniques
vanished.

—Dragon on Fire *(1978)*
Used in "Duel of the Iron Mic," from Liquid Swords

The huge wave that carried Wu-Tang throughout most of
the nineties crashed onto the shores of a new millennium
with a force powerful enough to pull the once tight-knit
unit apart, flinging them all in different directions. Certain
members landed on their feet—RZA, following his passion
for film, started getting into scoring while making cameo
appearances in such movies as Jim Jarmusch's *Ghost Dog:
The Way of the Samurai* (1999), while Method Man made
a pivot to acting in HBO's first TV series *Oz* and later *The
Wire*. Others attempted to focus on their solo careers without the benefit of the collective mentality that had brought
them there in the first place. Clan had always meant family, but, predictably, egos, fame, and money pushed a wedge
between the brothers. In the early 2000s, all the individual
members (except GZA, who never had a contract, and ODB,

who was incarcerated) asked to be released from their initial contracts with Wu-Tang Productions, and RZA relented over the protests of his brother and business partner Divine. But if the Abbott practiced what he preached, he really had no other choice. His only condition was that when he threw up the *W*, the Clan would still come together for the odd tour and album—like 2001's uninspiring *Iron Flag* (Loud/Columbia)—but the glory days were just a fading point in their rearview mirror.

Competition was fierce on the roulette wheel of rap, and serious contenders like Jay-Z, the newly dubbed P. Diddy, Eminem, Outkast, and Lil Wayne were already vying for supremacy in the new millennium. But Wu-Tang's demise did not come suddenly—more like a slow-burning fire, as missteps and mishaps, along with infighting and the public airing of grievances, took their cumulative toll over the course of the decade. Ghostface and U-God went so far as to bring lawsuits against RZA for withholding royalties. Raekwon didn't sue but went on record on the radio to criticize the man responsible for taking him off the streets and setting him up with a reputable career. But more than any single incident, Ol' Dirty's downward spiral during this period, leading to his tragic death, offered a metaphor for the group's problems as they struggled to stay together and remain relevant.

In a group of mostly ex-felons, Dirty certainly wasn't the worst. Offenses like shoplifting and brawling that got him into trouble were nothing compared to more serious crimes of weapons possession, armed robbery, or the distribution of controlled substances that had put his fellow Clansmen behind bars. One could even argue that he had a leg up on the other guys, coming from the only two-parent household where both parents worked. But even though Wu-Tang made the leap to a legitimate income, their past was constantly coming back to bite them. Take Ghost, for instance, who had also seen his share of trouble and still had one foot in the streets. His problems with the law almost foreshadow Dirty's, but the way in which each handled their respective situations made all the difference in the outcomes.

On the night of December 10, 1997, Ghost was rolling through Harlem with his crew when police stopped his homeboy Dupree Lane for a traffic violation near 139th Street and FDR Drive. Ghost, who was following behind them, allegedly started acting disorderly, prompting the officers to search his vehicle. In a hidden compartment behind the glove box, they found an unregistered .357 Magnum, loaded with hollow-point bullets—prohibited for anyone outside of law enforcement in New York State. As a result, Ghost and the two other occupants of the vehicle were charged with third-degree criminal possession of a weapon, a felony. Since the rapper was wearing a bulletproof vest, they also charged him with wearing body armor during the commission of a felony, which was an additional felony.[1]

He was promptly arrested, released on bail, and then remanded into custody again after it was discovered that he had missed a court date the week before for an incident that took place in August 1995 at the Palladium club in Manhattan. In that instance, Ghost and his crew allegedly got into it with the club's parking lot attendants after discovering that their car's tires had been slashed. Demanding to be recompensed, they allegedly tried to take $3,000 from the attendants, for which Ghost was charged with attempted robbery.

So, following his arrest in Harlem, he was locked up for twenty-five days after his bail was revoked from the Palladium case. Then, on January 12, he pleaded guilty to that charge. "He was forced into a situation where if he went to trial and was convicted, he could have gotten a sentence of five to 15 years in jail," said his lawyer, Jeremy Schneider.[2] Instead, he got five years' probation and had to serve four months at the notorious Rikers Island facility while in the middle of working on his second album, *Supreme Clientele*. Meanwhile, his latest charge of weapons and vest possession, set for a later hearing, never produced an indictment due to police "error." The cops claimed he fled the scene, when, in fact, he had been arrested and then released by them.

Such an example illustrated how difficult it was to extricate oneself from the criminal justice system once caught up inside it—especially for a Black man and doubly so for one with celebrity status. Minor incidents had a way of escalating into much bigger problems. To Ghost's credit, however, he served his time without incident and double downed on his album, one reason *Supreme Clientele* stood out among the second round of mediocre Wu-Tang solo releases. He even turned a bad situation into inspiration, rapping, "Check the grays on the side of my waves / I grew those on Rikers Island, stressed out, balled up in a cage" on "Buck 50." But most importantly, he took these incidents to heart, making a conscious effort to stay out of trouble after his release. Prior to his incarceration, an advanced condition of type 2 diabetes had already forced him to take his health more seriously, cutting out all drugs and alcohol. He even went as far as traveling to Benin in Africa to receive nontraditional treatment. But Dirty, who lacked the discipline and resolve to get ahold of his situation, needed help. As his addiction spiraled out of control, fueling chronic run-ins with the law, it led to his eventual incarceration, a devastating turn for this free spirit.

A closer examination of Dirty's rap sheet revealed that the great majority of offenses were minor and concentrated in the comparatively short period between 1998 and 1999. He was arrested for the first time in 1987 for petty larceny, following one of the shoplifting missions he used to make as a teenager with RZA. In 1992, he was charged with assault after a fight in a bar, for which he received a $5,000 fine and five years' probation.[3] Following that incident, he managed to avoid any trouble with the law for the next six years, until April 1998, when he was charged with second-degree harassment of his wife, Icelene; endangering the welfare of children; and failure to pay child support for an incident that occurred on November 12, 1997. Even so, he was granted a conditional release after agreeing to pay her $35,000 in child support, since she retained full custody of their three kids.

Back in high school, Icelene had known Dirty as the sweet, charming guy who had once taken off his coat and placed it over a puddle so she could cross. He had always had his problems with alcohol, but his personality was shifting under the influence of drugs. "It got really bad at the end of the nineties," she says. "He just started disappearing and becoming this Ol' Dirty Bastard person for real. He had problems way before that, but they really got bad around then."[4] The Drunken Master had always been known for his affection for forty ounces of Olde English and wine, which served to stimulate his already raucous personality. But on his initiation into the music industry, he was introduced to another more deadly vice, cocaine, which was all too accessible for a rapper with money. The white powder was not only a status symbol—a rich man's high that made you feel like a million bucks—but it also unleashed paranoia in heavy users.

That may or may not have been a factor on the night of November 16, 1994, when Dirty was walking home alone in Brooklyn during the wee hours and he noticed a car slowly following him. After turning a couple of corners in an attempt to unsuccessfully shake the suspicious vehicle, he decided to duck into someone's backyard. As luck would have it, however, he found himself face-to-face with three snarling Rottweilers, and his only escape was through a doggy door into the house. Crawling through on his hands and knees, he promptly instructed the owner of the house, who had been awakened by the barking, to call the cops—a bizarre request from someone creeping into her abode. As she spoke to the 911 dispatcher, the dogs bounded in after Dirty, chasing him upstairs. Finally, in a last-ditch effort to escape his attackers, he jumped out a second-story window onto the street below. A few blocks away, he was picked up by the cops, who didn't believe his story, thinking he was under the influence of something. Without pending charges from the dogs' owner, however, they had to let him go.

Hardly twelve hours later, Dirty was going to see a girl on Kingston Avenue in Bed-Stuy when he was robbed at gunpoint. Scuffling with the robbers, he got shot in the back—the bullet piercing his spleen—but still managed to jump in his car and drive to the hospital. Not two weeks afterward, on November 30, Tupac Shakur was shot five times in an alleged robbery attempt at Quad Studios in Manhattan. Perhaps Dirty wasn't being so paranoid after all.

According to RZA, "In the old days when Big Daddy Kane and Biz and the Juice Crew was the most popular crew making money, it's like back then you couldn't talk about how much money you had and think you gonna walk through the streets of Brooklyn and not get touched. And the times is going back to that."[5] Long before it became the title of a Spike Lee joint, Crooklyn had a notorious reputation for crews of "boosters" (shoplifters) known as the Lo Lifes, who stole only expensive Polo gear, and street gangs like the infamous Decepticons, who took their name from the villains in the Transformer series and engaged primarily in armed robbery and muggings. "Stick up kids is out to tax," said Greg Nice in Nice & Smooth's "Funky for You" (1990). That line was sampled for the hook of Gang Starr's "Just to Get a Rep," a song that detailed the motivations of these street criminals. Gang Starr's Guru (Keith Elam), who wrote that song, received firsthand experience after being robbed and pistol-whipped at a studio in Queens on January 8, 1999.

In a strange twist, then, rappers, who routinely reported on the violence and crime in their neighborhoods, were increasingly becoming its victims, culminating in the deaths of two of the biggest names in hip-hop—Tupac Shakur on September 13, 1996, and the Notorious B.I.G. on March 9, 1997, murdered in drive-by shootings roughly six months apart. For the rap community, it was the equivalent of Malcolm and Martin being assassinated, and conspiracy theories abounded—especially since no one has been charged for these crimes to this day. Dirty strongly believed that the government (i.e., the FBI and CIA) was responsible. While these two senseless killings helped exacerbate a nonexistent East Coast / West Coast rivalry in hip-hop that was played up to the hilt by the media, they also clouded the real issue, which was that rappers better beware because they were between the crosshairs of both cops and criminals.

Still, Dirty, who loved the borough of his birth as much as he did his fellow ghetto dwellers, refused to take the appropriate precautions. Unlike other rappers, he didn't roll with an entourage, a bodyguard, or even a gun. On the afternoon of June 30, 1998, he arrived back in New York after a show in LA. Instead of going directly home, he decided to stop off at his cousin's place in Bed-Stuy's notorious Brevoort Houses, where he often hung out. He parked his new Infiniti QX4 SUV outside his cousin Tracey Richardson's building, at 254 Ralph Avenue. On his way to her first-floor apartment, he passed a couple of guys smoking a blunt outside.

It turns out that these two were members of an underground criminal organization known as the G-Squad or BGS (Brevoort Gangster Squad), which became known on the streets and to law enforcement as "the Commission." In their case, *commission* was a verb because they basically took whatever they wanted with impunity. What began as a loose collective of Brooklyn stick-up kids from the borough's most notorious projects—most of them not even out of high school—soon evolved into a sophisticated crime ring targeting rappers. They developed contacts inside the industry— sometimes even a rapper's own bodyguard—to tip them off about a potential victim's whereabouts and movements, as well as a fence in the diamond district. The guy specialized in making customized bling for rappers while also buying their stolen jewelry from the Commission, who made ODB one of their first high-profile marks.

The group's leader, known on the streets as Da Kommander, and one of his associates, who went by D-Mac, had peeped the shiny ornament dangling from Dirty's neck. Seeing that he was alone, they couldn't pass up the opportunity to "yap" him. First, they went back to Da Kommander's apartment to retrieve two ski masks, one red and one black, and a 9 mm handgun. They returned at about five o'clock to stake out apartment 1-B and, after observing a woman leaving, sprang into action. Fortunately for them, she had left the door unlocked so her kids could come and go as they pleased. After sneaking in, the perps found Dirty asleep on the couch.[6]

Da Kommander approached first, slapping Dirty and telling him to wake up. Startled, the rapper jumped up and tried to grab the gun that was pointed at him. In the scuffle that ensued, the weapon fired, a bullet striking Dirty in the back and exiting through his left arm. That was enough to dissolve his courage; he told them, "Take it! Take the jewelry just don't kill me."[7] D-Mac snatched the $10,000 gold chain and a ring, and he and Da Kommander took off, hiding on a nearby rooftop. The next day, they sold Dirty's jewelry at a pawn shop on Pitkin Avenue, splitting the proceeds, a measly $500.[8]

In the immediate aftermath, Dirty drove himself to the Interfaith Medical Center in Bed-Stuy, where he was treated for his wounds. According to his mother, who went to see him there, he was in good spirits and wanted her to sing for him despite the harrowing ordeal he had just survived. The doctors wanted to keep him overnight for observation; however, when Dirty saw a TV news report about the shooting, he wasn't eager to speak to police, whom he knew would be showing up. Still wearing his hospital gown, he sneaked out on his own at around two in the morning, climbing out a window. A couple of days later, RZA scooped him up in the Bobby Digital van, and they drove down to Virginia Beach together, blasting one of Dirt's favorite songs, "Good Morning Heartache," as sung by Natalie Cole, for the duration of the eight-hour ride. RZA said he could feel his cousin's pain.[9]

Dirty's robbery was no isolated incident, however, as the Commission was just hitting their stride. Da Kommander was personally involved in the home invasion of rapper Foxy Brown (Inga Marchand) on July 8, 1998, and his colleagues were also responsible for robbing Busta Rhymes not once but twice, allegedly stealing jewelry worth $100,000 from him.[10] The robbing of high-profile rappers became so prevalent that an up-and-coming artist named 50 Cent (Curtis Jackson), who derived his alias from an infamous Brooklyn robber from the eighties, Kelvin Martin, even made a song about it. Though he prefaces his debut single, "How to Rob (an Industry Nigga)" (Columbia, 1999) with a disclaimer saying, "Don't take this shit serious, we just buggin' the fuck out," he talks about robbing no fewer than forty-six rap and R&B artists, which obviously did not go down too well with many of them in the frenzied climate of the time. But 50 used such a controversy to distinguish himself from the competition and kindle that crucial buzz—even though Columbia eventually dropped him. Ironically, after making a name for himself, he, too, became a victim when someone pumped nine bullets into him the following year. This attempt on his life as well as his miraculous survival only enhanced his rap résumé, however, and he was signed by Eminem and Dr. Dre in 2002.

After getting shot in two separate incidents, one would imagine that Dirty would keep a low profile and stay far away from trouble, but just days after fleeing the hospital, he was caught at a Sneakers Stadium in Virginia Beach, trying to walk out with a pair of fifty-dollar kicks. Despite having money in his pocket, he just couldn't resist that familiar adrenaline rush that boosting provided. He spent the Fourth of July in jail before making bail. Though he could have easily squashed the matter by appearing in court and possibly paying a fine or doing community service, he elected instead to leave for a tour of the West Coast. As a result of his no-show, the Virginia court issued a bench warrant for his arrest.

While in California, he got in trouble again—twice. The first incident occurred at the House of Blues in LA on September 17, while Dirty was attending a show by the English singer Des'ree. After being kicked out for acting drunk and disorderly, he allegedly threatened to return and kill the bouncers—the equivalent of a "terrorist threat" in California, where it was considered a felony offense. West Hollywood deputy sheriffs also discovered an outstanding traffic warrant and held him in jail overnight, after which Dirty was released on a $50,000 bail.[11]

Then, on November 6, like déjà vu, he was arrested again for the very same offense. This time the action occurred in Carson, California, where Dirty threatened to kill ex-girlfriend Krishana Ruckers, twenty-seven, with whom he had a one-year-old child. Police apprehended him at one o'clock in the afternoon as he attempted to scale the security gate at her jobsite. This time, his bail was set at $500,000, though Ruckers ultimately dropped the charges.[12] Meanwhile, back in Virginia, Judge Robert L. Simpson issued a second bench warrant for Dirty's arrest and quadrupled the penalty after the rapper failed to appear in court for a second time.[13] All these infractions were unforced errors on Dirty's part and completely avoidable, but as they snowballed into much bigger legal problems, he risked being crushed by them. Of course, it didn't help that he was also developing a full-blown addiction to cocaine, which wasn't known for making a person more clearheaded and responsible.

Dirty's trouble with the law came to a head in the new year. On the night of January 15, 1999—MLK Jr.'s birthday—he and his cousin 60 Second Assassin (Fred Cuffie Jr.) were headed to their aunt's house in Brooklyn in Dirty's Chevy Tahoe when he noticed a vehicle following them in the rear-view mirror. Cocaine aside, his paranoia had reached manic levels following the murders of Tupac and Biggie, as well as the attempts on his own life, and rightfully so. Sixty wasn't buying it, but when Dirty made a couple of turns and still couldn't shake the vehicle, he, too, became convinced that they were being tailed. Finally, the mystery car made a move, forcing Dirty to pull over. Two plainclothes officers jumped out with guns drawn, ordering the cousins out of the car. At first, the rapper rolled down his window and yelled, "Don't shoot, man! It's me. It's Ol' Dirty Bastard," as if his name would mean anything to two white cops.[14] As they continued to slowly advance, he panicked and floored it. The officers responded by pumping eight shots at the car, and they weren't aiming for their tires.

In their report, the cops later lied and said that Dirty fired at them first, but no weapon was found on either him or his cousin, and the only spent shell casings at the scene came from the officers' guns. Somehow, in the midst of a hairy high-speed car chase around Brooklyn, Dirty managed to call his mother of all people, using the cell phone she had given him for Christmas. A former 911 dispatcher herself, she told him to go to his aunt's place at 1341 East New York Avenue and wait for her there. Upon arrival, he and his cousin made a run for the building before finally surrendering to the cops in front of his mom and aunt. Who knows what would have happened to them had those women not been there?

Back at the Seventy-Seventh Precinct house, they interrogated Dirty and his cousin separately, as per protocol, trying to get them to rat each other out as the shooter. Problem was, neither was guilty as charged, providing yet another example of police harassment of Black men who were minding their own business. Initially pulled over for no probable cause, they were fired upon, unprovoked, and finally framed for attempted murder when the cops were the only ones doing the shooting. It was most likely quota time, and these cops hadn't collared enough bad guys yet.

The two plainclothes officers also turned out to be members of an elite 380-member squad known as the Street Crimes Unit, who were tasked with removing guns from New York's streets. One of the controversial tactics they employed was "stop and frisk." According to the *New York Times*, "The unit's officers frisked 18,023 people in 1997 and 27,061 last year [1998]. Those numbers alarmed some civil rights advocates because the unit made only 4,899 arrests in 1997 and 4,647 the next year, meaning that nearly 40,000 people were stopped and frisked during the last two years simply because a street crimes officer mistakenly thought they were carrying guns."[15] Since stop and frisk was primarily used in low-income minority neighborhoods, it should not be surprising that the great majority of people stopped were young Black and Hispanic males and that racial profiling obviously lay at the heart of this strategy.

Not two weeks later, on February 4, Amadou Diallo, a twenty-three-year-old Guinean immigrant, was returning to his Bronx apartment after dinner when four members of the Street Crimes Unit rolled up on him. They said he matched the description of a serial rapist in the area or was possibly working as a lookout for a drug gang. For his part, Diallo may have thought he was being robbed because the undercover officers never identified themselves as cops, and when confronted by them, he pulled out his wallet. Mistaking it for a gun, they fired forty-one shots at him without warning, hitting him nineteen times and ending his life. The clincher was that—surprise, surprise—all four cops were acquitted of the murder. But a huge public outcry over Diallo's senseless death ensured that the Street Crimes Unit's days were numbered, and they were officially disbanded in April 2002.

But around 1999, a new, even more secretive off-the-books squad was being formed within NYPD. Spearheaded by Detective Derrick Parker, a Black officer from the middle-class enclave of Hollis, Queens, who was actually a fan of hip-hop, this rap intel squad, more popularly called the "hip-hop cops," was officially known by the less sexy title of Enterprise Operations Unit. Their job was basically to monitor rappers and develop intelligence about them—especially regarding their association with known criminals—another blatant example of racial profiling. They also worked with the feds to bring cases under the RICO (Racketeer Influenced and Corrupt Organizations) Act. By 1999, according to Parker, "There were already two major RICO investigations going on in the rap community: one was the Commission case, and the other involved the Staten Island, New York based rap supergroup the Wu-Tang Clan. Wu-Tang Clan were being investigated for murder, racketeering, and money laundering by Staten Island detectives who were also collaborating with the Feds."[16] Dirty's intuition had been right all along.

On January 24, 1999, the *New York Post* confirmed this news with the headline "Wu-Tang Rappers Eyed in Fed Weapons Probe." Dirty's paranoia had reached new heights after his close call with the cops. He already knew crooks were gunning for him on the streets of his beloved Brooklyn, but also, apparently, so were the ones who were supposed to "protect and serve." Though rife with inaccuracies—such as the fact that the police had yet to find the gun that Dirty had supposedly fired at them—the article confirmed his worst fears of surveillance by the feds (under a 2012 FOIA request, the full ninety-five-page FBI file was finally made public). Following this revelation, he started taking no more chances. RZA bought him a bulletproof vest and surveillance equipment worth $50,000. On February 3, a Brooklyn grand jury failed to indict Dirty on any charges regarding the shooting, but despite the rapper's threats to hold the cops responsible, he never filed any lawsuits against them.

On November 13, 1994—exactly ten years to the day before ODB's death—Officer James Guelff, a ten-year veteran of the San Francisco Police Department, approached carjacking suspect Victor Boutwell at the corner of Pine and Franklin Streets. Wearing a ballistic helmet and flak jacket, Boutwell was in the process of transferring hundreds of rounds of ammunition between stolen cars when he turned his semi-automatic weapon on Guelff. The police officer responded, unloading his six-shot service revolver at the suspect. While reloading, however, he was fatally shot by Boutwell, who also wounded another officer, a paramedic, and a civilian before the SWAT team finally took him down.

A similar incident occurred on February 28, 1997, in North Hollywood—not far from Ameraycan Studios, where Wu-Tang Clan was busy recording *Forever*—when two ex-cons, both heavily armed with automatic weapons and clad in body armor, robbed a Bank of America branch at 6600 Laurel Canyon Boulevard. After one of the biggest gun battles in US history, in which an estimated two thousand rounds were fired, the perps, Larry Phillips Jr. and Emil Mătăsăreanu, were finally neutralized, but not before wounding twelve police officers and eight civilians and causing huge amounts of property damage. Such high-profile cases spurred California to pass the James Guelff Body Armor Act, which prohibited anyone convicted of a violent felony from purchasing, owning, or possessing body armor. The law went into effect on January 1, 1999.

Dirty probably had no idea what he was in for as he sat in his car in LA on the night of February 16, double-parked on Yucca Street. The cops approached him at about ten thirty, asking him to move. He complied but parked illegally again. When the officer asked to see a driver's license, he produced a passport instead and, at this time, was asked to step out of the vehicle. That was when the cops noticed the bulk of a bulletproof vest under his clothes. After running his name, they turned up the aggravated assault charge from 1992, the only violent offense on his record. Therefore, as a result of a mere technicality, Dirty became the first person in the state arrested under the James Guelff Body Armor Act, a law that, incidentally, was overturned in 2010 for being unconstitutional. After being taken in and booked, he was released on $115,000 bail.

At a press conference following the incident, Dirty was unapologetic, saying, "Hell yeah, I was wearing a vest. I'm scared like a motherfucker. Dirty don't pull no guns on cops. Not saying I'm a soft-ass nigga, but I don't want no grandmothers and shit thinking this crazy shit about me, I'm scared like a motherfucker and you got rappers dying and shit and it's in my blood."[17] That last comment aside, everything he said made perfect sense. Only a day before Dirty's arrest, on February 15, a rising talent from Harlem, Big L (Lamont Coleman), was gunned down in his own neighborhood by an unknown assassin. The following month, on

March 28, rapper Freaky Tah (Tahliq Raymond Rogers) of the group the Lost Boyz was shot in the head in Queens. It seemed like open season on rappers, who were caught in a difficult place between the cops and robbers. In such a climate of violence, Dirty would have been crazy not to wear a vest. Despite pending cases in three different states, this felony charge, more than anything, dragged him further into the depths of a skewed and biased criminal justice system, from which there seemed to be no salvation.

Between his numerous court appearances—as well as the ones he missed—Dirty was working on his second album for Elektra for most of 1999. He was also, apparently, smoking a lot of crack cocaine. On March 22, he was arrested for drug possession after cops found three vials of crack in his brand-new Range Rover without plates, which had been double-parked in front of a Bushwick, Brooklyn, bodega at one in the morning. Because his license had been suspended, he gave the cops RZA's real name, not knowing that his cousin's license had also been suspended.[18] Then, in May, he was pulled over in Brooklyn for driving without plates. Of course, he had no license either, and the cops, once again, turned up a few vials of crack.

The situation came to a head on July 31, 1999, when Dirty was stopped for running a red light on Linden Boulevard in Queens at 2:28 a.m. With his license still suspended, he was driving a red convertible Mercedes this time, and when police searched the vehicle, they found twenty glassine envelopes containing more than five hundred milligrams of cocaine powder as well as one envelope with marijuana. Due to the quantity of controlled substances, he was arrested for possession with intent to sell, a much more serious charge than his priors. In only a few short months, he had managed to rack up ten drug arrests, most of which were triggered by traffic stops. It begs the question, what would have happened had he just had a driver or a dealer who delivered? In spite of these unforced errors, his high-priced lawyers managed to keep him out of jail by getting him admitted into various rehab programs.

Dirty's rampant drug use was a far cry from the "firewater" that inspired his drunken style on the mic. In fact, what greater cry for help could there be? "Dirty didn't take drugs to be Ol' Dirty Bastard," says Buddha Monk. "Dirty took the drugs to escape a world where everybody wanted something. It was his way of having fun and enjoying himself and relaxing after so many people wanted him to come to a meeting or come to the studio or were stressing him out about shit, so every now and then he'd have some drugs and just hide and wouldn't answer the phone and wouldn't talk to nobody."[19] In the beginning, Buddha was complicit, getting high with Dirty until coke took its toll on him. Then, after he stopped snorting, he says, "I was trying to help Dirty get off drugs, but any time I started to get really heavy on him about it, that's when he didn't want me around."[20] It was a fine line to tread for a man who had taken on the unenviable role as ODB's handler. Not only did he have to deal with Dirty's endless antics, but he also served as the unofficial liaison between the rapper and his record company and even between the Clan, who expected Dirty's attendance at shows.

Besides Buddha, the only people aware of the extent of Dirty's drug problem were the people closest to him—his mother, Cherry, and ex-wife, Icelene, who, despite their estrangement, still cared deeply for him. His cousins RZA and GZA were busy growing careers, as were the other members of the group. Even if they knew how far their fellow

Clansman was slipping, they had no control over it. Plus, a laissez-faire attitude pervaded the hood, maintaining the misconception that a grown man could take care of himself. This same macho stance precluded any thought of intervention and silenced any serious discussion of mental health or therapy.

Yet, even in the midst of the maelstrom, Dirty pulled off the seemingly impossible and released a second album. He wanted to call it *The Black Man Is God, White Man Is the Devil* but, due to label objection, settled on *Nigga Please*. On September 14, 1999, the album entered the Billboard 200 chart at number ten, selling a healthy ninety-three thousand copies in its first week with hardly any promotion. Hailed by fans and critics alike, it took only three months to go gold. Like most of the second round of Wu-Tang solo releases, RZA's participation was minimal, producing only three tracks, and there were zero cameos from the rest of the Clan. The only guest rappers on it included Raison the Zukeeper, 12 O'Clock, La the Darkman, and Shorty Shitstain (on "Gettin' High"). It was as if Dirty, who felt abandoned, was asserting his independence.

Regardless, it was an entertaining album that spawned the Neptunes-produced hit "Got Your Money," featuring Kelis, which helped kick off Pharrell Williams and Chad Hugo's run as one of the most sought-after production teams of the new millennium. Far from being out of it, Dirty seemed very self-aware. On the title track, he raps, "My words can't be held against me / I'm not caught up in your law," acknowledging his fight with the system while also admitting, "I'm immune to all viruses / I get the cocaine, it clears up my sinuses." Later in the same song, he pokes fun at his own fondness for conspiracy: "Kill all the government microchips in my body /

I'm the paranoid nigga at your party." The album-cover shot had him wearing a yellow-and-white polyester jumpsuit and a long, ridiculous curly wig, posing with exaggerated swagger while aping his idol Rick James, another dynamic talent consumed by his addiction to cocaine. By the time the record dropped, Dirty was getting himself ironed out from the confines of another boring inpatient rehab facility.

On November 19, he had to appear in California court to answer both the previous year's terrorist threat charge from the House of Blues and the bulletproof vest charge. Accompanying him was his attorney, Robert Shapiro, a member of OJ's "Dream Team," who was attempting to argue that California's body armor law was unconstitutional—as it was eventually declared a full decade later in 2010. Dirty, who had days earlier turned thirty-one, showed up in Judge Marsha Revel's LA courtroom wearing Killa Beez colors—a loose yellow shirt over black pants. He was calm, respectful, and, of course, his own charming self as he defended his position. "I keep it real. I mean I am not no terrorist you know what I mean. I'm not the one who made those accusations like they said I made those accusations," he said. "A terrorist is someone that bombs somebody's house or hijacks planes and holds people hostage or bombs big buildings like the United Nations. Me, I'm just a regular rap artist who loves women, who loves partying, who loves to fuck, who loves people not to lie about him. That's basically it. I'm no terrorist or nothing like that."[21] With a defense like that, it was surprising that he wasted money on Shapiro, who wasn't even able to negotiate a reprieve for Dirty to work on the upcoming Wu-Tang album *The W*.

This judge was certainly no pushover. When Dirty expressed concern about possible harassment by the NYPD, she told him to move out of the city. He countered by saying his kids lived there, so she advised him not to put himself in a position where he would have to confront the cops. She must have had some sympathy for the guy, however, as she ended up giving him only three years' probation, a $500 fine, and twelve months at an inpatient rehab facility, with credit for eighty-six days already served. Considering he escaped jail time, he should have kissed the judge's feet, but on leaving, the rapper—who had just assumed another alias, "Big Baby Jesus"—told her, "Jesus loves you," to which she responded, smiling, "Thank you. I need all the love I can get."[22] At least she understood what Dirty desperately needed. By court order, he checked into Impact House in Pasadena, a top-dollar exclusive facility where stars like Lindsay Lohan went to sober up. Though still a fugitive in Virginia, with two outstanding cases for crack possession in New York, he was now a prisoner in a place with no walls.

After only a couple of months in rehab, Dirty was given permission to go back to New York to appear in court for his Queens drug offense—accompanied, of course, by an Impact House counselor. He certainly didn't look like a person on the road to recovery, as he fell asleep in court, picked his nose, and, at one point, inexplicably asked the female prosecutor if she found him horny. Once more, his big mouth was ruining the day. The judge found him in contempt of court before issuing a postponement in the case.

Because Dirty was constantly clashing with his rehab counselor, they ended up taking separate flights back to LA, which could only lead to no good. Sure enough, when Dirty landed, he was found clutching a bottle of Hennessy. Impact House had no choice but to kick him out for violating probation, and he was transferred to Biscaoluz Recovery Center in the LA County Jail. In March, he returned to court to answer these most recent charges, and the judge ordered him to undergo three months of psychological tests before he was remanded back to Impact House for six months.[23]

During his last stint there, Dirty was finally making progress. He was behaving himself and following the rules, and he even earned the privilege of making supervised day trips outside the facility again. With the Clan finishing up *The W* in LA, Dirty secured a weekend furlough to go work with them. But he was late returning to Impact House, and, afraid that they'd throw him back in jail again for violating parole, he simply fled. It was October 21, 2000, only two months short of his discharge date. Dirty had no real excuses for fucking up this time. He had no substances, judges, or cops to blame, only his own bad judgment. His history within the criminal justice system and the inevitable stress it engendered could have been a factor, however, making him so scared he couldn't think straight. Regardless, skipping out on rehab when he had almost completed his sentence proved to be the slipup that pushed Dirty past the point of no return.

On the lam from the cops, he somehow made it back to New York, where he bounced between his mother's Park Slope brownstone, which he had bought her, and the homes of RZA and other family. On November 21, the Clan was performing at New York's Hammerstein Ballroom to celebrate the release of their third album, *The W*. Most of the sellout crowd were aware of news reports that Dirty was on the run, but the last place they expected to find him was here. The excitement to see at least eight of the original nine members together after such a long time, however, was palpable, and the night had all the makings of a momentous one.

Wu-Tang smashed it, living up to all the expectations as they plowed through the hits before a pumped-up home-town crowd. Then RZA slowed things down midset to announce a special guest. An unknown figure appeared, lurking around stage in a bright orange parka like Kenny from *South Park*. The fur-trimmed hood obscured his face, but when he pushed it back, the place went apeshit. ODB launched into "Shame on a Nigga" with four thousand hype men and women reciting every word of the hook with him. RZA remarked that this was the first time the whole Clan had been onstage together in three years. Dirty, who only had time for one song, announced, "The whole fuckin' world is after me." With plenty of uniformed officers outside, and the hip-hop cops obviously staking out the venue, it was nothing short of a miracle that he made it out of there undetected in his Day-Glo orange disguise. The furry hood, no doubt, saved the day.

This time, he didn't go back to Brooklyn but hid out with his boys, the Zu Ninjaz, in Willingboro, New Jersey. The Ninjaz—K-Blunt, Popa Chief, and 5-Foot Hyper Sniper—were a rap group that Dirty and Buddha Monk often hung out with when they wanted to get away from it all. They liked to party, and they put up with Dirty's shit. Merdoc and Shorty Shitstain from the Brooklyn Zu were also there, everyone staying at Popa Chief's house in the woods. Dirty spent most of the time sleeping, but when K-Blunt had to go pick up his car at a body shop in nearby Philly on the morning of November 27, he insisted on going along. After arguing about it, the stubborn Dirty got his way, as always.[24]

When they arrived at the body shop, however, the car wasn't quite ready. Impatient and probably a wee bit para-noid, Dirty made a fuss, saying he wanted to go back to Jersey instead of waiting the half hour until the car was done. He got his way again, but just as they were about to get on the Walt Whitman Bridge toward the Garden State, he told Blunt he needed to piss really badly. Of course he wouldn't wait, so they detoured to a nearby McDonald's. On his way to the bathroom, Dirty got a sudden hankering for a Filet-O-Fish, so Blunt said he would wait in line to order for him. When he returned, Dirty was trying to pay for the food when two teenage girls in line recognized him. The rapper deepened his voice and tried to deny it: "Nah that ain't me." Blunt had to practically push him out the door while he stayed and waited for the food.[25]

But Dirty couldn't even make the short walk from McDonald's front entrance to the car without getting distracted. Blunt came outside to find him bent over some girl's car window, chatting her up as she waited in the drive-through. By this time, he also saw a squad car pull into the parking lot. "We gotta go!" Blunt screamed. When Dirty saw the cops, he finally headed to the car but told Blunt to get the girl's number. Two more squad cars arrived, blocking the exits. Blunt made an absurd attempt to escape by driving over a concrete median, but at this point, the cops had service revolvers pointing at them while a police helicopter provided maximum intimidation from above. The cops pulled Blunt, Merdoc, and Chief out of the car one by one and threw them on the ground and cuffed them. When they asked Dirty to identify himself, he produced a fake ID, saying he was Robert Brown, but he wasn't fooling anybody. Law enforcement around the country had his mugshot, and, apparently, a couple of the arresting officers also happened to be fans. When they placed Dirty in the paddy wagon, he made a hell of a ruckus, slamming himself against the sides of the vehicle while screaming at the top of his lungs that he was, indeed, Robert Brown. He never got a chance to enjoy that Fish-O-Filet—the cause of his arrest in the first place, since a McDonald's employee had recognized him and called in to a radio station.[26]

The free spirit was once again in captivity for the foreseeable future, and this time he wouldn't be spending it at some cushy rehab facility without walls. Denied bail because he had already proven himself a flight risk, in jail he had to deal with the threats and intimidation that came with being a celebrity inmate. Dirty was no softy and could handle himself on the streets, but the self-professed momma's boy was out of luck in a place where he was surrounded by hardened criminals and had a target on his back. His lawyer, Peter Frankel, told the *Daily News*, "His mental health is bad. He's trying to get some mental health counseling and trying to get some spiritual counseling."[27] In April, prosecutor Ken Holder offered him a plea deal for the charge of possession with intent to sell, which would see him serving two to four years in New York while also fulfilling two years of his California sentence. The alternative was going to trial and getting as much as eight years if convicted. Despite the difficulties he had faced in jail so far, he really had no choice but to cop the plea.

On July 18, 2001, Judge Joseph A. Grosse sentenced Dirty to two to four years for the twenty glassine bags of cocaine. The rapper would receive eight months credit for time already served since his arrest in Philly. The judge was good enough to recommend that Dirty serve his time at the Arthur Kill Correctional Facility in Staten Island, so it would be easier for his family and fellow group members to visit him, but the decision was ultimately up to the Department of Corrections. On August 7, Dirty was transferred from the Kings

County Jail in East Flatbush, Brooklyn, to the Clinton Correctional Facility, located three hundred miles north of the city in Dannemora, New York. The place, known as "Little Siberia," was in one of the coldest and most isolated corners of the state. It also wasn't far from the former site of the Matteawan State Hospital for the Criminally Insane, where Five Percent Nation founder Clarence 13X had been committed. More recently, in 1995, Tupac had served eight months of a sexual abuse conviction in Clinton. Coinciding with Dirty's sentence, rapper Shyne (Jamal Barrow) was doing a ten-year bid for assault, criminal weapons possession, and reckless endangerment for his part in the 1999 Club New York shooting involving Puff Daddy and Jennifer Lopez. After doing his time, he was deported to his native Belize.

Prison was probably the worst place for a man already struggling with addiction and mental health issues. "Dirty got hit in the face with a telephone. Some niggas jumped him and broke his leg. But none of the prison officers wanted to help him," says Buddha. "Other inmates wanted money from him, they wanted to take something from him, or build a reputation as the nigga who beat down Ol' Dirty Bastard. They were threatening his life. They were threatening to set him on fire in his bunk."[28]

At one point, Dirty set himself on fire so he could be taken out of general population, according to Popa Wu, but that only led to a psychiatric evaluation and the prescribing of scary psychotropic drugs like Haldol. The meds made him gain weight and become listless and lethargic, like a zombie. His only regular visitors were his mom and Icelene and the kids. RZA visited him while he was still jailed in Brooklyn, but neither he nor any of the Clan bothered to make the eight-hour ride upstate. RZA did share his concerns on the Wu-Tang website, however, saying, "Ol' Dirty Bastard fears his life is in jeopardy and that a conspiracy is in effect to kill him. These concerns have been presented to the DA and prison officials have been alerted to the threat to his life. None of these state officials have given any regard to this matter. If something happens while ODB is in the custody of these officials, his family, his thirteen children, and Wu-Tang will seek full retribution in a civil resolution."[29] Dirty spent a total of eighteen months in the hellhole that was Clinton before being released to the Manhattan Psychiatric Center for three more months of observation. On May 1, 2003, he finally gained his freedom.

If his life up to then had been something of a bad reality show gone awry, his postprison life was the subject of an actual VH1 hatchet job called *Ol' Dirty Bastard on Parole*. Done in seemingly poor taste, the show was the brainchild of Jarred Weisfeld, a twenty-three-year-old recent college graduate. Credit him, however, with having the chutzpah to pitch a show to the network when he was only a production assistant peon who didn't even know Dirty personally at the time. All that changed when Buddha introduced him to Cherry Jones, who was her son's acting manager at the time. Aware that Dirty had no deal and, therefore, no income after Elektra dropped him, she had her son's best interests at heart when she offered Weisfeld access to Dirty if he would agree to be his comanager.

Around the same time, Damon Dash of Roc-A-Fella Records got wind of Dirty's impending release and, for whatever reason, offered to sign the rapper for a cool million-dollar advance. It was a surprising move considering Dirty's rough, anything-goes aesthetic was hardly what the slick, jiggy label represented. Weisfeld's role in securing that deal, if any, is unknown. After having very little contact with his Wu-Tang brothers over the past few years, Dirty probably didn't know where he stood. Even so, in the documentary, RZA stated that he had half a million dollars waiting for him, a place to stay, and a studio so Dirty could start doing what he did best again. But first, he said, he was going to put Dirty in the gym to get him healthy and in shape, to prepare him for public life. At a minimum, rest, relaxation, and time away from the spotlight were what Dirty really needed instead of having cameras poking in his face all the time.

The show documents all of this, including a press conference at Manhattan's RIHGA Royal Hotel just hours after Dirty's release, where Dash presents the husky rapper with a Roc-A-Fella medallion chain to welcome him to the label as a beaming Mariah Carey and proud Mama Jones look on. It also airs out the Clan's internal conflicts as RZA, Divine, and Dirty butt heads over his signing to a rival organization. After ripping up all his contracts with the individual members of Wu-Tang, RZA has no choice but to grant Dirty his independence too.

Witnessing Dirty's interactions with the fake industry types at Roc-A-Fella, a powerful and influential label at the time, one can plainly see that he's completely out of his element and making yet another bad move. In fact, everything about *ODB on Parole* is painful to watch. It's surprising they didn't include a segment of him buying and smoking crack because, under the circumstances, it didn't take Dirty long to relapse and start using drugs again.

At the last show he ever performed, before a sold-out crowd at the Aggie Theatre in Fort Collins, Colorado, Dirty was a hot mess. He allegedly lit up a crack pipe onstage, started speaking incoherently to the audience, and could barely get through a song. He also fell off the stage at one point, reinjuring the leg he had broken in prison. Popa Wu, who was supposed to accompany him but never received a ticket from Weisfeld, got a frantic call from the show promoters asking him what they should do. Apparently, Dirty had already missed a show in Vail, for which he had been paid, blowing the whole amount on drugs. Powerless to help, Popa Wu could only tell them to send him back, but even that didn't go well. Dirty missed the flight home after going on a serious bender in his hotel room that night. What he couldn't finish, he wrapped in plastic and swallowed before catching the next flight home. Arriving at JFK the following evening, when he was supposed to be performing with the Clan at a sold-out show at the Meadowlands in New Jersey, he went instead to his sister's house in Brooklyn to sleep. Method Man, for one, was not amused by his absence that night; he told the crowd, "There's no one person bigger than the Wu-Tang Clan, and when you see Ol' Dirty Bastard, tell him that. His family needs him. If you see Dirty, tell him we love him."

The next day, November 13, 2004, only two days shy of Dirty's thirty-sixth birthday, RZA picked his cousin up and drove him to 36 Chambers studio on Thirty-Fourth Street and Eleventh Avenue in Manhattan. On arrival, Dirty was sweating profusely, so he asked for some cold water and took off his shirt. The excruciating pain in his leg was also bothering him, so he took a Tramadol, a prescription painkiller that had been approved by his parole officer. Recording tracks for his Roc-A-Fella debut with members of Brooklyn Zu, Dirty worked for a bit before taking a break. Then he ordered a limo to pick up his kids so he could spend a little time with them. At one point, he took fifteen-year-old Barson into the lounge with him while he smoked a joint. After sending the kids back to their mother's, he lay down on the floor of the lounge to take a nap.

When 12 O'Clock and the rest of the Zu finished their session, they woke up Dirty, who said he felt like shit. He gobbled up a bowl of cereal, thinking that might help, but it didn't, so 12 suggested taking him to the hospital. After his ordeal, however, Dirty was not down with doctors and wasn't going anywhere. So they left, and he curled up on the floor again and went back to sleep. At about five o'clock, someone discovered that Dirty was not breathing and called 911, but when the paramedics arrived, they couldn't revive him. According to the autopsy that followed, the combination of the painkiller and the cocaine he had previously swallowed proved to be lethal. When his mother, Cherry, arrived and saw him lying there with the faintest impression of a smile on his face, she said she was unable to shed any tears because she knew Dirty had finally found peace.

"I was fucked up, crying nigga, you know what I mean? I'm on the highway like this. I had to pull over," says Raekwon of the moment he heard of ODB's passing, "'cause when you know somethin' is wrong with one of your brothers and you see him going down, but there's no way you could really save him, and then you hear it, and it's like you almost predicted it."[30] Like everyone else—including Dirty himself—Rae saw it coming: "But at the end of the day, we just let a grown man be a grown man. You gotta let him do that though. You let a nigga be who he is because that's who he want to be, you know what I mean?"[31]

RZA went a little further toward admitting his own guilt or complicity, telling CNN, "If you let a man that you love or anybody—man, woman, or child that you love—sit there and destroy themselves in front of you, you're neglecting them. Everybody let him do what he wanted to do. There were times when I took his drugs and threw them down the toilet. When I do that, he would get so pissed off I don't see him for weeks after that. So, it got to a point, I was like 'Fuck it, let him do his drugs,' just to have him around me, just to keep him there. But that's still neglect, yo."[32] In truth, most of the Clan felt the exact same way.

Inspectah Deck echoed these sentiments in his verse on "Life Changes," a dedication to Dirty from the Wu-Tang album *8 Diagrams* (2007), in which he raps, "And I share the blame 'cause you were calling for help kid / Should've, would've, could've, had the time I was selfish / I carry on your struggle, each day, it really hurts me / I really miss you, Russell, hope you forgive me Dirty." Although he and Dirty were polar opposites, he says, "As crazy and wild as he was, though, I have to make that point that he was definitely a civilized person. He wasn't no savage, like people paint the picture of him bein'—a dude that just didn't give a fuck about nothing. That's not true, man. He cared about his lady, he cared about his babies, he cared about the people around him, know what I'm sayin'? He just didn't want nobody tellin' him what to do or how to do it, know what I'm sayin', he didn't take orders or take commands from nobody. Yunno, he wanted to do everything his way. And that's why I salute the brother because I learned a lot from him."[33]

Coming from a position of tough love, U-God says, "If I had to do it all over again, I would fuck his ass up, throw handcuffs on him, and throw him in the fuckin' rehab. But that ain't gonna stop a mothefucker from doin' what he want to do and livin' his life the way he wanted to live his life.

Yunno, he wanted to have fun. He liked fuckin' bitches and takin' drugs—that was his thing, man. That's what he liked to do. Yunno, it's like how you gonna stop a motherfucker from doin' shit he liked to do."[34] At the same time, he acknowledged that Dirty's passing was "like losing a leg."

"ODB to me was always the nucleus to the movement we created," says Raekwon. "Dirty was the one that actually was the cheerleader, the mascot, then he became a general, then he became the psychologist to us to really keep us motivated, and you know, let us know who we are. It's like he was a father to niggas. He was goofy; he would make us step into a place super confident about what we are—like he been knew that Wu-Tang rocks the world. Like, that was always his attitude, and that was to me the battery that we needed to get to the next level."[35] With that energy no longer around, however, the Clan was at a definite disadvantage. While his death may have brought the other members closer together for a brief moment, it also ensured that they could never go back to the way things were when Wu-Tang ruled. Even with Cappadonna on board as an official member, moving forward without the heart and soul of the group seemed more like a job and less of an adventure.

CHAPTER 17

A MONUMENT IN HIP-HOP

If the entire Wu-Tang catalog consisted solely of their first two albums, bookending the five solo releases that appeared in between, the group's name would still be etched in stone on the holy tablets of hip-hop. Establishing a dynasty was no easy feat, and longevity in the rap game just as difficult to maintain, but the Clan's creative output, musical and otherwise, continued unabated into the new millennium. Even while chasing former glory, they unexpectedly acquired a new kind of cachet—as a cultural phenomenon and movement that existed independent of hip-hop.

This acknowledgment had to do, in part, with the many ways the band successfully transformed themselves into a brand, diversifying their portfolio with unprecedented business moves and savvy marketing opportunities. The DIY spirit had always pervaded hip-hop, but Wu-Tang was taking it to the next level—as in the artist as entrepreneur. First came Wu Wear in 1995, one of the earliest and most successful examples of an artist-run clothing label. Central to its appeal was the instantly recognizable *W* logo, of which Cappadonna said, "It's like a Timberland stamp, whenever you see that symbol, you can bet it's the best of hip-hop."[1] The group fully capitalized on their status, venturing into the video game market with a fighting game for PlayStation called *Wu-Tang: Shaolin Style*, followed by their own comic book series, *Nine Rings of Wu-Tang*. Both projects seemed a natural fit for a group so influenced by the various currents of pop culture.

In addition, they also made their mark on the big screen. While several Clansmen made cameo appearances in such films as *Belly* (1998), *Black and White* (1999), and *Ghost Dog: The Way of the Samurai* (1999), which RZA also scored, Meth went on to bigger roles in HBO's *The Wire* and *The Deuce* on his way to becoming a full-blown actor. RZA, too, graduated from scoring work or playing bit parts to writing and directing his own feature, *The Man with the Iron Fists* (2012), and establishing a career behind the lens. As someone accustomed to wearing many hats, he also served as showrunner for a fictionalized Hulu series about the group called *Wu-Tang: An American Saga* (2019) and was pivotal in putting together the four-part docuseries about the group, *Wu-Tang Clan: Of Mics and Men* (2019), which aired on Showtime. Coming on the heels of the group's twenty-fifth anniversary, these twin projects helped cement the Clan's legacy as the greatest hip-hop group the world has ever known. Besides N.W.A, Notorious B.I.G., and Tupac, no other rap artists have even come close to receiving the Hollywood treatment.

Though rooted in nostalgia, the Clan has always had an eye firmly fixed on the future and preserving their legacy. This quest for immortality, in fact, extended far beyond the title of their magnum opus, *Wu-Tang Forever*. In 2015, RZA and associate Cilvaringz, a Dutch Moroccan rap artist and Wu-Tang obsessive, announced the novel concept of releasing a one-off copy of a new album, which would be auctioned off to the highest bidder in the same manner as a piece of fine art. The CD would be packaged in an intricately carved, custom-made silver and nickel box, which itself deserved to be in a museum. This highly ambitious and unprecedented project became Wu-Tang's seventh studio album, *Once Upon a Time in Shaolin*. Eventually sold to "Pharma Bro" Martin Shkreli for $2 million, it inevitably stirred up a lot of controversy, as well as publicity, for the Clan.

When Wu-Tang first emerged from the underground as unknowns, their mystique was a powerful part of their appeal. Today, despite every internal conflict and controversy spilling into public view, they are loved more than ever, but for a newfound familiarity. They represent the dysfunctional family with whom everyone could identify, embodying universal archetypes such as the curmudgeonly Raekwon, ODB the jester, and so forth. People saw themselves in those nine distinct personalities. Yet the Clan was also very special.

Here was a group of young Black men from the ghetto—mostly high school dropouts and ex-felons—whom society had written off. Statistically speaking, they should have been dead or in jail by age twenty-five. But, overcoming the odds, they came together for a common cause, using the power of music to channel their anger, pain, and discontent, totally transcending their environment and circumstances. In the process, they changed not only their own lives and those of their families but also the art form of rap and the way business is done in the music industry. Often mistaken for a bat, their iconic *W* logo, a phoenix rising from the ashes, is considered one of the most recognizable symbols in the world, up there with the corporate logos of Nike or Apple or the trademark lips and tongue of musical legends the Rolling Stones. That *W* has become a monument in hip-hop, representing authenticity, innovation, creativity, and excellence, all qualities on which the art form and culture were built.

"The Wu-Tang logo is definitely up there with Batman or the actual WB, Warner Brothers, know what I'm saying," says Inspectah Deck. "Even now, man, I see Wu-Tang tattoos, Wu-Tang merchandise, memorabilia, and things like that, whether it's commercially available or fan created, man, it's just beautiful to me like to be a part of this movement, and to be twenty years later still, like we got die-hard fans and we don't got them fans that, yunno, they like you today and they're gone tomorrow. Our fans are down with us from day one. They don't allow us to do other things, we have to do Wu-Tang at all times, you know what I mean, but I appreciate that because they stuck with us through the ups and downs. And that *W*, that really shows me that it's bigger than me, it's transcended me already."[2]

The eternal clash between art and commerce seems to have been resolved in the development of hip-hop, an art form that openly celebrates capitalism and the accumulation of wealth. From its earliest incarnation in the parks, where broke MCs exhorted their indigent audiences to "make money, money!"—a chant immortalized in Jimmy Spicer's 1983 twelve-inch "Money (Dollar Bill Y'all)"—rampant material-ism and consumerism have found a champion in rap. In 1986, when Run-DMC asked the capacity crowd at Madison Square Garden to hold their sneakers in the air while they performed "My Adidas"—thrilling executives at the shoe company, who had been invited to the show—they revealed the marketing potential of this rebel sound, which was soon exploited. But more often than not, name-dropping popular brands in their rhymes was nothing more than free advertising, and rappers received nothing out of it.

Then, Naughty by Nature, a trio out of East Orange, New Jersey, whose "O.P.P." dominated the airwaves in 1991, flipped the script. Instead of advertising other people's products, they would promote their own. Piggybacking off the success of Black-owned brands like FUBU, Cross Colours, and Karl Kani, who catered to a young Black clientele, they became the first rap group to establish their own clothing line. Naughty Gear, a line of T-shirts, hats, and hoodies emblazoned with their distinctive baseball bat logo, was sold exclusively out of their own flagship store in Newark as well as via mail order (which still operates online). At the time, it may have seemed like going out on a limb, but as long as their records were selling and everyone wanted to be "down with O.P.P.," they had stumbled onto a potent form of cross-promotion.

Oliver "Power" Grant checked out the Naughty Store in Brick City and figured he could do better. Neither an artist nor manager, Power, a childhood buddy of Divine, had been instrumental in the formation of Wu-Tang, but as the group established themselves in the industry, he was trying to see where he could fit in. A born hustler who, at one point, commanded a drug organization of roughly two dozen people, he was so successful on the streets that he owned his first car, a black 1986 Audi Quattro, by the time he was sixteen. But, like his brothers in the struggle, he saw no future in the illegal life, and when he found an opening to go legit, he was going to get it in.[3]

Power was the guy who had the Wu-Tang logo silk-screened on T-shirts when Meth shot his first video for "Method Man." Recognizing the powerful pull of the W, with its ill resemblance to the Batman symbol, he made more shirts when the group went on tour, using those profits to re-up and expand. From simple silk-screening, he graduated to embroidery and started adding new items such as hockey jerseys, headbands, and throwback jerseys to his growing inventory. The response was tremendous, and he spent his days fulfilling mail orders. But drawing on previous retail experience in crack sales, he knew he needed a physical spot from which to hawk his wares. Taking a calculated risk, he rented an eight-hundred-square-foot storefront at 61 Victory Boulevard in Staten Island, midway between the St. George ferry terminal and Stapleton, investing about $50,000 to stock it with all manner of Wu-Tang branded garments. In addition to the Wu Wear store, it was Power's idea to include a mail-order catalog within the CD sleeve of Raekwon's *Only Built 4 Cuban Linx*. Both debuted in August 1995.[4]

Wu Wear expanded exponentially from there, paralleling the rise of the group. Power inked manufacturing and distribution deals with bigger companies that could provide a steady flow of product and get it into the appropriate stores around the country—including Macy's flagship store in Herald Square in Manhattan, where they became the first urban brand to get a window display. Wu Wear, in fact, became the battering ram behind which other Black designers were able to break into mainstream fashion outlets. Sales in that first year alone topped $10 million, and Power was set to open additional Wu Wear boutiques in Atlanta; Norfolk, Virginia; and LA.[5]

The clothing line naturally benefitted from a cross-promotion with the group's music and vice versa. In 1996, RZA, Method Man, and Cappadonna made it official, recording "Wu Wear: The Garment Renaissance" for the soundtrack to the film *High School High* (1996). In RZA's verse, he references a guy who stops wearing popular designers after gaining knowledge of self:

Then he became highly civilized
and spent time amongst the wise

Went through a garment renaissance and stopped wearing
    Benetton
Tommy Hill, Perry Ellis, Nautica or Liz Claiborne
Ocean Pacific, Fila, Bill Blass and leave fitted
Quit the Armani sweaters with the Gucci wool knitted
Mecca, Pelly Pell, 88, North Q, Bear and a few others
For the new year, strictly Wu-Wear.

Aside from a directive to "buy Black," he asserted that it was about time rappers stopped flogging other people's products and started promoting their own. In a *New York Times* article appearing at the end of the year entitled "Brash Hip-Hop Entrepreneurs," professor of business administration at the Harvard Business School James I. Cash said of the group, "What these guys have done—without taking a single business school course—is go right to the head of the class in terms of strategy development."[6] Of course, the next generation of hip-hop moguls was taking notes, and people like Sean Combs and Shawn Carter, who launched their own highly successful lines—Sean John and Rocawear, respectively—followed a path paved by the Wu.

For their part, group members were initially skeptical about Wu Wear, but that didn't stop them from walking into the Victory Boulevard store and helping themselves to the wares whenever they felt like it. This was the price of doing business with your homeboys; Power had no choice but to write it off. As far as running the day-to-day operations and the creative aspect of designing product, he says, "That was all me. I had a crew of people who worked with me and helped me achieve and do the things that I wanted to do. But that was all my direction, based on how I saw it. At the end of the day, it was just something I made for us, for them to project to the people. They [the group] never really actively took a part in it like that, although they were influential in the styling of what it was, just from being who they are and me knowing them as my friends, and now, my business partners."[7] It's unclear, however, how much of a financial stake the individual Clansmen had in Wu Wear. But Wu-Tang was setting a precedent among hip-hop crews that not everyone had to rap or make music. There were plenty of other opportunities to get paid. Power had spotted an opening and ran to fill it, turning his passion and hustle into a multimillion-dollar operation.

Although Wu Wear was officially discontinued in 2008, Power continued to forge exclusive collaborations with such partners as Nike—for the Wu-Tang Dunk shoe—and respected street apparel brands such as Alife and DC Shoes. He says, "When we started back then, everything was in its own corner. Music dudes ain't give a fuck about clothes. They was busy trying to sell music. Movie cats ain't care about clothes or music because they too busy trying to sell movies and vice versa. Now, everybody's strategically partnering where it's beneficial, and that's the growth and expansion of where all of this came from."[8] Wu Wear was most definitely on the vanguard of this new cross-pollination of marketing across various platforms.

Sometimes it worked, and sometimes it didn't, as in the case of the Wu-Tang video game and comic book, which appeared toward the end of 1999. *Wu-Tang: Shaolin Style* for PlayStation, released in October by gaming world giant Electronic Arts (EA), broke ground in becoming the first 3D fighting game to accommodate four players at once. It was based on an engine created by game developer Paradox for a shelved product called *Thrill Kill* that was deemed too sexually explicit for release at the time. They salvaged the fighting component, however, making the Clan into muscle-bound marauders with their own unique superpowers. Though it managed to move several hundred thousand copies on their name alone, it might have been even more successful with greater participation from the group, who come off as nothing more than generic characters.

The same might be said for *Nine Rings of Wu-Tang*, a comic book series issued by Gibraltar Entertainment, whose first of five issues ran in November 1999. Written by Aaron Bullock and illustrated by Brian Haberlin, the comic reimagines the Wu as burly superheroes, who look nothing like themselves, in Moorish Spain. Instead of exploiting the group's existing kung fu ethos, or even their individual personas, the comic served as a romp in generic fantasy. One would expect, given the Clan's influences, that such projects would have been right up their alley, yet they failed to maximize their potential. Still, pursuing such opportunities showcased the group's tireless grind, further expanding the Wu-Tang imprint into areas beyond music.

Silent partner Power was on a roll in the late nineties, setting up deals while also copping some of the spotlight for himself, making his big-screen debut as the lead in James Toback's *Black and White* (1999). The role supposedly fell into his lap when the director approached him to license some music for the film, which turned out to be a rambling wreck, heavy on star cameos—including Mike Tyson, Ben Stiller, Robert Downey Jr., and Claudia Schiffer—but light on substance and story line. While teasing an in-depth examination of the powerful influence of Black culture on white youth, things quickly went south once Brooke Shields appeared in faux dreadlocks, playing a documentary filmmaker, with Downey Jr. as her closeted husband. In one humorous scene, he even attempts to hit on Tyson, and even though they're acting, he looks like he was taking his life into his own hands.

But while everybody else was busy playing the fool, Power and his Wu-Tang cohorts—including Raekwon, who features prominently as rapper "Cigar"; Method Man; Ghostface; Masta Killa; and Inspectah Deck, who all make cameos playing themselves—provide the film's only anchor in reality. In fact, the best scenes blur the lines between fiction and documentary—Raekwon rhyming a cappella in the studio or Method Man explaining the significance of the infamous graffiti wall at Killah Hill, where the names of the deceased are remembered. Their truth and authenticity actually showed why white kids were attracted to Black culture. But the confused movie really goes nowhere, which was reflected at the box office, where it didn't even recoup half of its $12 million budget.

That same year, cult director Jim Jarmusch released *Ghost Dog: Way of the Samurai* (1999), an infinitely better film of the arthouse variety. The $2 million budget independent starred Forest Whitaker as an unlikely Mob hitman and loner who happens to follow *Hagakure, the Book of the Samurai*. Though the critically lauded picture bears comparisons to Jean-Pierre Melville's *Le Samourai* (1967) as well as the sixties gangster films of Japanese director Seijun Suzuki, Wu-Tang proved to be as much of an inspiration for Jarmusch, who wrote the script while listening to their music. It was hardly a stretch, then, to invite RZA to compose the film's original score. Hair braided in cornrows, he even makes a brief cameo like a camouflage monk, mirroring Whitaker's character, the honorable assassin. When you hear Ghost

Dog reciting the wisdom of the *Hagakure* in voice-overs, you can see the extent to which his whole being is simply a reflection of the humble urban-warrior spirit that Wu-Tang exemplified.

The first Clansman to land on the big screen and make a lasting career of it was none other than their breakout star, Method Man. Before Meth, you could count the number of rappers who had made an impact on Hollywood on one hand—Will Smith, LL Cool J, Ice-T, Ice-Cube, and Tupac. After playing bit roles in *Cop Land* (1997) and *Belly* (1998), Meth shared the lead in the stoner comedy *How High* (2001) with Redman, a frequent musical collaborator (on *Blackout 1 & 2* on Def Jam). That led to the short-lived Fox comedy series *Method & Red* (2004). But it was his appearance on HBO's *The Wire* (2003–2008) as recurring character Melvin "Cheese" Wagstaff that really put him on the map as a serious actor. He followed that with an even bigger role on HBO's *The Deuce* (2017) about Times Square in the seventies, in which he plays a principled pimp. Today, his onscreen résumé runs thick, and he's known as much for his acting chops as for lyrical ones.

The only other member of the Clan to carve out a whole new career for himself in Hollywood was RZA, who has not only appeared on camera but also worked behind the lens as a director. In hindsight, looking back at the important role movies played in his life—especially kung fu films—RZA's transition into the medium seems as natural and organic as his relationship with music. He had to proceed through various stages like San Te's transformation into a Shaolin monk in *36 Chambers of Shaolin*. But, instead of film school, he had the benefit of apprenticing under such cinematic talents as Jarmusch; Quentin Tarantino, whose *Kill Bill: Vol. 1* soundtrack he produced; and even legendary Hong Kong director John Woo.

After years of scoring movies and appearing in bit roles, RZA graduated to writing and directing his own feature, *The Man with the Iron Fists* (2012)—starring himself, Russell Crowe, and Lucy Liu—which he described as an homage to the Shaw Brothers' films he grew up watching. Shooting on location in China on a $15 million budget, RZA realized a childhood dream, working with some of the same martial arts legends he used to marvel at on the big screen. Though the film received mixed reviews, it did turn a small profit and, most importantly, put RZA on the map as a viable director and most certainly as the first rapper to direct a major studio release. Adding to that his two *New York Times'* best-selling books, *The Wu-Tang Manual* (Riverhead Books, 2004), co-written by Chris Norris, and *The Tao of Wu* (Riverhead, 2009), and RZA had turned into a truly renaissance talent.

The cumulative effect of all these outside endeavors was to keep the group's name alive and relevant, as none of the guys were perceived as solo entities but rather as part of Wu-Tang. With film and television occupying the top of the entertainment hierarchy, it was also a step-up from simply making music and considered an advancement rather than a detriment to their careers. At the end of the day, America respects money and celebrity above all else, and while no one lamented the end of Will Smith's rapping career or was clamoring for a new album from him, they would line up to see his next film. The Clansmen were obviously keeping all their options open.

Wu-Tang's outside-the-box mentality has taken them where few rap groups have ventured before, and in 2015, they made international headlines, landing in the Guinness World

Records for selling the most expensive album ever made. After releasing *8 Diagrams* (2007) and *A Better Tomorrow* (2014) to a lukewarm reception and vastly diminishing sales—in the US, the records sold 202,000 and 60,000 copies, respectively—it was obvious that the music industry's once-lucrative business model had been blown to smithereens by the advent of digital technologies such as downloading and streaming. Without a need for the physical form of vinyl, CD, or cassette, music had basically lost all monetary value when it could be accessed for free on the internet. This situation left many artists without a means for making a living besides, of course, touring. The Clan's response was to secretly record an album, of which they produced only a single copy, to be auctioned off to the highest bidder as if it were a piece of fine art. On May 3, 2015, their circuitous six-year plan came to fruition when Martin Shkreli, the controversial pharmaceutical CEO, bought the album, *Once Upon a Time in Shaolin*, for a reported $2 million, also making this project one of the biggest publicity stunts in history.

The gargantuan effort that culminated in this singular release was documented in the book *Once Upon a Time in Shaolin: The Untold Story of Wu-Tang Clan's Million-Dollar Secret Album, the Devaluation of Music, and America's New Public Enemy No. 1* (Flatiron Books / Macmillan, 2017), by Cyrus Bozorgmehr, one of the principal advisers behind the project. Despite the unwieldly title, it's an entertaining read, and the fact that Plan B Entertainment, a company jointly owned by Brad Pitt and Netflix, acquired the rights to the story is proof that this project was, indeed, a publicity grab of the magnitude that would make Edward Bernays blush.

Ironically, such an audacious idea did not originate within the Clan but rather from the mind of Tarik Azzougarh, a.k.a.

Cilvaringz, a then-unknown but highly motivated Dutch Moroccan rapper, producer, manager, and fan, who successfully insinuated himself within the Wu-Tang organization over a number of years. He first reportedly crossed paths with the Clan after their concert at Amsterdam's Melkweg in 1997, where he impressed ODB and Meth at a spontaneous freestyle session. A brief audience with RZA, however, was interrupted by a stage-clearing brawl, and he lost contact with the group. Undaunted, Cilvaringz traveled to New York no fewer than five times between 1997 and 1999 in the hopes of reconnecting with his mentor. In the process, he met RZA's mother and uncle, making a positive impression on them. He even dropped his demo tape off at the Wu Nails salon on Staten Island, a boutique run by RZA's sister Sophia, who was instrumental in finally getting him the face-to-face meeting that he desperately sought.

The unbelievable outcome of that encounter—his signing to Wu-Tang Records—had all the trimmings of a fan fantasy come to life. But it appears that RZA was more impressed by Cilvaringz's hustle and persistence than his actual skills on the mic, and he set his new disciple on a long journey to prepare his debut album. Concurrently, the neophyte rapper was completing a degree in entertainment law, so his album, *I* (RPEG, 2007), heavily studded with appearances from the Clan, took six years to produce. In the meantime, as part of his law school graduation project, Ringz arranged a massive 2003 world tour for RZA that went through 163 cities in 56 countries.[9] He served not only as the booking agent but as the opening act as well.

Without a doubt, being on the road with someone day in and day out offered plenty of opportunity for bonding, and it was during this time that his relationship with RZA solidified to the point that they even became friends. Then, in 2004, the Abbott invited Ringz to accompany him on a voyage of discovery to the pyramids in Egypt—not only the first wonder of the world but probably one of the most enduring examples of art as well. As they climbed up the ancient megaton blocks of granite, perfectly carved and fitted together with geometric precision, this brush with eternity had a profound effect—especially on Cilvaringz.

In 2007, his album finally dropped to virtual crickets. Frustrated by the sorry state of the music industry that had been decimated by downloading, he came up with the concept of a one-off album that was not mass-produced but sold in auction to the highest bidder. Taking a cue from the fine art world, in which paintings routinely sold for millions of dollars, he wanted to apply the same concept to music—specifically the Clan's music, which he knew could command top dollar. Bringing the idea to RZA, who could not resist such a daring scheme, which, at a minimum, was bound to generate loads of publicity, he found an effective partner in crime.

But since the Clan was now a collection of solo entities with their own separate management, Cilvaringz had the arduous task of approaching each MC and convincing him to sign off on the idea and contribute to the album, which he would be producing. Though he had already collaborated with members of the Clan on his own record, this time the stakes were much higher, since it was a Wu-Tang project (though none of the individual members were aware of this fact). For six years, he kept his nose to the grindstone, working on tracks that RZA green-lighted and getting all nine living members of the Clan to bless them—all the while keeping a tight lid on leaks. He obviously had to pay all the MCs for services rendered, and the only way he could do so was to secure an unnamed investor, who is known in the book as simply "Mr. S."

The album demanded packaging worthy of something that was to be sold as a fine art piece, a component supplied by British Moroccan artist Yahya, a favorite of the Moroccan royal court, who designed a box within a box within a box. The outer box consisted of a sleek wooden container about the size of a footlocker, emblazoned with the W. Inside it lay an intricately carved silver and nickel box, also branded with the logo but slightly smaller than the first and only accessible by lock and key. Opening this box revealed a smaller silver box with logo that held the only physical copy of the album on two CDs. The entire presentation gave new meaning to the term *jewel box*.

In March 2015, after years of secrecy, Cilvaringz and RZA were finally ready to go public at MoMA's PS 1 in Queens, exhibiting *Once Upon a Time in Shaolin* for the first and only time before a crowd of about 150 art collectors, dealers, media, and a gaggle of thirty-six lucky fans who had won tickets through a Power 105.1 giveaway. Not only was its lavish packaging on display—everything except the leather-bound, 174-page liner notes with lyrics, credits, and anecdotes about the production—but RZA and Cilvaringz actually played thirteen minutes of snippets from the thirty-one-track 110-minute opus.

Complex magazine wrote, "The project sounds raw and rugged down to the mixing and mastering. The dusty yet crisp signature sound that evokes a fierce blade, both razor-sharp and rusted would feel very familiar to fans of vintage Wu-Tang. Lyrically the album also felt like a return to form. Two decades later, the MCs managed to channel the mid-'90s

Shaolin mindset, with the gritty storytelling and eclectic references fans know to expect."[10] While the review sounded positive, it was obviously tough to render a meaningful opinion after only hearing about 10 percent of the music. But the listening session also revealed that the album featured Redman, some FC Barcelona football players, a *Game of Thrones* actress, and Cher, only underscoring the bizarre nature of the project.

At one point in their career, Wu-Tang's strategy had been to flood the market with their branded product, but now they were going in the complete opposite direction toward exclusivity. A website dedicated to the release declared, "The intrinsic value of music has been reduced to zero. Contemporary art is worth millions by virtue of its exclusivity. . . . By adopting a 400-year-old Renaissance-style approach to music, offering it as a commissioned commodity and allowing it to take a similar trajectory from creation to exhibition to sale . . . we hope to inspire and intensify urgent debates about the future of music."[11] Couched in such hype, the cause almost seemed noble, but it was by no means going to solve the problem of the devaluation of music or close the lid on Pandora's box of free downloads. Some douche of a billionaire was always destined to buy the album, thus pissing off hard-core Wu-Tang fans everywhere, and only a group as celebrated as the Clan had a shot in hell at pulling off such a heist in the first place. No doubt everyone involved had their own ulterior motives as well.

For Cilvaringz, the project represented the culmination of a long journey that took him straight outta Tilburg, the Netherlands—his hometown—and into the inner circle of a group with whom he so desperately wanted to be down. Investors like Mr. S., for whom money was not an issue, were vying for their place in history. RZA, on the other hand, who had only to act as a spokesperson and adviser while doing none of the heavy lifting, had the most to gain, canonizing the mighty *W* for eternity. "This is the seal to a musical legacy," he boasted at PS1, showing off a shiny new object that trumped all the trunk jewelry on Canal Street.[12] This was clearly a play not for hearts and minds but for the imagination—a stunt the most interesting man in the world might pull off just because he could.

While they approached both the top auction houses for art, Sotheby's and Christie's, to sell the album, it eventually made more sense to go with New York–based online auction firm Paddle8, who had previously sold works by such well-known artists as Jeff Koons, Julian Schnabel, and Damien Hirst. The auction proceeded in May, and by August the sale was finalized, as both legal teams hammered out terms. The deal stipulated that the album could not be commercially available for a period of eighty-eight years while giving the buyer discretion to release it for free or exhibit it before that time. In December, it was finally revealed who that buyer was—Martin Shkreli, thirty-two, CEO of Turing Pharmaceuticals.

That might have been the end of the story, and another victory for the Clan, if not for the fact that Shkreli and his company had recently been in the news for price-gouging prescription medicine. Earlier in September, they had purchased the expired patent to Daraprim, a medication used by HIV/AIDS patients that was not available in a generic version. Overnight, Shkreli raised the price of a single dose of the drug from $13.50 to $750, an increase of more than 5,000 percent. The news attracted the attention of Congress, who summoned Shkreli to appear before them in a hearing, and even then-candidate for president Trump was quick to criticize Shkreli as "a spoiled brat" (oh, the irony). In an election year in which the rising cost of health care and prescription drugs was on the ballot, the young, snotty CEO was swiftly vilified in the media and became the face of unbridled corporate greed—especially within big pharma, for whom there was no love lost. In truth, however, he simply brought standard operating procedure within the for-profit industry into focus, becoming a convenient scapegoat.

When RZA discovered that *Bloomberg Businessweek* was outing Shkreli as the new owner of the single-copy Wu-Tang album, he preemptively issued a statement: "The sale of *Once Upon a Time in Shaolin* was agreed upon in May, well before Martin Skhreli's [*sic*] business practices came to light. We decided to give a significant portion of the proceeds to charity."[13] RZA obviously felt like he was in a tight situation, having sold this much-hyped album to someone who was fast becoming the most hated man in America. In addition, he had to face static from within his own crew—the most outspoken being Method Man.

"I dug the whole idea in the beginning. I'm like, 'Wow, this has never been done before.' I was cool with shit," said Meth. "But now, this is ridiculous. 88 years? Really? If that shit is true, that shit is stupid. You have to wait 88 years to hear some shit? By that time, it's going to be fuckin' played out. If it ain't already played out."[14] Meth, like the other members of the group, wasn't aware of the contingencies that allowed the music to be heard. It seemed, once again, as if miscommunication lay at the heart of the problem, as other members of the Clan also complained that they had been misled by Cilvaringz, even though RZA was complicit in the idea all along.

In a scene from *Of Mics and Men*, you can see exactly how they felt as the whole group trashes Cilvaringz and the album, while RZA, behind dark shades, remains conspicuously quiet. Here they make explicitly clear that they had no idea *Once Upon a Time in Shaolin* was going to be an official Wu-Tang release. Still, at the end of the day, they say all publicity is good publicity, and despite the backlash against Shkreli, everyone was talking about a mysterious Wu-Tang album that nobody ever heard—including Shkreli himself, who said he was saving it for a rainy day.

Throwing the controversial, almost comical CEO into the mix added all kinds of crazy to this story. To endear himself with the public even more, Shkreli went on to diss RZA and the Clan and start a personal beef with Ghostface. According to Bozorgmehr's book, this all started as part of Cilvaringz's plan B to ratchet up publicity, though Shkreli, a fan of pro wrestling, seemed to relish the faux conflict as well as his role as the super villain, which he played to the hilt. In 2016, he offered a free online sample of the album if Trump won the presidency but ended up playing only a couple of songs. By this time, he was well-ensconced in a securities fraud investigation by the FBI that had nothing to do with Daraprim and was in and out of court.

In August 2017, he was convicted on two counts of security fraud and conspiracy to commit securities fraud. Finally, on March 9, 2018, Shkreli was sentenced to seven years in federal prison and ordered to forfeit nearly $7.4 million in assets, thought to include *Once Upon a Time in Shaolin*. The seizure of assets, however, was deferred, as he appealed the case. While Shkreli serves his time at the minimum-security federal prison in Allentown, Pennsylvania, the album's whereabouts are currently unknown, and its future remains uncertain. But publicity like this was priceless and further bolstered the Clan's legendary status.

Compared to the hoopla surrounding *Once Upon a Time*, the last publicly released Wu-Tang album dropped quietly and with little fanfare. Released by Canadian entertainment outfit eOne, *The Saga Continues* (2017) was billed as a compilation, as it did not include any contributions from GZA or U-God, who had an active lawsuit against the group. The beats were produced entirely by Mathematics, the group's deejay, to whom RZA was throwing a bone after all his years of loyal service.

"There was a young brother that was our deejay," he said, explaining the album's genesis. "He was working construction. I hired him to draw the Wu-Tang logo. His name was Allah Mathematics. And he always was in the shadows doing the knowledge. He learned how to make beats and produce and after a while—when I became a composer I became further and further away from the sound of Wu-Tang, I mean I don't use the ASR-10 anymore—Mathematics stayed right there with it. So, he was really given the task and he took the task upon himself to go and start having the members re-energize their verses to the classic Wu-Tang sound. After he got it to a certain degree, he was like, 'I'm going to come over and show you where we're at.' He showed me and I was like, 'Yo, *The Saga Continues*.'"[15] But aside from Masta Killa, who called it "a definitive Wu-Tang project," none of the other Clan members bothered to comment on the release.[16] It still remains the least successful of their seven albums, moving fewer than twenty-five thousand units.

The attitude toward this mediocre release ultimately foreshadows how fans will likely view *Once Upon a Time in Shaolin* if it ever sees light. While Cilvaringz took a lot of flak, emerging from the experience like Yoko Ono, he does deserve credit for his incredible vision, as well as the dedication and commitment to pulling it off. In the big picture, however, while he might produce tracks that sound like RZA's, he is no RZA, which is quite apparent when you listen to his music on the internet—even leaked instrumentals from *Once Upon a Time in Shaolin*. For fans, a Wu-Tang album, by definition, begins with RZA's beats. Therefore, *Once Upon a Time in Shaolin* will always be regarded as a very expensive imitation. From the Renaissance on up to modern times, they still call that a forgery.

Few artists in hip-hop can boast twenty-five years in the game, so when Wu-Tang made it to this remarkable milestone, they made sure to milk the most out of it. Between 2018 and 2019, the group reconvened for a world tour that saw them performing at huge festivals, as well as such iconic venues as the Sydney Opera House in Australia. Following the music industry crash in the early aughts, touring was really the main income source for artists, and the Clan had learned their lesson after the ill-fated Rage tour in 1997. Utilizing his connections in film and TV, RZA was also focused on preserving the Clan's legacy through two major projects—*Of Mics and Men*, a four-part docuseries for Showtime, and *Wu-Tang: An American Saga*, a scripted series for Hulu. Though RZA didn't helm the first project, he personally selected its director, Sacha Jenkins, a veteran music journalist, filmmaker, graf writer, and overall hip-hop raconteur, who, as a member of the culture, brought authenticity and an insider's perspective. The Hulu series was a collaboration between RZA and screenwriter Alex Tse, whose credits included *Superfly* (2019) and *Watchmen* (2009), which he cowrote. These dual depictions of the Wu could not have been more different.

Of Mics and Men does a pretty amazing job of capturing the Clan's story in four hour-long episodes that feature in-depth conversations with each member interlaced with a considerable amount of previously unseen archival footage shot by the group and their affiliates, creating a real feeling of intimacy. For example, there's a priceless scene, obviously shot on grainy VHS, where the fellas are gathered in RZA's basement, deconstructing each other's verse from "Protect Ya Neck" as if they're in English class. One is struck not only by their youthful appearance but also how fervent and passionate they are about the art of rhyming. Jenkins also pulls a lot out of them in his interviews, usually conducted as they sit on a fancy throne against a black background. Ghost, for example, recalls how depressed he felt caring for two brothers with muscular dystrophy, admitting that, at the time, he didn't even know he was depressed. The film also uses an effective device of gathering all the members at the majestic St. George Theatre in Staten Island, which just celebrated its ninetieth anniversary, where Jenkins screens clips from their past that they discuss collectively as a group. In their interactions, one sees, firsthand, the kind of respect and brotherly love they have toward one another, which is both a reason for their longevity as well as why so many people worldwide hold them at the pinnacle of hip-hop.

The film's only shortcoming is its length, which seems like the wrong critique to make about a four-hour documentary unless the Wu themselves weren't so deep. Many aspects of their history, influences, and mythology were omitted, obviously due to time constraints. Also, instead of delving into their classic catalog of music, the source from which their power emanated, a whole episode was devoted to the story behind *Once Upon a Time in Shaolin*, an album that may not be heard for many years to come. But the doc made an overwhelmingly positive impression, and it was well worth the time commitment to watching, not least because it trafficked in the truth.

The same could not be said for *Wu-Tang: An American Saga*, which premiered on Hulu on September 4, 2019. This series faced more of a challenge because it involved young actors portraying the members of the group in their pre-fame days in the early nineties. For the purposes of plotting a ten-episode story, RZA also chose to fictionalize parts of their past. The only problem was that the Clan's story needed no embellishment—you couldn't add a thing to make it more interesting or compelling. Also, for a group concerned with authenticity, "keeping it real" was more than a slogan; it was a way of life. In effect, RZA was responsible for the Hollywood-ization of his own story. Curiously, both he and Method Man were executive producers on the project, and the rest of the Clan and the estate of Ol' Dirty Bastard were credited as consulting producers, so any one of them could have raised concerns. But perhaps it was their intention to purposely muddy their past to preserve some sense of mystique. In any case, Raekwon, a tough critic, gave it a six out of ten rating. What the series lacked in authenticity, however, was made up for by the talented cast, who brought to life these compelling characters. Regardless of Rae, the show got picked up for a second season in January 2020. Though there have been rumors of an upcoming ODB biopic, nothing has panned out so far.

"I didn't make myself the Abbot, this was a title that was given to me by the other Wu-Tang members," says RZA. "So you gave me the title, you gave me the power, I'll use it. But I'll use it not just for my personal benefit, not just for their personal benefit, but for the benefit of what the Wu-Tang stands for."[17] Clarifying this last point, he adds, "Wu-Tang has become a source of information and not just about our ghetto and our roughness and toughness and our personal entities, but a source of information for people to get their own thing and move on. So, when I do Wu-Tang, I don't do it for myself, I do it for the world."[18] His statement implicitly acknowledges that whatever Wu-Tang started out as, it has evolved into something far greater.

This sense of responsibility to something beyond the small circle of the group is unique among rappers. In a 1996 interview on BET's *Rap City*, Raekwon sounded downright prescient when he observed, "We bigger than just a rap group, man. 'Cause it's like, yo, we startin' generations, man, and we realize the power we bringin' to the people. It's like, yo, all we tryin' to show you is, yo, I know there's somebody out there that's livin' like how we livin'. If you got a crew take care of each other and that's gonna lead to prosperity for all y'all."[19] Certainly, the Clan's DIY approach and business savvy inspired legions of artists who followed, but it was their unity and brotherhood that allowed them to have such a huge impact. The fact that they are still standing, mostly intact, continuing to cast a long shadow after all these years, challenges the idea of relevance and begs the question: Why them?

"You know what our secret is?" says U-God. "Our mothers know each other, so that's one thing we had over other crews—our internal family knows each other. We have respect for that." Supporting these sentiments, Cappadonna adds, "What makes the Wu so special to me is that we not a manufactured group. We grew up together. We really grew up together, and when I think about that the way I say it, it's amazing that we all still homeboys, right? We all still together, we gonna be out here tomorrow, nah mean, me and all my boys, and it's like we been together since third grade—that's how far we go back. That's why we can't break up. We are the Wu-Tang Clan, like, we always gonna be the Wu-Tang Clan. There's nothing you can do about that, man."[20]

Clan has always represented family, and "family is the foundation," says Cappa.[21] But even among families, conflict is also inevitable. "There's always fighting, there's always egos," GZA admits, "but there's not one family that don't fight. It's controlling the fights you have. It's having them under control, man. It's like extinguishing a flame. We all fight. We all argue. We all have disagreements, but we not savages, so we can maintain that shit, man, and deal with them the best way we can." Deck adds, "We argue, snap, laugh, we fuckin' scream at niggas—top of your lungs—but later on, man, we gonna be laughing and shit."

Despite the strongest bonds of brotherhood, life inevitably intrudes, and people find themselves pulled in different directions according to the dictates of their families and personal situations, conditions to which Wu-Tang was not immune. "We all used to be at the Wu Mansion together, everybody, plus might have Sunz of Man, Shyheim might come through, yunno, Black Knights," Cappa recalls. "But that was our spot, and that's where we used to get the best songs—all a that Wu-Tang swordplay and all a that. A lot of stuff came out of there. But when we was in there, why it was so effective because we was able to lay down verses 24-7. We ain't have to look for nobody, email wasn't out yet, you couldn't email nobody a track. Had to come and get that!"[22]

Being around each other created the spark, according to Masta Killa, who says, "When I stopped seeing everybody at the studio at one time, yunno, to me that started [the decline]. What made it special was us bein' together, you know what I'm sayin', just vibin' off each other's vibe. It's nothing like bein' in the studio together and feelin' the energy and bein' creative right there on the spot."[23] Such moments of spontaneous collaboration were behind the magic. "It starts from the creativeness—what got us here," he says. "But if I'm not seeing you as often as I used to because you have responsibilities, I have responsibilities, and we get together every so often to maybe make a song or to do a show, our gelling is not as tight as it once was."[24]

Ghost also acknowledged a vital source of Wu-Tang's power when he says, "Being in a group where everybody is nice, there's competition. You know the powers of this guy and the powers of that guy, so, when everybody's in the studio, it's like damn! I take a while to write, you know what I mean, a lot of brothers is faster than me. So, being in there amongst Meth and Rae and Deck and RZA and GZA, it's like, yo, you better make sure you really get this right. And that's what it was. It was almost like a battle royale goin' on in there, like a friendly game of stickball or something."[25]

Steel sharpens steel, and for the Wu-Tang swordsmen, battling within the crew kept everyone at the top of their game, yielding amazing results. "'Cause you dealin' with dart masters," Ghost adds. "Once you dealin' with brothers that's focused and highly conscious, and they're wordsmiths—know how to put words together—it's like, yo, if you can't deal with a Genius and meet the requirements up there, it's like, yo, you feel like you're illiterate."[26]

"I'm proud to say, yo, I'm Wu-Tang for life," says Deck. "No matter how you feel, like Wu-Tang's smoked out or they over the hill, washed up. I'm like, nigga, the only way I'm washed up is fresh out the shower, you feel me? I'll go toe-to-toe with any MC in this game right now. They don't want to go lyrically, know what I'm sayin'? I don't make them cats eat trap hooks, I don't make a bunch of stripper music, know what I'm sayin', I make that shit that you listen to, man."[27] Putting his money where his mouth is, Deck recently released his fourth studio album, *Chamber No. 9* (2019), through Music Generation Corp. and continues to record with his side project Czarface, whose additional members include the MC Esoteric and producer 7L.

Grappling with the issues older artists face, Raekwon, who independently released his seventh studio album, *The Wild* (Ice H20 / Empire, 2017), says, "I think that you could only become irrelevant if you allow yourself to become irrelevant. I think we are the definition of keep going."[28] Diversifying his portfolio, Rae launched his own brand of premium wine in 2018, Licataa Lambrusco, a sparkling Italian red that retails for thirty-five dollars a bottle. RZA, who has his hands into everything, agrees, saying, "I have a slogan: intelligence is always relevant."[29] No argument there.

Wu-Tang appeals to all sorts of people for many different reasons, but one thing most fans will agree on is that the Clan never lacks substance or the capacity to surprise. There is always something to learn from these OGs, who impart hard-won wisdom from experience. So who said hip-hop was a young person's game? As MCs, poets, and writers, their skills can only improve over time like a fine vintage wine. Perhaps that's what drives continued interest in the group long after their heyday. In a career characterized by exceeding all expectations and making the impossible happen, the Clan continues to hold the trump card, controlling their own destiny, as they have from day one. By now, fans know that they are capable of anything—from another album or tour to something completely new and groundbreaking. Twenty-five years and counting, Wu-Tang remains a work in progress, their final chapter yet to be written, as the saga continues.

ACKNOWLEDGMENTS

It takes a village to make a book. Thanks to my agent, William Loturco; my editor, Ben Schafer; Carrie Napolitano; everyone at Hachette Publishing and Da Capo Press; my mother, Chandra Fernando; Uncle Cyril; Sid and Cynthia; Joe and Morgan; Siromi; Tiger; Michael Gonzales; Vikki Toback; Sacha Jenkins; Alan Light; Erin Burke; Tresa Sanders; Shecky Green; Ben Merlis; Matt Life; Schott Free; Ramsey Jones; Cherry Jones; Popa Wu; Melquan Smith; Carlos Bess; Scotty Hard; Chris Gehringer; Easy Mo Bee; Yoram Vazan; Prince Paul; Gerald Barclay; Wendy Goldstein; Osmo Walden; Kurt Anthony; Jonathan Carroll; Al Pereira; Alice Arnold; Ernie Paniccioli; Eddie Otchere; David Corio; and Christian Lantry. Special thanks to the entire Clan, especially RZA, GZA, ODB, Rae, Ghost, Meth, Deck, U-God, Masta Killa, and Cappadonna. All praises due to the Mighty Unseen Force that makes all things possible.

NOTES

RUCKUS IN B MINOR (THE PRELUDE)

1. David Smith, "Whitey's on the Moon: Why Apollo 11 Looked So Different to Black America," *Guardian*, July 14, 2019.

CHAPTER 1: SOMETHIN' IN THE SLUM WENT RA-PA-PUM-PUM

1. Jeff Chang, *Can't Stop Won't Stop: A History of the Hip-Hop Generation* (New York: St. Martin's, 2005), 75.

2. Ibid., 69.

3. djvlad, "Grandmaster Caz on Coke La Rock Being Hip-Hop's First MC," YouTube video, 5:32, May 31, 2015.

4. Michael Gonzales, "Jive Talkin': The Coke La Rock Story," *Wax Poetics*, issue 51, June 20, 2012.

5. GZA, "The Jam," Pitchfork video, 3:40, April 16, 2012, pitchfork .com/tv/14-frames/117-gza-the-jam/.

6. Harriet Gibson, "Introducing the Band: Mogwai's Stuart Braithwaite Interviews Wu-Tang's GZA," *Guardian*, June 19, 2015, 1, www .theguardian.com/music/musicblog/2015/jun/19/mogwai-stuart-braith waite-interviews-wu-tang-clan-gza-atp.

7. CNET, "Wu-Tang Clan Celebrates 25 Years of Music and the Future of Music," YouTube video, 9:12, June 17, 2018.

8. The RZA, *The Tao of Wu* (New York: Riverhead Books, 2009), 14.

9. Ibid., 14.

10. Sydney Opera House, "Wu-Tang's RZA and Briggs in Conversation," In Conversation: Sydney Opera House, YouTube video, 23:29, December 28, 2018.

11. GZA, "The Jam."

12. Gibson, "Introducing the Band," 2.

13. RZA, *Tao of Wu*, 11.

14. Ibid., 12.

15. Joseph Lelyveld, "Brownsville Erupts in Violence over Huge Accumulations of Garbage," *New York Times*, June 13, 1970.

16. RZA, *Tao of Wu*, 13.

17. Dan Charnas, *The Big Payback: The History of the Business of Hip-Hop* (New York: New American Library, 2010), 433.

18. RZA, *Tao of Wu*, 23.

19. djvlad, "Grandmaster Caz."

20. BigBoyTV, "RZA on Wu-Tang: An American Saga, Current State of Hip Hop, Scoring Movies + More," YouTube video, 53:11, October 9, 2019.

CHAPTER 2: LIFE AS A SHORTY

1. Henry C. Murphy, *The Voyage of Verrazzano: A Chapter in the Early History of Maritime Discovery in America* (Whitefish, MT: Kessinger, 2004), 90.

2. Montreality, "RZA x Montreality—Interview," YouTube video, 16:02, June 26, 2013.

3. Joshua Jelly-Schapiro, "Wu-Tang's RZA on the Mysterious Land of Shaolin: Staten Island," in *Nonstop Metropolis: A New York City Atlas*, ed. Rebecca Solnit and Joshua Jelly-Schapiro (Oakland: Univeristy of California Press, 2016).

4. Ibid.

5. Ibid.

6. Andrew Lipman, "A Hard Bargain: The Munsee Indians Sold Staten Island under Duress—but Not Before They Got the Colony of New York to Make Some Surprising Concessions," *Slate*, April 28, 2015, 1–2.

7. Ibid.

8. John Corry, "Staten Island: The City's Offshore Bucolic Niche," *New York Times*, July 18, 1972, www.nytimes.com/1972/07/18/archives/staten-island-the-citys-offshore-bucolic-niche-staten-island-offers.html.

9. Gerald Barclay, "Killa Hill—the Park Hill Documentary," Vimeo video, 1:36:04, 2015, vimeo.com/120611149.

10. Lamont "U-God" Hawkins, *Raw: My Journey into the Wu-Tang* (New York: Picador Books, 2018), 7.

11. Ibid., 15.

12. Alexander Fruchter, "Raekwon on the Meaning of Wu-Tang, Getting Out of Staten Island, and His Motivation to Be a Great Emcee," *Ruby Hornet*, June 25, 2018, 2.

13. Ibid., 2.

14. Hawkins, *Raw*, 23.

15. Gerald K. Barclay with Jessica Gerlach-Petrovic, *Shooting the Clan: An Eyewitness to the Rise of the Wu-Tang Clan* (self-pub., Dream-Starters, 2008), 17.

16. Montreality, "Inspectah Deck (Wu-Tang) x Montreality," YouTube video, 16:50, August 23, 2012.

17. Noisey, "Wu Wisdom: Back & Forth with Wu-Tang Clan—Episode14 Part 1/2," YouTube video, 6:28, June 21, 2013.

18. Andres Tardio, "Inspectah Deck Confirms Lost 'C.R.E.A.M.' Verse & Wu-Tang Reunion Album," HipHopDX, November 14, 2013, hiphopdx.com/interviews/id.2221/title.inspectah-deck-confirms-lost -c-r-e-a-m-verse-wu-tang-reunion-album.

19. Le Banlieuzart, "Inspectah Deck Interview Pt 1 / Banlieuzart TV," YouTube video, 12:28, July 5, 2013.

20. Anthony Decurtis, "Wu-Tang Family Values," *Rolling Stone*, July 10, 1997, 3.

21. Montreality, "Ghostface Killah x Montreality—Interview," You-Tube video, 22:59, February 19, 2013.

22. Hawkins, *Raw*, 43–44.

23. Kotori Magazine, "Wu-Tang's RZA Talks to Kotori about His Producing History," YouTube video (channel discontinued), November 20, 2007.

24. Hawkins, *Raw*, 44.

25. Stephon Turner (a.k.a. Raison Allah), director, *Dirty: One Word Can Change the World: The Official ODB Biography* (Zu Films, 2009), DVD.

26. Ibid.

27. Sam McDonald, "O.D.B.'s Dad," *NewPort News Daily Press*, December 20, 2004, 2.

28. Montreality, "RZA x Montreality."

29. ChasinDatPaperMedia, "Ol Dirty Bastard—Dirty Thoughts (Documentary)," YouTube video, 39:47, May 20, 2011.

CHAPTER 3: SUPREME CLIENTELE

1. Khalik Allah, "Popa Wu a 5% Story," YouTube video, 1:30:03, December 17, 2019.

2. Ibid.

3. Ibid.

4. Michael Muhammad Knight, *The Five Percenters: Islam, Hip-Hop and the Gods of New York* (London: One World, 2007), 64.

5. Ibid., plate 11.

6. Ibid., 263.

7. Ibid., 38–39.

8. Ibid., 37.

9. Rachel Dretzin and Phil Bertelsen, directors, *Who Killed Malcolm X?* (Ark Media, 2020), on Netflix.

10. Knight, *The Five Percenters*, 59–61.

11. Ibid., 120.

12. The RZA, *The Tao of Wu* (New York: Riverhead Books, 2009), 30–31.

13. Ibid., 93.

14. San Francisco Public Library, "2005 RZA of Wu-Tang Clan at San Francisco Public Library," YouTube video, 1:07:35, August 29, 2019.

15. RZA, *Tao of Wu*, 40–41.

16. Rakim with Bakari Kitwana, *Sweat the Technique: Revelations on Creativity from the Lyrical Genius* (New York: Amistad, 2019), 16.

17. Ibid., 18.

18. ABORT TV, "ABORT TV Presents: The GZA/Genius—The ABORT Interview," Vimeo video, 7:45, September 10, 2008, Random Pictures, vimeo.com/aborttv.

19. RZA, *Tao of Wu*, 39.

20. Allah, "Popa Wu."

21. Montreality, "Raekwon X Montreality—Interview 2013," YouTube video, 17:04, July 2, 2013.

22. Lamont "U-God" Hawkins, *Raw: My Journey into the Wu-Tang* (New York: Picador Books, 2018), 35.

23. SXSW, "U-God / Wu-Tang Clan / SXSW 2018," YouTube video, 52:02, March 16, 2018.

24. Hawkins, *Raw*, 37.

25. RZA, *Tao of Wu*, 40.

CHAPTER 4: SHAOLIN VS. WU-TANG

1. Michael Gonzales, "Live Girls, Lonely Boys," *Catapult*, September 7, 2016, 1.

2. Janos Marton, "Today in NYC History: In 1904, Longacre Square Renamed 'Times Square,'" Untapped New York, April 8, 2015, untapped cities.com/2015/04/08/today-in-nyc-history-in-1904-longacre-square -renamed-times-square/.

3. Bill Landis and Michelle Clifford, *Sleazoid Express: A Mind-Twisting Tour through the Grindhouse Cinema of Times Square* (New York: Fireside, 2002), 3.

4. Ibid., 272.

5. Ibid., 273.

6. Ibid., 3.

7. SXSW, "RZA Keynote / SXSW Live 2015 / SXSW ON," YouTube video, 1:02:55, April 20, 2015.

8. Joshua Jelly-Schapiro, "Wu-Tang's RZA on the Mysterious Land of Shaolin: Staten Island," in *Nonstop Metropolis: A New York City Atlas*, ed. Rebecca Solnit and Joshua Jelly-Schapiro (Oakland: University of California Press, 2016), 4.

9. Ibid.

10. Vanity Fair, "Wu-Tang's RZA Breaks Down 10 Kung Fu Films He's Sampled / Vanity Fair," YouTube video, 13:34, September 3, 2019.

11. Dr. Craig D. Reid, *The Ultimate Guide to Martial Arts Movies of the 1970s: 500+ Films Loaded with Action, Weapons & Warriors* (Seoul: Black Belt Communications, 2010), 102.

12. KickinAzz Entertainment, "The RZA Interview 36th Chamber of Shaolin," YouTube video, 9:57, April 18, 2012.

13. SXSW, "RZA Keynote."

14. KickinAzz, "RZA Interview."

15. Vijay Prashad, *Everybody Was Kung Fu Fighting: Afro-Asian Connections and the Myth of Cultural Purity* (Boston: Beacon, 2001), 127.

16. Sundiata Keita Cha-Jua, "Black Audiences, Blaxploitation and Kung Fu Films, and Challenges to White Celluloid Masculinity," in *China Forever: The Shaw Brothers and Diasporic Cinema*, ed. Poshek Fu (Urbana: University of Illinois Press, 2008), 216.

17. Bruce Lee, *Tao of Jeet Kune Do* (Santa Clarita, CA: Ohara, 1975), 12.

18. Cha-Jua, "Black Audiences," 215.

19. Darius James, *That's Blaxploitation: Roots of the Baadasssss 'Tude (Rated X by an All-Whyte Jury)* (New York: St. Martin's Griffin, 1995), 23.

20. Cha-Jua, "Black Audiences," 217.

21. David Remnick, *King of the World: Muhammad Ali and the Rise of an American Hero* (New York: Random House, 1988), 287.

22. David Desser, "The Kung Fu Craze: Hong Kong Cinema's First American Reception," in *The Cinema of Hong Kong: History, Arts, Identity*, ed. Poshek Fu and David Desser (New York: Cambridge University Press, 2000), 38.

23. Fanon Che Wilkins, "Shaw Brothers Cinema and the Hip-Hop Imagination," in *China Forever: The Shaw Brothers and Diasporic Cinema*, ed. Poshek Fu (Urbana: University of Illinois Press, 2008), 230.

24. 88Nine Radio Milwaukee, "An Interview with Wu-Tang Clan's RZA," YouTube video, 29:41, August 30, 2018.

25. The RZA, *The Tao of Wu* (New York: Riverhead Books, 2009), 52–53.

26. Stephen Teo, *Hong Kong Cinema: The Extra Dimensions* (London: British Film Institute, 1997), 108.

27. Wilkins, "Shaw Brothers," 233.

28. Shaolin Gung Fu Institute, "History of Shaolin Temples," accessed February 2020, www.shaolin.com/shaolin_history.aspx (site discontinued).

29. 88Nine Radio, "Wu-Tang Clan's RZA."

30. RZA, *Tao of Wu*, 53.

31. 88Nine Radio, "Wu Tang Clan's RZA."

32. KickinAzz, "36 Chambers of Shaolin."

33. Ibid.

34. RZA, *Tao of Wu*, 56.

35. 88Nine Radio, "Wu Tang Clan's RZA."

36. Troy Styles, "GZA from Wu Tang Clan Interview with DJ Troy Styles at the Cop Shop," YouTube video, 16:38, September 9, 2018.

37. Mr. Cass, "Hip Hop Icons the GZA Interview," YouTube video, 1:00:25, August 24, 2016.

38. Ibid.

39. RZA, *Tao of Wu*, 109.

CHAPTER 5: THE CRIME SIDE

1. Richard Lowe and Martin Torgoff, *Planet Rock: The Story of Hip-Hop and the Crack Generation* (Prodigious Media, 2011), VH1 Rock Docs.

2. Ibid.

3. David Farber, *Crack: Rock Cocaine, Street Capitalism, and the Decade of Greed* (Cambridge: Cambridge University Press, 2019), 40.

4. Ibid., 41.

5. Art Harris, "The Drug Game," *Washington Post*, March 11, 1984.

6. Farber, *Crack*, 43.

7. Ibid., 76.

8. Michael Massing, "Crack's Destructive Sprint across America," *New York Times Magazine*, October 1, 1989.

9. Alexander Fruchter, "Raekwon on the Meaning of Wu-Tang, Getting Out of Staten Island, and His Motivation to Be a Great Emcee," *Ruby Hornet*, June 25, 2018, rubyhornet.com/rh-interview-raekwon-on-the-meaning-of-wu-tang-getting-out-of-staten-island-and-his-motivation-to-be-a-great-emcee/.

10. Ibid.

11. Lamont "U-God" Hawkins, *Raw: My Journey into the Wu-Tang* (New York: Picador, 2018), 68.

12. Fruchter, "Raekwon."

13. Hawkins, *Raw*, 68.

14. Ibid., 70.

15. B High ATL, "U GOD: *Raw: My Journey into the Wu-Tang*, Son Getting Shot, Ol Dirty Bastard," YouTube video, 37:29, March 13, 2018.

16. Farber, *Crack*, 133.

17. Madison Gray, "New York's Rockefeller Drug Laws," *Time*, April 2, 2009, 1.

18. Montreality, "Method Man x Montreality—Interview," YouTube video, 10:24, January 21, 2013.

19. AerlaFawn, "Bonnie Chats with Hip-Hop Legend RZA (Wu-Tang Clan)," YouTube video, 7:34, October 26, 2009.

20. Ibid.

21. Fruchter, "Raekwon."

22. Andres Tardio, "Inspectah Deck Confirms Lost 'C.R.E.A.M.' Verse & Wu Tang Reunion Album," HipHopDX, November 14, 2013, hipho pdx.com/interviews/id.2221/title.inspectah-deck-confirms-lost-c-r-e-a -m-verse-wu-tang-reunion-album.

23. Ibid.

24. Le Balieuzart, "Inspectah Deck Interview Pt 1 / Banlieuzart TV," YouTube video, 12:25, July 5, 2013.

25. REVOLT TV, "Wu Tang Clan: Drink Champs (Full Episode)," YouTube video, 3:10:19, December 27, 2017.

26. Breakfast Club Power 105.1 FM, "Method Man Tells Crack Stories, Talks Playing a Pimp, Wu-Tang & More," YouTube video, 35:30, October 6, 2017.

27. Hawkins, *Raw*, 111.

28. Ibid., 118.

29. DJBooth, "Raekwon Interview: My Hip-Hop Heroes, RZA & GZA's Influence," YouTube video, 3:07, May 7, 2015.

30. Hot 97, "RZA Responds to Raekwon on Hot 97Morning," YouTube video, 40:27, April 21, 2014.

31. REVOLT TV, "Drink Champs."

32. Gerald Barclay, "Killa Hill—the Park Hill Documentary," Vimeo video, 1:36:04, 2015, vimeo.com/120611149.

33. Lowe and Torgott, *Planet Rock*.

CHAPTER 6: LABELS

1. Brian Coleman, *Check the Technique: Liner Notes for Hip-Hop Junkies* (New York: Villard, 2007), 451.

2. Ibid., 452.

3. GlobalGrindTV, "RZA Explains the Origins of the Wu-Tang to Funkmaster Flex," YouTube video, 5:35, October 17, 2012.

4. Kotori Magazine, "Wu-Tang's RZA Talks to Kotori about His Producing History," YouTube video (channel discontinued), November 20, 2007.

5. Wu-Tang Clan, "Wu-Tang Clan—Ghostface Shares How He First Got Down with the Wu (247HH Exclusive)," YouTube video, 3:58, December 13, 2014.

6. Kotori Magazine, "RZA Talks to Kotori."

7. Coleman, *Check the Technique*, 454.

8. Ibid., 455.

9. Vinny141, "Inspectah Deck Interview," YouTube video, 3:52, February 14, 2008.

10. Phillip Mlynar, "Q&A: Rapper 9th Prince on His Older Brother RZA and the Early Days of Wu-Tang Clan," *Spin*, October 4, 2010.

11. The RZA, *The Tao of Wu* (New York: Riverhead Books, 2009), 57–58.

12. The RZA, with Chris Norris, *The Wu-Tang Manual* (New York: Penguin Books, 2005), 62–63.

13. Canadian Music Week, "2008: RZA Interview," YouTube video, 39:25, December 2, 2014.

14. Ben Merlis, *Goin' Off: The Story of the Juice Crew and Cold Chillin' Records* (BMG Books, 2019), 169.

CHAPTER 7: FORM LIKE VOLTRON

1. Rory D. Webb, "Wu-Tang's RZA Found His Second Chance in Steubenville," *Pittsburgh City Paper*, April 10, 2013.

2. The RZA, *The Tao of Wu* (New York: Riverhead Books, 2009), 89.

3. Ibid., 89.

4. Ibid., 90.

5. Ibid., 93.

6. Jake Paine, "RZA Explains How His Attempted Murder Case Transformed Him," Ambrosia for Heads, October 6, 2018, ambrosiaforheads.com/2018/10/rza-ohio-charge-case-transformation-wu-tang-clan/.

7. RZA, *Tao of Wu*, 90–91.

8. San Francisco Public Library, "2005 RZA of Wu-Tang Clan at San Francisco Public Library," YouTube video, 1:07:35, August 29, 2019.

9. *Wu-Tang Clan: Of Mics and Men*, directed by Sacha Jenkins, aired May 10–31, 2019, on Showtime.

10. Paine, "RZA Explains."

11. San Francisco Public Library, "2005 RZA of Wu-Tang Clan."

12. Paine, "RZA Explains."

13. RZA, *Tao of Wu*, 94.

14. Ibid., 95.

15. Canadian Music Week, "2008: RZA Interview," YouTube video, 39:25, December 2, 2014.

16. "The RZA Interview," *Fat Lace*, December 2007, fatlacemagazine.com/2007/12/rza-interview/.

17. Canadian Music Week, "2008 RZA Interview."

18. Ibid.

19. Sacha Jenkins, "Looking for Jesus," *Vibe Magazine*, December 1999/January 2000, 169.

20. djvlad, "Inspectah Deck: After 'C.R.E.A.M.' Dropped I Knew Wu-Tang Made It," YouTube video, 7:39, June 17, 2015.

21. Lamont "U-God" Hawkins, *Raw: My Journey into the Wu-Tang* (New York: Picador Books, 2018), 145.

22. djvlad, "Raekwon: Method Man Had Most Passion in Wu-Tang," YouTube video, 4:22, March 17, 2013.

23. Ibid.

24. Gerard Barclay, "Killa Hill—the Park Hill Documentary," Vimeo video, 1:36:04, 2015, vimeo.com/120611149.

25. RZA, *Tao of Wu*, 105.

26. Kotori Magazine, "Wu-Tang's RZA Talks to Kotori about His Producing History," YouTube video (channel discontinued), November 20, 2007.

27. Ibid.

28. Ibid.

29. RZA, *Tao of Wu*, 105, 111.

30. Hawkins, *Raw*, 145.

31. djvlad, "Raekwon Details Friction between Wu-Tang Members (Flashback)," YouTube video, 10:09, September 12, 2019.

32. Ibid.

33. "RZA Interview," *Fat Lace*.

34. ForbesDVDPromo, "Popa Wu Says Rae & Ghost Used to Shoot Guns at Each Other Until RZA Brought Them Together Musically," YouTube video, 12:12, December 30, 2013.

35. EdLover4Real, "Ed Lover Show: Raekwon Interview," YouTube video, 27:14, March 17, 2015.

36. Paine, "RZA Explains."

37. Hot 97, "Rosenberg Interviews . . . Masta Killa of Wu Tang Clan," YouTube video, 41:29, October 12, 2017.

38. Ibid.

39. NatureSoundMusic, "Masta Killa Speaks on Early Days of Wu-Tang," YouTube video, 4:59, December 20, 2012.

40. Ibid.

41. RusteT1, "Enter the Wu-Tang Documentary (1994)," YouTube video, 20:30, January 28, 2013.

42. Ibid.

43. EdLover4Real, "Raekwon Interview."

44. Brian Coleman, *Check the Technique: Liner Notes for Hip-Hop Junkies* (New York: Villard, 2007), 463.

45. Ibid., 463.

46. Breakfast Club Power 105.1 FM, "RZA + Mathematics Break Down the New Album and Discuss Wu History," YouTube video, 42:08, October 16, 2017.

47. Frannie Kelley, "The Wu-Tang Clan's 20-Year Plan," NPR: The Record Music News from NPR, April 8, 2013, www.npr.org/sections /therecord/2013/04/08/176519640/the-wu-tang-clans-20-year-plan.

48. DubCNN, "Inspectah Deck: After 'Cream' Dropped I Knew Wu Tang Made It," October 24, 2012.

49. Kelley, "20-Year Plan."

50. DubCNN, "Inspectah Deck."

CHAPTER 8: ENTER THE WU-TANG

1. djvlad, "Steve Rifkind on Signing Wu-Tang, Only Label That Let Members Get a Solo Deal," YouTube video, 12:37, May 1, 2017.

2. Ibid.

3. Dan Charnas, *The Big Payback: The History of the Business of Hip-Hop* (New York: New American Library, 2010), 442.

4. Ibid., 444.

5. Ibid., 445.

6. Ibid., 446.

7. Alan Page, *Enter the Wu-Tang: How Nine Men Changed Hip-Hip Forever* (self-pub., Lone Gunman Media, 2014), 19.

8. EdLover4Real, "Ed Lover Show—Raekwon Interview," YouTube video, 27:14, March 17, 2015.

9. djvlad, "Steve Rifkind on Signing Wu-Tang."

10. Charnas, *The Big Payback*, 448.

11. Ibid., 448.

12. Canadian Music Week, "2008: RZA Interview," YouTube video, 39:25, December 2, 2014.

13. Vinny141, "Old Wu-Tang Interview, Pt. 1," YouTube video, 7:31, February 17, 2008.

14. Ibid.

15. Kenny Goodman, "The Making of Wu-Tang Clan's Enter the Wu-Tang (36 Chambers) Album Cover (1993) with Photographer Daniel Hastings," Egotripland.com (site discontinued), July 12, 2016.

16. Ibid.

17. Ibid.

18. Ibid.

19. Ibid.

20. Phillip Mlynar, "Engineering the Wu-Tang Clan: An Oral History of What Happened Behind the Console during the Making of One of the Most Important Debut Albums in Hip-Hop," Red Bull Music Academy, June 19, 2018, daily.redbullmusicacademy.com/2018/06/engineering-wu-tang-clan.

21. Phillip Mlynar, "Clan in the Back: The Behind-the-Scenes Oral History of 'Enter the Wu-Tang: 36 Chambers,'" *Spin Magazine*, November 5, 2013.

22. "The RZA Interview," *Fat Lace*, December 2007, fatlacemagazine .com/2007/12/rza-interview/.

23. Mlynar, "Clan in the Back."

24. Ibid.

25. Tim Noakes, "RZA's Ghetto Symphonies," *Dazed & Confused*, August 2013, www.dazeddigital.com/music/article/16679/1/dazed93-rzas -ghetto-symphonies.

26. ROLI, "Soundpack Stories: RZA's Spoonful of Grit," YouTube video, 6:17, January 5, 2017.

27. Mlynar, "Clan in the Back."

28. Ashley Heath, "Crosstown Trafffic," *The Face*, 1998, 78.

29. Noakes, "Ghetto Symphonies."

30. Heath, "Crosstown Trafffic."

31. EdLover4Real, "Raekwon Interview."

32. WuuuTangStyle, "Exclusive Interview w/ RZA (1997)," YouTube video, 14:34, August 20, 2011.

33. NatureSoundMusic, "Masta Killa Speaks on Early Days of Wu-Tang," YouTube video, 4:59, December 20, 2012.

34. Ibid.

35. Davy Reed, "Are the Wu-Tang Clan Related to a Native American Tribe? 10 Myths Busted," *The Face*, May 14, 2019, theface.com/music /wu-tang-clan-mythbusters.

36. Brian Coleman, *Check the Technique: Liner Notes for Hip-Hop Junkies* (New York: Villard, 2007), 465.

37. Andres Tardio, "Inspectah Deck Confirms Lost 'C.R.E.A.M.' Verse & Wu-Tang Reunion Album," HipHopDX, November 14, 2013, hipho pdx.com/interviews/id.2221/title.inspectah-deck-confirms-lost-c-r-e-a -m-verse-wu-tang-reunion-album.

38. 247HH.com, "Raekwon—My Homie Made Me Rewrite My 'C.R.E.A.M.' Verse (247HH Exclusive)," YouTube video, 3:34, August 26, 2015.

39. Ibid.

40. djvlad, "U-God on Issues with RZA, Mike Tyson Robbery, Leonardo Dicaprio, Son Getting Shot," YouTube video, 57:41, May 28, 2019.

41. Lamont "U-God" Hawkins, *Raw: My Journey into the Wu-Tang* (New York: Picador Books, 2018), 184–185.

42. djvlad, "U-God on Issues."

43. Coleman, *Check the Technique*, 466.

44. Ibid., 466.

45. Reed, "10 Myths Busted."

46. Ghetto Communicator, "Wu-Tang Clan: Enter the Wu-Tang (36 Chambers)," *The Source*, February 1994.

47. Ibid.

48. Toure Neblett, "Album Review: Wu-Tang Clan: Enter the Wu-Tang (36 Chambers)," *Rolling Stone*, April 7, 1994.

49. Ibid.

50. Coleman, *Check the Technique*, 460.

CHAPTER 9: METHOD MAN / TICAL

1. Insanul Ahmed, "Method Man Breaks Down His 25 Most Essential Songs," *Complex*, October 19, 2011, www.complex.com/music/2011/10/method-man-25-essential-songs/.

2. Phillip Mlynar, "Clan in the Back: The Behind-the-Scenes Oral History of 'Enter the Wu-Tang (36 Chambers),'" *Spin Magazine*, November 3, 2013.

3. Hot 97, "Amazing Method Man Interview!! Too Good to Title!!," YouTube video, 42:47, March 12, 2015.

4. Ibid.

5. Gerald K. Barclay, with Jessica Gerlach-Petrovic, *Shooting the Clan: An Eyewitness to the Rise of the Wu-Tang Clan* (self-pub., Dream-Starters, 2018), 86.

6. Bill Adler, Dan Charnas, Rick Rubin, and Russell Simmons, *Def Jam Recordings: The First 25 Years of the Last Great Record Label* (New York: Rizzoli, 2011).

7. djvlad, "Raekwon: Method Man Had Most Passion in Wu-Tang," YouTube video, 4:22, March 17, 2013.

8. Hot 97, "Amazing Method Man Interview."

9. Ahmed, "Method Man Breaks Down His 25."

10. Paul Meara, "RZA Discusses Losing Hundreds of Wu Tang Clan Beats & 2 Albums in Floods," Ambrosia for Heads, October 8, 2018, ambrosiaforheads.com/2018/10/rza-wu-tang-clan-lost-albums/.

11. Donnell Alexander, "Life Is Hectic: The Wu-Tang Clan's Success Is Dampened by Personal Tragedy," *The Source*, June 1994.

12. Zeke62 Nostalgia, "Wu-Tang Clan 1994 Interview," YouTube video, 3:42, March 20, 2017.

13. Ibid.

14. Ibid.

15. Joe Vitale, "How District Attorney's Investigation into 1994 Police Custody Death Unfolded," *Staten Island Advance*, August 6, 2014.

16. Gerald Barclay, "Killa Hill—the Park Hill Documentary," Vimeo video, 1:36:04, 2015, vimeo.com/120611149.

17. Ahmed, "Method Man Breaks Down His 25."

18. BornBlessed2011, "ODB & Method Man Interview," YouTube video, 31:22, April 1, 2012.

19. Chris Poggiali, "Drive-In Movie on WNEW Metromedia Channel 5," DVD Drive-In, dvddrive-in.com/TV%20Guide/driveinmovie5.htm.

20. Ahmed, "Method Man Breaks Down His 25."

21. Kotori Magazine, "Wu-Tang's RZA Talks to Kotori about His Producing History," YouTube video (channel discontinued), November 20, 2007.

22. Razor Blade, "Wu-Tang Clan on MTV Ultra Sound Pt. 1," YouTube video, 6:47, April 20, 2010.

23. Ibid.

24. Ahmed, "Method Man Breaks Down His 25."

25. Ibid.

26. Ibid.

27. David Weiss, "Chung King Ceases Varick Street Operations," *Sonic Scoop*, January 6, 2010.

28. Daniel Isenberg, "Raekwon Breaks Down His 25 Most Essential Songs," *Complex*, March 9, 2011, www.complex.com/music/2011/03/rae kwon-25-essential-songs/.

29. Ahmed, "Method Man Breaks Down His 25."

30. ROLI, "RZA in Conversation with Roland Lamb at CES 2017," YouTube video, 29:09, January 13, 2017.

31. Ibid.

32. J. Nadir Omowale, "Uniquely Blue Raspberry," *BLAC*, September 23, 2011, www.blac.media/arts-culture/uniquely-blue-raspberry.

33. Wu4ever90, "Method Man at Def Jam Offices 1994," YouTube video, 4:48, October 15, 2009.

34. Anton and Erin Garcia-Fernandez, "Sarah Vaughan's Snowbound: Songs for a Snowy Day," *The Vintage Bandstand* (blog), February 28, 2015, vintagebandstand.blogspot.com/2015/02/sarah-vaughans-snowbound -songs-for.html.

CHAPTER 10: OL' DIRTY BASTARD / RETURN TO THE 36 CHAMBERS

1. Stephon Turner (a.k.a. Raison Allah), director, *Dirty: One Word Can Change the World: The Official ODB Biography* (Zu Films, 2009), DVD.

2. Amazon Music, "Ol' Dirty Bastard and the Legacy of 'Return to the 36 Chambers,' Mini-Doc / Amazon Music," YouTube video, 16:52, March 26, 2020.

3. The Break Is Over, "Dante Ross Talks Signing Old Dirty Bastard," YouTube video, 7:35, January 21, 2014.

4. Ibid.

5. Buddha Monk and Mickey Hess, *The Dirty Version: On Stage, in the Studio, and in the Streets with Ol' Dirty Bastard* (New York: Dey Street Books, 2015), 41.

6. Ibid.

7. Sacha Jenkins, "Looking for Jesus," *Vibe*, December 1999/January 2000, 170.

8. Frank151, "John King (Chung King Studios) Interview for Chapter 51: Leaders—Frank151," YouTube video, 3:19, May 22, 2013.

9. Mike Stree, "RZA of the Wu-Tang Clan at ODB's Funeral," YouTube video, 8:00, July 25, 2009.

10. Ali Shaheed Muhammad and Frannie Kelly, "Dante Ross: 'We Wanted Our Own Universe,'" NPR: Microphone Check, November 14, 2014, www.npr.org/sections/microphonecheck/2014/11/04/361414881/dante-ross-we-wanted-our-own-universe.

11. Worldwidelegends5, "Ol Dirty Bastard Pickin Up Food Stamps in a Limo!!!!," YouTube video, 3:41, May 23, 2013.

12. Ibid.

13. Frank Broughton, "You Phat Bastard," *Hip-Hop Connection*, March 1995.

14. Vinny141, "Old Wu-Tang Interview, part 2," YouTube video, 6:55, February 17, 2008.

15. Martiansurvivalkit, "RZA Speaks on Using Roland MV8000 Sampler," YouTube video, 10:25, February 26, 2008.

16. Insanul Ahmed, "Method Man Breaks Down His 25 Most Essential Songs," *Complex*, October 19, 2011. www.complex.com/music/2011/10/method-man-25-essential-songs/.

17. Monk and Hess, *The Dirty Version*.

18. Turner, *One Word Can Change the World*.

19. Cian Traynor, "Keepin' It Dirty: A Celebration of ODB's Return to the 36 Chambers," *The Quietus*, March 30, 2015, thequietus.com/articles/17525-odb-return-to-the-36-chambers-ol-dirty-bastard.

20. Ibid.

CHAPTER 11: RAEKWON / ONLY BUILT 4 CUBAN LINX

1. Dan Charnas, *The Big Payback: The History of the Business of Hip-Hop* (New York: New American Library, 2010), 480.

2. Ibid., 481.

3. Sway's Universe, "Raekwon Talks Early Dynamics of the Wu-Tang Clan and Details of Forthcoming Album 'F.I.L.A.,'" YouTube video, 58:42, February 25, 2015.

4. Raekwon, "Raekwon—Ghostface and I Have a Great Chemistry (247HH Exclusive)," YouTube video, 3:24, August 25, 2015.

5. TimWestwoodTV, "Ghostface Killah 'Don't Make Me Old School' Interview—Westwood," YouTube video, 9:45, June 16, 2011.

6. Raekwon, "Great Chemistry."

7. Alvin Blanco, "Wu-Tang Clan," Red Bull Music Academy, 2012, www.redbullmusicacademy.com/lectures/wu-tang-lecture.

8. 247HH.com, "Raekwon—Wrote Only Built 4 Cuban Linx in the Bahamas with Ghostface (247HH Exclusive)," YouTube video, 1:39, August 25, 2015.

9. Paul W. Arnold, Paul Cantor, Jon Caramanica, Andrea Duncan, Toshitaka Kondo, Chairman Mao, Adam Matthews, and Vannessa Satten, compilers, "The Making of Only Built 4 Cuban Linx," *XXL*, August 1, 2010, www.xxlmag.com/raekwon-the-making-of-only-built-for-cuban-linx/.

10. Sway's Universe, "Early Dynamics."

11. David Ma, "Raekwon Speaks on Only Built 4 Cuban Linx . . . Pt. II," *Wax Poetics*, July 30, 2009.

12. 923 Entertainment, "#Raekwon and #RZA #ThePurpleTape #OnlyBuilt4CubanLinx #25thAnniversary," YouTube video, 30:27, August 2, 2020.

13. Arnold et al., "Making of Only Built 4 Cuban Linx."

14. EdLover4Real, "Ed Lover Show—Raekwon Interview," YouTube video, 27:14, March 17, 2015.

15. Ibid.

16. Blanco, "Wu-Tang Clan."

17. Arnold et al., "Making of Only Built 4 Cuban Linx."

18. Ibid.

19. Ma, "Raekwon Speaks."

20. Arnold et al., "Making of Only Built 4 Cuban Linx."

21. Ibid.

22. Ibid.

23. Ibid.

24. Daniel Isenberg, "Raekwon Breaks Down His 25 Most Essential Songs," *Complex*, March 9, 2011, www.complex.com/music/2011/03/raekwon-25-essential-songs/.

25. DJBooth, "Raekwon Interview—Grabbing 'Criminology' from RZA and Wu-Tang's Early Recording Process," YouTube video, 2:37, May 7, 2015.

26. Isenberg, "Raekwon Breaks Down His 25."

27. DJBooth, "Raekwon Interview—'Criminology,' Scarface Samples and Ghostface's Robes," YouTube video, 3:45, May 7, 2015.

28. Ibid.

29. Ibid.

30. Arnold et al., "Making of Only Built 4 Cuban Linx."

31. Isenberg, "Raekwon Breaks Down His 25 Most Essential Songs."

32. Ibid.

33. Ibid.

34. Arnold et al., "Making of Only Built 4 Cuban Linx."

35. Ibid.

36. Ibid.

37. Ibid.

38. Lamont "U-God" Hawkins, *Raw: My Journey into the Wu-Tang* (Picador Books: New York, 2018), 137.

39. Arnold et al., "Making of Only Built 4 Cuban Linx."

40. Blanco, "Wu-Tang Clan."

41. Arnold et al., "Making of Only Built 4 Cuban Linx."

42. Ibid.

43. Ibid.

44. Ibid.

45. Blanco, "Wu-Tang Clan."

46. Arnold et al., "Making of Only Built 4 Cuban Linx."

47. Ibid.

48. Ma, "Raekwon Speaks."

49. Isenberg, "Raekwon Breaks Down His 25."

50. Arnold et al., "Making of Only Built 4 Cuban Linx."

51. 247HH.com, "Cappadonna—'Ice Cream' Was My First Wu Work, Trying to Cash a $60,000 Check," YouTube video, 5:48, November 3, 2018.

52. Ibid.

53. Ibid.

54. Ibid.

55. Ibid.

56. Ibid.

57. Ibid.

58. Arnold et al., "Making of Only Built 4 Cuban Linx."

59. Ibid.

60. Ibid.

61. Isenberg, "Raekwon Breaks Down His 25."

62. Ibid.

63. Ma, "Raekwon Speaks."

64. Arnold et al., "Making of Only Built 4 Cuban Linx."

CHAPTER 12: GZA / LIQUID SWORDS

1. The RZA with Chris Norris, *The Wu-Tang Manual* (New York: Riverhead Freestyle, 2005), 8–9.

2. Eric Diep, "'Liquid Swords' Turns 20: GZA Looks Back on His Recently-Platinum Magnum Opus," *Billboard*, November 7, 2015, www.billboard.com/articles/columns/hip-hop/6754004/gza-liquid-swords-anniversary-interview.

3. Harriet Gibsone, "Introducing the Band: Mogwai's Stuart Braithwaite Interviews Wu-Tang's GZA," *Guardian*, June 6, 2015, www.theguardian.com/music/musicblog/2015/jun/19/mogwai-stuart-braithwaite-interviews-wu-tang-clan-gza-atp.

4. Tim Noakes, "RZA's Ghetto Symphonies," *Dazed & Confused*, July 22, 2013, www.dazeddigital.com/music/article/16679/1/dazed93-rzas-ghetto-symphonies.

5. Diep, "Liquid Swords."

6. Ibid.

7. Alex Shtaerman, "GZA Interview: Wu-Tang Clan's Grandmaster of Rhymes," *Riotsound*, February 18, 2016.

8. David Ma, "Wu-Tang Clan's GZA Runs Down Every Track off Liquid Swords," *Wax Poetics*, May 30, 2014.

9. Corbin Reiff, "20 Years, 20 Questions: GZA Revisits 'Liquid Swords,'" *Spin*, November 6, 2015, www.spin.com/2015/11/gza-liquid-swords-20-years-anniversary-interview/.

10. Diep, "Liquid Swords."

11. Ibid.

12. FridaeTV, "Fab 5 Freddy Interviews GZA," YouTube video, 7:55, June 23, 2009.

13. Ibid.

14. Matt Hall, "Out of the Dogghouse," *Select*, January 1996, 86.

15. Noakes, "Ghetto Symphonies."

16. Ma, "Liquid Swords."

17. Sherron Shabazz, "A Conversation with GZA," *The Real Hip-Hop*, August 26, 2019, therealhip-hop.com/a-conversation-with-gza/.

18. Ma, "Liquid Swords."

19. Ibid.

20. Ibid.

21. Ibid.

22. Ibid.

23. Ibid.

24. Angus Batey, "20 Years On: Angus Batey on Liquid Swords by GZA," *The Quietus*, July 27, 2015, thequietus.com/articles/18399-gza-liquid-swords-review-anniversary.

25. Ma, "Liquid Swords."

26. Ibid.

27. Mr Cass, "Hip-Hop Icons: The GZA Interview," YouTube video, 1:00:25, August 23, 2016.

28. Ma, "Liquid Swords."

29. Ibid.

30. San Francisco Public Library, "2005 RZA of Wu-Tang Clan at San Francisco Public Library," YouTube video, 1:07:35, August 29, 2019.

CHAPTER 13: GHOSTFACE KILLAH / IRONMAN

1. Desus & Mero, "The Legendary Method Man (Extended Cut)," YouTube video, 22:18, October 6, 2017.

2. djvlad, "Inspectah Deck Details Losing First Album to RZA's Flood," YouTube video, 7:08, June 25, 2015.

3. Ibid.

4. "Classic Material: Ghostface Killah on Ironman," *XXL*, Fall 2016.

5. Ibid.

6. Carter Higgins, "Ghostface Killah: On a Mission to Make Diabetes Ghost," BlackDoctor.org, May 9, 2016, blackdoctor.org/ghostface-killah-making-diabetes-ghost/.

7. Andres Tardio, "Ghostface Killah Says 'Illmatic' Made Him 'Step His Pen Game Up,'" HipHopDX, May 30, 2013, hiphopdx.com/interviews/id.2116/title.ghostface-killah-says-illmatic-made-him-step-his-pen-game-up#.

8. Ibid.

9. "Ghostface Killah on Ironman," *XXL*.

10. Jeff Weiss, "Ghostface Killah: *Supreme Clientele*," *Pitchfork*, June 4, 2017, pitchfork.com/reviews/albums/23207-supreme-clientele/.

11. Razor Blade, "Wu-Tang Clan on MTV Ultra Sound, Pt. III," YouTube video, 6:29, April 20, 2010.

12. Wilson Morales, "*The Education of Sonny Carson*: An Interview with Michael Campus," BlackFilm.com, November 2002, www.blackfilm.com/20021122/features/michaelcampus.shtml.

13. Ibid.

14. Jonathan Ben-Menachem, "Consequence on the '96 Def Jam Holiday Party Brawl," *Complex: The 1996 Project: Looking Back at the Year Hip-Hop Embraced Success*, February 22, 2016, www.complex.com/music/2016/02/the-1996-project-consequence-def-jam-holiday-party-fight.

15. "Ghostface Killah on Ironman," *XXL*.

16. Ibid.

17. Ibid.

18. ForbesDVDPromo, "Cappadonna from Wu-Tang Talks about When He Was a Cab Driver and Rappers Wearing Fake Jewelry," YouTube video, 11:12, March 31, 2014.

19. Hot 97, "Rosenberg Interviews . . . Masta Killa of Wu Tang Clan," YouTube video, 41:29, October 12, 2017.

20. Daniel Isenberg, "Raekwon Breaks Down His 25 Most Essential Songs," *Complex*, March 9, 2011, www.complex.com/music/2011/03/raekwon-25-essential-songs/.

21. Ibid.

22. Ibid.

CHAPTER 14: WU-TANG FOREVER

1. Dan Charnas, *The Big Payback: The History of the Business of Hip-Hop* (New York: New American Library, 2010), 505.

2. Insanul Ahmed, "Method Man Breaks Down His 25 Most Essential Songs," *Complex*, October 19, 2011.

3. Brendan I. Koerner, "Judge Kuffner's Fifteen Minutes," Microkhan (blog), posted May 22, 2009, www.microkhan.com/2009/05/22/judge-kuff ners-fifteen-minutes/.

4. Power 106 Los Angeles, "RZA Breaks Down Production on Wu-Tang's 'Triumph' and 'C.R.E.A.M.,'" YouTube video, 6:04, September 21, 2017.

5. Le Banlieuzart, "Inspectah Deck Interview, P 1 / Banlieuzart TV," YouTube video, 12:28, July 5, 2013.

6. Ibid.

7. Ibid.

8. Ibid.

9. AirMarshal Productions, "ODB / Method Man—Throwback Interview [1997]," YouTube video, 21:12, March 17, 2013.

10. Ahmed, "Method Man Breaks Down His 25."

11. Music Generation, "Ghostface Killah—The Best Verse I Wrote for Wu-Tang Clan (247HH Exclusive)," YouTube video, 2:31, December 13, 2014.

12. Ibid.

13. Ahmed, "Method Man Breaks Down His 25."

14. Ibid.

15. Roy Wilkinson, "One of These Men Is God," *Select*, July 1997.

CHAPTER 15: FOR THE CHILDREN

1. The RZA, *The Tao of Wu* (New York: Riverhead Books, 2009), 133–134.

2. Dan Charnas, *The Big Payback: The History of the Business of Hip-Hop* (New York: New American Library, 2010), 345–348.

3. Lamont "U-God" Hawkins, *Raw: My Journey into the Wu-Tang* (New York: Picador Books, 2018), 240.

4. Thomas Golianopoulos, "The Oral History of Hot 97's Summer Jam," *Complex*, June 5, 2015, www.complex.com/music/2015/06/hot-97 -summer-jam-oral-history.

5. James Sullivan, "Rage Doesn't Subside / Wu-Tang Drops Out of Tour, but Machine Plows Ahead," *SFGate*, September 14, 1997, www.sfgate .com/entertainment/article/Rage-Doesn-t-Subside-Wu-Tang-drops-out -of-tour-2827701.php.

6. Chris Nelson, "Loud Records Rep Details Alleged Wu-Tang Beating," *MTV News*, September 11, 1997, www.mtv.com/news/1188/loud -records-rep-details-alleged-wu-tang-beating/.

7. Ibid.

8. MTV News Staff, "Wu-Tang Talks about Leaving Rage Tour / Chicago Assault Allegations," *MTV News*, September 9, 1997, www.mtv .com/news/1429513/wu-tang-talks-about-leaving-rage-tour-chicago-as sault-allegations/.

9. Buddha Monk and Mickey Hess, *The Dirty Version: On Stage, in the Studio, and in the Streets with Ol' Dirty Bastard* (New York: Dey Street Books, 2015), 96.

10. Hawkins, *Raw*, 262.

11. Ibid.

12. Christopher John Farley, "Hip-Hop Nation," *Time*, February 8, 1999, 56.

13. djvlad, "U-God on Issues with RZA, Mike Tyson Robbery, Leonardo DiCaprio, Son Getting Shot," YouTube video, 57:41, May 28, 2019.

14. djvlad, "Cappadonna Tells Story of ODB Taking Mic from BIG," YouTube video, 3:53, November 10, 2013.

15. Monk and Hess, *The Dirty Version*, 103.

16. 247HH.com, "Steve Rifkind on RZA Friendship and ODB Grammy Interruption Was Because Wu-Tang Lost (2477HH Exclusive)," YouTube video, 2:50, November 10, 2018.

17. Jeff Weiss, "Ghostface Killah: *Supreme Clientele*," *Pitchfork*, June 4, 2017, pitchfork.com/reviews/albums/23207-supreme-clientele/.

CHAPTER 16: TEARZ

1. Chris Nelson, "Jailed Ghostface Killah to Answer Weapons Charge," *MTV News*, February 9, 1999, www.mtv.com/news/512033/jailed -ghostface-killah-to-answer-weapons-charge/.

2. Chris Nelson, "Wu-Tang's Ghostface Killah Pleads Guilty to Attempted Robbery," *MTV News*, January 6, 1998, www.mtv.com/news /2412/wu-tangs-ghostface-killah-pleads-guilty-to-attempted-robbery/.

3. Buddha Monk and Mickey Hess, *The Dirty Version: On Stage, in the Studio, and in the Streets with Ol' Dirty Bastard* (New York: Dey Street Books, 2015), 92.

4. Jaime Lowe, *Digging for Dirt: The Life and Death of ODB* (New York: Faber & Faber, 2008), 116.

5. Anthai (71RAW), "RZA Speaks the Truth on Tim Westwood pt 2," YouTube video, 12:10, May 3, 2011.

6. Derrick Parker and Matt Diehl, *Notorious C.O.P.: The Inside Story of the Tupac, Biggie, and Jam Master Jay Investigations from NYPD's First "Hip-Hop Cop"* (New York: St. Martin's, 2006), 213.

7. Monk and Hess, *The Dirty Version*, 110.

8. Parker and Diehl, *Notorious C.O.P.*, 222.

9. Stephon Turner (a.k.a. Raison Allah), director, *Dirty: One Word Can Change the World: The Official ODB Biography* (Zu Films, 2009), DVD.

10. Parker and Diehl, *Notorious C.O.P.*, 224.

11. MTV News Staff, "Ol' Dirty Bastard Out on Bail After Hollywood Club Arrest," *MTV News*, September 17, 1998.

12. MTV News Staff, "Ol' Dirty Bastard Arrested on Threat Charges Again," *MTV News*, November 6, 1998, www.mtv.com/news/1429462/ol -dirty-bastard-arrested-on-threat-charges-again/.

13. Lowe, *Digging for Dirt*, 118.

14. Monk and Hess, *The Dirty Version*, 112.

15. David Kocieniewski, "Success of Elite Police Unit Exacts Toll on the Streets," *New York Times*, February 15, 1999.

16. Parker and Diehl, *Notorious C.O.P.*, 229.

17. Monk and Hess, *The Dirty Version*, 117.

18. Ibid., 124.

19. Ibid., 66.

20. Ibid., 67.

21. MTV News Staff, "ODB Sentenced to One Year in Drug Rehab," *MTV News*, November 19, 1999, www.mtv.com/news/520173/odb-sen tenced-to-year-in-drug-rehab/.

22. Lowe, *Digging for Dirt*, 138.

23. Ibid., 159.

24. Monk and Hess, *The Dirty Version*, 130–131.

25. Ibid., 132.

26. Ibid., 134.

27. Nomatazele, "ODB Ponders Plea to Send Him to Jail for 4 Years," HipHopDX, March 19, 2001, hiphopdx.com/news/id.21/title.odb-pon ders-plea-to-send-him-to-jail-for-4-years.

28. Monk and Hess, *The Dirty Version*, 139.

29. Village Voice Staff, "Music: Who Wants to Kill Joe Bananas?," *Village Voice*, August 28, 2001, vvstaging.villagevoice.com/2001/08/28 /music-87/.

30. djvlad, "Raekwon: ODB Had Face of Bravery When He Died," YouTube video, 5:19, March 23, 2013.

31. Ibid.

32. Eliott C. McLaughlin, "RZA: Wu-Tang a Drive-By Away from Never Existing," CNN Entertainment, October 12, 2009, www.cnn.com /2009/SHOWBIZ/Music/10/12/rza.tao.wu.tang/.

33. djvlad, "Inspectah Deck Recalls Funny Moment ODB Fought Akinyele on Stage," YouTube video, 8:46, July 2, 2015.

34. djvlad, "U-God on ODB Attempting Suicide More than Once While at Rikers Island (Part 6)," YouTube video, 6:40, May 21, 2019.

35. 247HH.com, "Raekwon—ODB Played a Huge Role in the Clan & PCP Pushup Competition Story (247HH Archives)," YouTube video, 6:22, August 19, 2016.

CHAPTER 17: A MONUMENT IN HIP-HOP

1. Matt Diehl, "Brash Hip-Hop Entrepreneurs," *New York Times*, December 8, 1996, www.nytimes.com/1996/12/08/arts/brash-hip-hop -entrepreneurs.html.

2. djvlad, "Inspectah Deck Speaks on Cultural Impact of Iconic Wu-Tang Logo," YouTube video, 2:55, June 28, 2015.

3. Dan Charnas, *The Big Payback: The History of the Business of Hip-Hop* (New York: New American Library, 2010), 483.

4. Ibid., 485–486.

5. Ibid., 490.

6. Diehl, "Hip-Hop Entrepreneurs."

7. Jian DeLeon, "Wu-Tang Forever: The History of Wu Wear," *Complex*, October 12, 2011, www.complex.com/style/2011/10/wu-tang-forever-the-history-of-wu-wear/.

8. Ibid.

9. Cyrus Bozorgmehr, *Once Upon a Time in Shaolin: The Untold Story of Wu-Tang Clan's Million-Dollar Secret Album, the Devaluation of Music, and America's New Public Enemy No. 1* (New York: Flatiron Books, 2017), 25.

10. Matt Rasmussen, "You'll Never Hear the New Wu-Tang Album, but This Is What It Sounds Like," *Complex*, March 3, 2015, www.complex.com/music/2015/03/wu-tang-clan-rza-once-upon-a-time-in-shaolin.

11. Sean Michaels, "Wu-Tang Clan Producing One Copy of New Album, *Once Upon a Time in Shaolin*," *Guardian*, March 27, 2014, www.theguardian.com/music/2014/mar/27/wu-tang-clan-one-copy-new-album-once-upon-a-time-in-shaolin.

12. Rasmussen, "You'll Never Hear."

13. Devin Leonard and Annmarie Hordern, "Who Bought the Most Expensive Album Ever Made?," *Bloomberg Businessweek*, December 9, 2015, www.bloomberg.com/features/2015-martin-shkreli-wu-tang-clan-album/.

14. Miranda J., "Method Man Thinks Waiting 88 Years to Release 'Once Upon a Time in Shaolin' Is Stupid," *XXL*, March 4, 2015.

15. Brian Josephs, "What Exactly Is This New Wu-Tang Album?," *Spin*, October 13, 2017, www.spin.com/2017/10/wu-tang-clan-saga-continues-album/.

16. Ibid.

17. "The RZA Interview," *Fat Lace*, December 2007, fatlacemagazine.com/2007/12/rza-interview/.

18. Ibid.

19. noblechild456, "Ghostface Classic Interview 1996 (Rare)," YouTube video, 9:31, February 19, 2013.

20. 247HH.com, "Cappadonna—Wu-Tang Is a Family, We Can't Break Up, How We Changed the Industry," YouTube video, 8:08, November 1, 2018.

21. DooMWellp, "Cappadonna—Da Struggle (DVD)," YouTube video, 1:02:12, June 12, 2018.

22. 247HH.com, "Cappadonna—I Miss Working Out at the Wu Mansion," YouTube video, 5:12, November 20, 2018.

23. djvlad, "Masta Killa: What Made Wu-Tang Special Was Having All Members in the Studio Together (Part 5)" YouTube video, 7:11, December 7, 2017.

24. Ibid.

25. No Jumper, "The Ghostface Killah Interview," YouTube video, 1:12:02, April 30, 2018.

26. Ibid.

27. djvlad, "Inspectah Deck Believes Mismanagement Is Hurting Wu-Tang," YouTube video, 7:54, July 12, 2015.

28. Butter Sydney, "Butter Presents (Ep. #6): The Wu-Tang Clan," YouTube video, 24:43, February 18, 2019.

29. Ibid.

SELECTED BIBLIOGRAPHY

Ashon, Will. *Chamber Music: About the Wu-Tang [in 36 Pieces]*. London: Granta, 2018.

Barclay, Gerald, with Jessica Gerlach-Petrovic. *Shooting the Clan: An Eyewitness to the Rise of the Wu-Tang Clan*. Self-published, DreamStarters, 2018.

Blount, Jackson, and George "Rack-Lo" Billups. *Lo-Life: An American Classic*. Brooklyn: powerHouse Books, 2016.

Bozorgmehr, Cyrus. *Once Upon a Time in Shaolin: The Untold Story of the Wu-Tang Clan's Million-Dollar Secret Album, the Devaluation of Music, and America's New Public Enemy No. 1*. New York: Flatiron Books, 2017.

Charnas, Dan. *The Big Payback: The History of the Business of Hip-Hop*. New York: New American Library, 2010.

Coleman, Brian. *Check the Technique: Liner Notes for Hip-Hop Junkies*. New York: Villard, 2007.

Farber, David. *Crack: Rock Cocaine, Street Capitalism, and the Decade of Greed*. Cambridge: Cambridge University Press, 2019.

Fernando, S. H., Jr. *The New Beats: Exploring the Music, Culture, and Attitudes of Hip-Hop*. New York: Anchor/Doubleday, 1994.

Ferranti, Seth. *The Supreme Team: The Birth of Crack and Hip-Hop, Prince's Reign of Terror and the Supreme / 50 Cent Beef Exposed*. Self-published, Gorilla Convict Publications, 2012.

Fu, Poshek, ed. *China Forever: The Shaw Brothers and Diasporic Cinema*. Urbana: University of Illinois Press, 2008.

Hawkins, Lamont (U-God). *Raw: My Journey into the Wu-Tang*. New York: Picador, 2018.

Knight, Michael Muhammad. *The Five Percenters: Islam, Hip-Hop and the Gods of New York*. London: One World Publications, 2007.

Landis, Bill, and Michelle Clifford. *Sleazoid Express: A Mind-Twisting Tour Through the Grindhouse Cinema of Times Square.* New York: Fireside, 2002.

Lowe, Jaime. *Digging for Dirt: The Life and Death of ODB.* London: Faber & Faber, 2008.

Merlis, Ben. *Goin' Off: The Story of the Juice Crew & Cold Chillin' Records.* BMG, 2019.

Monk, Buddha, and Mickey Hess. *The Dirty Version: On Stage, in the Studio, and in the Streets with Ol' Dirty Bastard.* New York: Dey Street Books, 2014.

Page, Alan. *Enter the Wu-Tang: How Nine Men Changed Hip-Hip Forever.* Self-published, Lone Gunman Media, 2014.

Parker, Derrick, and Matt Diehl. *Notorious C.O.P.: The Inside Story of the Tupac, Biggie, and Jam Master Jay Investigations from the NYPD's First "Hip-Hop Cop."* New York: St. Martin's, 2006.

Prashad, Vijay. *Everybody Was Kung-Fu Fighting: Afro-Asian Connections and the Myth of Cultural Purity.* Boston: Beacon, 2001.

Rakim, with Bakari Kitwana. *Sweat the Technique: Revelations on Creativity from the Lyrical Genius.* New York: Amistad, 2019.

Reid, Dr. Craig D. *The Ultimate Guide to Martial Arts Movies of the 1970s: 500+ Films Loaded with Action, Weapons and Warriors.* Seoul: Black Belt Communications, 2010.

The RZA. *The Tao of Wu.* New York: Riverhead Books, 2009.

The RZA, with Chris Norris. *The Wu-Tang Manual.* New York: Penguin, 2005.

Webb, Gary. *Dark Alliance: The CIA, the Contras, and the Crack Explosion.* New York: Seven Stories, 1998.

DISCOGRAPHY

WU-TANG CLAN

Enter the Wu-Tang: 36 Chambers (Loud, 1993)
Forever (Loud, 1997)
The W (Columbia, 2000)
Iron Flag (Columbia, 2001)
8 Diagrams (SRC, 2007)
A Better Tomorrow (Warner Bros., 2014)
Once Upon a Time in Shaolin (EZCLZIV Scluzay, 2015)

Compilations

The Swarm (Priority, 1998)
Wu-Chronicles (Wu-Tang Records, 1999)
Wu-Chronicles, Chapter 2 (Priority, 2001)
The Sting (Koch, 2002)
Disciples of the 36 Chambers, Chapter 1 (Sanctuary, 2004)
Legend of the Wu-Tang Clan (BMG Heritage, 2004)
Wu-Tang Meets the Indie Culture (Babygrande, 2005)
Mathematics Presents Wu-Tang Clan & Friends (Nature Sounds, 2007)
Wu-Box: The Cream of the Clan (Cleopatra, 2007)
Return of the Swarm (101 Distribution, 2007)
Return of the Swarm, Vol. 4 (CMP Entertainment, 2007)
Wu XM Radio (Think Differently, 2007)
Lost Anthology (Think Differently, 2007)
Return of the Swarm, Vol. 5 (101 Distribution, 2008)
Soundtracks from the Shaolin Temple (Wanderluxe, 2008)
Wu: The Story of the Wu-Tang Clan (Loud/Legacy, 2008)

Killa Bees Attack (J-Love Enterprises, 2008)
Wu-Tang Chamber Music (E1 Music, 2009)
Wu-Tang Meets the Indie Culture, Vol. 2 (Ihiphop, 2009)
Legendary Weapons (E1 Music, 2011)
The Essential Wu-Tang Clan (Loud/Legacy 2013)
The Saga Continues (eOne, 2017)

RZA

Bobby Digital in Stereo (Gee Street / V2 / BMG, 1998)
Digital Bullet (Koch, 2001)
Birth of a Prince (Sanctuary/BMG, 2003)
Digi Snacks (Koch, 2008)

Collaborations

Gravediggaz / *Six Feet Deep* (Gee Street / Island / Polygram, 1994)
Gravediggaz / *The Pick, the Sickle, and the Shovel* (Gee Street / V2 /
　　BMG, 1997)
Banks & Steelz (Paul Banks) / *Anything but Words* (Warner Bros., 2016)

Compilations

The RZA Hits (Razor Sharp / Epic, 1999)
The World According to RZA (Virgin/EMI, 2003)

Soundtracks

Ghost Dog: The Way of the Samurai (Razor Sharp / Epic / Sony, 2000)
Kill Bill Vol. 1: Original Soundtrack (A Band Apart / Maverick / Warner
　　Bros., 2003)
Kill Bill Vol. 2: Original Soundtrack (Maverick, 2004)
Soul Plane (2004)
Blade: Trinity (New Line Records, 2004)
The Protector (Bulletproof, 2006)
Blood of a Champion (2006)
Afro Samurai: The Album (Koch, 2007)
Babylon A.D. (Varèse Sarabande, 2008)

Afro Samurai: Resurrection (E1 Music, 2009)
The Man with the Iron Fists (Soul Temple, 2012)

GZA

Words from the Genius (Cold Chillin' / Warner, 1991)
Liquid Swords (Geffen, 1995)
Beneath the Surface (MCA, 1999)
Legend of the Liquid Sword (MCA/Universal, 2002)
Pro Tools (Babygrande, 2008)

Collaborations

DJ Muggs / *Grandmasters* (Angeles, 2005)

OL' DIRTY BASTARD

Return to the 36 Chambers: The Dirty Version (Elektra, 1995)
Nigga Please (Elektra, 1999)
A Son Unique (E1, 2005)
Message to the Other Side, Osirus Part 1 (Capitol, 2009)

Compilations

The Dirty Story: The Best of Ol' Dirty Bastard (Elektra, 2001)
The Trials and Tribulations of Russell Jones (D3, 2002)
The Definitive Ol' Dirty Bastard Story (Elektra, 2005)
In Memory Of . . . Vol. 3 (101 Distribution, 2007)
The Last Tape (Greatest Hits) (Wu Music Group, 2011)

METHOD MAN

Tical (Def Jam, 1994)
Tical 2000: Judgement Day (Def Jam, 1998)
Tical 0: The Prequel (Def Jam, 2004)
4:21 . . . The Day After (Def Jam, 2006)
The Meth Lab (Hanz on Music / Tommy Boy, 2015)
Meth Lab Season 2: The Lithium (Hanz on Music, 2018)

Collaborations

Redman / *Blackout!* (Def Jam, 1999)
Redman / *How High Soundtrack* (Def Jam, 2001)
Redman / *Blackout! 2* (Def Jam, 2009)
Raekwon and Ghostface Killah / *Wu-Massacre* (Def Jam, 2010)

RAEKWON

Only Built 4 Cuban Linx (Loud/RCA/BMG, 1995)
Immobilarity (Loud/Columbia/SME, 1999)
The Lex Diamond Story (Universal, 2003)
Only Built 4 Cuban Linx, Pt. II (Ice H20 / EMI, 2009)
Shaolin vs. Wu-Tang (Ice H20 / EMI, 2011)
Fly International Luxurious Art (Ice H20 / Caroline, 2015)
The Wild (Ice H20 / Empire, 2017)

Collaborations

Ghostface Killah and Method Man / *Wu Massacre*
   (Def Jam, 2010)

GHOSTFACE KILLAH

Ironman (Razor Sharp / Epic, 1996)
Supreme Clientele (Razor Sharp / Epic, 2000)
Bulletproof Wallets (Epic, 2001)
The Pretty Toney Album (Def Jam, 2004)
Fishscale (Def Jam, 2006)
More Fish (Def Jam, 2006)
The Big Doe Rehab (Def Jam, 2007)
Ghostdini: Wizard of Poetry in Emerald City (Def Jam, 2009)
Apollo Kids (Def Jam, 2010)
Twelve Reasons to Die (Soul Temple, 2013)
36 Seasons (Tommy Boy, 2014)
Twelve Reasons to Die II (Linear Labs, 2015)
Ghostface Killahs (Music Generation Corp., 2019)

Collaborations

Theodore Unit / *718* (Sure Shot, 2004)
Trife Diesel / *Put It on the Line* (Starks Enterprise, 2005)
Raekwon and Method Man / *Wu-Massacre* (Def Jam, 2010)
Sheek Louch / *Wu Block* (E1, 2012)
BadBadNotGood *Sour Soul* (Lex, 2015)
Big Ghost Ltd. / *The Lost Tapes* (Cleopatra, 2018)
Czarface / *Czarface Meets Ghostface* (Silver Age, 2019)

Compilations

Shaolin's Finest (Epic, 2003)
Hidden Darts: Special Edition (Starks Enterprise, 2007)
The Wallabee Champ (Starks Enterprise, 2008)
Ghostdeini the Great (Def Jam, 2008)
Best of Ghostface Killah (Def Jam, 2014)

INSPECTAH DECK

Uncontrolled Substance (Loud, 1999)
The Movement (Koch, 2003)
The Resident Patient (Universal, 2006)
Manifesto (Urban Icons, 2010)
Chamber No. 9 (Music Generation Corp., 2019)

Collaborations with Czarface

Czarface (Brick / Silver Age, 2013)
Every Hero Needs A Villain (Brick, 2015)
A Fistful of Peril (Silver Age, 2016)
First Weapon Drawn (Silver Age, 2017)
Czarface Meets Metal Face (Get on Down, 2018)
Czarface Meets Ghostface (Silver Age, 2019)
The Odd Czar Against Us (Silver Age, 2019)

U-GOD

Golden Arms Redemption (Priority, 1999)
Mr. Xcitement (Free Agency, 2005)

Dopium (Babygrande, 2009)
The Keynote Speaker (Soul Temple, 2013)
Venom (Babygrande, 2018)

Collaborations

UGodz-Illa Presents: The Hillside Scramblers (Synergy Music, 2004)

MASTA KILLA

No Said Date (Nature Sounds, 2004)
Made in Brooklyn (Nature Sounds, 2006)
Selling My Soul (Nature Sounds, 2012)
Loyalty Is Royalty (Nature Sounds, 2017)

Collaborations

Masta Killa Presents the Next Chamber (Royal Lion, 2010)

CAPPADONNA

The Pillage (Razor Sharp / Epic, 1998)
The Yin and the Yang (Razor Sharp, 2001)
The Struggle (Code Red Entertainment, 2003)
The Cappatilize Project (Cappadonna, 2008)
Slang Prostitution (Chambermusik, 2009)
The Pilgramage (Media Fire, 2011)
Eyrth, Wynd and Fyre (RBC, 2013)
Hook Off (God Love Family, 2014)
The Pillage 2 (God Love Family, 2015)
Ear Candy (God Love Family, 2018)
Black Is Beautiful (God Love Family, 2020)
Show Me the Money (God Love Family, 2020)

Collaborations

Iron Fist Pillage (Soundtrack) (2001)
Ratchet Rush / *Wu South Volume 1* (ChamberMusik, 2005)
Ratchet Rush / *Wu South Welfare Volume II* (2009)
Bronze Nazareth, Canibus, and M-Eighty / *The 2nd Coming* (RBC, 2013)

INDEX